United Nations Economic Commission for Europe

Statistical Division

UNECE Countries in Figures 2007

www.unece.org

UNITED NATIONS
New York and Geneva, 2007

NOTE

The designations employed and the presentation of the material do not imply the expression of any opinion whatsoever on the part of the United Nations concerning the legal status of any country, territory, city or area, or its authorities or concerning the delimitation of its frontiers or boundaries.

UNITED NATIONS PUBLICATION

Sales No. E.07.II.E.8

ISBN: 978-92-1-116960-7

ISSN: 1020-5799

Introduction

Created in 1947, the United Nations Economic Commission for Europe (UNECE) aims to promote pan-European economic integration. The UNECE region covers 56 countries in Europe, North America, in the Caucasus, and Central Asia. *UNECE Countries in Figures* uses statistical indicators to give an overview of the social and economic structure of the countries and territories of this region.

This publication was prepared by the UNECE Statistical Division, and includes data collected from national and international sources of official statistics. The data are for the most recent year available, which is usually 2005. Most of these data are also available online through the UNECE Statistical Database (www.unece.org/stats/data.htm), which is regularly updated to include the latest available information.

Readers should be aware that differences in statistical methods might affect cross-country comparability, though every effort has been made to minimize the impact of this. The UNECE takes an active role in work to harmonize definitions and methodology wherever possible. The websites of UNECE, national statistical offices, and other international organizations provide more detailed descriptions, and technical notes, which can give users a greater insight into comparability issues.

UNECE Countries in Figures is intended to be of general interest to readers who are not necessarily familiar with statistical terminology or with interpreting statistical tables. A glossary of terms and list of references is available at the back of the publication.

I am pleased to present this publication and hope that it will help readers gain a better understanding of the socio-economic situation in countries and territories of the UNECE region.

Marek Belka
UNECE Executive Secretary

Acknowledgement

This publication was prepared with collective input from the staff of the UNECE Statistical Division. The cover design, maps and layout were prepared by the UNECE Graphics Design Unit.

About UNECE Countries in Figures

UNECE Countries in Figures presents a profile of social and economic indicators for each of the 56 UNECE member countries.

These profiles, prepared by the UNECE Statistical Division, are intended to be of general interest to readers not necessarily familiar with statistical terminology or with interpreting statistical tables. A glossary of terms and list of references is available at the back of the publication.

An online version of this publication can be found at www.unece.org/stats/profiles2007.

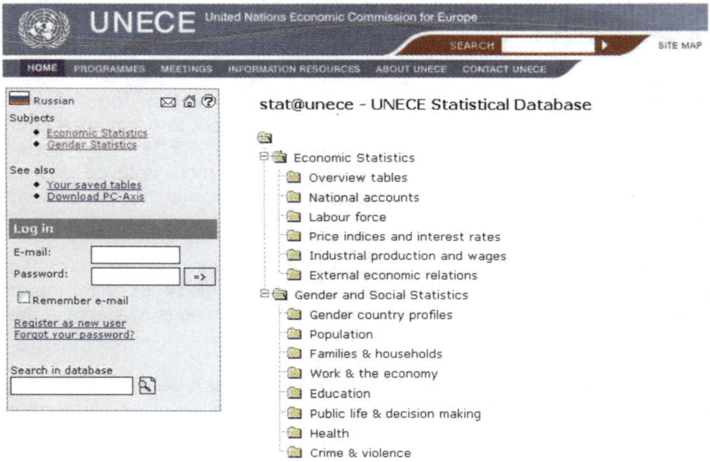

UNECE Statistical Database

This publication is an example of the information available through the UNECE Statistical Division online database. The database includes internationally comparable statistics and is continually updated by statistical experts. The latest data are available through the UNECE website (www.unece.org/stats/data.htm).

Contacts for More Information

Comments or questions about the data or content of this publication are welcomed. Please email support.stat@unece.org or telephone +41 22 917 2084 for further information.

About the UNECE Statistical Division

The UNECE Statistical Division services the Conference of European Statisticians (CES), promoting cooperation amongst national and international statistical organizations in the UNECE region. The Division implements the goals of the CES through provision of technical assistance programs, activities such as intergovernmental meetings and workshops, and the development of standards and guidelines. This work aims to achieve better international comparability of statistical data within and between regions. In addition, the division helps countries to bring their statistical systems in line with the UNECE Fundamental Principles of Official Statistics (www.unece.org/stats/archive/docs.fp.e.htm).

The division works across a wide range of subject areas, including economic statistics, national accounts, social and demographic statistics, gender statistics, dissemination of official statistics, and the management, organization and institutional frameworks of national systems of official statistics. Coordination of the statistical activities of international organizations active in UNECE region occurs through the division's maintenance of a Database of International Statistical Activities (unece.unog.ch/disa/). The UNECE makes available key statistical data about the countries of the region through online databases and publications (www.unece.org/stats/data.htm).

MEMBER

Albania	Bosnia and Herzegovina	Estonia	Iceland
Andorra	Bulgaria	Finland	Ireland
Armenia	Canada	France	Israel
Austria	Croatia	Georgia	Italy
Azerbaijan	Cyprus	Germany	Kazakhstan
Belarus	Czech Republic	Greece	Kyrgyzstan
Belgium	Denmark	Hungary	Latvia

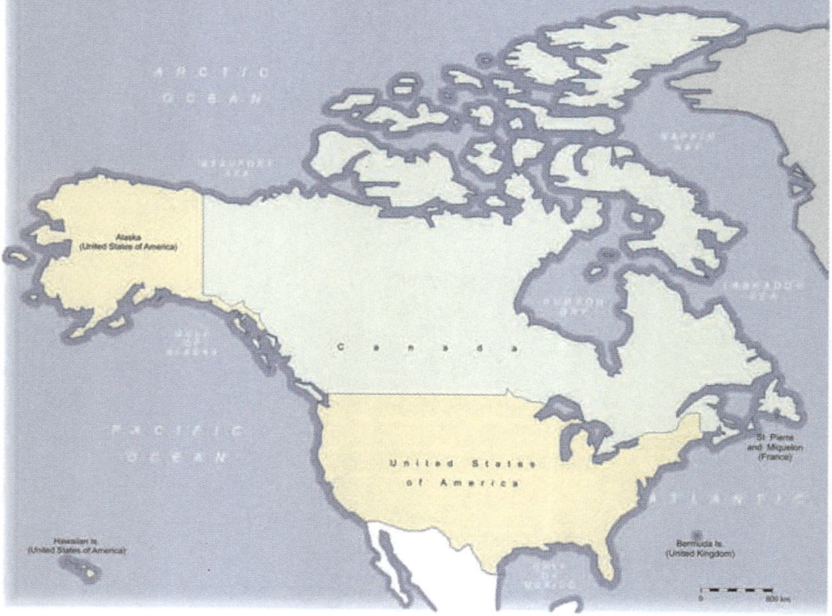

COUNTRIES

Liechtenstein
Lithuania
Luxembourg
Malta
Monaco
Montenegro
Netherlands
Norway
Poland
Portugal
Republic of Moldova
Romania
Russian Federation
San Marino
Serbia
Slovakia
Slovenia
Spain
Sweden
Switzerland
Tajikistan
The former Yugoslav Republic of Macedonia
Turkey
Turkmenistan
Ukraine
United Kingdom
United States
Uzbekistan

Explanatory Notes

UNECE Countries in Figures is based on a selection of official statistics prepared by the UNECE on its member countries.

Sources

The statistical data in these profiles were extracted from the UNECE Statistical Database (www.unece.org/stats/data.htm): an online collection of official statistics from national and international sources. Additional sources for this publication are listed on page 131.

Country and territory notes

Azerbaijan: with the exception of surface area, population and population density, data exclude Nagorno-Karabah.

Cyprus: in general, data refer to the government-controlled area. The exceptions are total population and area – these data refer to the whole of Cyprus.

Denmark: Separate profiles are provided for the territories of Greenland and Faroe Islands.

France: in general, geographical coverage of data includes the overseas departments (French Guiana, Guadeloupe, Martinique, and Réunion), and excludes overseas territories (French Polynesia, French Southern and Antarctic Lands, Mayotte, New Caledonia, Saint Pierre and Miquelon, Wallis and Futuna). Data relating to the surface area, economic activity rate, employment rate, unemployment rate, youth unemployment rate, percentage of women in the labour force, and employment by major economic sectors) exclude all aforementioned overseas departments and territories.

Georgia: in general, geographical coverage of data excludes the regions of Abkhazia and South Ossetia.

Guernsey: Total population excludes inhabitants of Alderney and Sark.

Israel: the coverage of the data provided by the Central Bureau of Statistics, Israel, does not always coincide with the map given in the country profiles of this publication.
The position of the United Nations on the question of Jerusalem is contained in General Assembly Resolution 181(II) of 29 November 1947, and subsequent resolutions of the General Assembly and the Security Council concerning this question.

Kosovo: United Nations Security Council Resolution 1244 (1999) provides a legal basis for the establishment, pending a final settlement, of substantial autonomy and self-government in Kosovo.

Moldova: in general, geographical coverage of data excludes the region of Transnistria.

Montenegro: This country was previously part of the State Union Serbia and Montenegro. Following the Declaration of Independence adopted by the National Assembly of Montenegro on 3 June 2006, Montenegro was admitted as a member country of the United Nations on 28 June 2006.

Norway: in general, geographical coverage of data excludes territories of Svalbard and Jan Mayen.

Serbia: This country was previously part of the State Union Serbia and Montenegro. After 1999, the data exclude Kosovo and Metohia.

Following the Declaration of Independence adopted by the National Assembly of Montenegro on 3 June 2006, the membership of the State Union Serbia and Montenegro in the United Nations (including all organs and organizations of the UN system) is continued by the Republic of Serbia.

Comparability of data

Readers should be aware that differences in statistical methods might affect cross-country comparability, though every effort has been made to minimize the impact of this. The UNECE takes an active role in work to harmonize definitions and methodology wherever possible. Primary sources, such as the websites of national and international statistical offices, provide more detailed statistics, descriptions, and technical notes, which can give users a greater insight into comparability issues.

Data not available

The indication 'data not available' signifies that these particular data are not currently available in the UNECE databases. It is possible the data are available from other official sources.

Time period

The data in this publication are for 2005, unless otherwise indicated.

Units of measurement

The units of measurement are indicated in each table. The metric tonne is the standard unit of weight used. The term "billion" signifies a thousand million.

Symbols and abbreviations

..	Data not available
0	Less than 0.5
65+	65 years of age or more
h	Hour(s)
km^2	Square kilometres
%	Percentage
CPI	Consumer Price Index
EUROSTAT	Statistical Office of the European Communities
GDP	Gross domestic product
ILO	International Labour Organization
n/a	Not applicable
PPP	Purchasing power parity
UN	United Nations
UNECE	United Nations Economic Commission for Europe
UNSD	United Nations Statistical Division
US	United States of America
USD	United States Dollars
UTC	Co-ordinated Universal Time

Contents

Country profiles

Territory profiles

International administered territory

Indicators used in country profiles

(A translation into French and Russian is available on page134)

General data

- Time zone
- Capital city (population)
- Two largest cities (population)
- Area (km^2)
- Official languages
- Date joined UN
- National currency
- Name and website of the national statistical agency

Population

- Total population
- Population density (per km^2)
- Population by age
- Life expectancy at birth and at age 65
- Median age
- Marital status of total population
- Foreign born
- Foreigners in population

Gender Statistics

- Women in labour force
- Gender pay gap
- Female government ministers
- Female central bank board members
- Female tertiary students
- Total fertility rate
- Parliament seats held by women

Employment

- Employment (% change over previous year)
- Unemployment rate (%)
- Youth unemployment rate (%)
- Economic activity rate (Women and Men)
- Employment in major sectors

Economy

- GDP at current prices in millions of US Dollars, PPP
- GDP at current prices in millions of national currency
- GDP at constant 2000 prices, per capita, in US Dollars, PPP
- GDP at constant 2000 prices, per capita, in national currency
- Final consumption expenditure, per capita, US Dollars, PPP
- Purchasing power parity (PPP)
- Gross external debt (in millions of US Dollars)
- Exchange rate (annual average, national currency per US Dollar)
- Real GDP growth rate (% change over previous year)
- GDP in agriculture, industry (including construction) and services
- Consumer price index, annual average (% change over previous year)
- GDP by major economic sectors
- Exports of goods and services (as % of GDP)
- Imports of goods and services (as % of GDP)
- External trade balance (as % of GDP)

Trade

- Major import partners from UNECE (% of imports from worldwide trading partners)
- Major export partners in UNECE (% of exports to worldwide trading partners)

COUNTRY PROFILES

ALBANIA

Capital:	Tirana (343 078)
Two largest cities:	Durrës (99 546)
	Elbasan (87 797)
Area (km²):	28 748
Total population:	3 127 265
Population density (per km²):	109
Official languages:	Albanian
Date joined UN:	14 December 1955
National currency:	Albanian lek (ALL)
National statistical office:	Institute of Statistics (INSTAT)
	http://www.instat.gov.al/

Time: *UTC +1h*

Population by age, 2004

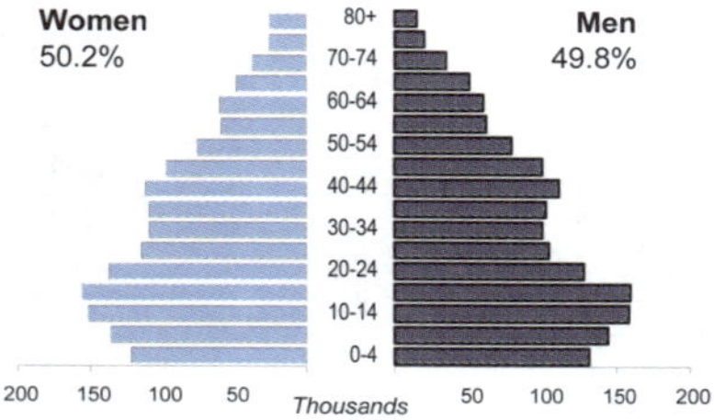

Life expectancy (in years), 2003:	at birth	at 65
Women:	79	18
Men:	73	15

Median age (in years), 2004:	
Women:	29
Men:	28

	percentage of total population
Foreign born:	..
Foreigners in population:	..

Legal marital status, population aged 18+

Data not available

never married
married
divorced
widowed

Women in the labour force, 2004:	39.3%
Gender pay gap, 2004:	34.6%
Female government ministers, 2002: percentage of total for both sexes	16.7%
Female central bank board members, 2005: percentage of total for both sexes	22.2%
Female tertiary students, 2002-2003: percentage of total for both sexes	62%

Total fertility rate

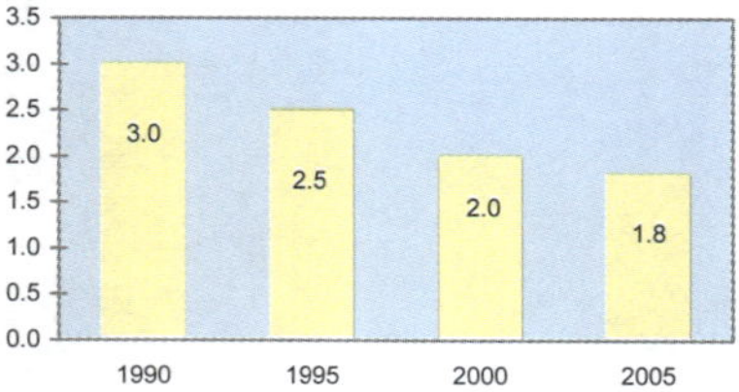

Parliament seats held by women (% of total)

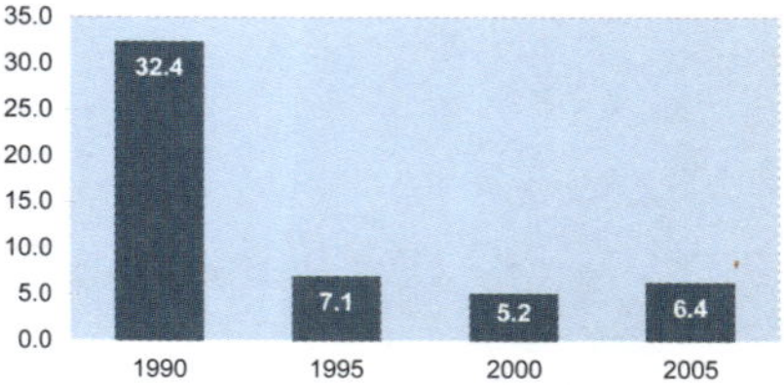

ALBANIA

	1999	2000	2001	2002	2003	2004	2005
Employment (% change over previous year)	-1.8	0.3	-13.9	0.0	0.7	0.5	0.1
Unemployment rate (%)	18.4	16.8	16.4	15.8	15.0	14.4	14.2
Youth unemployment rate (%)	..	..	..	..	..	..	..

Economic activity rate, 2001

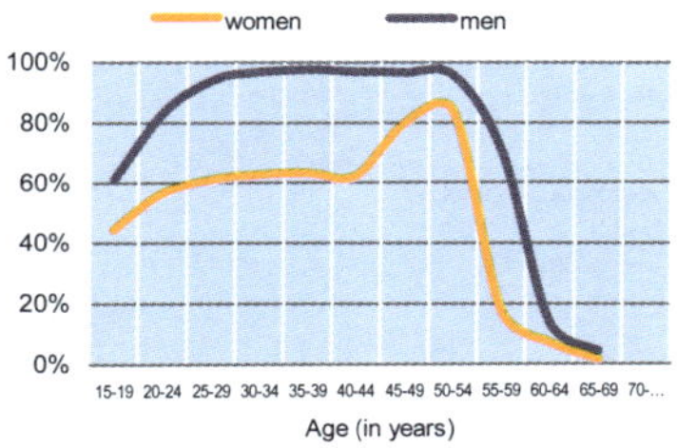

GDP at current prices	
in millions of US Dollars, PPP, 2004:	15 774
in millions of ALL, 2005:	822 035
GDP at constant 2000 prices, per capita	
US Dollars, PPP, 2005:	4 864
ALL, 2005:	224 866
Final consumption expenditure at 2000 prices, per capita, US Dollars, PPP, 2003:	3 248
Purchasing Power Parity (PPP)	
ALL per USD, 2004, US=1:	47.7
Gross external debt:	
in millions of US Dollars, 2004:	1 390
Exchange rate	
Annual average, ALL per USD, 2005:	99.87

Real GDP growth rate

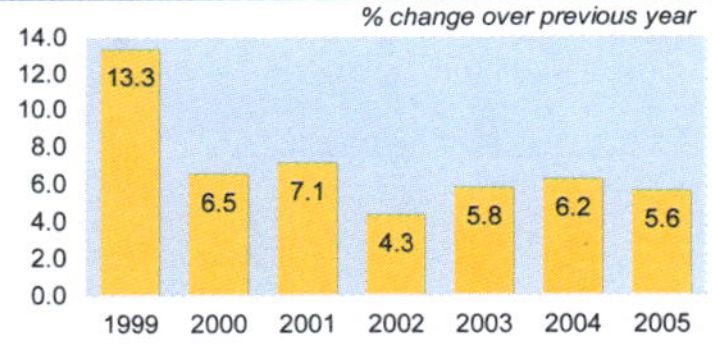

Consumer price index (annual average)

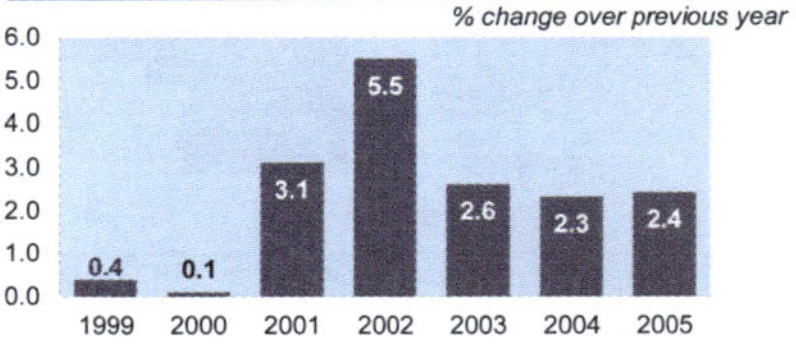

	% of GDP
Exports of goods and services:	21.9
Imports of goods and services:	44.2
External trade balance:	-22

GDP by major sectors

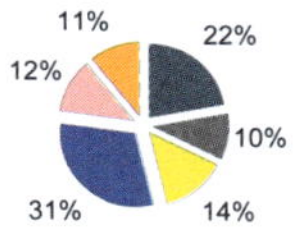

Employment in major sectors, 2004

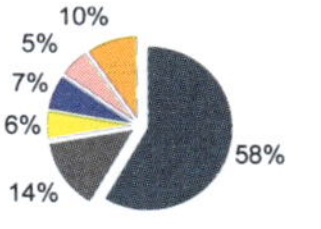

- Agriculture, hunting & forestry; fishing (ISIC A-B)
- Industry, including energy (ISIC C-E)
- Construction (ISIC F)
- Wholesale & retail trade, repairs; hotels & restaurants; transport & communications (ISIC G-I)
- Financial intermediation; real estate, renting & business activities (ISIC J-K)
- Other service activities (ISIC L-P)

GDP in agriculture, industry, and services (2000=100)

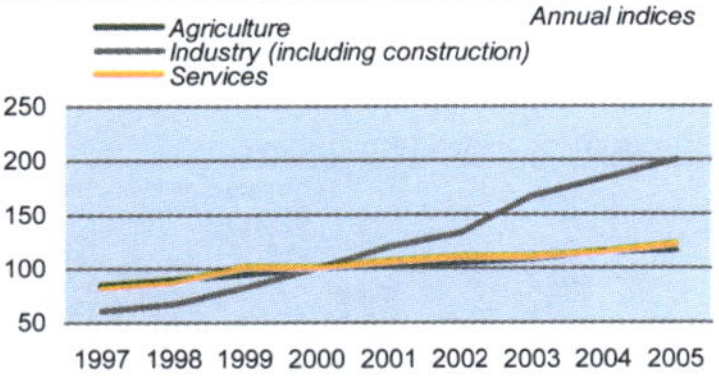

Major import partners from UNECE, 2005

Major export partners in UNECE, 2005

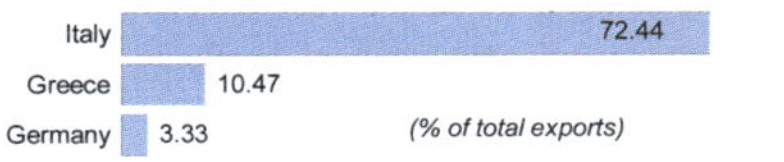

ANDORRA

Time: *UTC +1h*

Capital:	Andorra-La-Vella (22 035)
Two largest cities:	Escaldes-Engordany (16 402)
	Encamp (11 832)
Area (km^2):	470
Total population:	76 875
Population density (per km^2):	164
Official languages:	Catalan
Date joined UN:	28 July 1993
National currency:	Euro (EUR)
National Statistical Office:	Departament d'Estudis i d'Estadística (DEE)
	http://www.estadistica.ad

Population by age, 2004

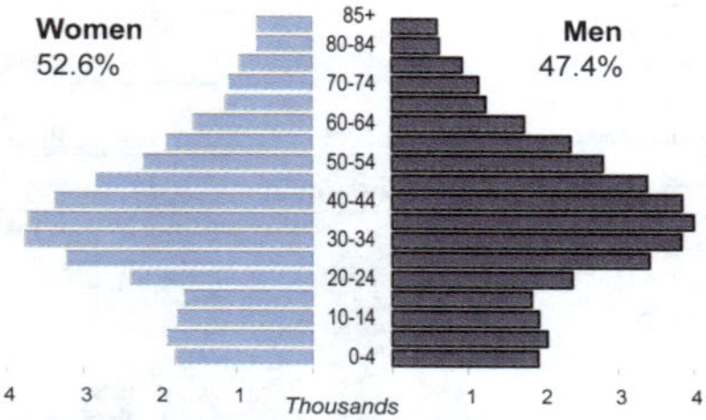

Life expectancy (in years), 2004:	at birth	at 65
Women:	83	..
Men:	77	..

Median age (in years), 2004:	
Women:	38
Men:	38

	percentage of total population
Foreign born, 1998:	88.48%
Foreigners in population, 2004:	63.35%

Legal marital status, population aged 18+

Data not available

never married
married
divorced
widowed

Total fertility rate

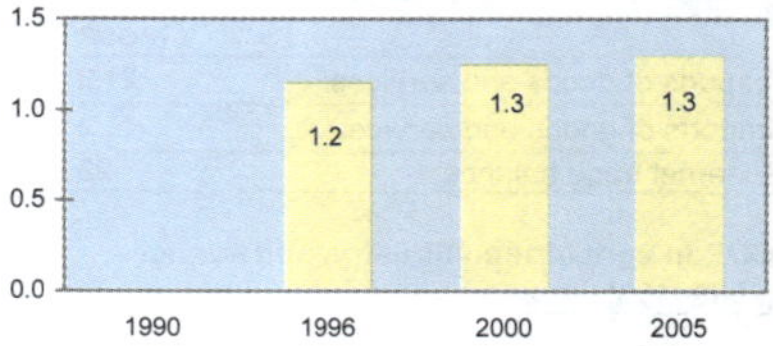

Real GDP growth rate

% change over previous year

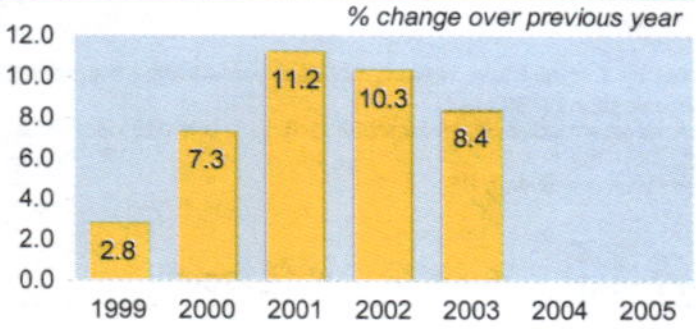

Consumer price index (annual average)

% change over previous year

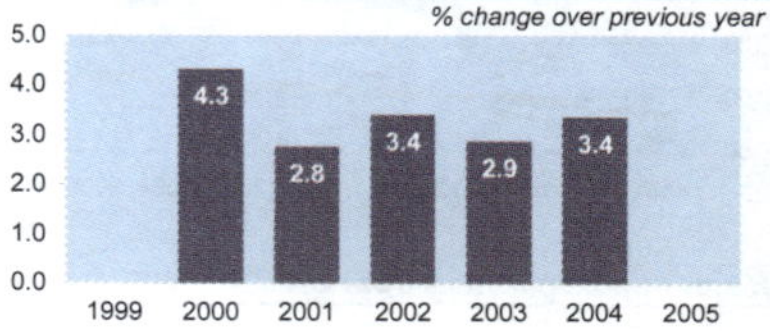

ANDORRA

GDP by major sectors

Employment in major sectors, 2004

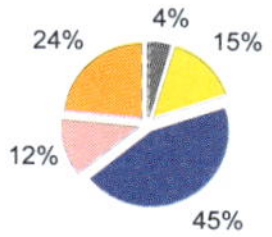

■ Agriculture, hunting & forestry; fishing (ISIC A-B)

■ Industry, including energy (ISIC C-E)

■ Construction (ISIC F)

■ Wholesale & retail trade, repairs; hotels & restaurants; transport & communications (ISIC G-I)

■ Financial intermediation; real estate, renting & business activities (ISIC J-K)

■ Other service activities (ISIC L-P)

GDP at current prices	
in millions of US Dollars, PPP, 2003:	1 485
in millions of EUR:	
GDP at constant 2000 prices, per capita	
US Dollars, PPP, 2004:	36 535
EUR:	
Final consumption expenditure at 2000 prices, per capita, US Dollars, PPP:	..
Purchasing Power Parities (PPP)	
EUR per USD, 2000, US=1:	0.765
Gross external debt:	
in millions of US Dollars:	..
Exchange rate	
Annual average, EUR per USD, 2005:	0.804

Major import partners from UNECE

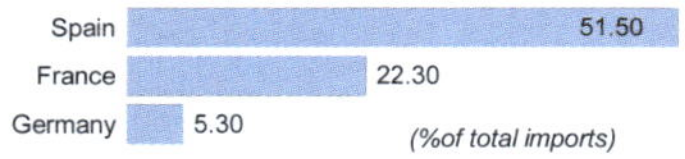

Major export partners in UNECE

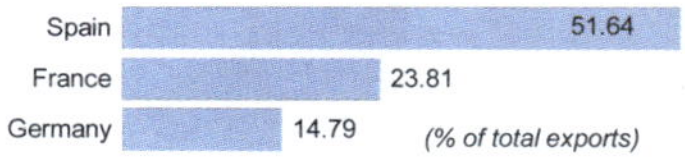

ARMENIA

Capital:	Yerevan (1 102 900)
Two largest cities:	Gyumri (148 900)
	Vanatzor (105 700)
Area (km^2):	29 743
Total population:	3 214 031
Population density (per km^2):	108
Official languages:	Armenian
Date joined UN:	2 March 1992
National currency:	Armenian dram (AMD)
National statistical office:	Ministry of Statistics (ARMSTAT)
	http://www.armstat.am/

Time: UTC +3h

Population by age, 2004

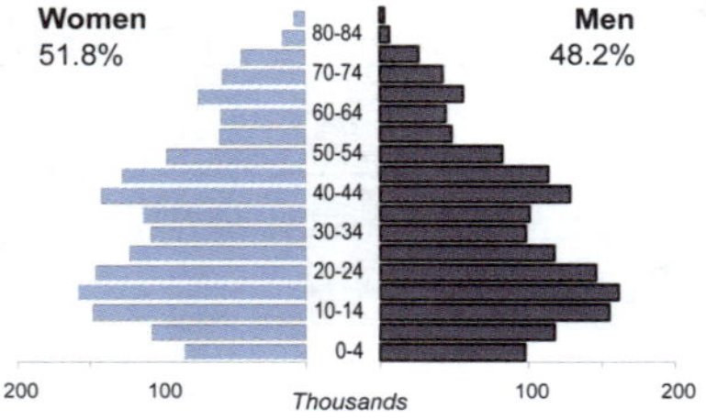

Life expectancy (in years), 2003:	at birth	at 65
Women:	76	15
Men:	70	13

Median age (in years), 2004:	
Women:	33
Men:	29

	percentage of total population
Foreign born:	..
Foreigners in population:	..

Legal marital status, population aged 18+

never married
married
divorced
widowed

Data not available

Women in the labour force, 2005:	48.5%
Gender pay gap, 2005:	44.3%
Female government ministers, 2006: percentage of total for both sexes	6%
Female central bank board members, 2005: percentage of total for both sexes	28.6%
Female tertiary students, 2002-2003: percentage of total for both sexes	53.7%

Total fertility rate

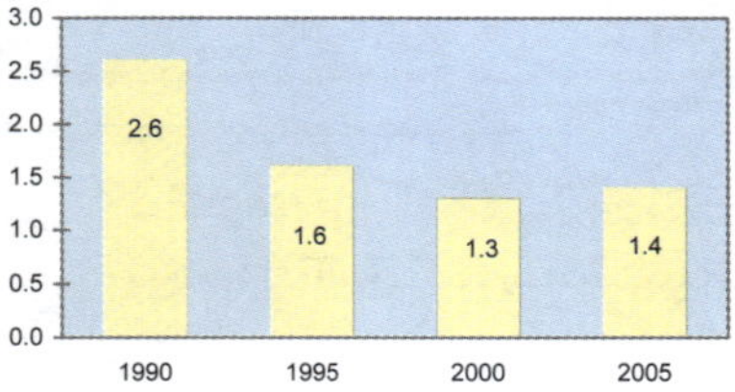

Parliament seats held by women (% of total)

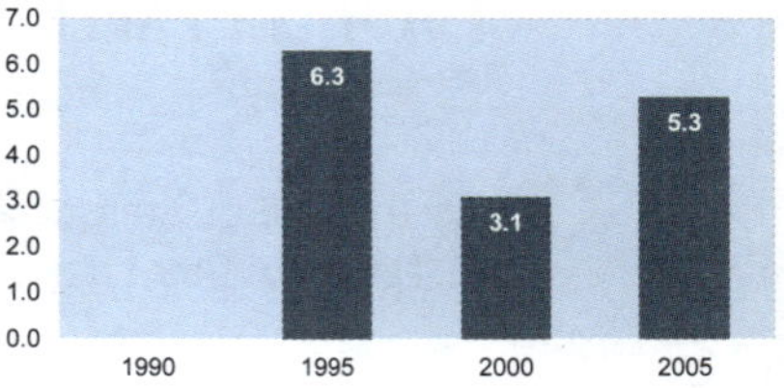

ARMENIA

	1999	2000	2001	2002	2003	2004	2005
Employment (% change over previous year)	-2.9	-1.6	-1.0	-12.5	0.1	-2.3	1.5
Unemployment rate (%)	11.5	10.9	9.8	10.5	10.2	9.4	7.6
Youth unemployment rate (%)	..	..	65.6	66.7	60.0	57.6	54.6

Economic activity rate, 2001

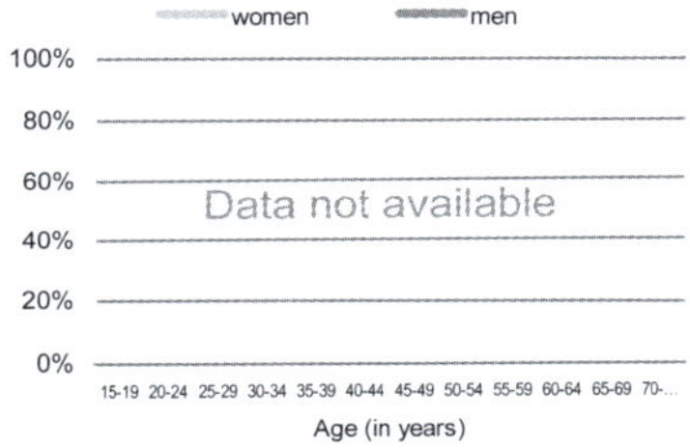

GDP at current prices	
in millions of US Dollars, PPP, 2005:	15 105
in millions of AMD, 2005:	2 243 953
GDP at constant 2000 prices, per capita	
US Dollars, PPP, 2005:	4 428
AMD, 2005:	619 018
Final consumption expenditure at 2000 prices, per capita, US Dollars, PPP, 2005:	4 020
Purchasing Power Parity (PPP)	
AMD per USD, 2005, US=1:	148.6
Gross external debt:	
in millions of US Dollars, 2005:	1 860
Exchange rate	
Annual average, AMD per USD, 2005:	457.7

Real GDP growth rate

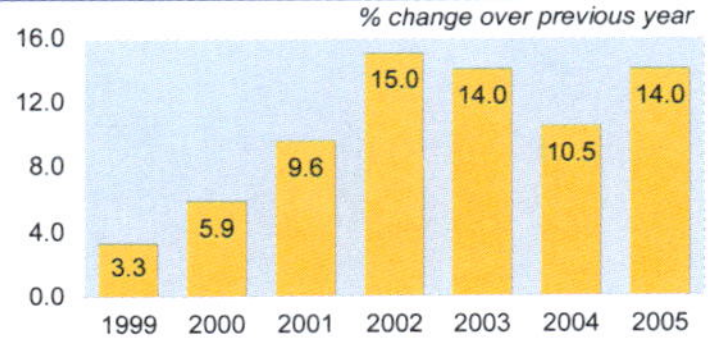

Consumer price index (annual average)

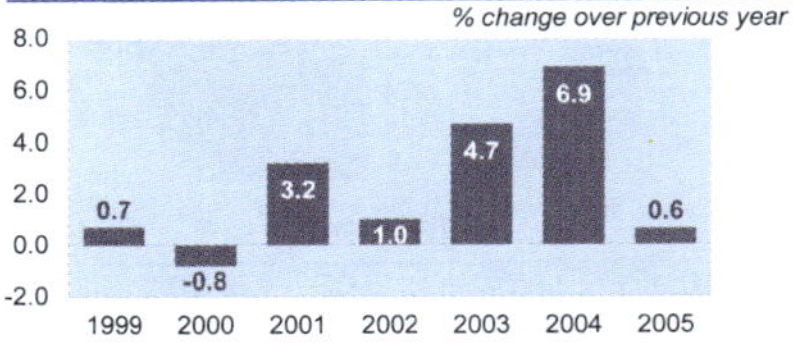

	% of GDP
Exports of goods and services:	26.9
Imports of goods and services:	39.9
External trade balance:	-13

GDP in agriculture, industry, and services (2000=100)

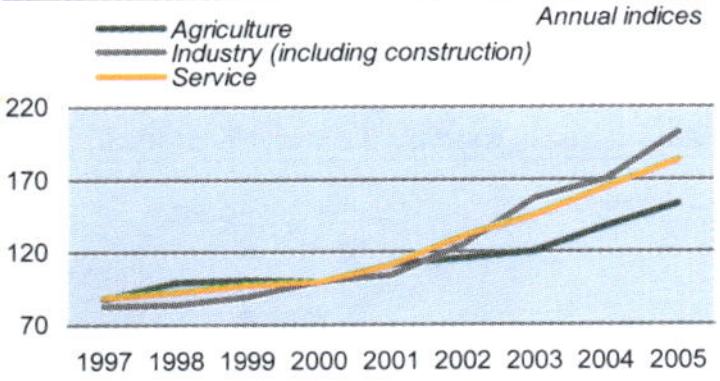

GDP by major sectors, 2005

Employment in major sectors, 2005

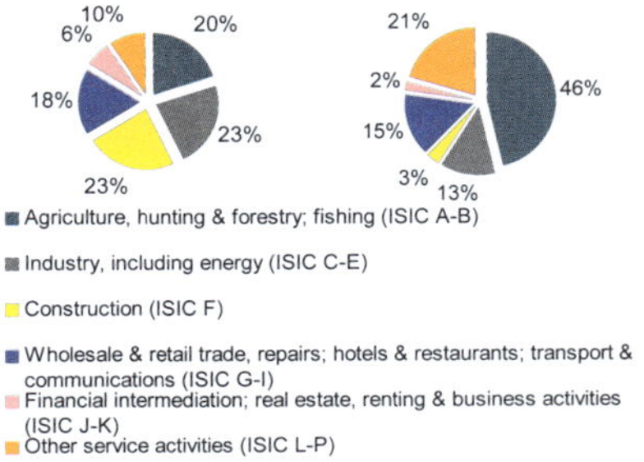

Major import partners from UNECE, 2005

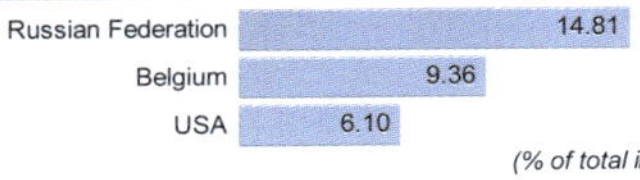

(% of total imports)

Major export partners in UNECE, 2005

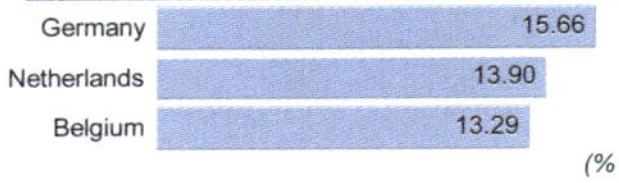

(% of total exports)

AUSTRIA

Capital:	Vienna (1 598 626)
Two largest cities:	Graz (235 477)
	Linz (185 530)
Area (km^2):	83 858
Total population:	8 236 225
Population density (per km^2):	98
Official languages:	German
Date joined UN:	14 December 1955
National currency:	Euro (EUR)
National statistical office:	Statistical Office of Austria http://www.statistik.at

Time: UTC +1h

Population by age, 2005

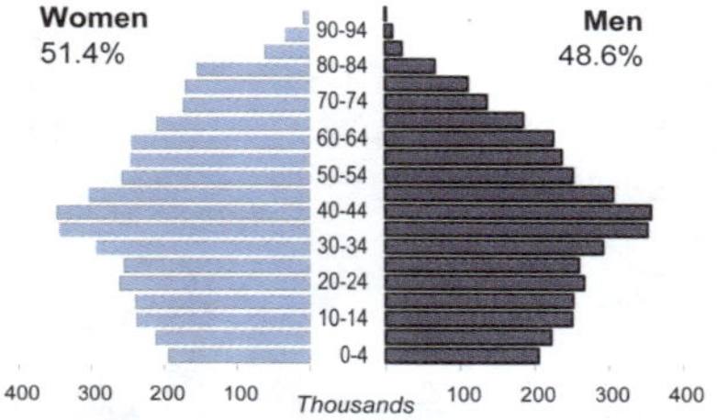

Life expectancy (in years), 2005:	at birth	at 65
Women:	82	21
Men:	77	17

Median age (in years), 2005:	
Women:	41
Men:	39

	percentage of total population
Foreign born:	..
Foreigners in population, 2005:	9.6%

Legal marital status, population aged 18+

never married
married
divorced
widowed

Data not available

Women in the labour force, 2005:	45.4%
Gender pay gap, 2005:	18%
Female government ministers, 2006: percentage of total for both sexes	33.3%
Female central bank board members, 2005: percentage of total for both sexes	..
Female tertiary students, 2003-2004: percentage of total for both sexes	53.3%

Total fertility rate

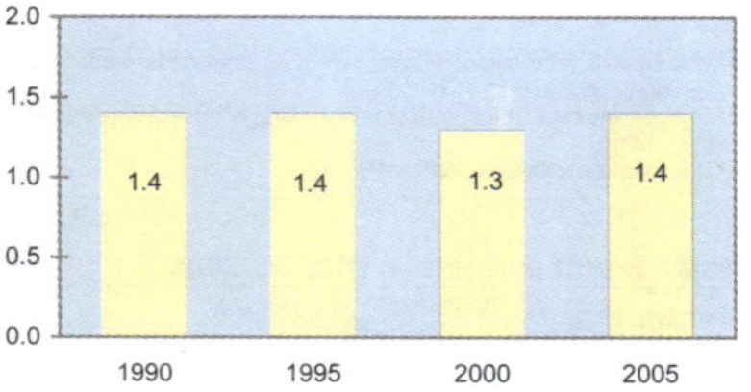

Parliament seats held by women (% of total)

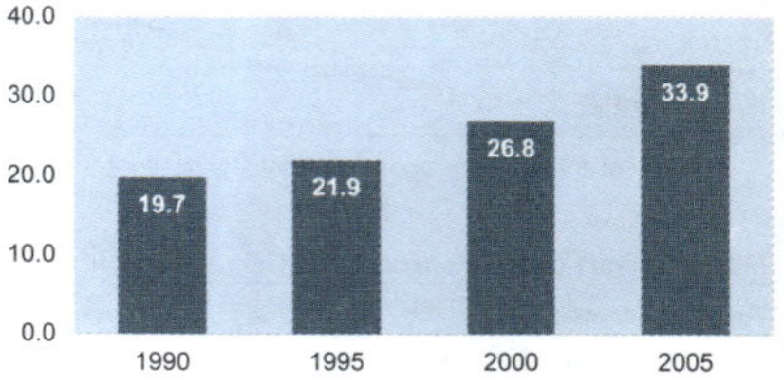

AUSTRIA

	1999	2000	2001	2002	2003	2004	2005
Employment (% change over previous year)	2.7	-0.1	1.0	1.2	0.2	-1.6	0.4
Unemployment rate (%)	3.9	3.6	3.6	4.2	4.3	4.8	5.2
Youth unemployment rate (%)	..	5.3	5.8	6.7	8.1	9.6	10.3

Economic activity rate, 2004

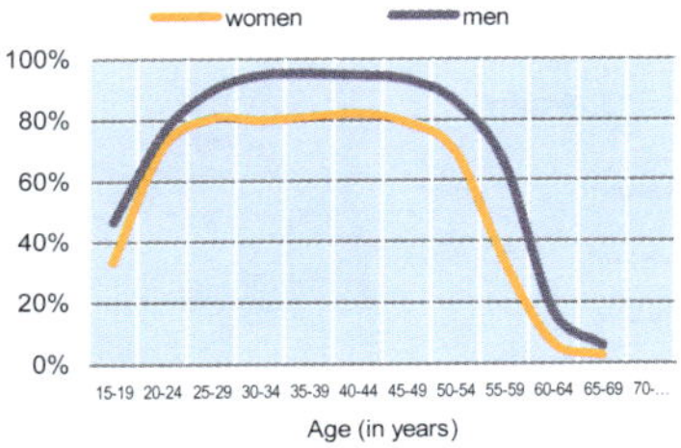

GDP at current prices	
in millions of US Dollars, PPP, 2005:	278 792
in millions of EUR, 2005:	245 103
GDP at constant 2000 prices, per capita	
US Dollars, PPP, 2005:	30 058
EUR, 2005:	27 489
Final consumption expenditure at 2000 prices, per capita, US Dollars, PPP, 2005:	22 251
Purchasing Power Parity (PPP)	
EUR per USD, 2005, US=1:	0.879
Gross external debt:	
in millions of US Dollars, 2005:	510 795
Exchange rate	
Annual average, EUR per USD, 2005:	0.804

Real GDP growth rate

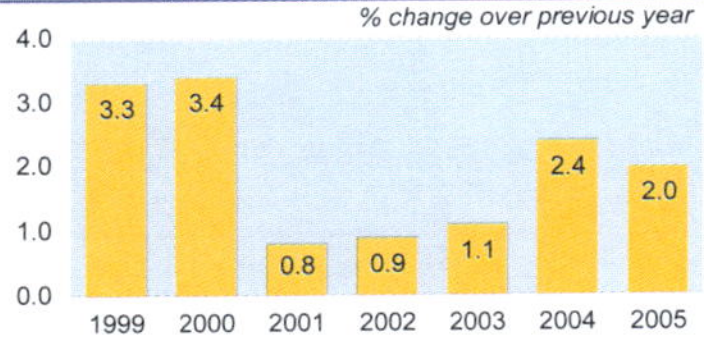

Consumer price index (annual average)

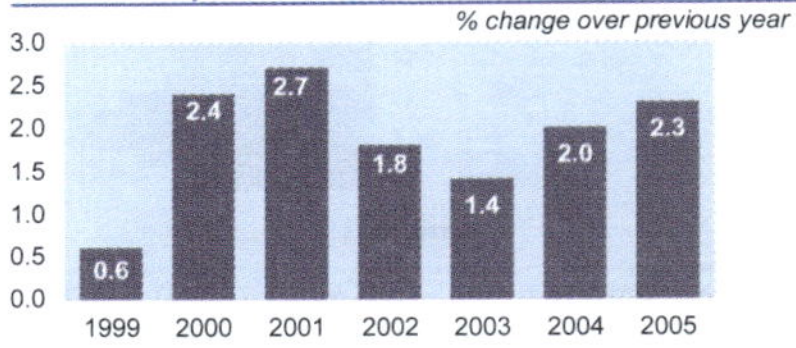

	% of GDP
Exports of goods and services:	54.3
Imports of goods and services:	49.5
External trade balance:	4.8

GDP by major sectors, 2005

Employment in major sectors, 2004

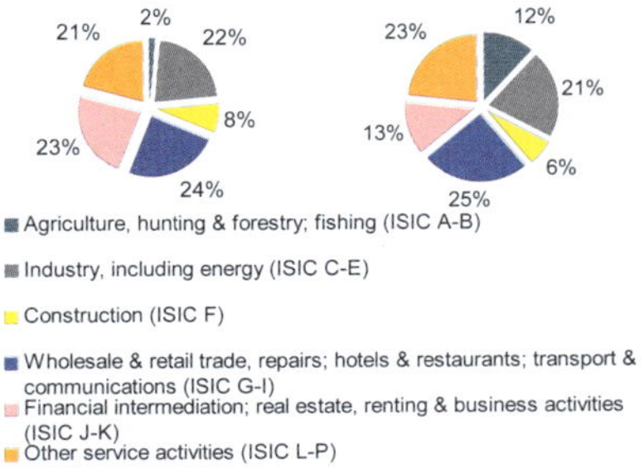

GDP in agriculture, industry, and services (2000=100)

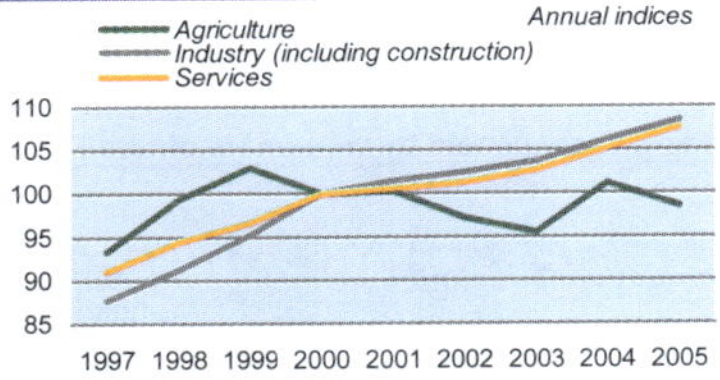

Major import partners from UNECE, 2005

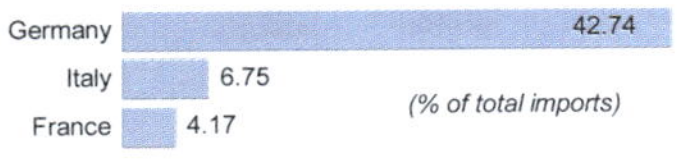

Major export partners in UNECE, 2005

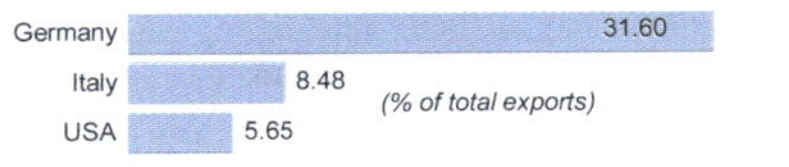

AZERBAIJAN

Capital:	Baku (1 066 800)
Two largest cities:	Ganca (291 900)
	Sumqayit (248 500)
Area (km^2):	86 600
Total population:	8 306 500
Population density (per km^2):	96
Official languages:	Azeri
Date joined UN:	2 March 1992
National currency:	Azerbaijanian new manat (AZN)
National statistical office:	
	State Statistical Committee of the Azerbaijan Republic
	http://www.azstat.org

Time: UTC +4h

Population by age, 2004

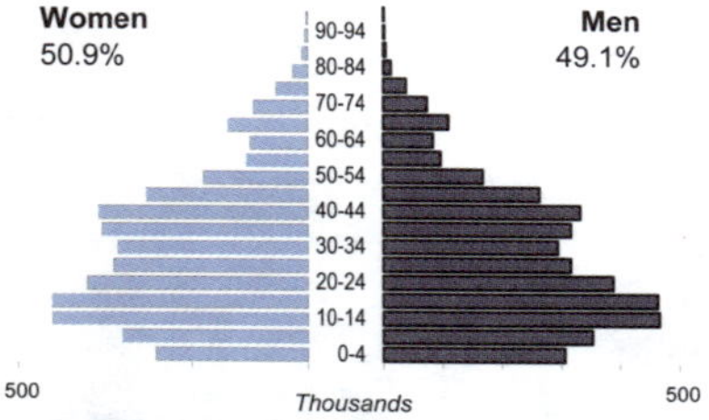

Legal marital status, population aged 18+

never married
married
divorced
widowed

Data not available

Life expectancy (in years), 2004:	at birth	at 65
Women:	75	17
Men:	70	15

Median age (in years), 2004:	
Women:	29
Men:	26

	percentage of total population
Foreign born:	..
Foreigners in population:	..

Women in the labour force, 2005:	47.7%
Gender pay gap:	..
Female government ministers: percentage of total for both sexes	..
Female central bank board members: percentage of total for both sexes	..
Female tertiary students: percentage of total for both sexes	..

Total fertility rate

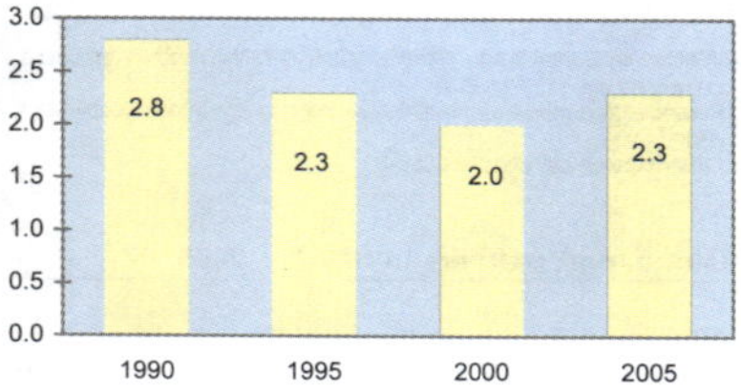

Parliament seats held by women (% of total)

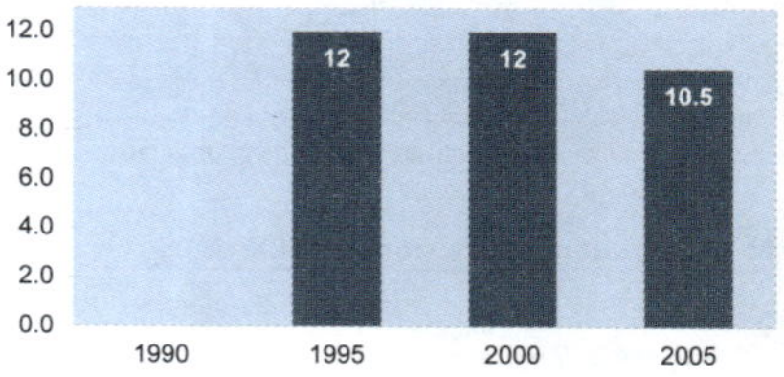

AZERBAIJAN

	1999	2000	2001	2002	2003	2004	2005
Employment (% change over previous year)	0.0	0.0	0.3	0.3	0.6	1.7	1.1
Unemployment rate (%)	1.2	1.2	1.3	1.3	1.4	1.4	1.4
Youth unemployment rate (%)	..	..	..	..	21.8	..	..

Economic activity rate

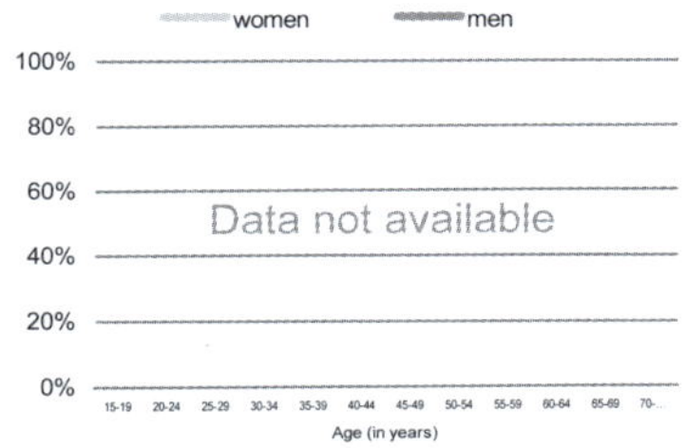

GDP at current prices	
in millions of US Dollars, PPP, 2005:	41 343
in millions of AZN, 2005:	11 876
GDP at constant 2000 prices, per capita	
US Dollars, PPP, 2005:	4 373
AZN, 2005:	1 058
Final consumption expenditure at 2000 prices, per capita, US Dollars, PPP, 2005:	3 003
Purchasing Power Parity (PPP)	
AZN per USD, 2005, US=1:	0.287
Gross external debt:	
in millions of US Dollars, 2004:	1 500
Exchange rate	
Annual average, AZN per USD, 2005:	0.945

Real GDP growth rate

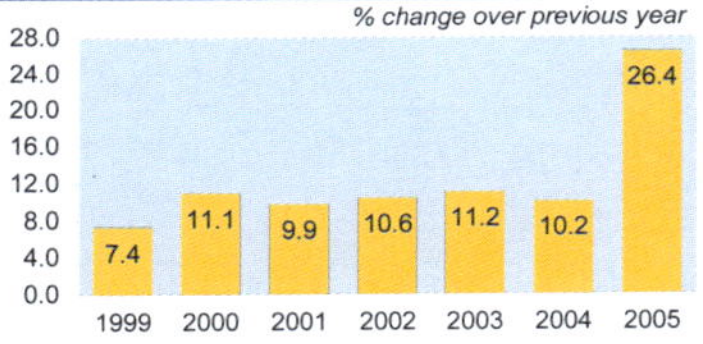

Consumer price index (annual average)

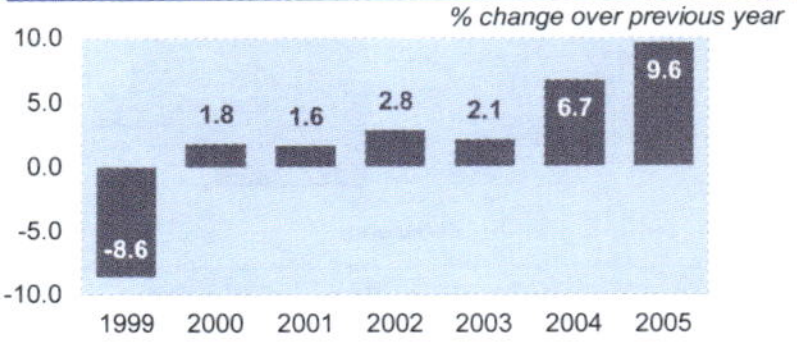

	% of GDP
Exports of goods and services:	66.4
Imports of goods and services:	55.8
External trade balance:	10.6

GDP by major sectors, 2005

Employment in major sectors, 2005

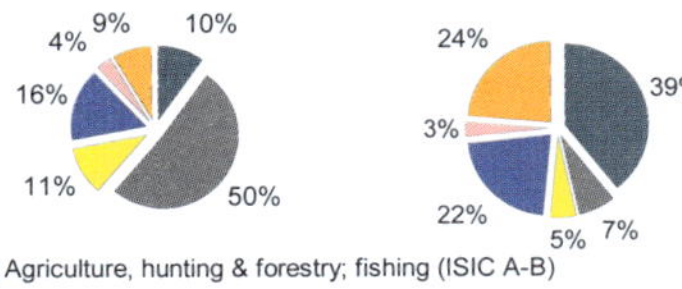

- Agriculture, hunting & forestry; fishing (ISIC A-B)
- Industry, including energy (ISIC C-E)
- Construction (ISIC F)
- Wholesale & retail trade, repairs; hotels & restaurants; transport & communications (ISIC G-I)
- Financial intermediation; real estate, renting & business activities (ISIC J-K)
- Other service activities (ISIC L-P)

GDP in agriculture, industry, and services (2000=100)

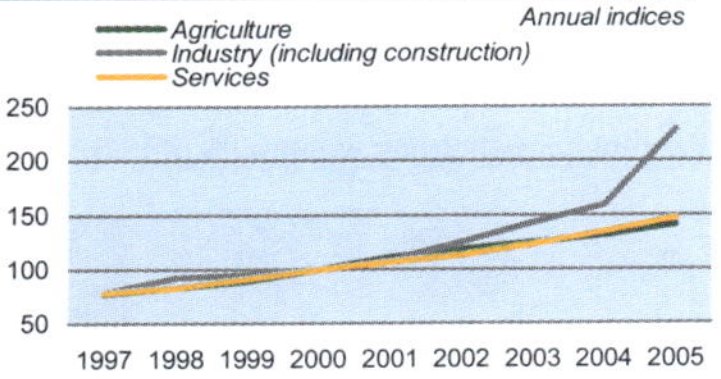

Major import partners from UNECE, 2005

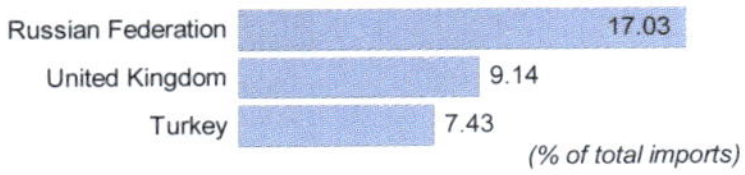

Major export partners in UNECE, 2005

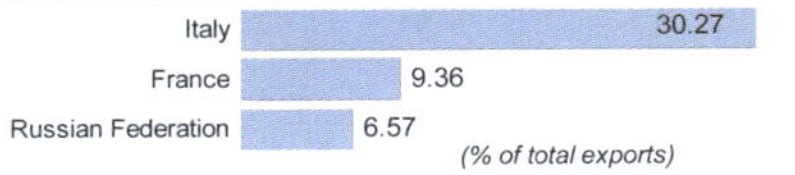

BELARUS

Capital:	Minsk (1 741 327)
Two largest cities:	Homel' (481 197)
	Mahilëu (365 102)
Area (km^2):	207 600
Total population:	9 824 568
Population density (per km^2):	47
Official languages:	Belarussian
Date joined UN:	24 October 1945
National currency:	Belarusian ruble (BYR)
National statistical office:	

Ministry of Statistics and Analysis of the Republic of Belarus
http://www.belstat.gov.by

Time: UTC +2h

Population by age, 2004

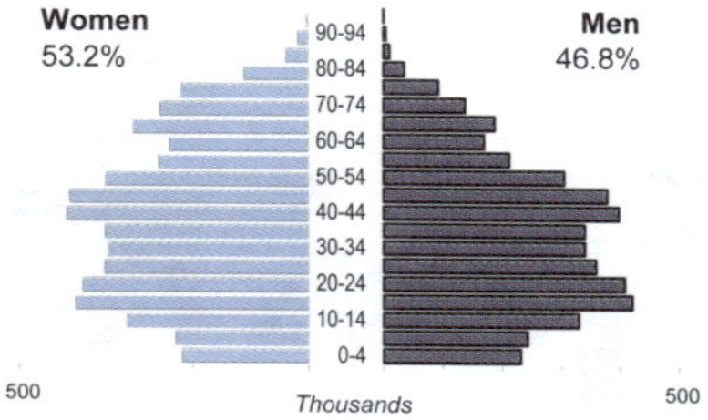

Life expectancy (in years), 2004:	at birth	at 65
Women:	75	16
Men:	63	11

Median age (in years), 2004:	
Women:	40
Men:	35

	percentage of total population
Foreign born:	..
Foreigners in population:	..

Legal marital status, population aged 18+

never married
married
divorced
widowed

Data not available

Women in the labour force, 2005:	53.1%
Gender pay gap, 2005:	20.9%
Female government ministers, 2006: percentage of total for both sexes	4%
Female central bank board members, 2005: percentage of total for both sexes	16.7%
Female tertiary students, 2001-2002: percentage of total for both sexes	56.8%

Total fertility rate

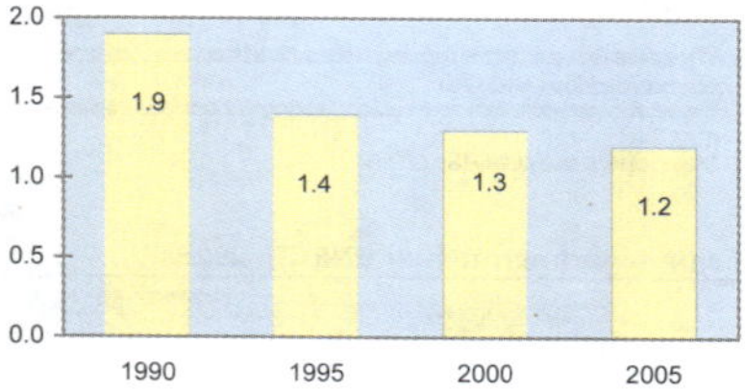

Parliament seats held by women (% of total)

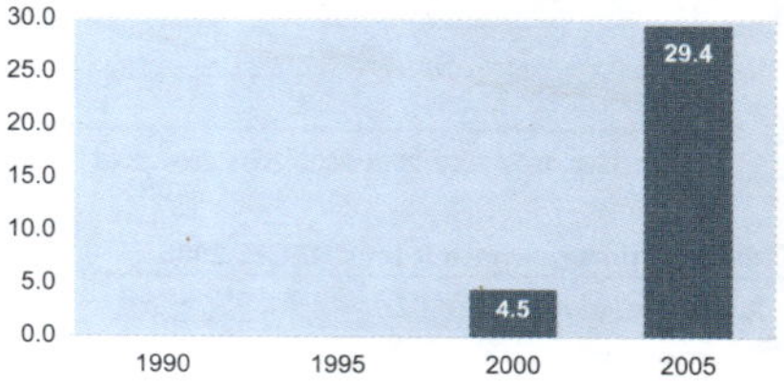

BELARUS

	1999	2000	2001	2002	2003	2004	2005
Employment (% change over previous year)	0.6	0.0	-0.5	-0.8	-0.9	-0.5	0.8
Unemployment rate (%)	2.1	2.1	2.3	3.0	3.1	1.9	1.5
Youth unemployment rate (%)	..	..	..	..	..	..	..

Economic activity rate, 2000

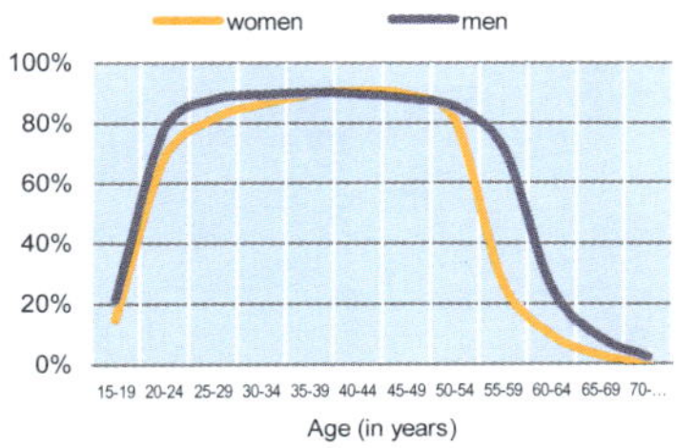

GDP at current prices	
in millions of US Dollars, PPP, 2005:	75 958
in millions of BYR, 2005:	63 678 893
GDP at constant 2000 prices, per capita	
US Dollars, PPP, 2005:	6 892
BYR, 2005:	1 338 071
Final consumption expenditure at 2000 prices, per capita, US Dollars, PPP, 2005:	5 620
Purchasing Power Parity (PPP)	
BYR per USD, 2005, US=1:	838.3
Gross external debt:	
in millions of US Dollars, 2005:	5 192
Exchange rate	
Annual average, BYR per USD, 2005:	2154

Real GDP growth rate

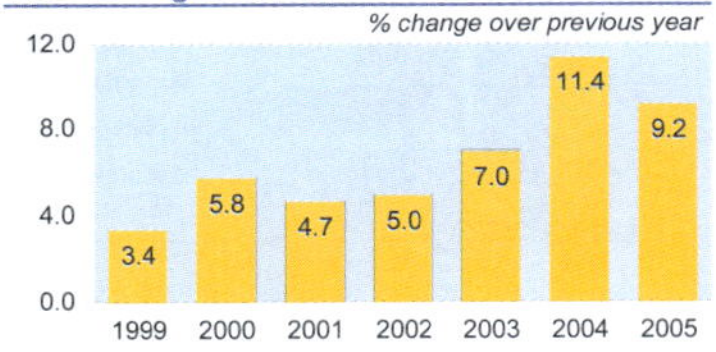

Consumer price index (annual average)

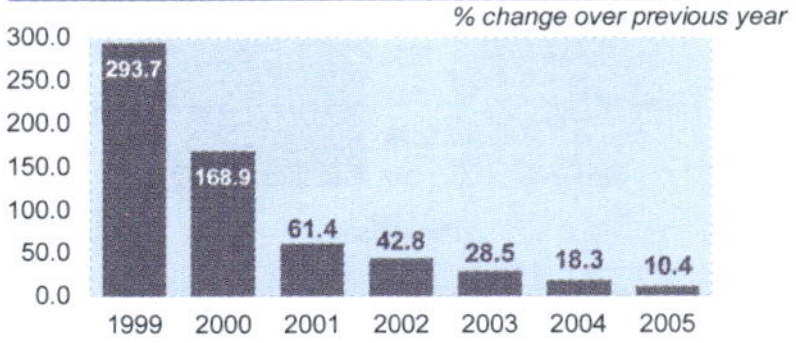

	% of GDP
Exports of goods and services:	61.4
Imports of goods and services:	60.4
External trade balance:	1

GDP by major sectors, 2005

Employment in major sectors, 2004

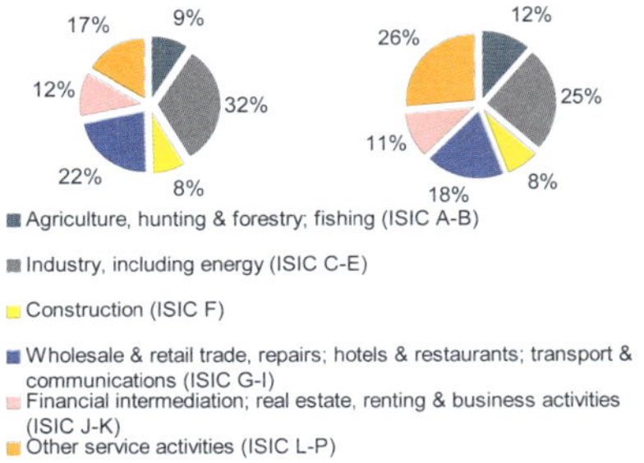

GDP in agriculture, industry, and services (2000=100)

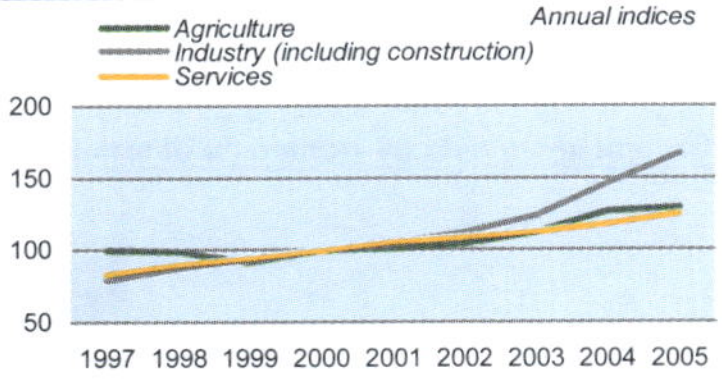

Major import partners from UNECE, 2005

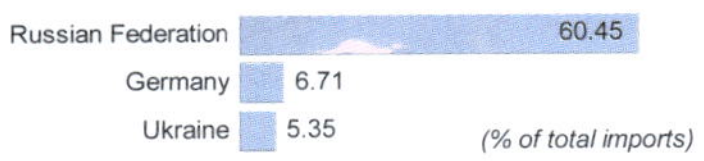

Major export partners in UNECE, 2005

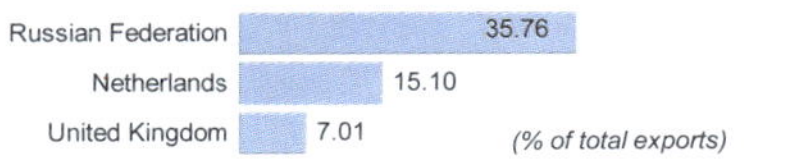

BELGIUM

Capital:	Brussels (141 312)
Two largest cities:	Antwerpen (455 148)
	Gent (229 344)
Area (km^2):	30 528
Total population:	10 421 137
Population density (per km^2):	341
Official languages:	Dutch, French and German
Date joined UN:	27 December 1945
National currency:	Euro (EUR)
National statistical office:	FPS Statistics Division Belgium http://www.statbel.fgov.be

Time: UTC +1h

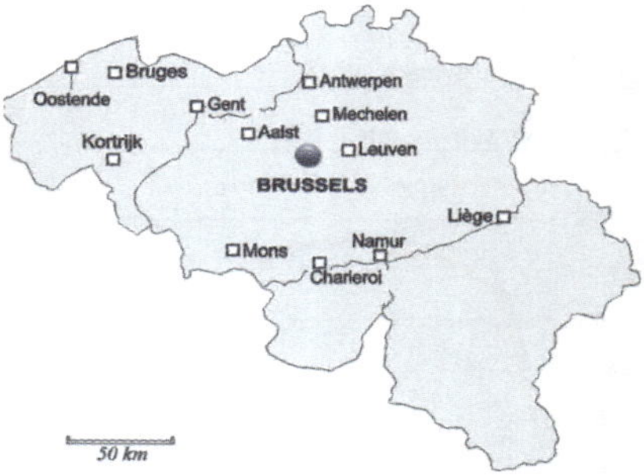

Population by age, 2004

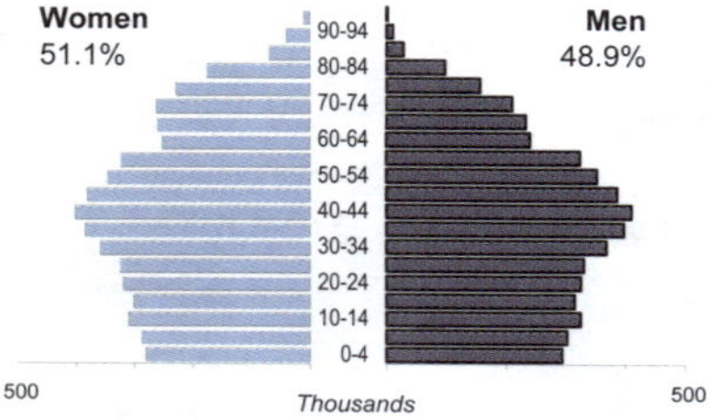

Legal marital status, population aged 18+, 2004

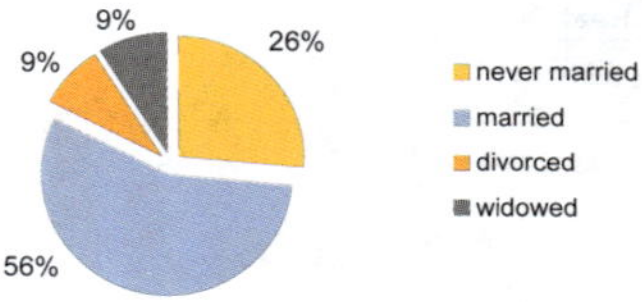

Life expectancy (in years), 2005:	at birth	at 65
Women:	82	20
Men:	77	16

Women in the labour force, 2005:	44.2%
Gender pay gap, 2005:	7%
Female government ministers, 2006: percentage of total for both sexes	23.8%
Female central bank board members, 2005: percentage of total for both sexes	25%
Female tertiary students, 2003-2004: percentage of total for both sexes	53.8%

Median age (in years), 2004:	
Women:	41
Men:	39

	percentage of total population
Foreign born:	..
Foreigners in population, 2005:	8.3%

Total fertility rate

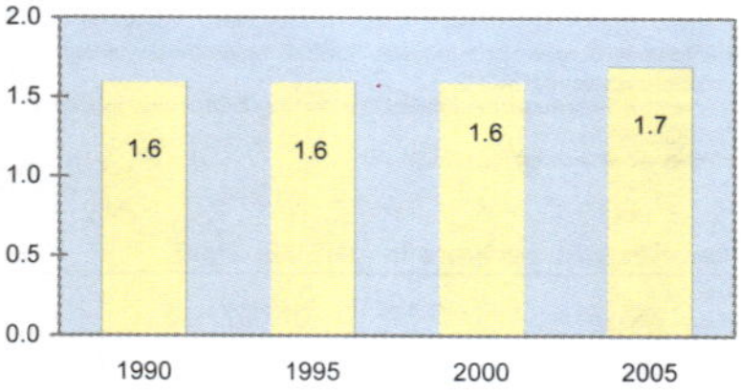

Parliament seats held by women (% of total)

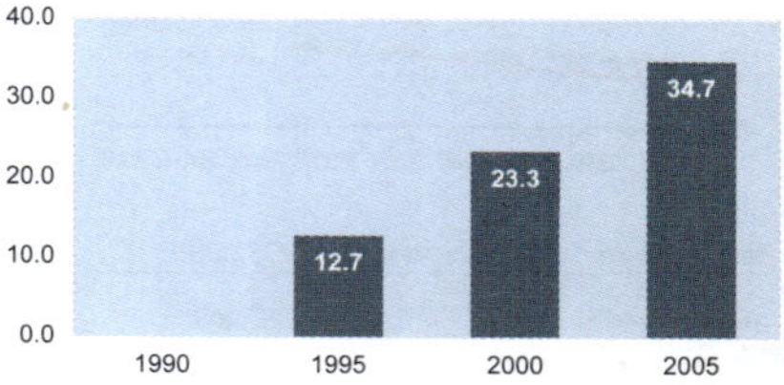

BELGIUM

	1999	2000	2001	2002	2003	2004	2005
Employment (% change over previous year)	1.3	2.0	1.4	-0.1	-0.1	0.6	0.9
Unemployment rate (%)	8.5	6.9	6.6	7.5	8.2	8.4	8.4
Youth unemployment rate (%)	..	16.7	16.8	17.7	21.8	21.2	21.5

Economic activity rate, 2004

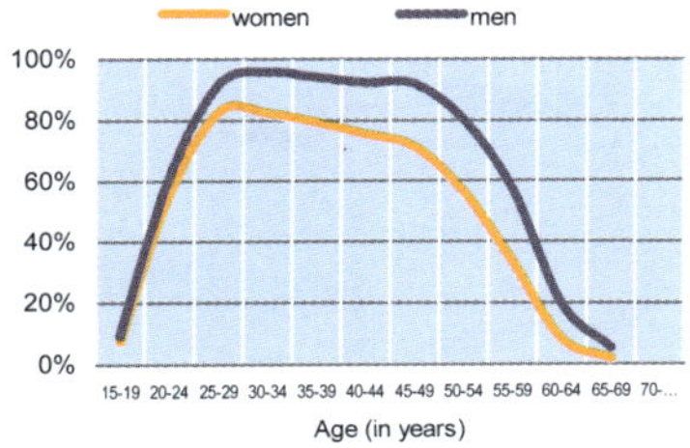

GDP at current prices	
in millions of US Dollars, PPP, 2005:	340 623
in millions of EUR, 2005:	298 180
GDP at constant 2000 prices, per capita	
US Dollars, PPP, 2005:	28 036
EUR, 2005:	25 845
Final consumption expenditure at 2000 prices, per capita, US Dollars, PPP, 2005:	20 912
Purchasing Power Parity (PPP)	
EUR per USD, 2005, US=1:	0.875
Gross external debt:	
in millions of US Dollars, 2005:	969 872
Exchange rate	
Annual average, EUR per USD, 2005:	0.804

Real GDP growth rate

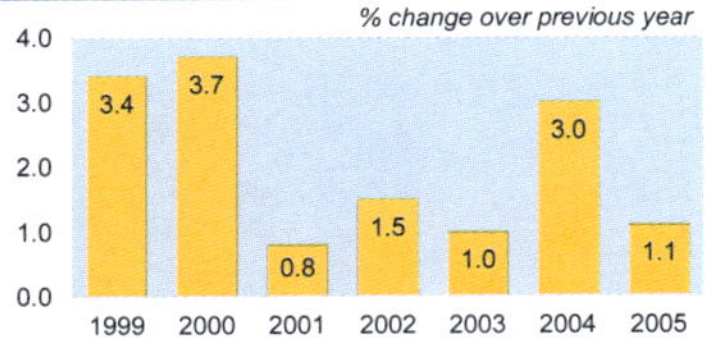

Consumer price index (annual average)

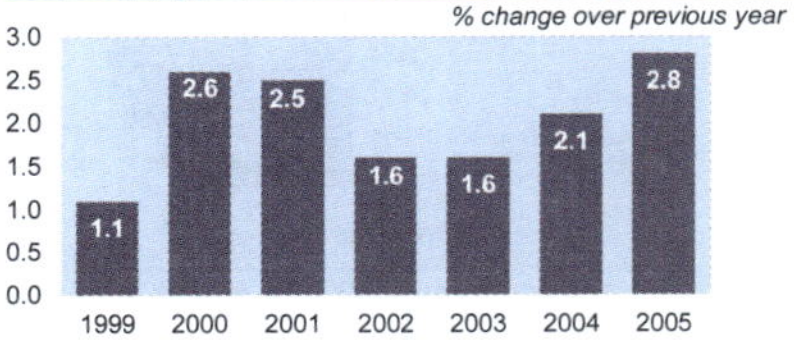

	% of GDP
Exports of goods and services, 2005:	87.1
Imports of goods and services, 2005:	84.8
External trade balance, 2005:	2.3

GDP in agriculture, industry, and services (2000=100)

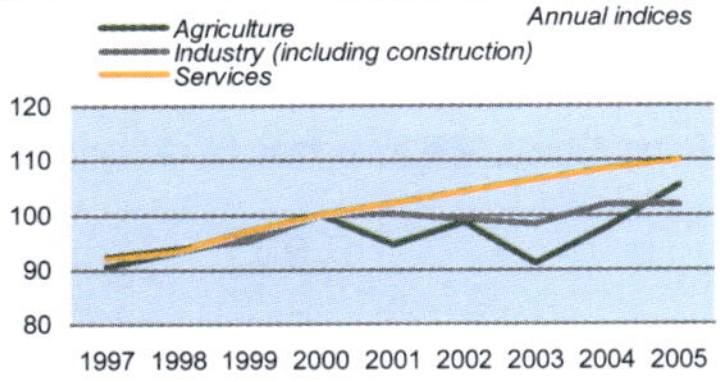

GDP by major sectors, 2005

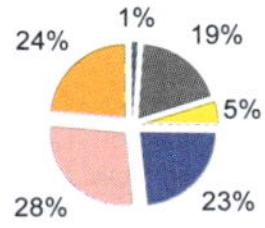

Employment in major sectors, 2005

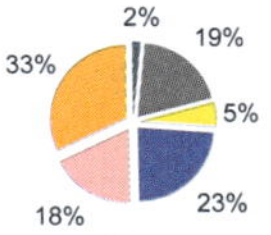

- Agriculture, hunting & forestry; fishing (ISIC A-B)
- Industry, including energy (ISIC C-E)
- Construction (ISIC F)
- Wholesale & retail trade, repairs; hotels & restaurants; transport & communications (ISIC G-I)
- Financial intermediation; real estate, renting & business activities (ISIC J-K)
- Other service activities (ISIC L-P)

Major import partners from UNECE, 2005

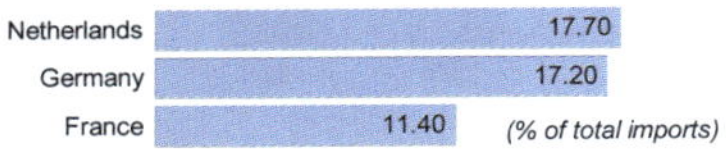

(% of total imports)

Major export partners in UNECE, 2005

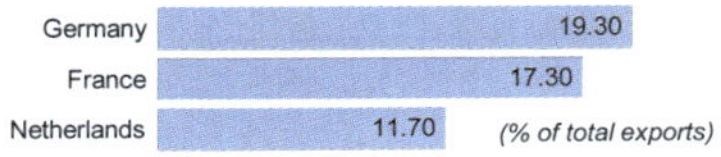

(% of total exports)

BOSNIA AND HERZEGOVINA

Time: UTC +1h

Capital:	Sarajevo (380 000)
Two largest cities:	Banja Luka (165 100)
	Zenica (84 300)
Area (km^2):	51 197
Total population:	3 906 000
Population density (per km^2):	76
Official languages:	Bosnian, Serbian, Croatian
Date joined UN:	22 May 1992
National currency:	Convertible mark (BAM)
National statistical office:	

Federal Office of Statistics of Bosnia And Herzegovina
http://www.fzs.ba/

Population by age, 2005

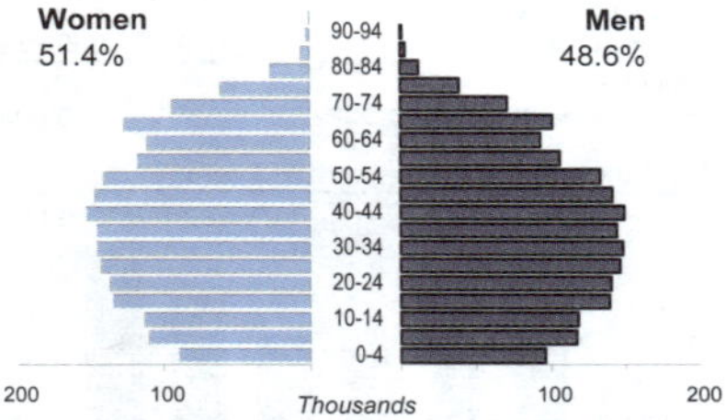

Life expectancy (in years), 2005:	at birth	at 65
Women:	77	..
Men:	70	..

Median age (in years), 2005:	
Women:	39
Men:	37

	percentage of total population
Foreign born:	..
Foreigners in population:	..

Legal marital status, population aged 18+

Data not available

never married
married
divorced
widowed

Women in the labour force:	..
Gender pay gap:	..
Female government ministers, 2006: percentage of total for both sexes	11.8%
Female central bank board members, 2005: percentage of total for both sexes	20%
Female tertiary students: percentage of total for both sexes	..

Total fertility rate

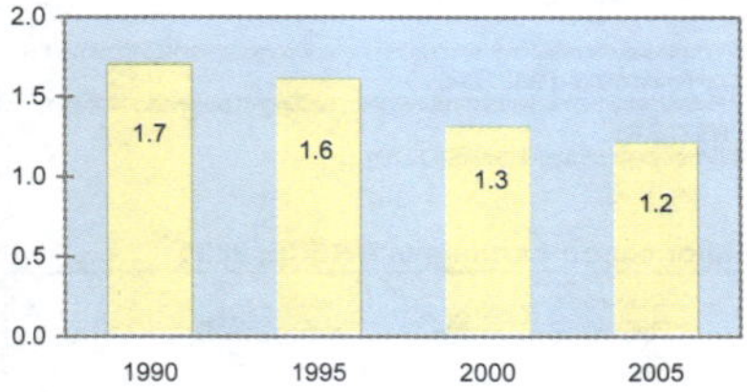

Parliament seats held by women (% of total)

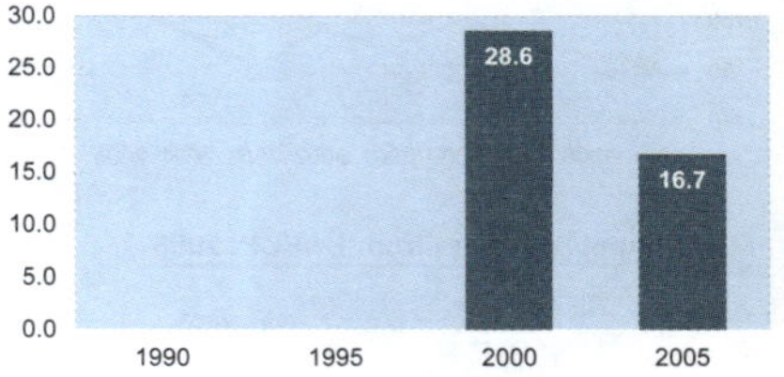

BOSNIA AND HERZEGOVINA

	1999	2000	2001	2002	2003	2004	2005
Employment (% change over previous year)	3.1	0.7	-0.9	-3.2	-1.7	0.2	0.0
Unemployment rate (%)	39.0	39.4	39.9	42.7	44.0	44.9	46.6
Youth unemployment rate (%)	..	..	..	..	..	..	..

Economic activity rate

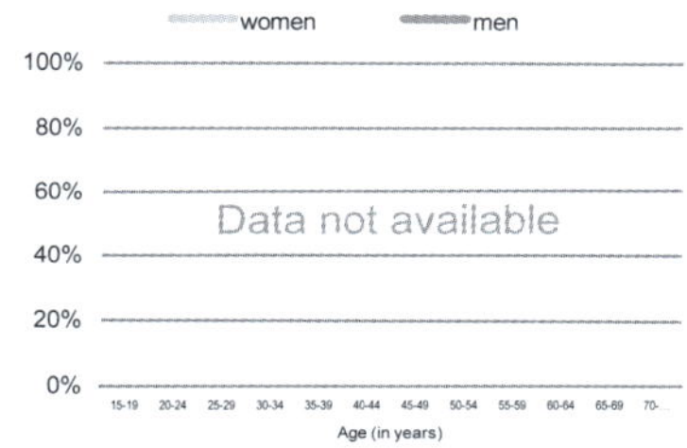

GDP at current prices	
in millions of US Dollars, PPP, 2005:	30 886
in millions of BAM, 2005:	15 750
GDP at constant 2000 prices, per capita	
US Dollars, PPP, 2005:	7 053
BAM, 2005:	3 145
Final consumption expenditure at 2000 prices, per capita, US Dollars, PPP:	..
Purchasing Power Parities (PPP)	
BAM per USD, 2005, US=1:	0.51
Gross external debt:	
in millions of US Dollars, 2004:	2 770
Exchange rate	
Annual average, BAM per USD, 2005:	1.573

Real GDP growth rate

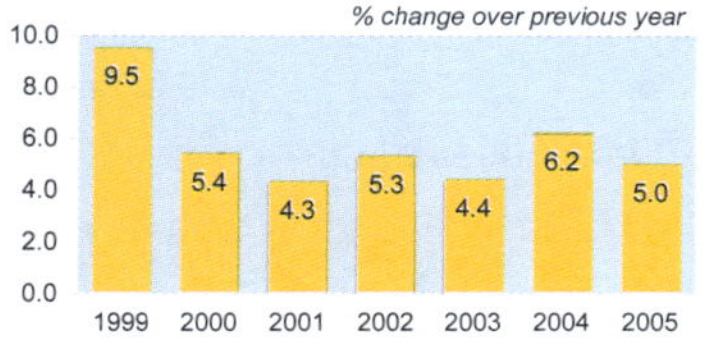

Consumer price index (annual average)

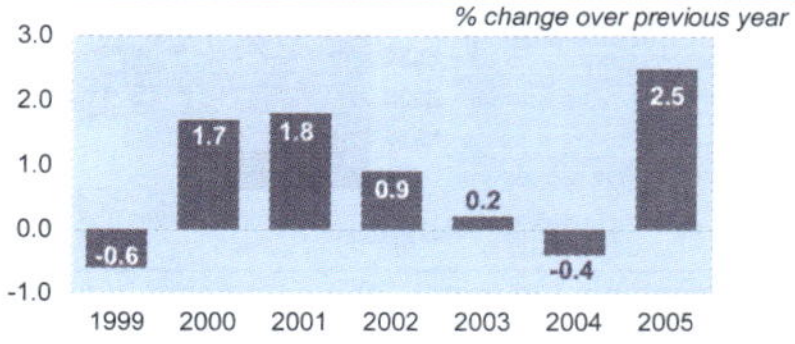

	% of GDP
Exports of goods and services:	..
Imports of goods and services:	..
External trade balance:	..

GDP in agriculture, industry, and services (2000=100)

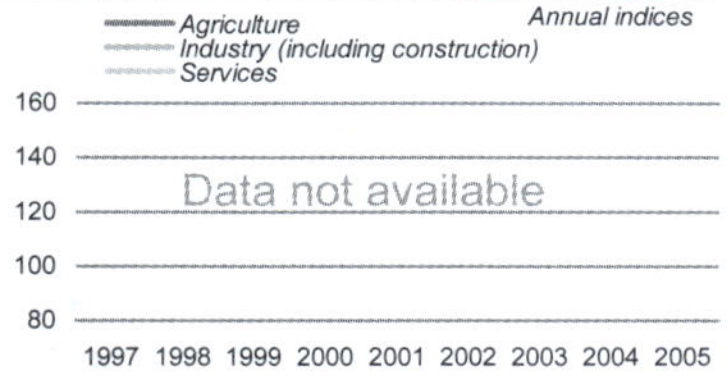

GDP by major sectors, 2005

Employment in major sectors, 2004

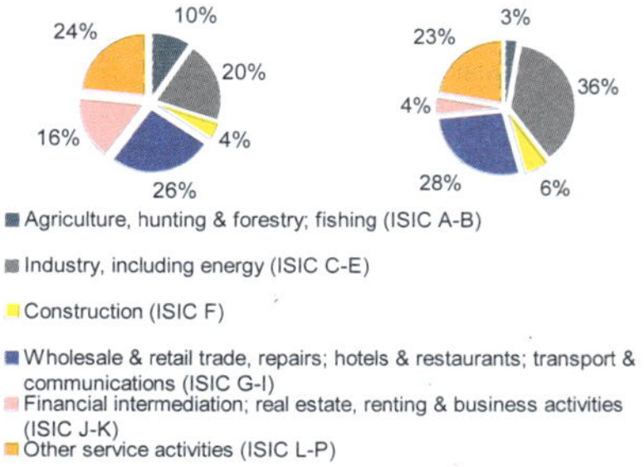

Major import partners from UNECE, 2005

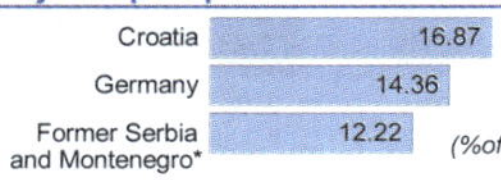

(%of total imports)

Major export partners in UNECE, 2005

(%of total exports)

* refers to trade with the former State Union Serbia and Montenegro.

BULGARIA

Capital:	Sofia (1 138 950)
Two largest cities:	Plovdiv (341 464)
	Varna (312 026)
Area (km²):	110 993
Total population:	7 781 161
Population density (per km²):	70
Official languages:	Bulgarian
Date joined UN:	14 December 1955
National currency:	Bulgarian lev (BGN)
National statistical office:	National Statistical Institute (NSI) http://www.nsi.bg/

Time: UTC +2h

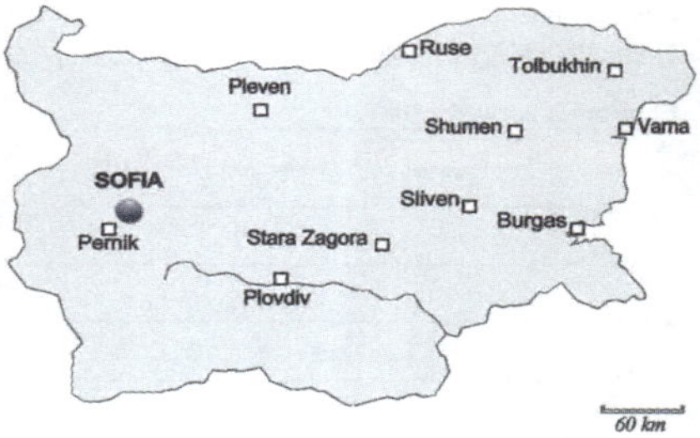

Population by age, 2004

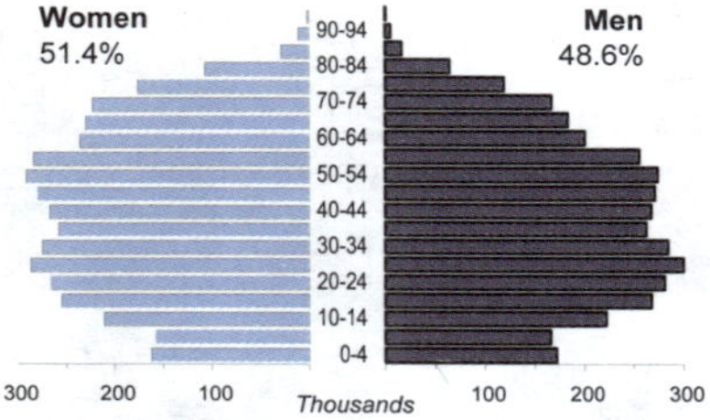

Life expectancy (in years), 2005:	at birth	at 65
Women:	76	16
Men:	69	13

Median age (in years), 2004:	
Women:	42
Men:	39

	percentage of total population
Foreign born, 2004:	0.6%
Foreigners in population, 2004:	0.3%

Total fertility rate

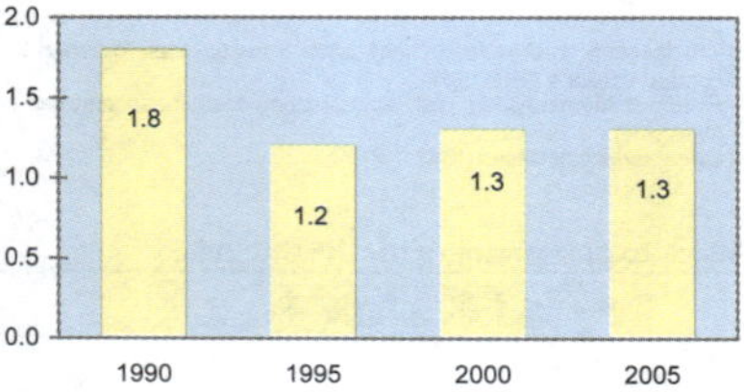

Legal marital status, population aged 18+

never married
married
divorced
widowed

Data not available

Women in the labour force, 2005:	46.5%
Gender pay gap, 2005:	16%
Female government ministers, 2006: percentage of total for both sexes	16.6%
Female central bank board members, 2005: percentage of total for both sexes	14.3%
Female tertiary students, 2003-2004: percentage of total for both sexes	52.5%

Parliament seats held by women (% of total)

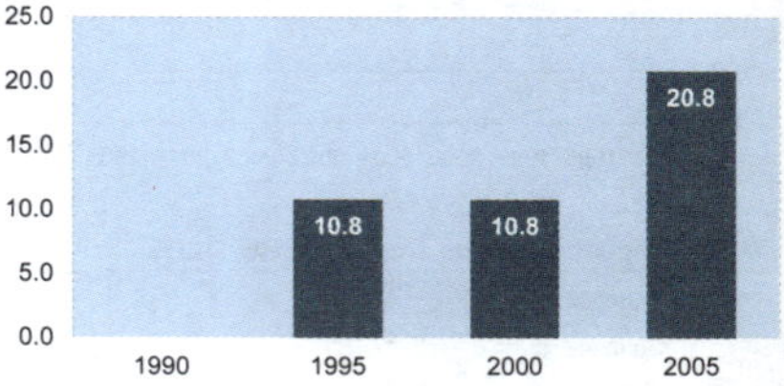

BULGARIA

	1999	2000	2001	2002	2003	2004	2005
Employment (% change over previous year)	-2.1	-3.5	-0.4	0.4	6.3	1.9	1.5
Unemployment rate (%)	15.7	16.4	19.5	18.1	13.7	12.0	9.9
Youth unemployment rate (%)	..	33.7	38.8	37.0	28.2	25.8	22.3

Economic activity rate, 2004

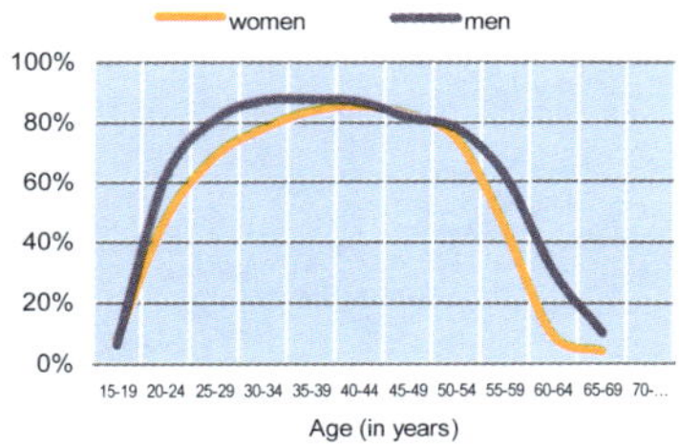

GDP at current prices	
in millions of US Dollars, PPP, 2005:	68 707
in millions of BGN, 2005:	41 948
GDP at constant 2000 prices, per capita	
US Dollars, PPP, 2005:	8 129
BGN, 2005:	4 398
Final consumption expenditure at 2000 prices, per capita, US Dollars, PPP, 2005:	7 202
Purchasing Power Parity (PPP)	
BGN per USD, 2005, US=1:	0.611
Gross external debt:	
in millions of US Dollars, 2005:	17 226
Exchange rate	
Annual average, BGN per USD, 2005:	1.574

Real GDP growth rate

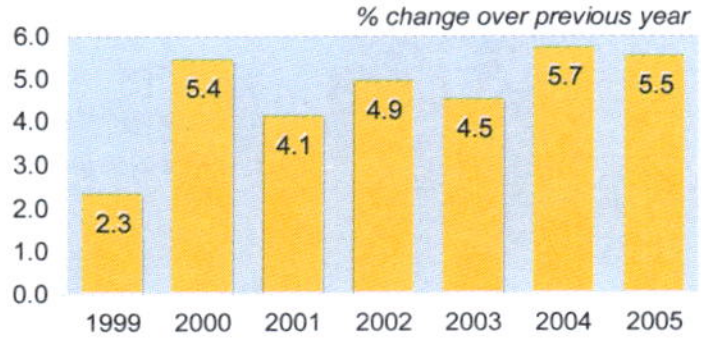

Consumer price index (annual average)

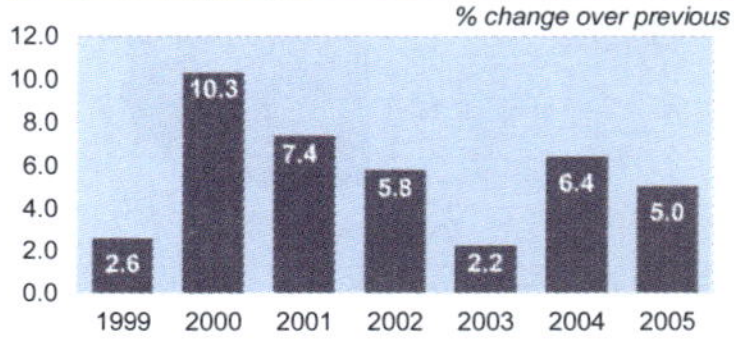

	% of GDP
Exports of goods and services, 2005:	60.8
Imports of goods and services, 2005:	77.4
External trade balance, 2005:	-17

GDP in agriculture, industry, and services (2000=100)

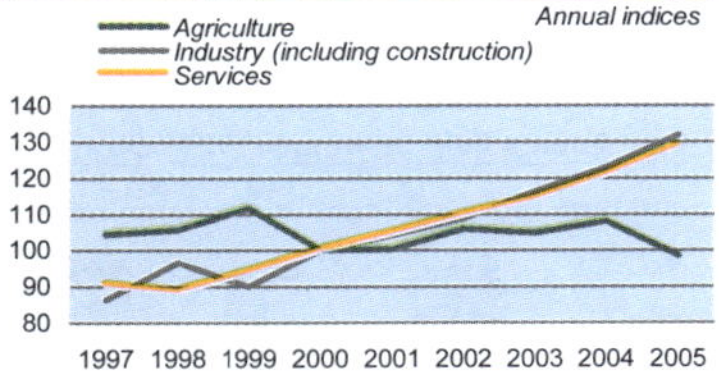

GDP by major sectors, 2005

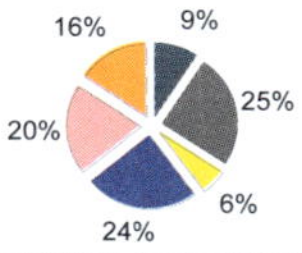

Employment in major sectors, 2005

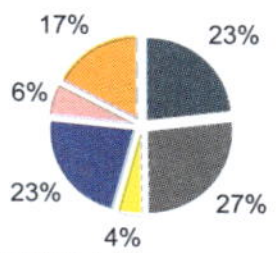

- Agriculture, hunting & forestry; fishing (ISIC A-B)
- Industry, including energy (ISIC C-E)
- Construction (ISIC F)
- Wholesale & retail trade, repairs; hotels & restaurants; transport & communications (ISIC G-I)
- Financial intermediation; real estate, renting & business activities (ISIC J-K)
- Other service activities (ISIC L-P)

Major import partners from UNECE, 2005

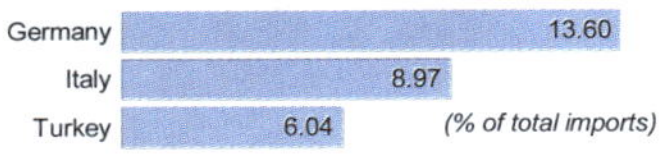

Major export partners in UNECE, 2005

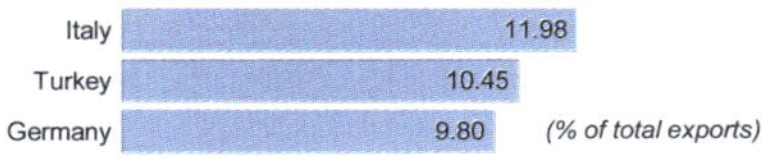

CANADA

Capital:	Ottawa (1 145 500)
Two largest cities:	Toronto (5 202 300)
	Montreal (3 607 200)
Area (km²):	9 970 610
Total population:	32 270 507
Population density (per km²):	3
Official languages:	English and French
Date joined UN:	9 November 1945
National currency:	Canadian dollar (CAD)
National statistical office:	Statistics Canada http://www.statcan.ca

Time: UTC -8h to -3h

Population by age, 2005

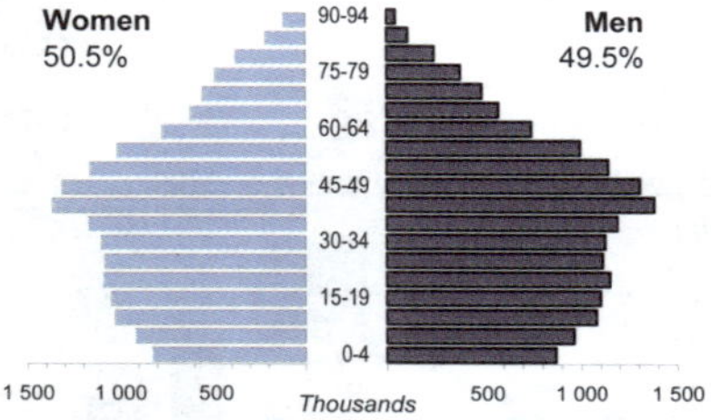

Life expectancy (in years), 2004:	at birth	at 65
Women:	82	21
Men:	77	17

Median age (in years), 2005:	
Women:	39
Men:	38

	percentage of total population
Foreign born, 2001:	18.4%
Foreigners in population:	..

Total fertility rate

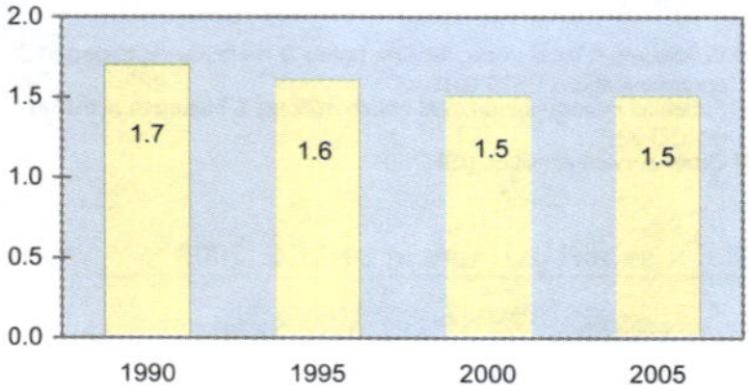

Legal marital status, population aged 18+, 2004

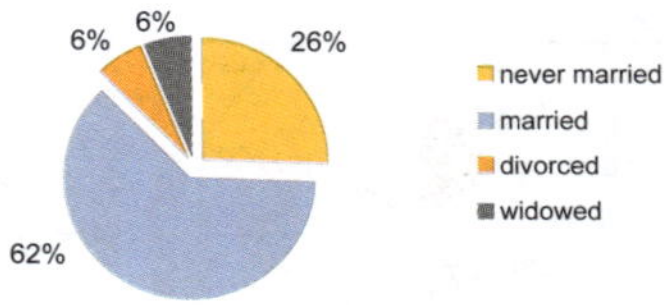

Women in the labour force, 2005:	46.7%
Gender pay gap, 2004:	30.1%
Female government ministers, 2007: percentage of total for both sexes	21.8%
Female central bank board members, 2005: percentage of total for both sexes	16.7%
Female tertiary students, 2004-2005: percentage of total for both sexes	58%

Parliament seats held by women (% of total)

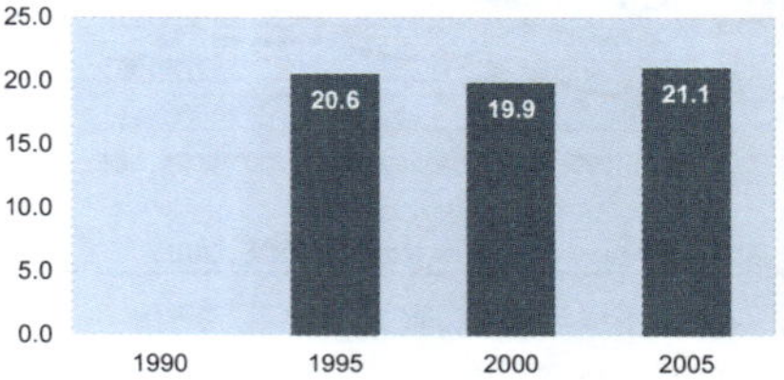

CANADA

	1999	2000	2001	2002	2003	2004	2005
Employment (% change over previous year)	2.8	2.4	0.9	2.2	1.9	1.7	..
Unemployment rate (%)	7.6	6.8	7.2	7.7	7.6	7.2	6.8
Youth unemployment rate (%)	..	12.7	12.9	13.6	13.6	13.4	12.4

Economic activity rate, 2004

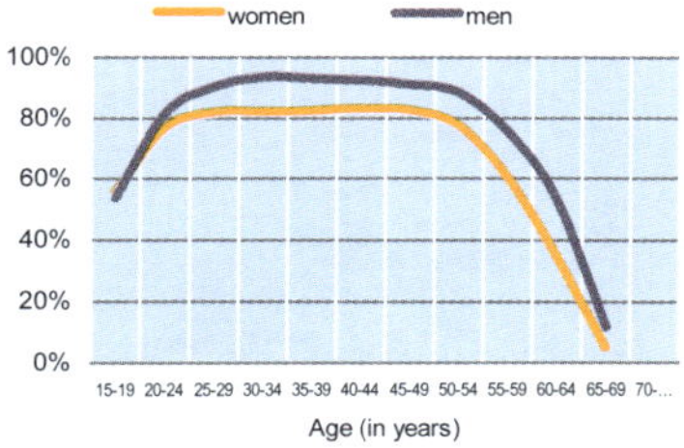

GDP at current prices	
in millions of US Dollars, PPP, 2005:	1 097 140
in millions of CAD, 2005:	1 371 425
GDP at constant 2000 prices, per capita	
US Dollars, PPP, 2005:	30 865
CAD, 2005:	37 964
Final consumption expenditure at 2000 prices, per capita, US Dollars, PPP, 2005:	23 538
Purchasing Power Parity (PPP)	
CAD per USD, 2005, US=1:	1.25
Gross external debt:	
in millions of US Dollars, 2005:	623 346
Exchange rate	
Annual average, CAD per USD, 2005:	1.212

Real GDP growth rate

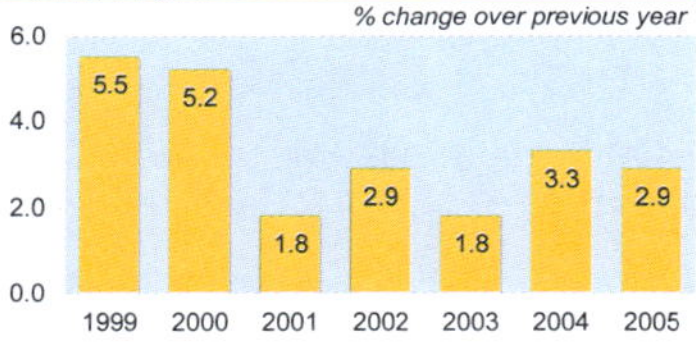

Consumer price index (annual average)

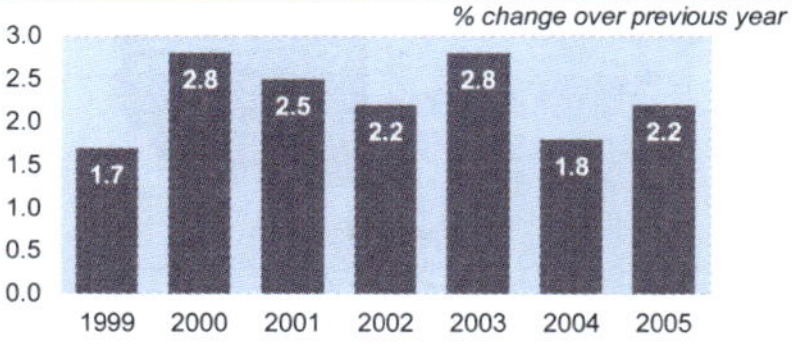

	% of GDP
Exports of goods and services, 2005:	37.9
Imports of goods and services, 2005:	34.1
External trade balance, 2005:	3.8

GDP in agriculture, industry, and services (2000=100)

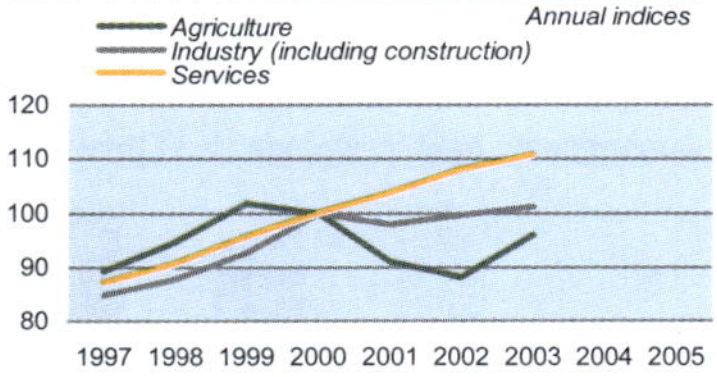

GDP by major sectors, 2001

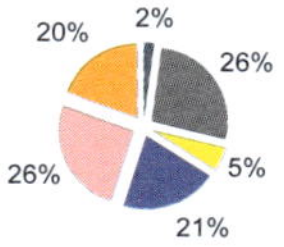

Employment in major sectors, 2004

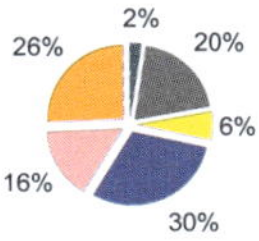

- Agriculture, hunting & forestry; fishing (ISIC A-B)
- Industry, including energy (ISIC C-E)
- Construction (ISIC F)
- Wholesale & retail trade, repairs; hotels & restaurants; transport & communications (ISIC G-I)
- Financial intermediation; real estate, renting & business activities (ISIC J-K)
- Other service activities (ISIC L-P)

Major import partners from UNECE, 2005

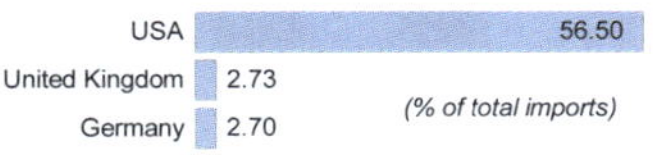

Major export partners in UNECE, 2005

CROATIA

Capital:	Zagreb (691 274)
Two largest cities:	Split (188 694)
	Rijeka (143 800)
Area (km^2):	56 542
Total population:	4 442 850
Population density (per km^2):	79
Official languages:	Croatian
Date joined UN:	22 May 1992
National currency:	Croation kuna (HRK)
National statistical office:	Central Bureau of Statistics Croatia http://www.dzs.hr

Population by age, 2004

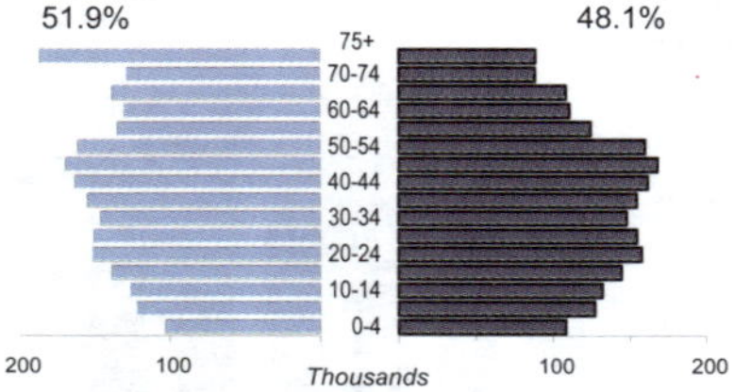

Life expectancy (in years), 2005:	at birth	at 65
Women:	79	17
Men:	72	14

Median age (in years), 2004:	
Women:	42
Men:	38

	percentage of total population
Foreign born:	..
Foreigners in population:	..

Total fertility rate

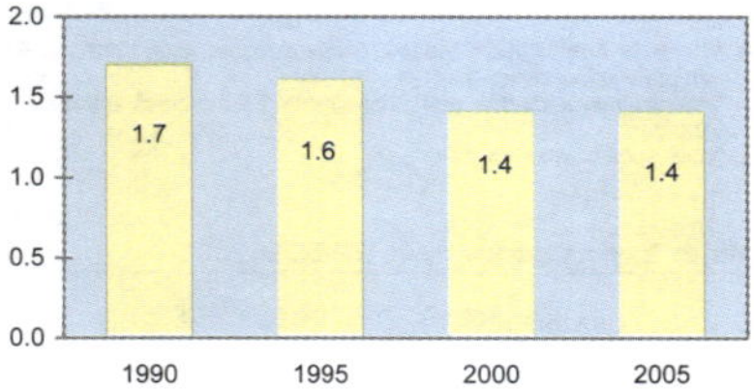

Time: UTC +1h

Legal marital status, population aged 18+

Data not available

never married
married
divorced
widowed

Women in the labour force, 2004:	45.6%
Gender pay gap:	..
Female government ministers, 2006: percentage of total for both sexes	28.6%
Female central bank board members, 2005: percentage of total for both sexes	12.5%
Female tertiary students, 2003-2004: percentage of total for both sexes	53.7%

Parliament seats held by women (% of total)

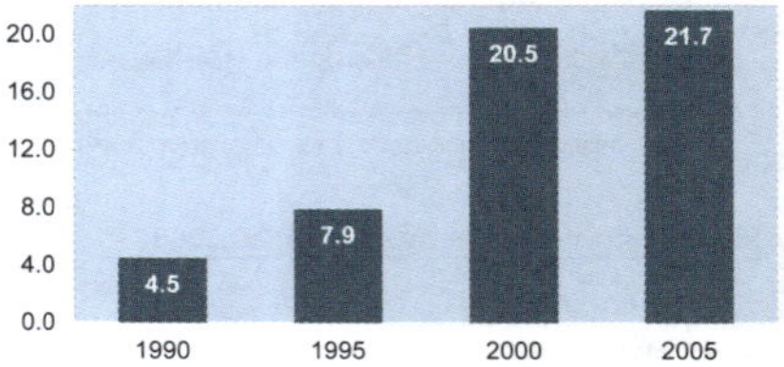

CROATIA

	1999	2000	2001	2002	2003	2004	2005
Employment (% change over previous year)	-3.4	4.1	-5.4	3.9	0.6	1.7	0.7
Unemployment rate (%)	13.6	16.1	15.8	14.8	14.3	13.8	12.7
Youth unemployment rate (%)	..	38.4	41.5	35.5	35.6	33.3	32.5

Economic activity rate, 2004

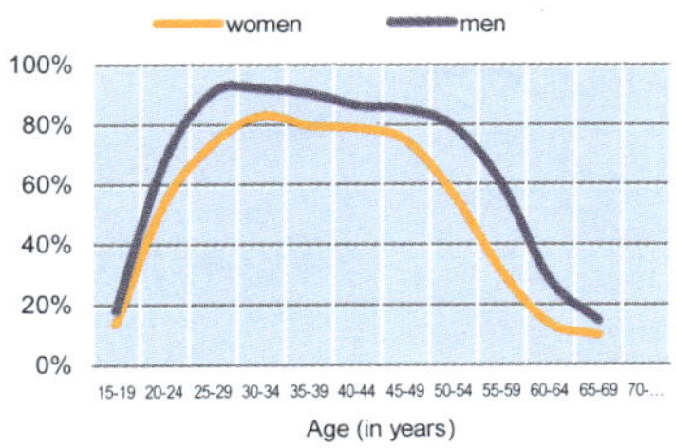

GDP at current prices	
in millions of US Dollars, PPP, 2005:	59 958
in millions of HRK, 2005:	229 031
GDP at constant 2000 prices, per capita	
US Dollars, PPP, 2005:	11 577
HRK, 2005:	43 162
Final consumption expenditure at 2000 prices, per capita, US Dollars, PPP, 2005:	9 256
Purchasing Power Parity (PPP)	
HRK per USD, 2005, US=1:	3.82
Gross external debt:	
in millions of US Dollars, 2005:	30 131
Exchange rate	
Annual average, HRK per USD, 2005:	5.947

Real GDP growth rate

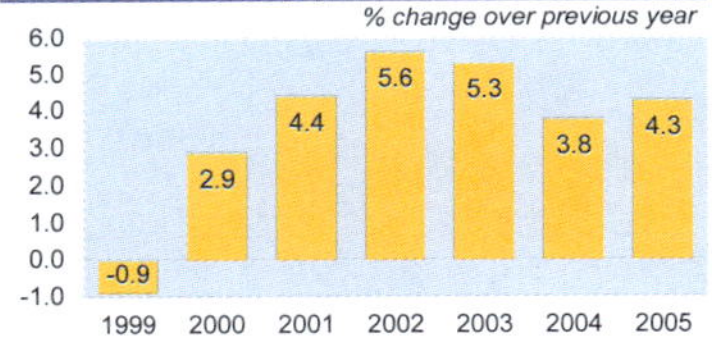

Consumer price index (annual average)

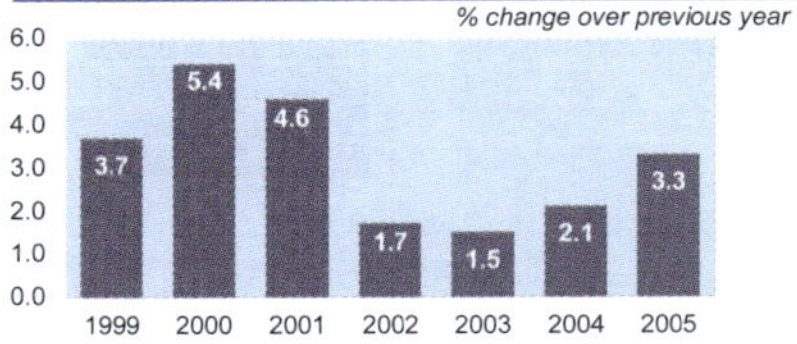

	% of GDP
Exports of goods and services, 2005:	47.1
Imports of goods and services, 2005:	55.8
External trade balance, 2005:	-8.7

GDP by major sectors, 2005 / Employment in major sectors, 2004

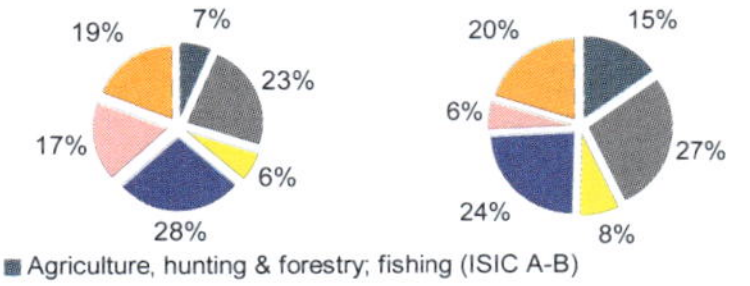

- Agriculture, hunting & forestry; fishing (ISIC A-B)
- Industry, including energy (ISIC C-E)
- Construction (ISIC F)
- Wholesale & retail trade, repairs; hotels & restaurants; transport & communications (ISIC G-I)
- Financial intermediation; real estate, renting & business activities (ISIC J-K)
- Other service activities (ISIC L-P)

GDP in agriculture, industry, and services (2000=100)

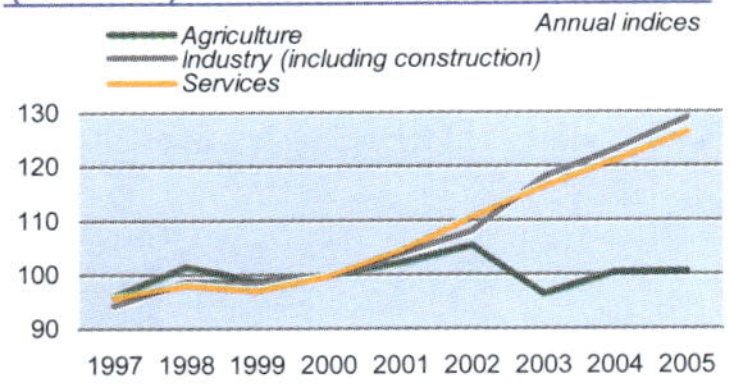

Major import partners from UNECE, 2005

Major export partners in UNECE, 2005

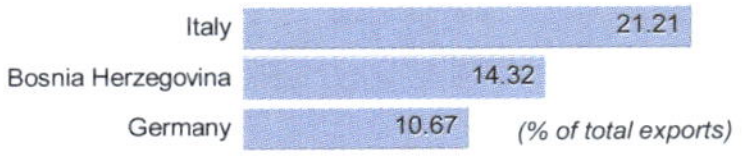

CYPRUS

Capital:	Nicosia (219 200)
Two largest cities:	Limassol (172 500)
	Larnaca (77 000)
Area (km²):	9 251
Total population:	739 771
Population density (per km²):	80
Official languages:	Greek and Turkish
Date joined UN:	20 September 1960
National currency:	Cypriot pound (CYP)
National statistical office:	Department of Statistics and Research http://www.mof.gov.cy/cystat

Time: UTC +2h

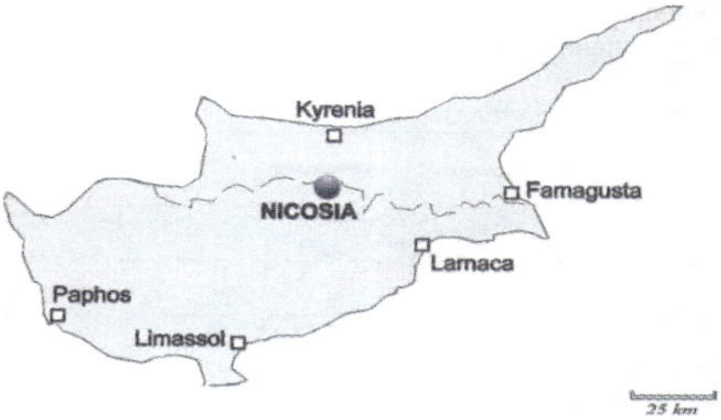

Population by age, 2004

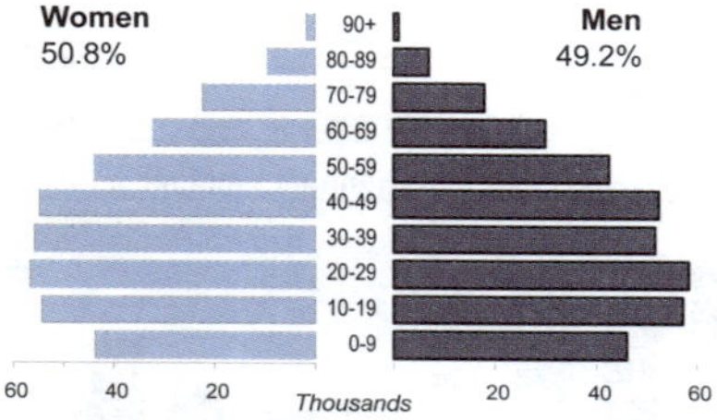

Life expectancy (in years), 2004:	at birth	at 65
Women:	82	20
Men:	77	17

Median age (in years), 2004:	
Women:	36
Men:	34

	percentage of total population
Foreign born:	..
Foreigners in population, 2005:	2.5%

Total fertility rate

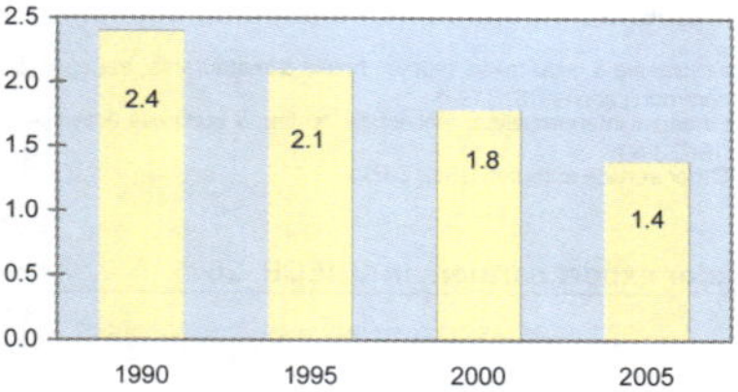

Legal marital status, population aged 18+

Women in the labour force, 2005:	43.8%
Gender pay gap, 2005:	25%
Female government ministers, 2000: percentage of total for both sexes	0%
Female central bank board members, 2005: percentage of total for both sexes	0%
Female tertiary students, 2003-2004: percentage of total for both sexes	47.9%

Parliament seats held by women (% of total)

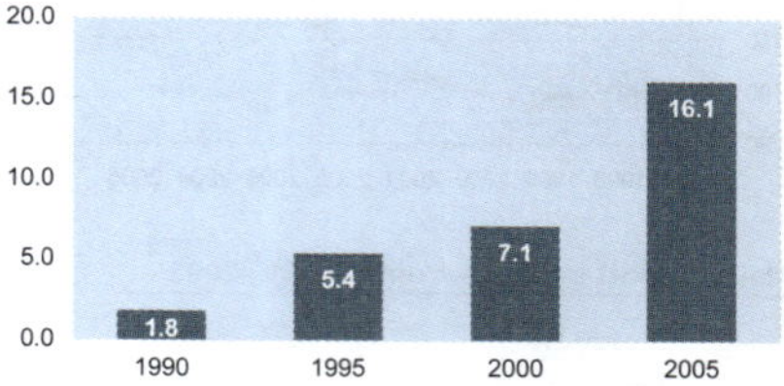

CYPRUS

	1999	2000	2001	2002	2003	2004	2005
Employment (% change over previous year)	1.8	2.3	4.8	2.0	0.8	1.7	1.4
Unemployment rate (%)	5.1	4.8	3.9	3.6	4.1	4.7	5.3
Youth unemployment rate (%)	..	10.1	8.1	8.1	8.9	10.5	13.0

Economic activity rate, 2004

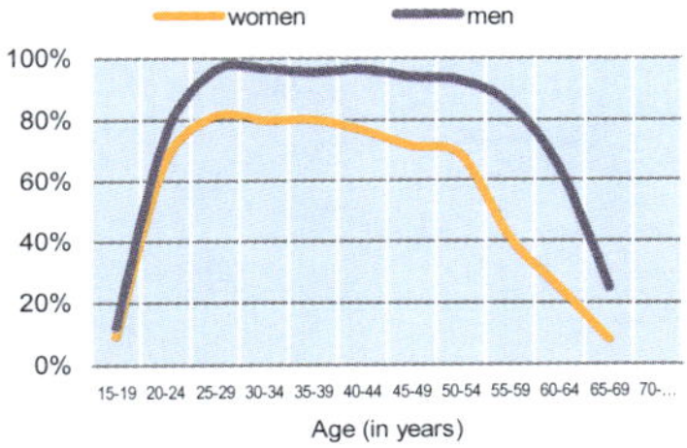

GDP at current prices	
in millions of US Dollars, PPP, 2005:	17 750
in millions of CYP, 2005:	7 862
GDP at constant 2000 prices, per capita	
US Dollars, PPP, 2005:	20 125
CYP, 2005:	8 917
Final consumption expenditure at 2000 prices, per capita, US Dollars, PPP, 2005:	16 743
Purchasing Power Parity (PPP)	
CYP per USD, 2005, US=1:	0.443
Gross external debt:	
in millions of US Dollars, 2004:	9 725
Exchange rate	
Annual average, CYP per USD, 2005:	0.464

Real GDP growth rate

% change over previous year

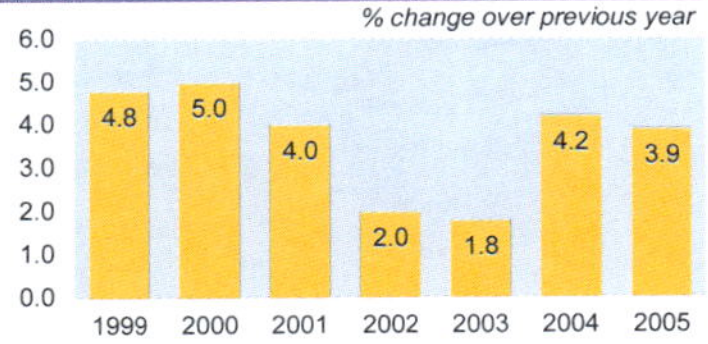

Consumer price index (annual average)

% change over previous year

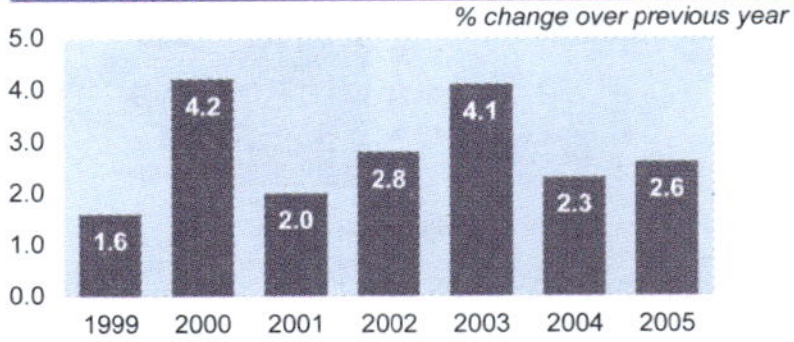

	% of GDP
Exports of goods and services, 2005:	48.4
Imports of goods and services, 2005:	51.0
External trade balance, 2005:	-2.6

GDP by major sectors, 2005

Employment in major sectors, 2005

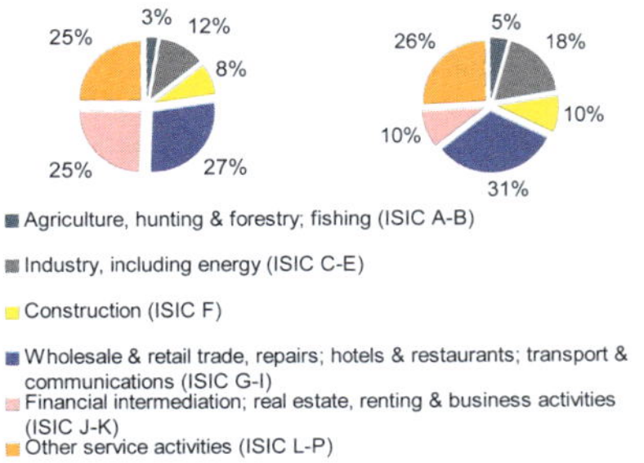

GDP in agriculture, industry, and services (2000=100)

Annual indices

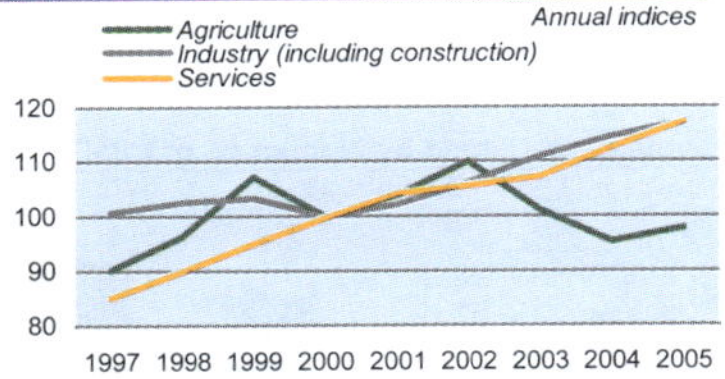

Major import partners from UNECE, 2005

Major export partners in UNECE, 2005

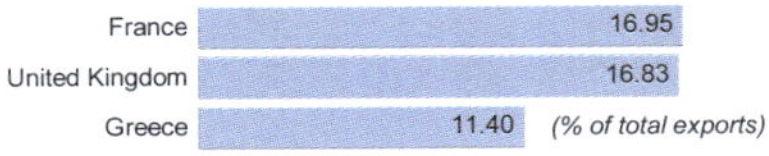

CZECH REPUBLIC

Capital:	Prague (1 165 581)
Two largest cities:	Brno (396 559)
	Ostrava (313 088)
Area (km^2):	78 866
Total population:	10 216 016
Population density (per km^2):	130
Official languages:	Czech
Date joined UN:	19 January 1993
National currency:	Czech koruna (CZK)
National statistical office:	Czech Statistical Office http://www.czso.cz

Time: UTC +1h

Population by age, 2004

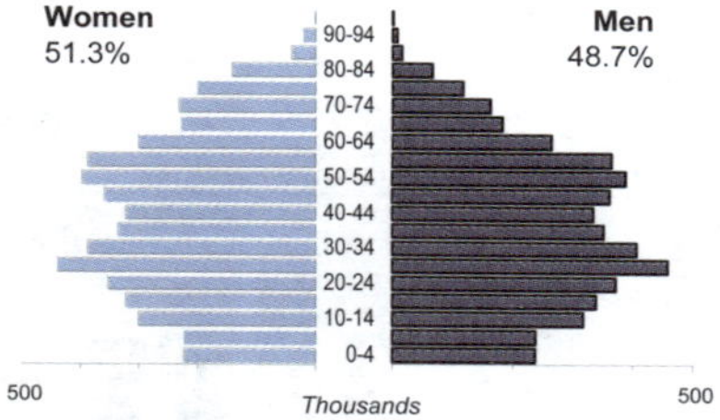

Life expectancy (in years), 2005:	at birth	at 65
Women:	79	18
Men:	73	15

Median age (in years), 2004:	
Women:	40
Men:	37

	percentage of total population
Foreign born:	..
Foreigners in population, 2005:	2.5%

Legal marital status, population aged 18+, 2004

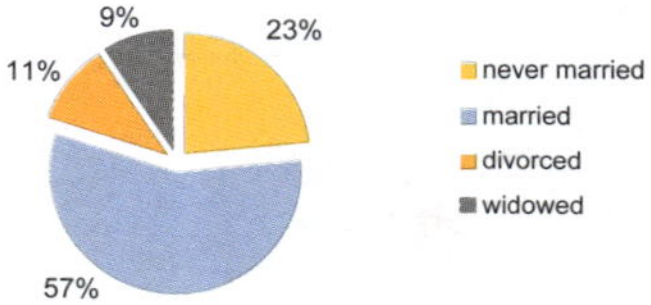

Women in the labour force, 2005:	44.1%
Gender pay gap, 2005:	19%
Female government ministers, 2006: percentage of total for both sexes	13.3%
Female central bank board members, 2005: percentage of total for both sexes	14.3%
Female tertiary students, 2003-2004: percentage of total for both sexes	51.7%

Total fertility rate

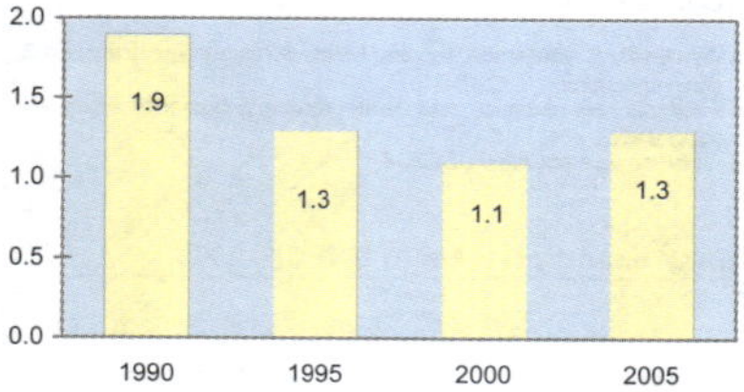

Parliament seats held by women (% of total)

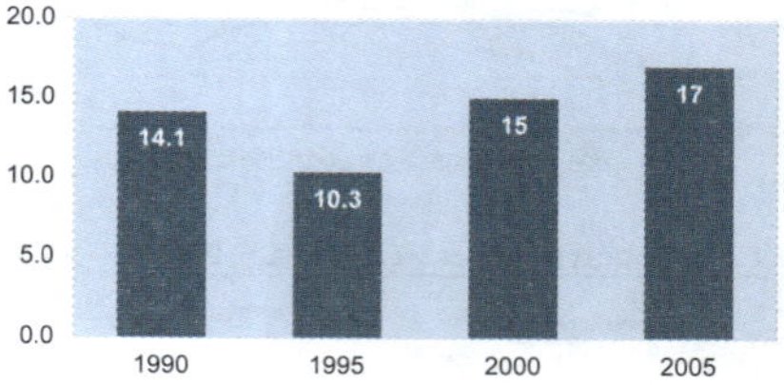

CZECH REPUBLIC

	1999	2000	2001	2002	2003	2004	2005
Employment (% change over previous year)	-4.1	-0.5	0.4	1.6	-1.4	0.1	-1.8
Unemployment rate (%)	8.6	8.7	8.0	7.3	7.8	8.3	7.9
Youth unemployment rate (%)	..	17.8	17.3	16.9	18.6	21.0	19.2

Economic activity rate, 2004

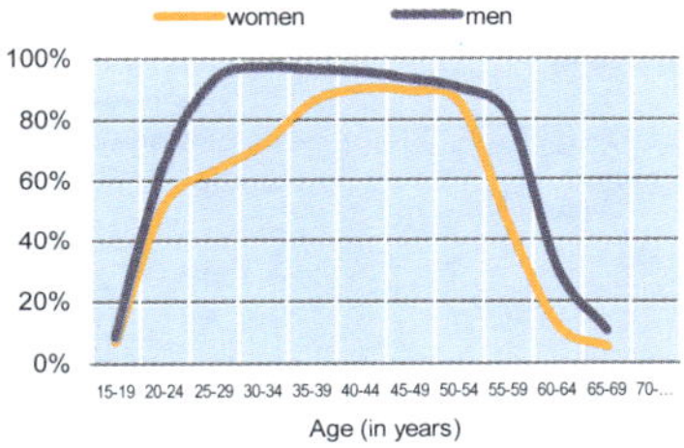

GDP at current prices	
in millions of US Dollars, PPP, 2005:	208 947
in millions of CZK, 2005:	2 970 261
GDP at constant 2000 prices, per capita	
US Dollars, PPP, 2005:	17 778
CZK, 2005:	255 776
Final consumption expenditure at 2000 prices, per capita, US Dollars, PPP, 2005:	12 727
Purchasing Power Parity (PPP)	
CZK per USD, 2005, US=1:	14.22
Gross external debt:	
in millions of US Dollars, 2005:	45 791
Exchange rate	
Annual average, CZK per USD, 2005:	23.96

Real GDP growth rate

% change over previous year

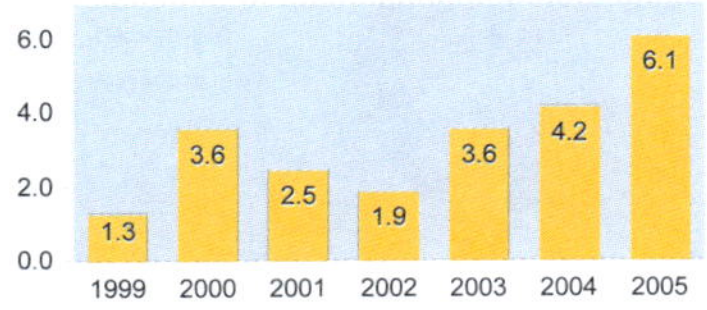

Consumer price index (annual average)

% change over previous year

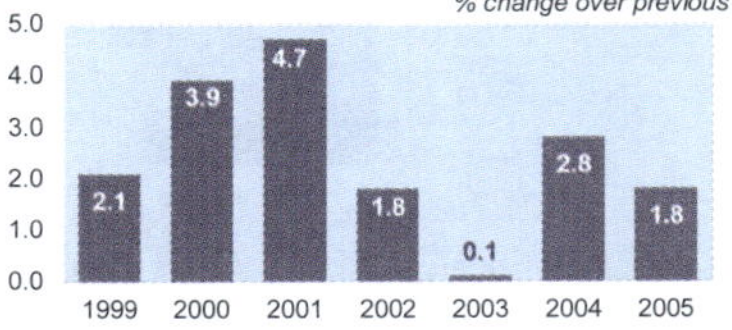

	% of GDP
Exports of goods and services, 2005:	71.7
Imports of goods and services, 2005:	69.8
External trade balance, 2005:	1.9

GDP by major sectors, 2005

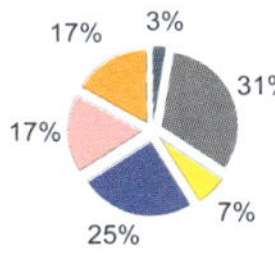

Employment in major sectors, 2005

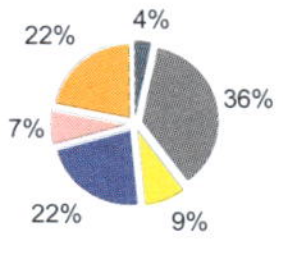

- Agriculture, hunting & forestry; fishing (ISIC A-B)
- Industry, including energy (ISIC C-E)
- Construction (ISIC F)
- Wholesale & retail trade, repairs; hotels & restaurants; transport & communications (ISIC G-I)
- Financial intermediation; real estate, renting & business activities (ISIC J-K)
- Other service activities (ISIC L-P)

GDP in agriculture, industry, and services (2000=100)

Annual indices

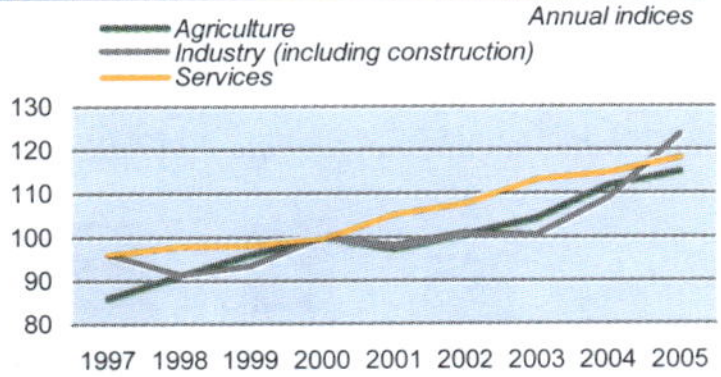

Major import partners from UNECE, 2005

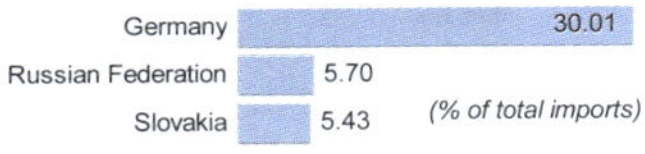

Major export partners in UNECE, 2005

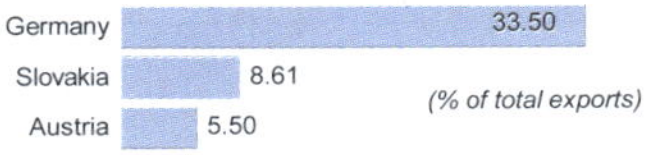

DENMARK

Capital:	Copenhagen (502 362)
Two largest cities:	Arhus (294 954)
	Odense (185 871)
Area (km^2):	43 094
Total population:	5 419 432
Population density (per km^2):	126
Official languages:	Danish
Date joined UN:	24 October 1945
National currency:	Danish krone (DKK)
National statistical office:	Statistical Office of Denmark http://www.dst.dk

Time: UTC +1h

Population by age, 2005

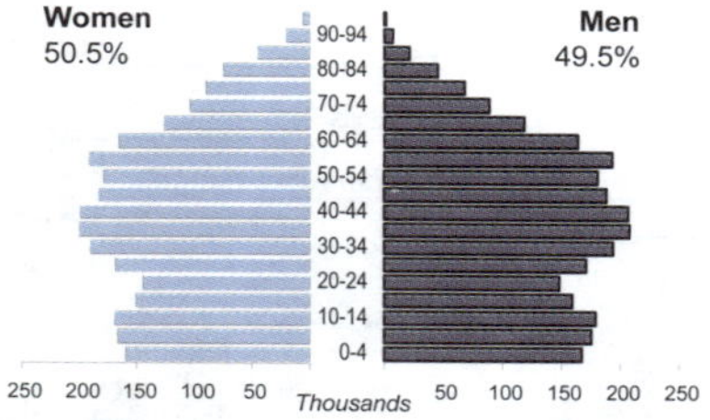

Life expectancy (in years), 2005:	at birth	at 65
Women:	80	19
Men:	76	16

Median age (in years), 2005:	
Women:	40
Men:	39

	percentage of total population
Foreign born, 2005:	7.7%
Foreigners in population, 2005:	4.9%

Legal marital status, population aged 18+, 2004

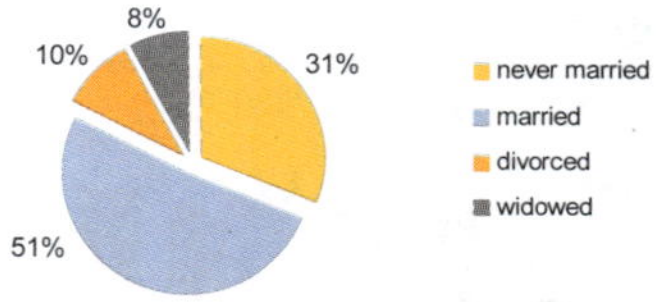

Women in the labour force, 2005:	46.8%
Gender pay gap, 2005:	18%
Female government ministers: percentage of total for both sexes	..
Female central bank board members, 2005: percentage of total for both sexes	33.3%
Female tertiary students, 2003-2004: percentage of total for both sexes	57.9%

Total fertility rate

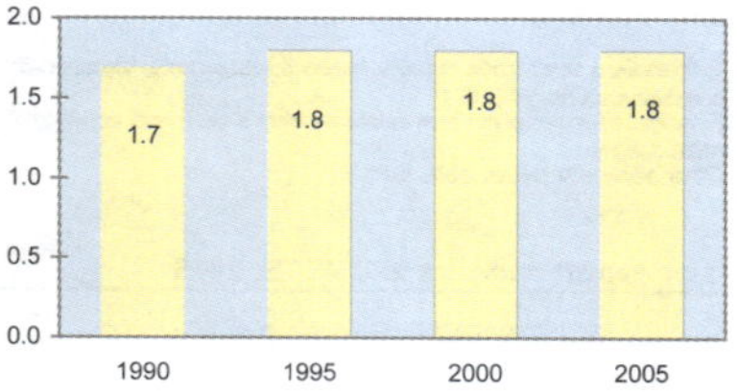

Parliament seats held by women (% of total)

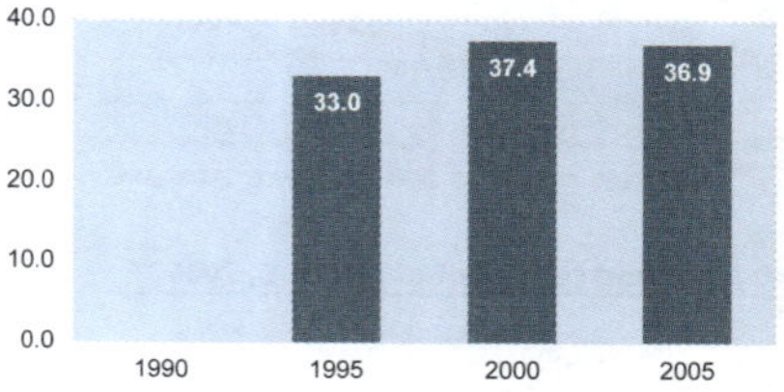

DENMARK

	1999	2000	2001	2002	2003	2004	2005
Employment (% change over previous year)	1.0	0.4	0.8	-0.1	-1.2	0.0	0.7
Unemployment rate (%)	5.2	4.3	4.5	4.6	5.4	5.5	4.8
Youth unemployment rate (%)	..	6.2	8.3	7.4	9.2	8.2	8.6

Economic activity rate, 2004

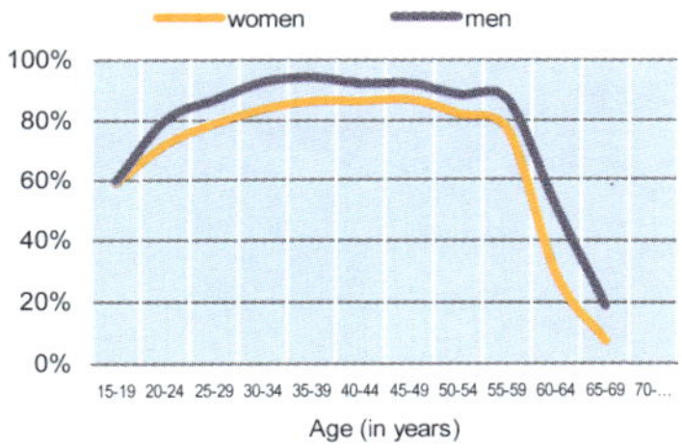

GDP at current prices	
in millions of US Dollars, PPP, 2005:	186 237
in millions of DKK, 2005:	1 554 044
GDP at constant 2000 prices, per capita	
US Dollars, PPP, 2005:	30 338
DKK, 2005:	255 194
Final consumption expenditure at 2000 prices, per capita, US Dollars, PPP, 2005:	22 690
Purchasing Power Parity (PPP)	
DKK per USD, 2005, US=1:	8.344
Gross external debt:	
in millions of US Dollars, 2005:	360 155
Exchange rate	
Annual average, DKK per USD, 2005:	5.997

Real GDP growth rate

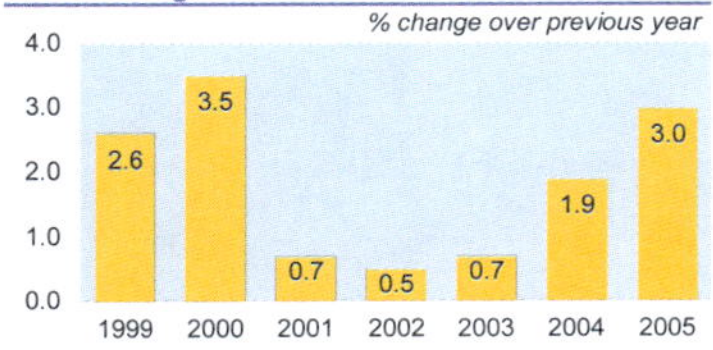

Consumer price index (annual average)

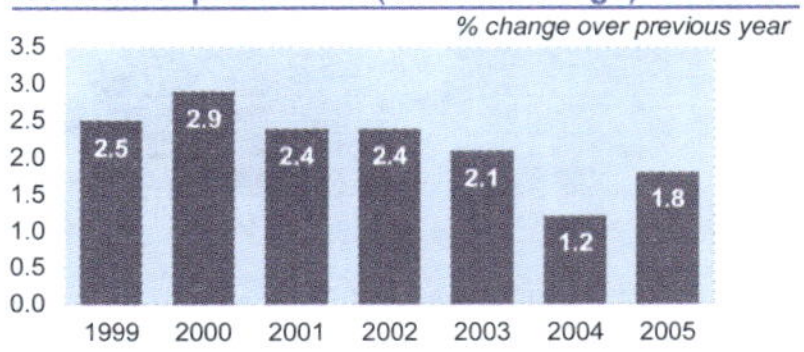

	% of GDP
Exports of goods and services, 2005:	48.5
Imports of goods and services, 2005:	43.8
External trade balance, 2005:	4.7

GDP in agriculture, industry, and services (2000=100)

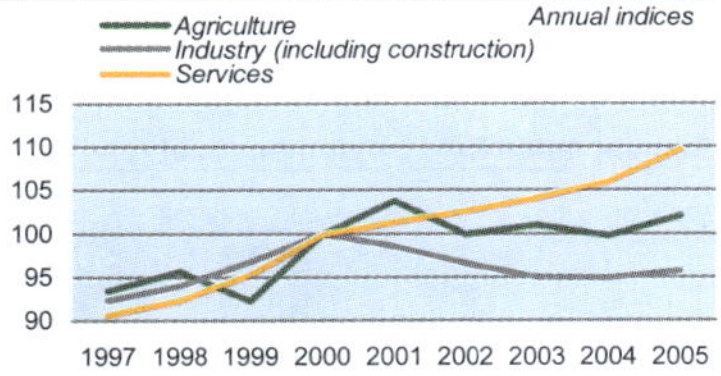

GDP by major sectors, 2005

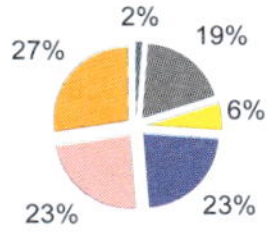

Employment in major sectors, 2005

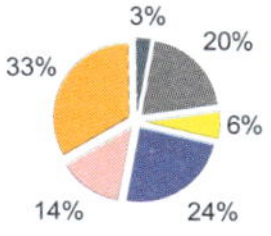

- Agriculture, hunting & forestry; fishing (ISIC A-B)
- Industry, including energy (ISIC C-E)
- Construction (ISIC F)
- Wholesale & retail trade, repairs; hotels & restaurants; transport & communications (ISIC G-I)
- Financial intermediation; real estate, renting & business activities (ISIC J-K)
- Other service activities (ISIC L-P)

Major import partners from UNECE, 2005

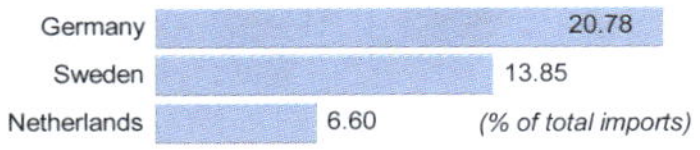

Major export partners in UNECE, 2005

ESTONIA

Capital:	Tallinn (397 150)
Two largest cities:	Tartu (101 190)
	Narva (67 752)
Area (km²):	45 228
Total population:	1 346 097
Population density (per km²):	30
Official languages:	Estonian
Date joined UN:	17 September 1991
National currency:	Estonian kroon (EEK)
National statistical office:	Statistical Office of Estonia http://www.stat.ee

Time: UTC +2h

Population by age, 2005

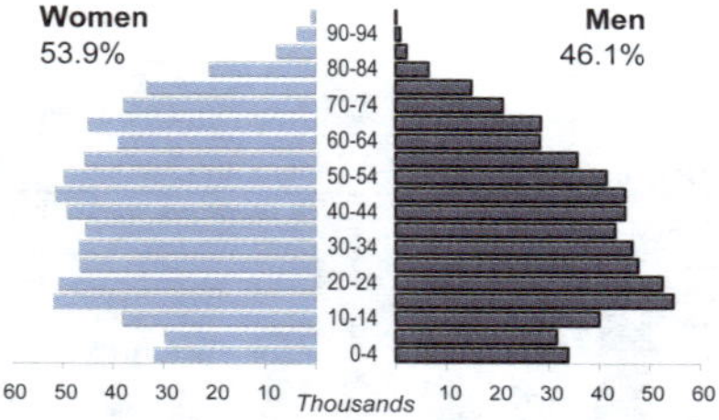

Life expectancy (in years), 2005:	at birth	at 65
Women:	78	18
Men:	67	13

Median age (in years), 2005:	
Women:	42
Men:	35

	percentage of total population
Foreign born:	..
Foreigners in population:	..

Legal marital status, population aged 18+

never married
married
divorced
widowed

Data not available

Women in the labour force, 2005:	50.1%
Gender pay gap, 2005:	25%
Female government ministers, 2006: percentage of total for both sexes	14.3%
Female central bank board members, 2005: percentage of total for both sexes	25%
Female tertiary students, 2003-2004: percentage of total for both sexes	61.8%

Total fertility rate

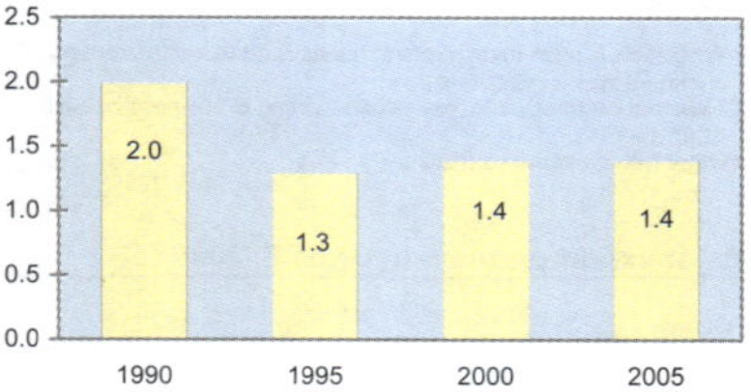

Parliament seats held by women (% of total)

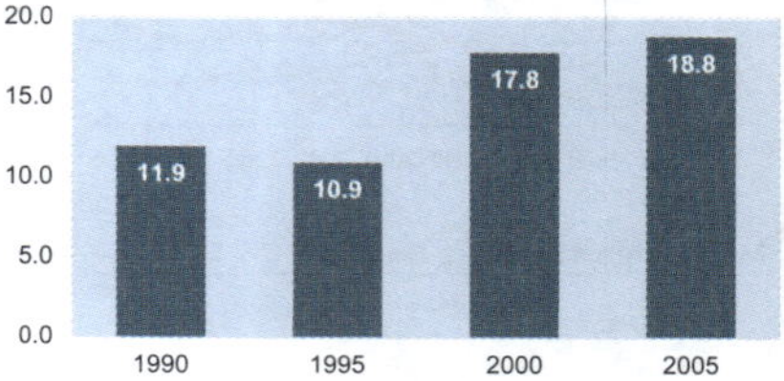

ESTONIA

	1999	2000	2001	2002	2003	2004	2005
Employment (% change over previous year)	-4.3	-1.5	0.9	1.2	1.5	0.0	1.9
Unemployment rate (%)	11.3	12.8	12.4	10.3	10.0	9.7	7.9
Youth unemployment rate (%)	..	23.9	23.2	17.6	20.6	21.7	15.9

Economic activity rate, 2004

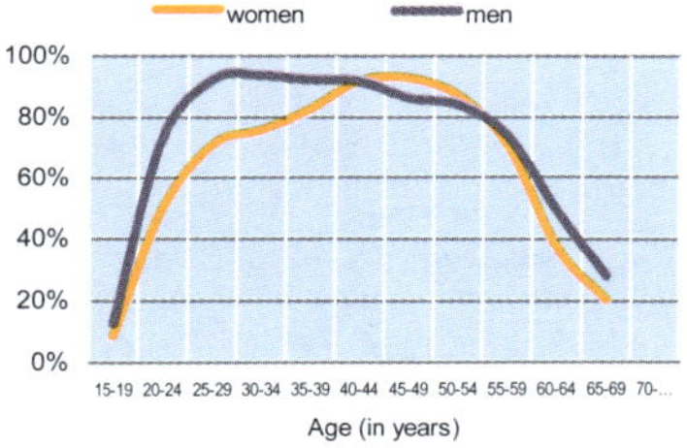

GDP at current prices	
in millions of US Dollars, PPP, 2005:	22 424
in millions of EEK, 2005:	173 062
GDP at constant 2000 prices, per capita	
US Dollars, PPP, 2005:	14 561
EEK, 2005:	105 318
Final consumption expenditure at 2000 prices, per capita, US Dollars, PPP, 2005:	10 080
Purchasing Power Parity (PPP)	
EEK per USD, 2005, US=1:	7.718
Gross external debt:	
in millions of US Dollars, 2005:	11 430
Exchange rate	
Annual average, EEK per USD, 2005:	12.58

Real GDP growth rate

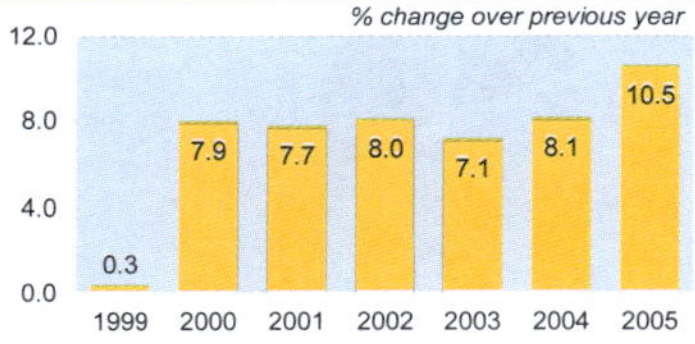

Consumer price index (annual average)

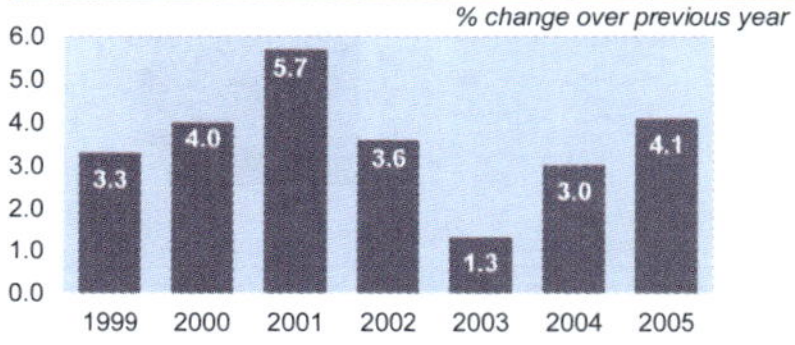

	% of GDP
Exports of goods and services, 2005:	80.0
Imports of goods and services, 2005:	86.1
External trade balance, 2005:	-6.1

GDP in agriculture, industry, and services (2000=100)

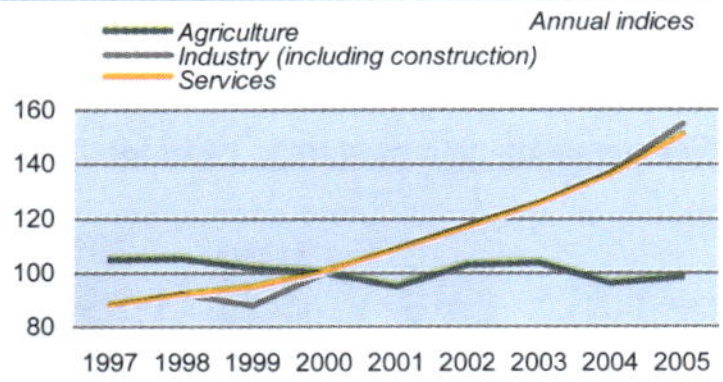

GDP by major sectors, 2005

Employment in major sectors, 2005

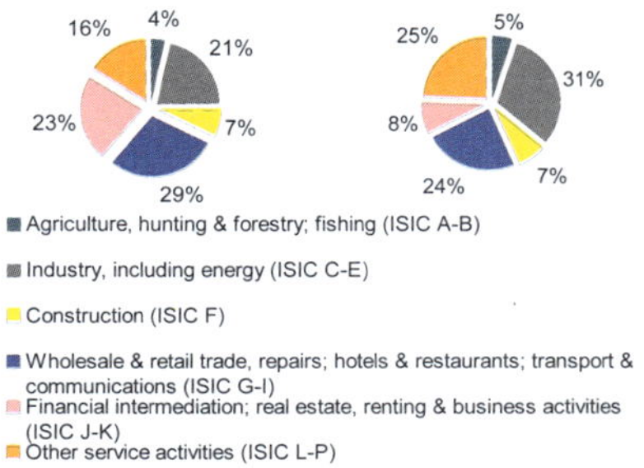

Major import partners from UNECE, 2005

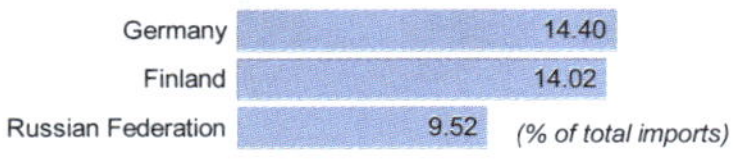

Major export partners in UNECE, 2005

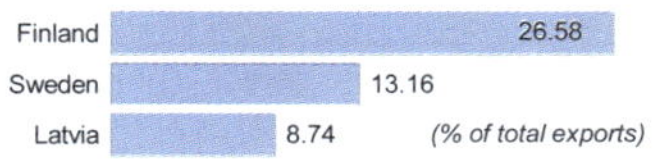

FINLAND

Capital:	Helsinki (559 046)
Two largest cities:	Espoo (227 472)
	Tampere (202 932)
Area (km²):	338 150
Total population:	5 246 096
Population density (per km²):	16
Official languages:	Finnish and Swedish
Date joined UN:	14 December 1955
National currency:	Euro (EUR)
National statistical office:	Statistics Finland http://www.stat.fi

Population by age, 2005

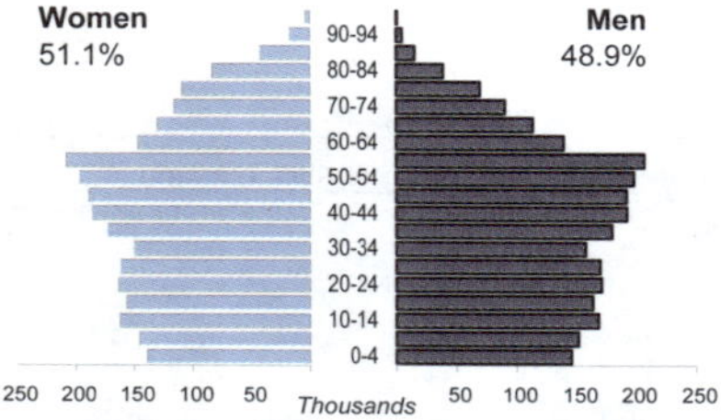

Life expectancy (in years), 2005:	at birth	at 65
Women:	82	21
Men:	76	17

Median age (in years), 2005:	
Women:	42
Men:	39

	percentage of total population
Foreign born, 2005:	3.2%
Foreigners in population, 2005:	2.1%

Total fertility rate

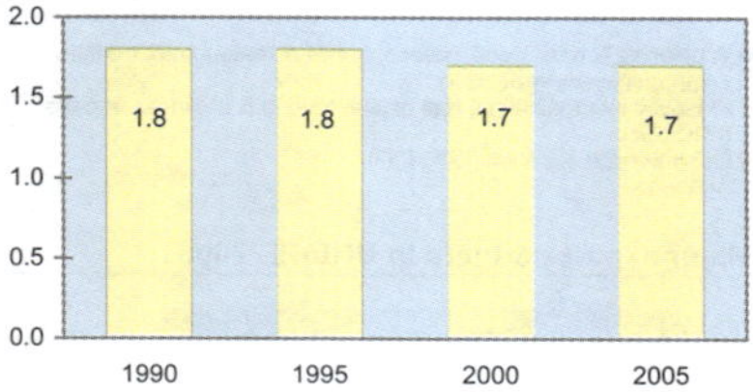

Time: UTC +2h

Legal marital status, population aged 18+, 2004

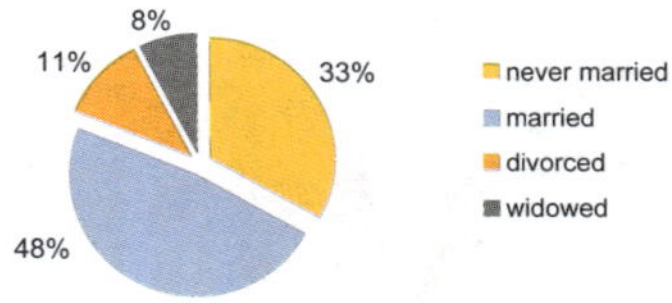

Women in the labour force, 2005:	48.4%
Gender pay gap, 2004:	19%
Female government ministers, 2006: percentage of total for both sexes	44.4%
Female central bank board members, 2005: percentage of total for both sexes	25%
Female tertiary students, 2003-2004: percentage of total for both sexes	53.4%

Parliament seats held by women (% of total)

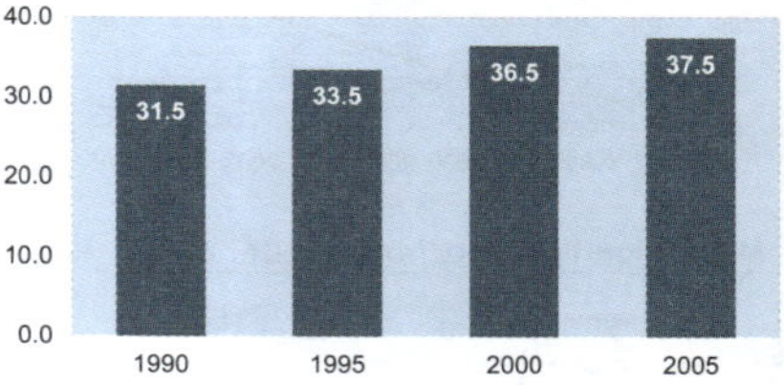

FINLAND

	1999	2000	2001	2002	2003	2004	2005
Employment (% change over previous year)	2.5	2.3	1.5	0.9	0.0	0.3	1.6
Unemployment rate (%)	10.2	9.8	9.1	9.1	9.0	8.8	8.4
Youth unemployment rate (%)	..	21.4	19.8	21.0	21.8	20.7	20.1

Economic activity rate, 2004

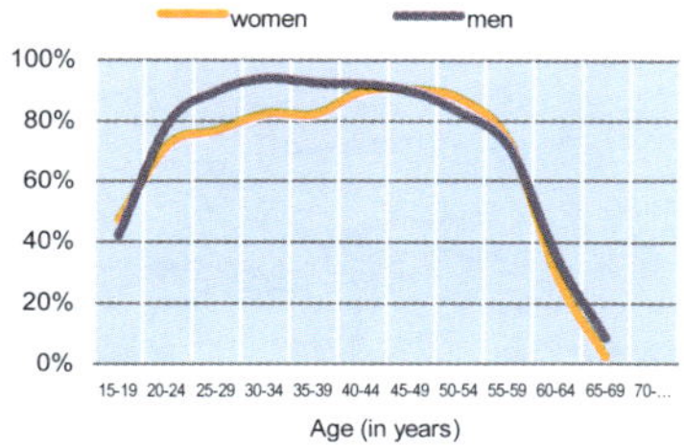

GDP at current prices	
in millions of US Dollars, PPP, 2005:	164 519
in millions of EUR, 2005:	157 377
GDP at constant 2000 prices, per capita	
US Dollars, PPP, 2005:	29 119
EUR, 2005:	28 525
Final consumption expenditure at 2000 prices, per capita, US Dollars, PPP, 2005:	20 707
Purchasing Power Parity (PPP)	
EUR per USD, 2005, US=1:	0.957
Gross external debt:	
in millions of US Dollars, 2005:	217 363
Exchange rate	
Annual average, EUR per USD, 2005:	0.804

Real GDP growth rate

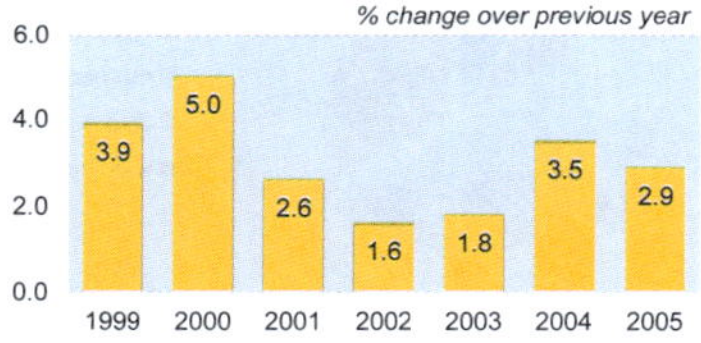

Consumer price index (annual average)

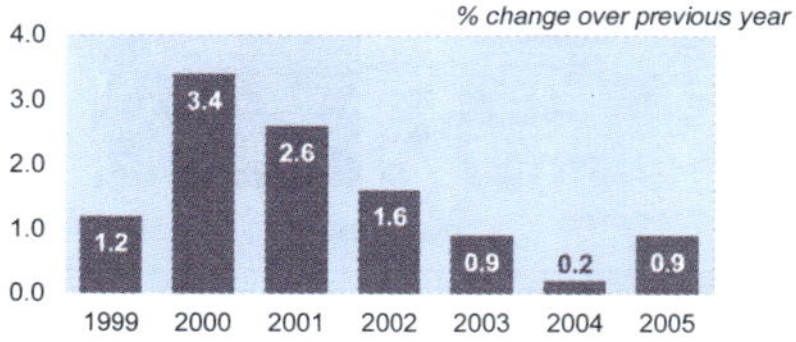

	% of GDP
Exports of goods and services, 2005:	41.8
Imports of goods and services, 2005:	36.1
External trade balance, 2005:	5.7

GDP in agriculture, industry, and services (2000=100)

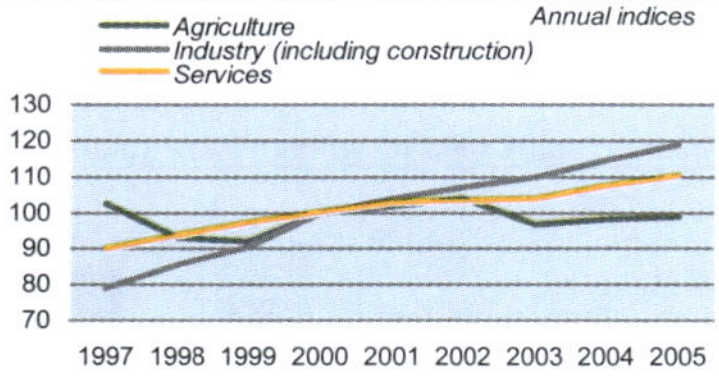

GDP by major sectors, 2005

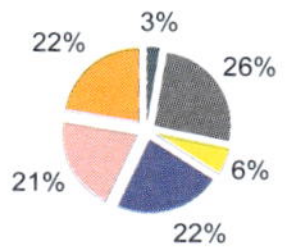

Employment in major sectors, 2005

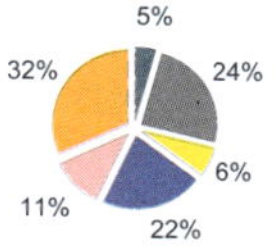

- Agriculture, hunting & forestry; fishing (ISIC A-B)
- Industry, including energy (ISIC C-E)
- Construction (ISIC F)
- Wholesale & retail trade, repairs; hotels & restaurants; transport & communications (ISIC G-I)
- Financial intermediation; real estate, renting & business activities (ISIC J-K)
- Other service activities (ISIC L-P)

Major import partners from UNECE, 2005

(% of total imports)

Major export partners in UNECE, 2005

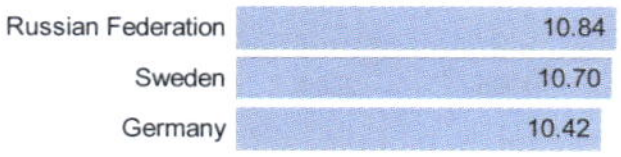

(% of total exports)

FRANCE

Capital:	Paris (2 142 800)
Two largest cities:	Marseille (795 600)
	Lyon (468 300)
Area (km^2):	551 500
Total population:	62 702 371
Population density (per km^2):	114
Official languages:	French
Date joined UN:	24 October 1945
National currency:	Euro (EUR)
National statistical office:	

National Institute of Statistics and Economic Studies (INSEE)
http://www.insee.fr

Time: UTC +1h

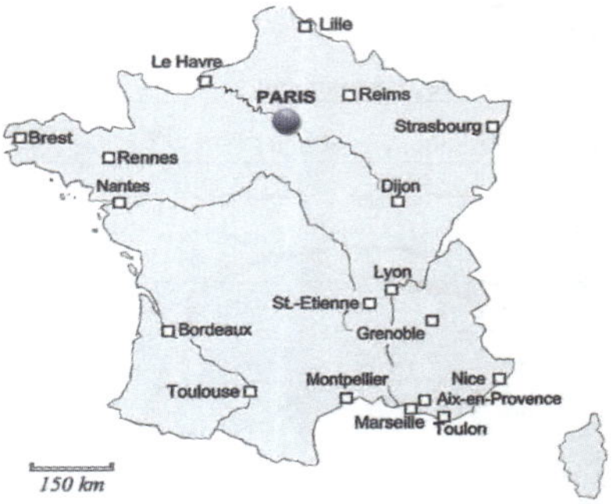

Population by age, 2005

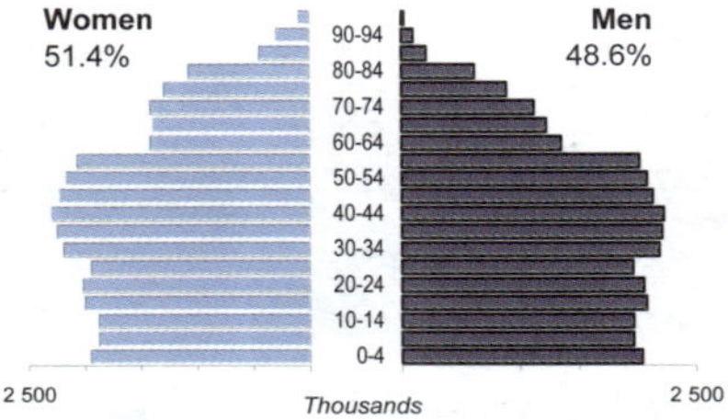

Legal marital status, population aged 18+, 2004

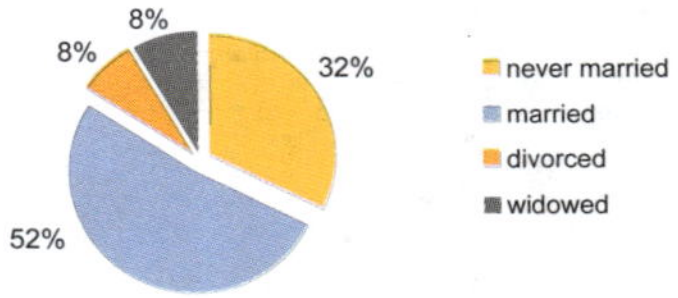

Life expectancy (in years), 2005:	at birth	at 65
Women:	84	21
Men:	77	17

Median age (in years), 2005:	
Women:	40
Men:	37

	percentage of total population
Foreign born, 1999:	10%
Foreigners in population, 1999:	5.6%

Women in the labour force, 2005:	46.7%
Gender pay gap, 2005:	12%
Female government ministers, 2006: percentage of total for both sexes	18.7%
Female central bank board members, 2005: percentage of total for both sexes	14.3%
Female tertiary students: percentage of total for both sexes	..

Total fertility rate

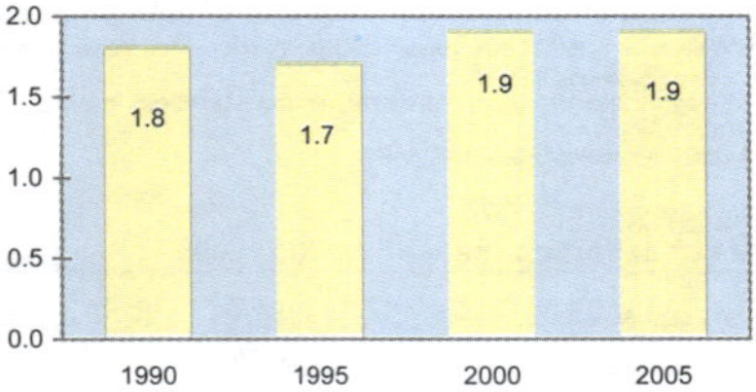

Parliament seats held by women (% of total)

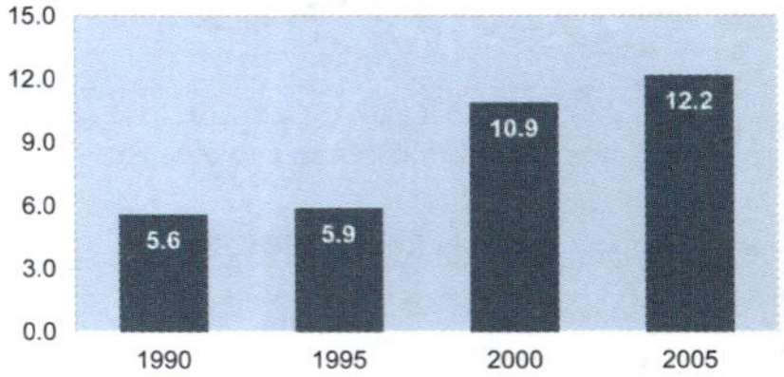

FRANCE

	1999	2000	2001	2002	2003	2004	2005
Employment (% change over previous year)	2.0	2.7	1.7	0.7	-0.1	0.0	0.2
Unemployment rate (%)	10.5	9.1	8.4	8.9	9.5	9.6	9.5
Youth unemployment rate (%)	..	20.1	19.4	20.0	21.1	21.8	22.7

Economic activity rate, 2004

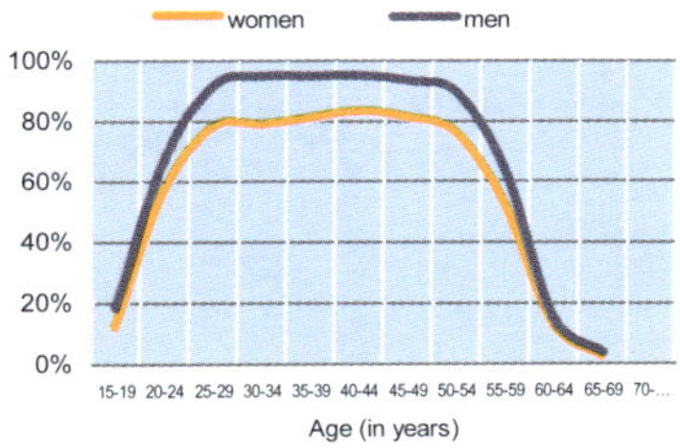

GDP at current prices	
in millions of US Dollars, PPP, 2005:	1 887 567
in millions of EUR, 2005:	1 710 024
GDP at constant 2000 prices, per capita	
US Dollars, PPP, 2005:	27 036
EUR, 2005:	24 756
Final consumption expenditure at 2000 prices, per capita, US Dollars, PPP, 2005:	21 882
Purchasing Power Parity (PPP)	
EUR per USD, 2005, US=1:	0.906
Gross external debt:	
in millions of US Dollars, 2005:	3 006 493
Exchange rate	
Annual average, EUR per USD, 2005:	0.804

Real GDP growth rate

% change over previous year

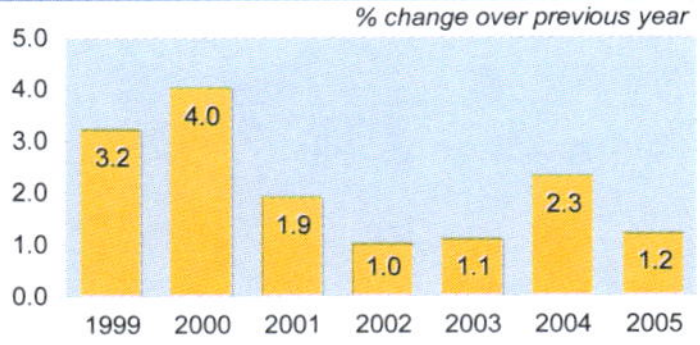

Consumer price index (annual average)

% change over previous year

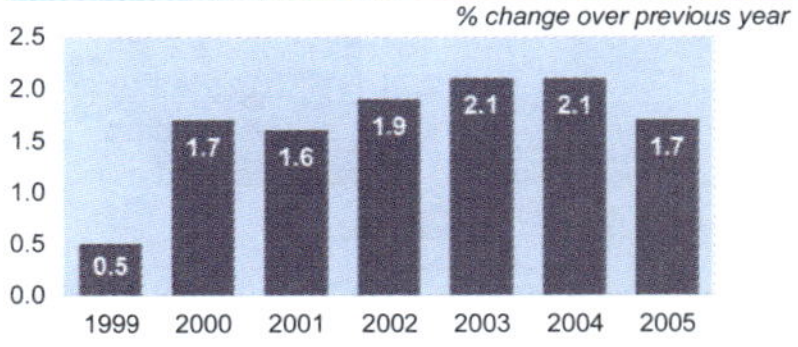

	% of GDP
Exports of goods and services, 2005:	26.1
Imports of goods and services, 2005:	27.1
External trade balance, 2005:	-1

GDP by major sectors

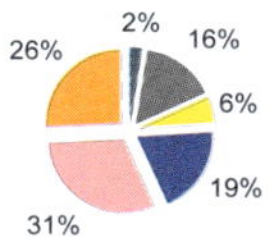

Employment in major sectors, 2004

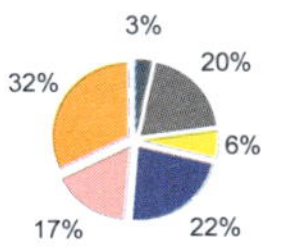

- Agriculture, hunting & forestry; fishing (ISIC A-B)
- Industry, including energy (ISIC C-E)
- Construction (ISIC F)
- Wholesale & retail trade, repairs; hotels & restaurants; transport & communications (ISIC G-I)
- Financial intermediation; real estate, renting & business activities (ISIC J-K)
- Other service activities (ISIC L-P)

GDP in agriculture, industry, and services (2000=100)

Annual indices

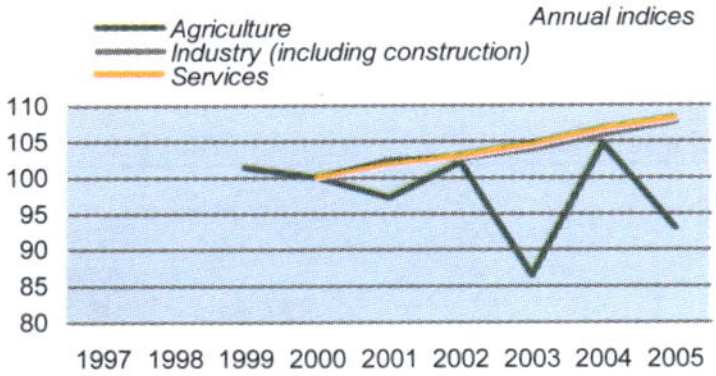

Major import partners from UNECE, 2005

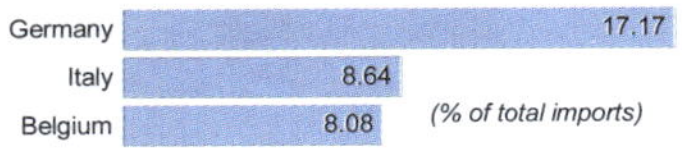

Major export partners in UNECE, 2005

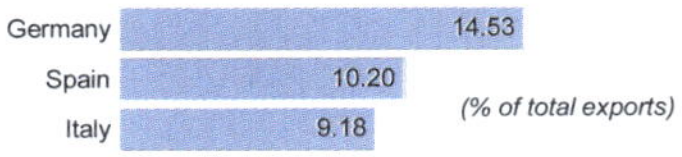

GEORGIA

Capital:	Tbilisi (1 073 345)
Two largest cities:	Kutaisi (185 965)
	Batumi (121 806)
Area (km²):	69 700
Total population:	4 361 400
Population density (per km²):	63
Official languages:	Georgian
Date joined UN:	31 July 1992
National currency:	Georgian lari (GEL)
National statistical office:	State Department for Statistics Georgia http://www.statistics.ge

Time: UTC +3h

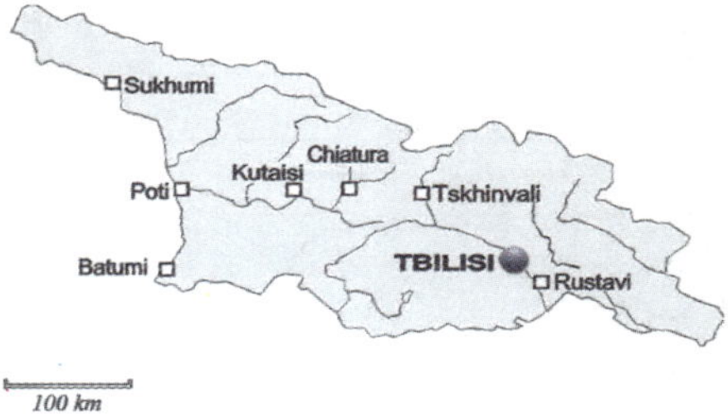

Population by age, 2005

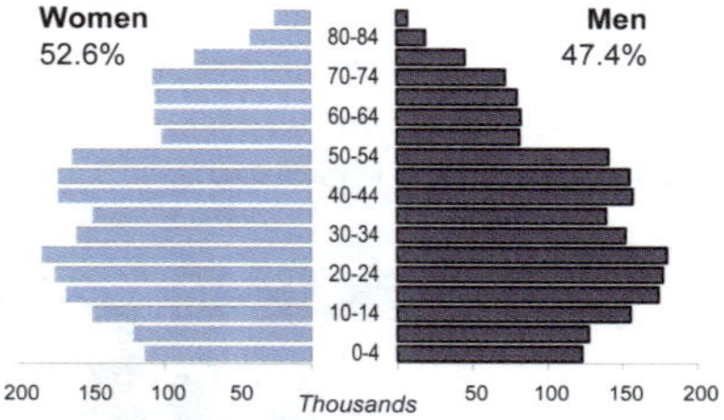

Life expectancy (in years), 2005:	at birth	at 65
Women:	77	..
Men:	69	..

Median age (in years), 2005:	
Women:	38
Men:	33

	percentage of total population
Foreign born:	..
Foreigners in population:	..

Total fertility rate

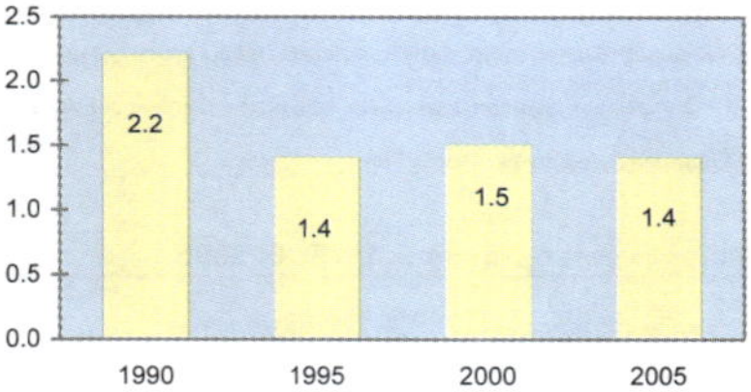

Legal marital status, population aged 18+

never married
married
divorced
widowed

Data not available

Women in the labour force, 2005:	46.9%
Gender pay gap, 2005:	50.9%
Female government ministers, 2005: percentage of total for both sexes	16.7%
Female central bank board members, 2005: percentage of total for both sexes	11.1%
Female tertiary students, 2002-2003: percentage of total for both sexes	48.8%

Parliament seats held by women (% of total)

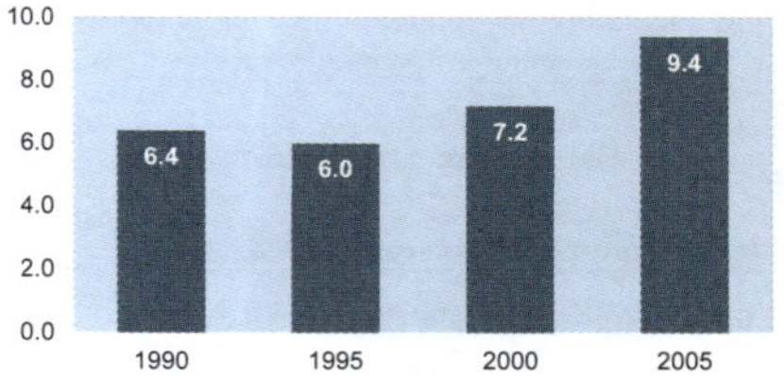

GEORGIA

	1999	2000	2001	2002	2003	2004	2005
Employment (% change over previous year)	0.1	6.2	2.1	-2.1	-1.3	-1.7	-2.2
Unemployment rate (%)	13.8	10.3	11.1	12.6	11.5	12.6	13.8
Youth unemployment rate (%)	..	20.0	20.1	28.0	24.9	28.3	28.3

Economic activity rate, 2001

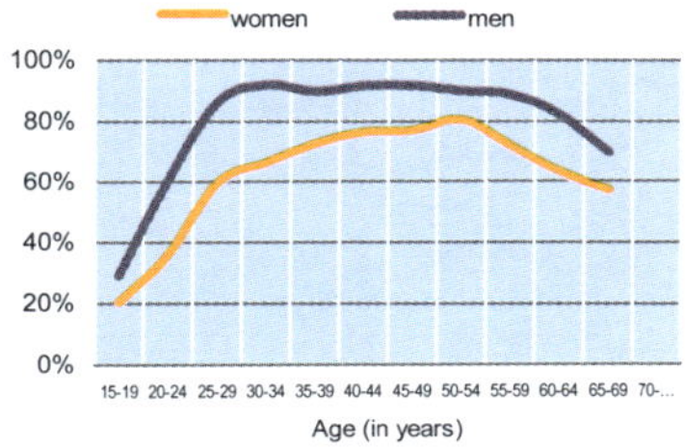

GDP at current prices	
in millions of US Dollars, PPP, 2005:	16 479
in millions of GEL, 2005:	11 592
GDP at constant 2000 prices, per capita	
US Dollars, PPP, 2005:	3 352
GEL, 2005:	1 969
Final consumption expenditure at 2000 prices, per capita, US Dollars, PPP:	..
Purchasing Power Parity (PPP)	
GEL per USD, 2005, US=1:	0.703
Gross external debt:	
in millions of US Dollars, 2004:	2 190
Exchange rate	
Annual average, GEL per USD, 2005:	1.813

Real GDP growth rate

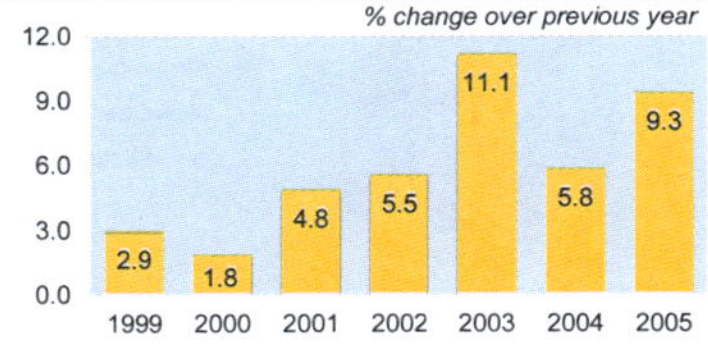

Consumer price index (annual average)

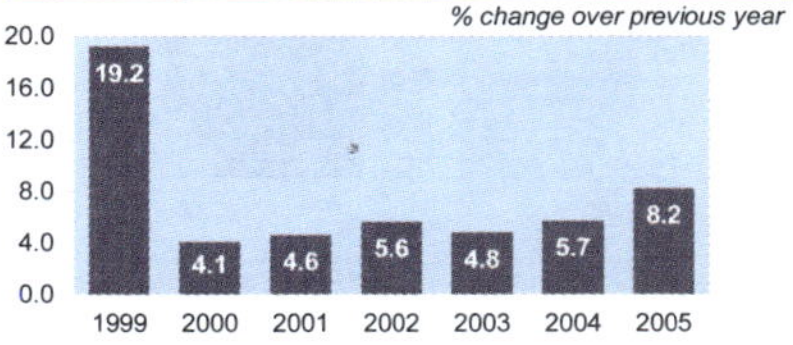

	% of GDP
Exports of goods and services, 2005:	33.9
Imports of goods and services, 2005:	51.7
External trade balance, 2005:	-18

GDP by major sectors, 2005

Employment in major sectors, 2004

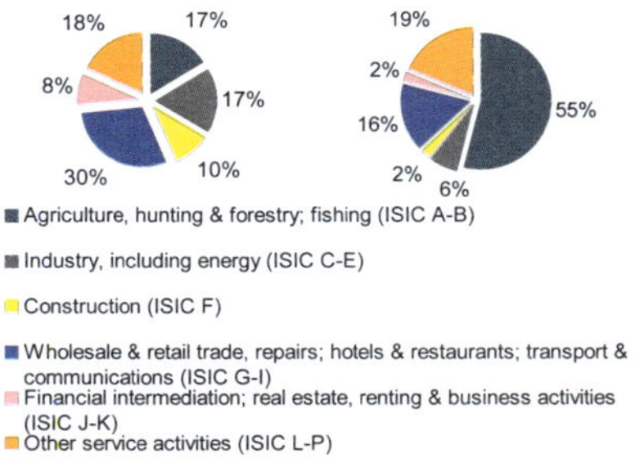

GDP in agriculture, industry, and services (2000=100)

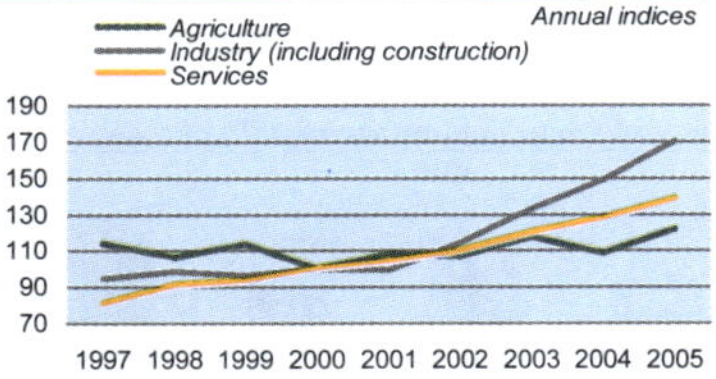

Major import partners from UNECE, 2005

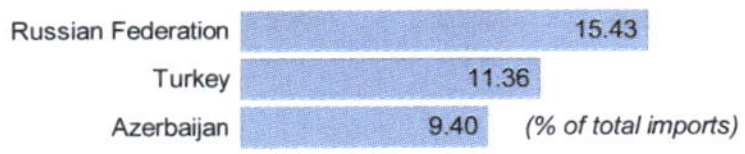

Major export partners in UNECE, 2005

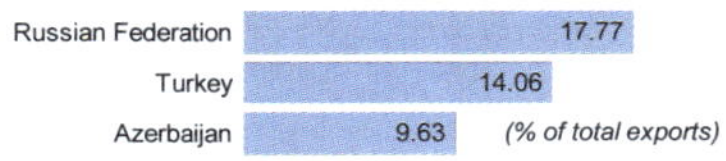

GERMANY

Capital:	Berlin (3 388 477)
Two largest cities:	Hamburg (1 734 083)
	München (1 247 873)
Area (km²):	357 030
Total population:	82 469 422
Population density (per km²):	231
Official languages:	German
Date joined UN:	18 September 1973
National currency:	Euro (EUR)
National statistical office:	Federal Statistical Office Germany http://www.destatis.de

Time: UTC +1h

Population by age, 2005

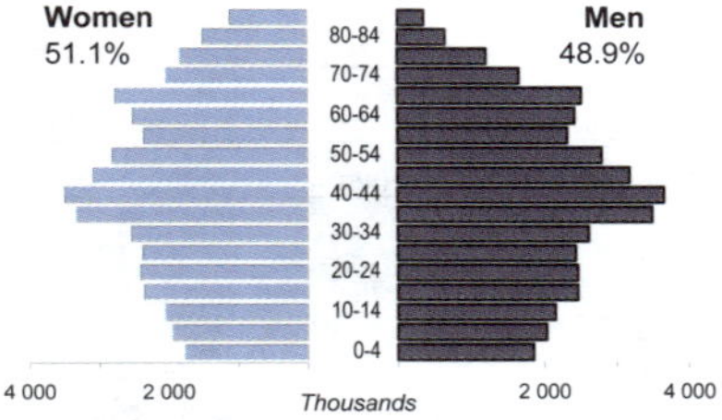

Legal marital status, population aged 18+, 2004

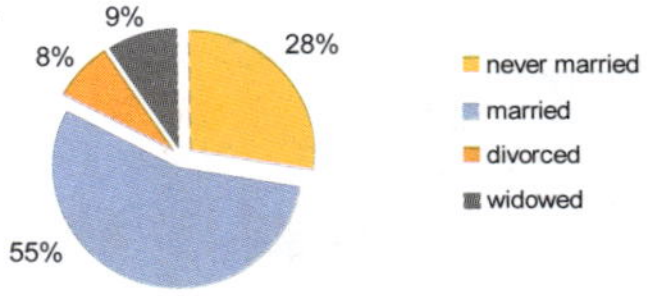

Life expectancy (in years), 2004:	at birth	at 65
Women:	82	20
Men:	76	17

Median age (in years), 2005:	
Women:	43
Men:	41

	percentage of total population
Foreign born:	..
Foreigners in population, 2005:	8.8%

Women in the labour force, 2005:	44.9%
Gender pay gap, 2005:	22%
Female government ministers, 2006: percentage of total for both sexes	37.5%
Female central bank board members: percentage of total for both sexes	..
Female tertiary students, 2003-2004: percentage of total for both sexes	49.4%

Total fertility rate

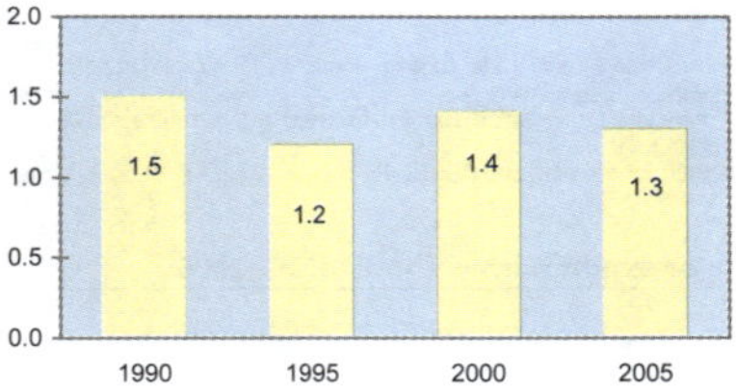

Parliament seats held by women (% of total)

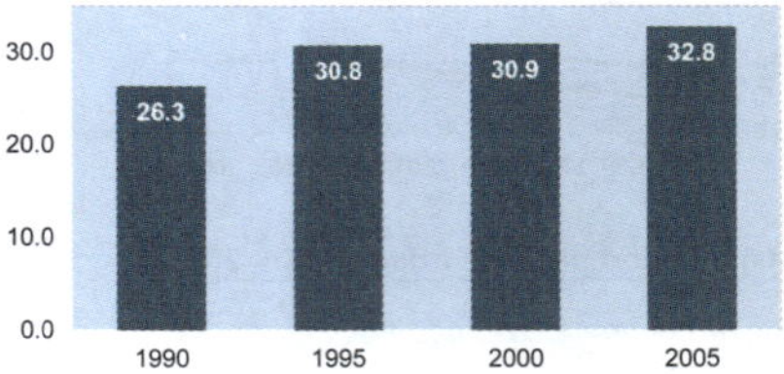

GERMANY

	1999	2000	2001	2002	2003	2004	2005
Employment (% change over previous year)	1.4	1.9	0.4	-0.6	-1.0	0.4	-0.2
Unemployment rate (%)	7.9	7.2	7.4	8.2	9.0	9.5	9.5
Youth unemployment rate (%)	..	10.6	12.8	14.2	14.6	15.0	14.8

Economic activity rate, 2003

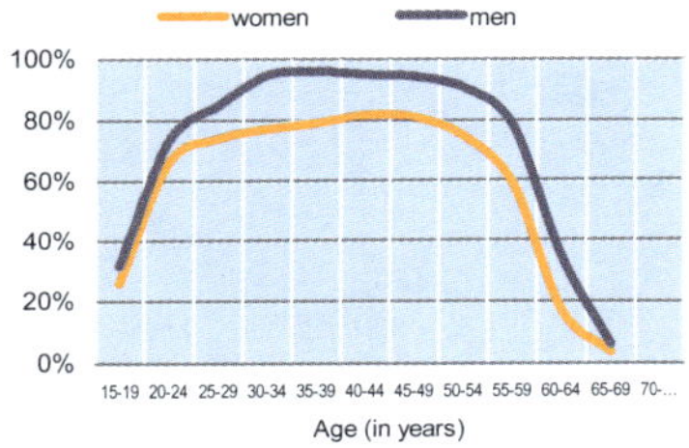

GDP at current prices	
in millions of US Dollars, PPP, 2005:	2 494 754
in millions of EUR, 2005:	2 241 000
GDP at constant 2000 prices, per capita	
US Dollars, PPP, 2005:	26 293
EUR, 2005:	25 821
Final consumption expenditure at 2000 prices, per capita, US Dollars, PPP, 2005:	20 092
Purchasing Power Parity (PPP)	
EUR per USD, 2005, US=1:	0.898
Gross external debt:	
in millions of US Dollars, 2005:	3 566 273
Exchange rate	
Annual average, EUR per USD, 2005:	0.804

Real GDP growth rate

% change over previous year

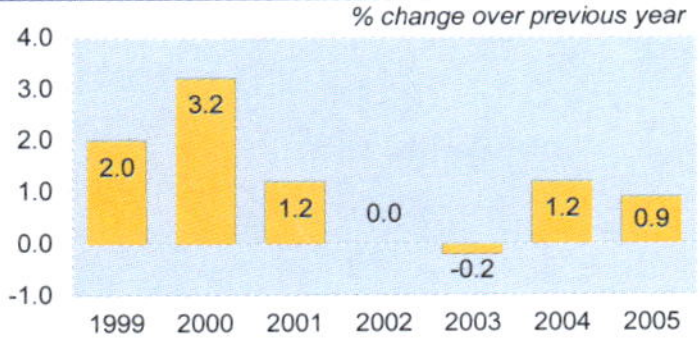

Consumer price index (annual average)

% change over previous year

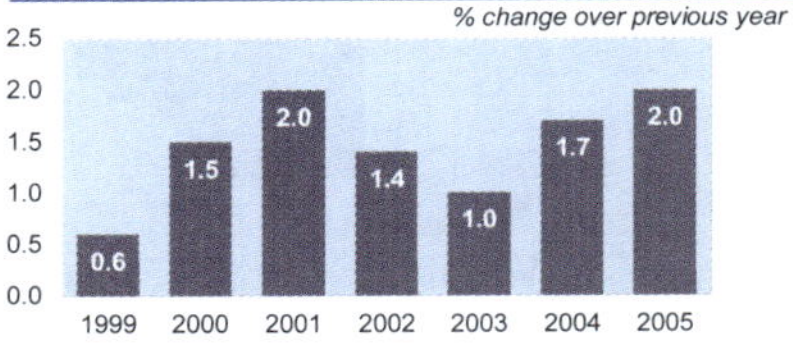

	% of GDP
Exports of goods and services, 2005:	40.7
Imports of goods and services, 2005:	35.5
External trade balance, 2005:	5.2

GDP by major sectors, 2005

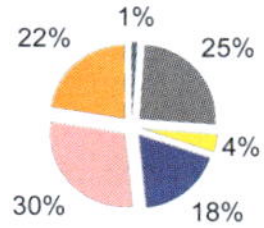

Employment in major sectors, 2005

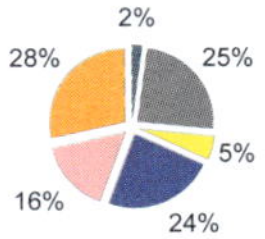

- Agriculture, hunting & forestry; fishing (ISIC A-B)
- Industry, including energy (ISIC C-E)
- Construction (ISIC F)
- Wholesale & retail trade, repairs; hotels & restaurants; transport & communications (ISIC G-I)
- Financial intermediation; real estate, renting & business activities (ISIC J-K)
- Other service activities (ISIC L-P)

GDP in agriculture, industry, and services (2000=100)

Annual indices

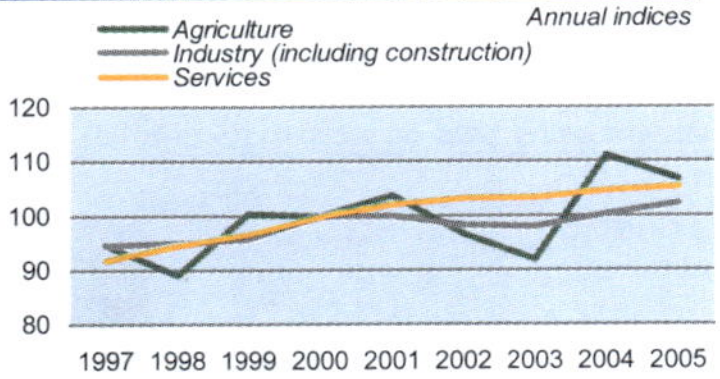

Major import partners from UNECE, 2005

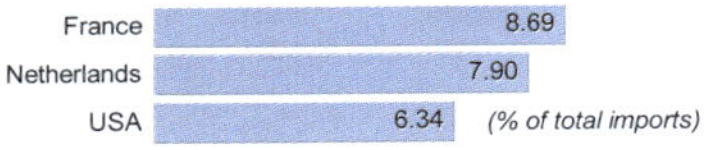

Major export partners in UNECE, 2005

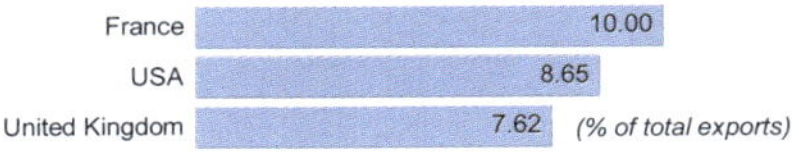

GREECE

Capital:	Athens (745 514)
Two largest cities:	Thessaloníki (363 987)
	Piraeus (175 697)
Area (km²):	131 957
Total population:	11 103 965
Population density (per km²):	84
Official languages:	Greek
Date joined UN:	25 October 1945
National currency:	Euro (EUR)
National statistical office:	National Statistical Service of Greece http://www.statistics.gr

Time: UTC +2h

Population by age, 2005

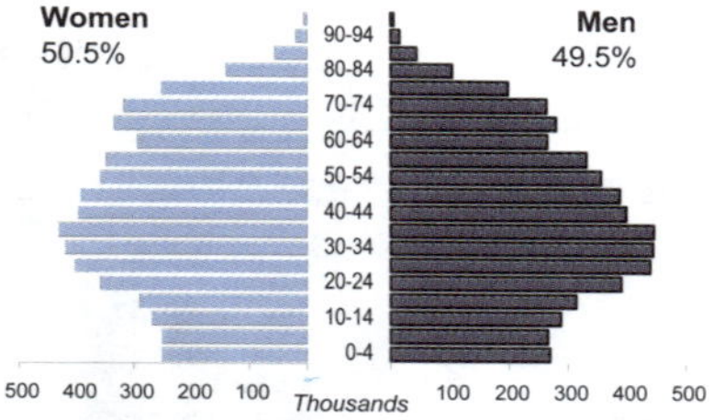

Life expectancy (in years), 2005:	at birth	at 65
Women:	82	19
Men:	77	17

Median age (in years), 2005:	
Women:	42
Men:	39

	percentage of total population
Foreign born:	..
Foreigners in population, 2004:	8.1%

Total fertility rate

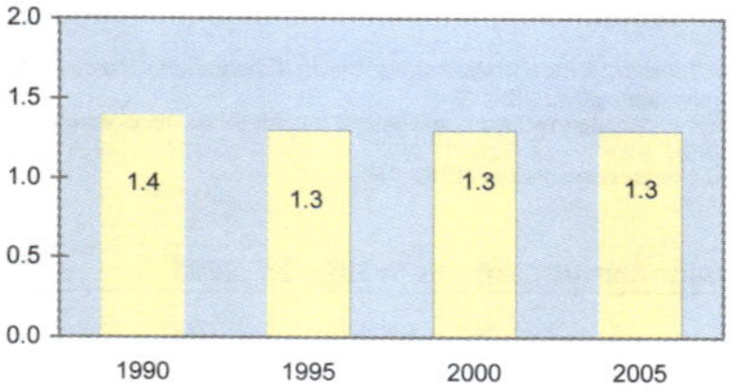

Legal marital status, population aged 18+

Data not available

never married
married
divorced
widowed

Women in the labour force, 2005:	40.7%
Gender pay gap, 2005:	9%
Female government ministers, 2006: percentage of total for both sexes	15.8%
Female central bank board members, 2005: percentage of total for both sexes	7.7%
Female tertiary students, 2003-2004: percentage of total for both sexes	51.7%

Parliament seats held by women (% of total)

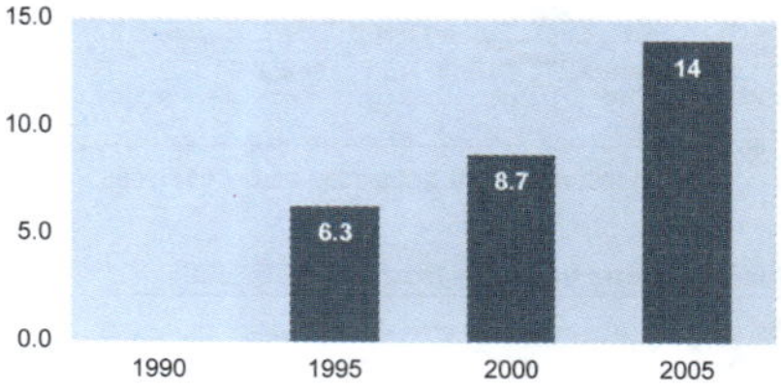

	1999	2000	2001	2002	2003	2004	2005
Employment (% change over previous year)	0.4	0.9	0.3	0.1	1.6	4.1	4.2
Unemployment rate (%)	12.0	11.3	10.8	10.3	9.7	10.5	9.8
Youth unemployment rate (%)	..	29.2	28.2	26.8	26.8	26.9	26.0

Economic activity rate, 2004

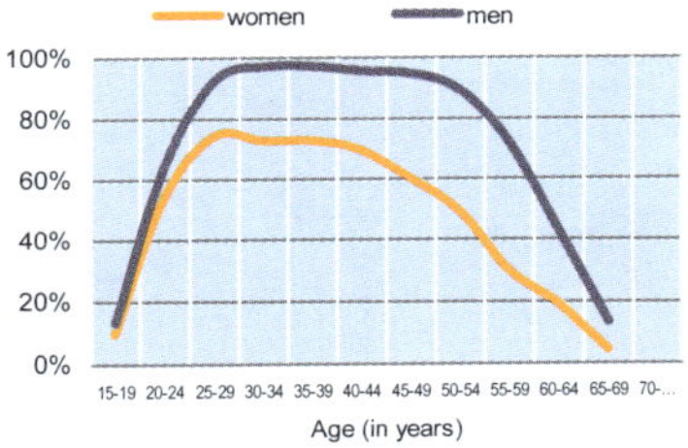

GDP at current prices	
in millions of US Dollars, PPP, 2005:	251 481
in millions of EUR, 2005:	181 088
GDP at constant 2000 prices, per capita	
US Dollars, PPP, 2005:	20 321
EUR, 2005:	13 919
Final consumption expenditure at 2000 prices, per capita, US Dollars, PPP, 2005:	17 162
Purchasing Power Parity (PPP)	
EUR per USD, 2005, US=1:	0.72
Gross external debt:	
in millions of US Dollars, 2005:	266 617
Exchange rate	
Annual average, EUR per USD, 2005:	0.804

Real GDP growth rate

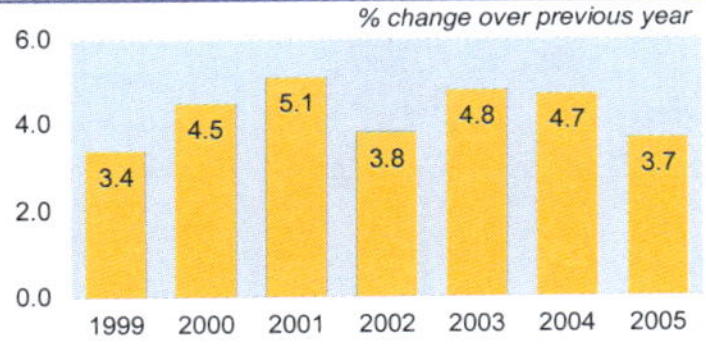

Consumer price index (annual average)

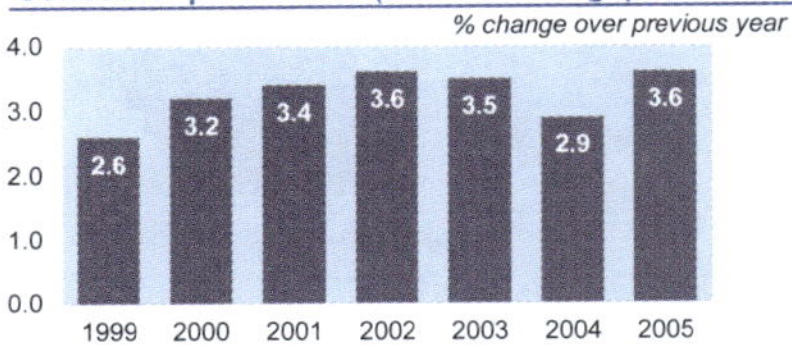

	% of GDP
Exports of goods and services, 2005:	20.8
Imports of goods and services, 2005:	28.0
External trade balance, 2005:	-7.2

GDP by major sectors, 2005

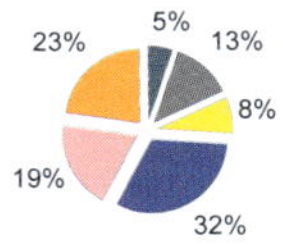

Employment in major sectors, 2005

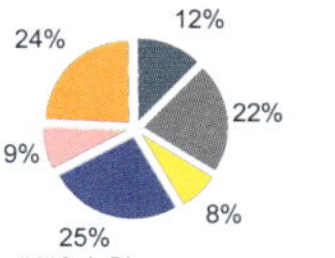

- Agriculture, hunting & forestry; fishing (ISIC A-B)
- Industry, including energy (ISIC C-E)
- Construction (ISIC F)
- Wholesale & retail trade, repairs; hotels & restaurants; transport & communications (ISIC G-I)
- Financial intermediation; real estate, renting & business activities (ISIC J-K)
- Other service activities (ISIC L-P)

GDP in agriculture, industry, and services (2000=100)

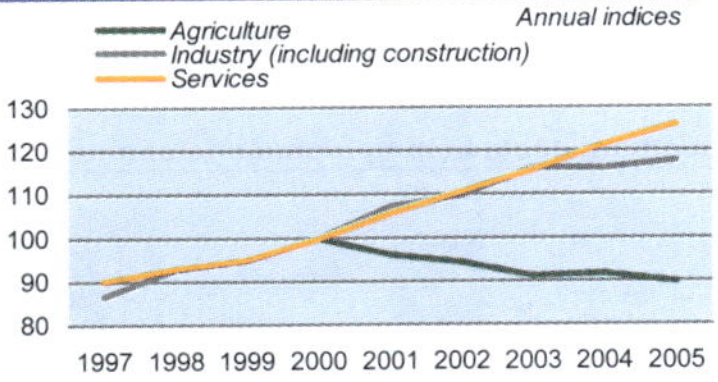

Major import partners from UNECE, 2005

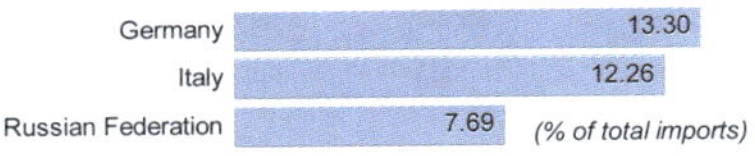

Major export partners in UNECE, 2005

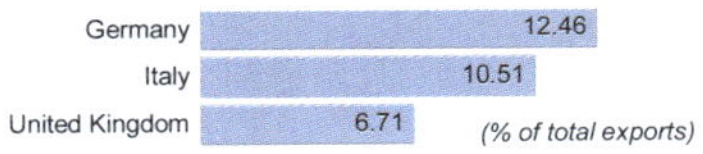

HUNGARY

Capital:	Budapest (1 719 342)
Two largest cities:	Debrecen (205 881)
	Miskolc (180 282)
Area (km^2):	93 030
Total population:	10 087 065
Population density (per km^2):	108
Official languages:	Hungarian
Date joined UN:	14 December 1955
National currency:	Hungarian forint (HUF)
National statistical office:	Hungarian Central Statistical Office http://www.ksh.hu

Time: UTC +1h

Population by age, 2005

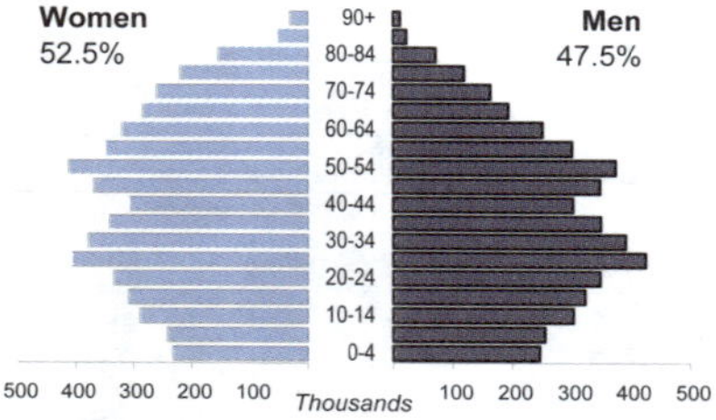

Life expectancy (in years), 2005:	at birth	at 65
Women:	77	17
Men:	69	13

Median age (in years), 2005:	
Women:	42
Men:	37

	percentage of total population
Foreign born:	..
Foreigners in population, 2005:	1.4%

Legal marital status, population aged 18+, 2004

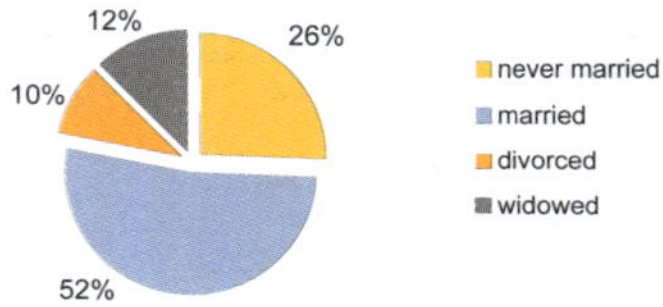

Women in the labour force, 2005:	45.9%
Gender pay gap, 2005:	11%
Female government ministers, 2006: percentage of total for both sexes	16.6%
Female central bank board members: percentage of total for both sexes	..
Female tertiary students, 2003-2004: percentage of total for both sexes	57.3%

Total fertility rate

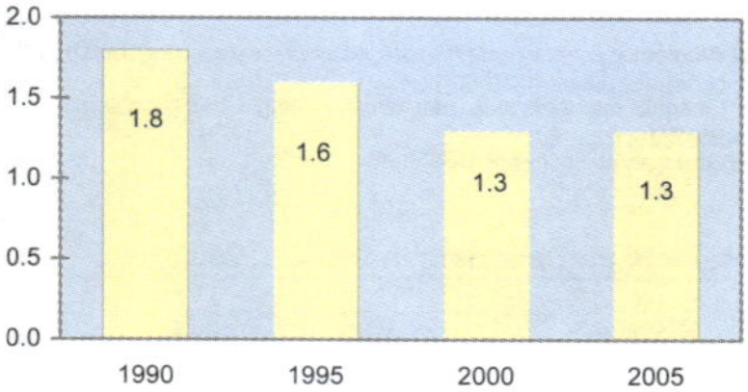

Parliament seats held by women (% of total)

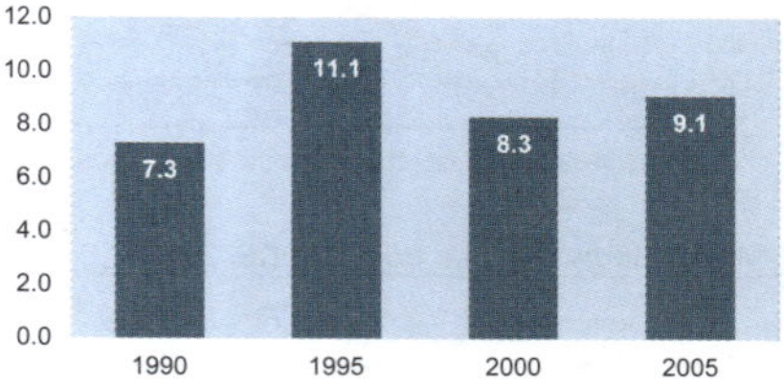

HUNGARY

	1999	2000	2001	2002	2003	2004	2005
Employment (% change over previous year)	3.4	1.3	0.3	0.1	1.3	-0.7	0.0
Unemployment rate (%)	7.0	6.4	5.7	5.8	5.9	6.1	7.2
Youth unemployment rate (%)	..	12.5	11.3	12.7	13.4	15.5	19.4

Economic activity rate, 2004

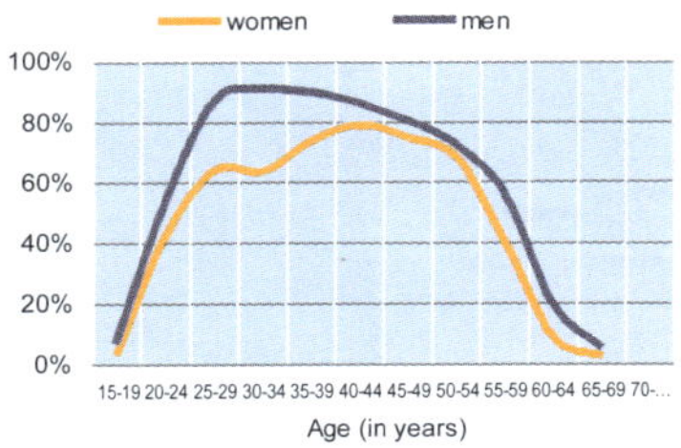

GDP at current prices	
in millions of US Dollars, PPP, 2005:	171 415
in millions of HUF, 2005:	22 026 763
GDP at constant 2000 prices, per capita	
US Dollars, PPP, 2005:	15 426
HUF, 2005:	1 658 637
Final consumption expenditure at 2000 prices, per capita, US Dollars, PPP, 2005:	11 974
Purchasing Power Parity (PPP)	
HUF per USD, 2005, US=1:	128.5
Gross external debt:	
in millions of US Dollars, 2005:	78 405
Exchange rate	
Annual average, HUF per USD, 2005:	199.6

Real GDP growth rate

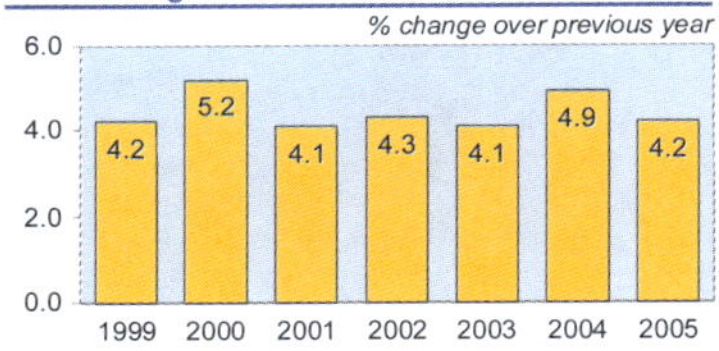

Consumer price index (annual average)

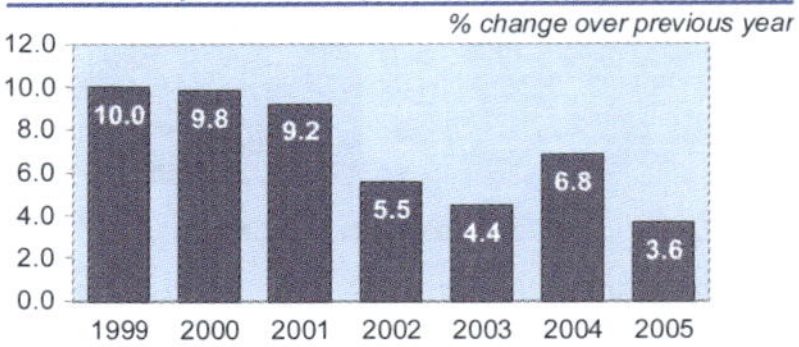

	% of GDP
Exports of goods and services, 2005:	66.4
Imports of goods and services, 2005:	67.8
External trade balance, 2005:	-1.4

GDP in agriculture, industry, and services (2000=100)

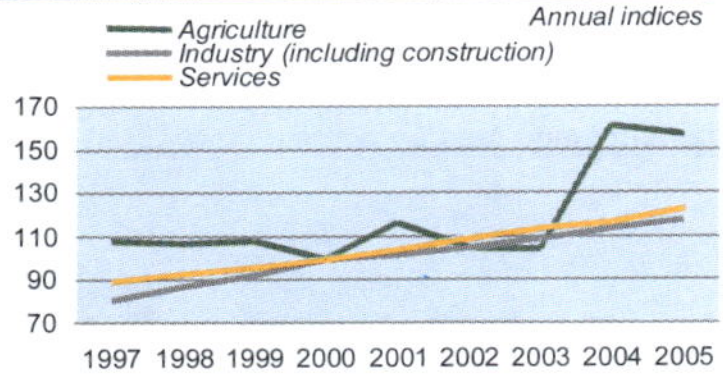

GDP by major sectors, 2005

Employment in major sectors, 2005

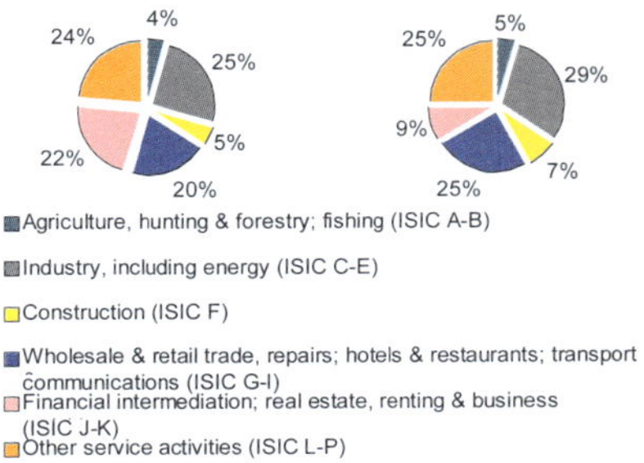

Major import partners from UNECE, 2005

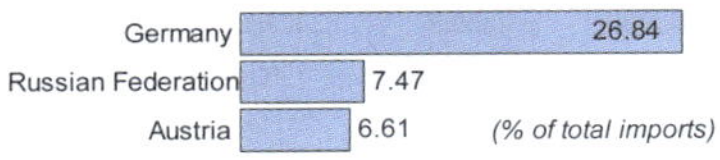

Major export partners in UNECE, 2005

ICELAND

Capital:	Reykjavik (113 730)
Two largest cities:	Kópavogur (25 784)
	Hafnarfjordhur (21 942)
Area (km²):	103 000
Total population:	296 734
Population density (per km²):	3
Official languages:	Icelandic
Date joined UN:	19 November 1946
National currency:	Icelandic krona (ISK)
National statistical office:	Statistical Office of Iceland
	http://www.statice.is

Time: UTC

Population by age, 2005

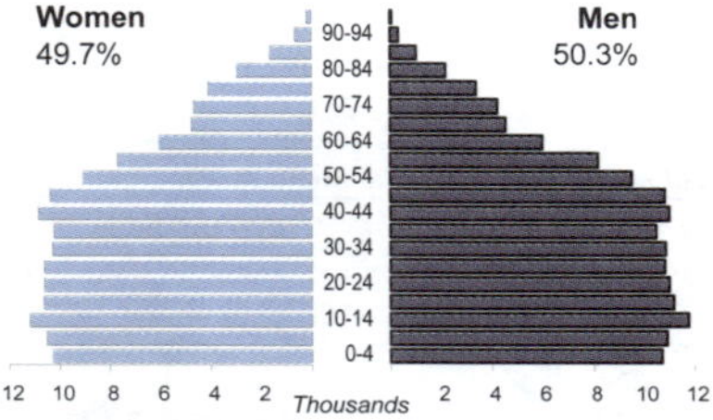

Legal marital status, population aged 18+, 2004

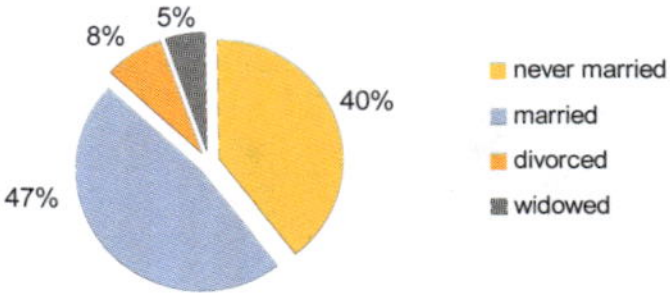

Life expectancy (in years), 2005:	at birth	at 65
Women:	83	20
Men:	79	18

Median age (in years), 2005:	
Women:	35
Men:	34

	percentage of total population
Foreign born:	..
Foreigners in population, 2003:	3.5%

Women in the labour force, 2005:	46.9%
Gender pay gap, 2003:	44.2%
Female government ministers, 2006: percentage of total for both sexes	33%
Female central bank board members: percentage of total for both sexes	..
Female tertiary students, 2003-2004: percentage of total for both sexes	64.5%

Total fertility rate

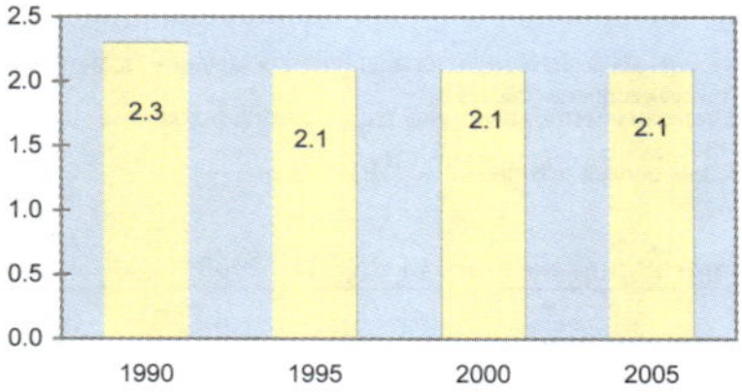

Parliament seats held by women (% of total)

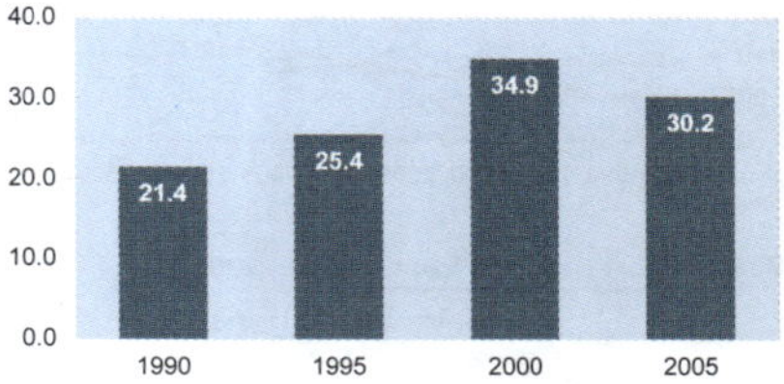

ICELAND

	1999	2000	2001	2002	2003	2004	2005
Employment (% change over previous year)	3.7	2.0	1.7	-1.5	1.5	0.0	1.3
Unemployment rate (%)	2.1	2.3	2.3	3.2	3.4	3.1	2.6
Youth unemployment rate (%)	..	4.8	4.7	..	8.3	8.1	7.2

Economic activity rate, 2005

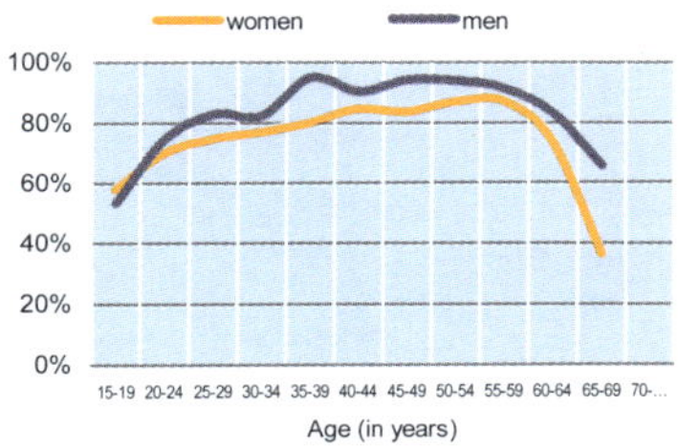

GDP at current prices	
in millions of US Dollars, PPP, 2005:	10 441
in millions of ISK, 2005:	1 012 200
GDP at constant 2000 prices, per capita	
US Dollars, PPP, 2005:	33 873
ISK, 2005:	2 818 103
Final consumption expenditure at 2000 prices, per capita, US Dollars, PPP, 2005:	28 038
Purchasing Power Parity (PPP)	
ISK per USD, 2005, US=1:	96.94
Gross external debt:	
in millions of US Dollars, 2005:	45 850
Exchange rate	
Annual average, ISK per USD, 2005:	62.98

Real GDP growth rate

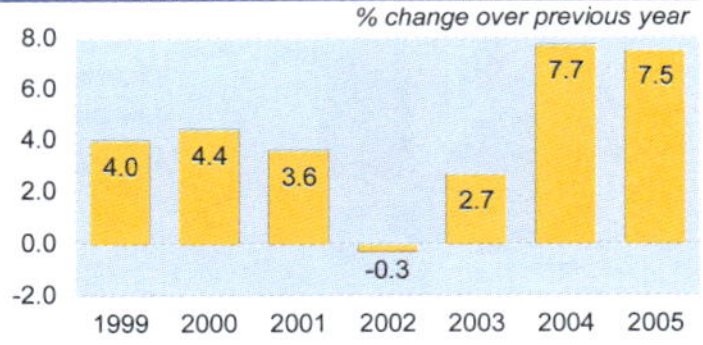

Consumer price index (annual average)

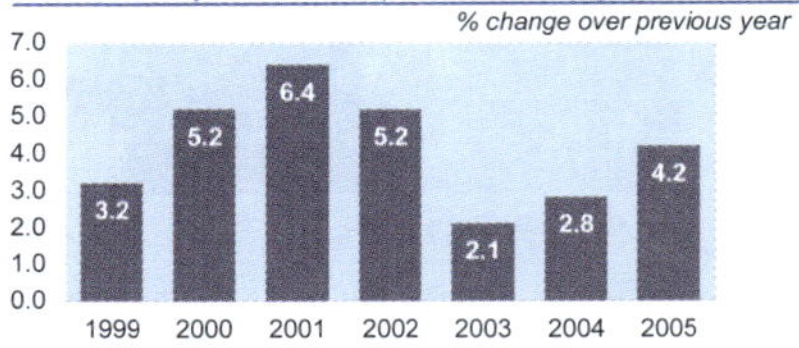

	% of GDP
Exports of goods and services, 2005:	32.0
Imports of goods and services, 2005:	44.5
External trade balance, 2005:	-13

GDP in agriculture, industry, and services (2000=100)

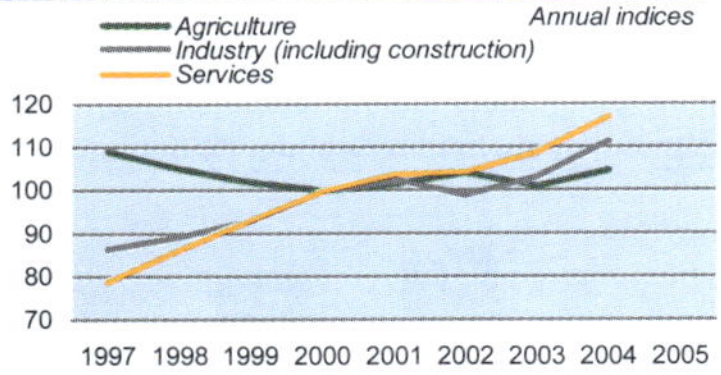

GDP by major sectors

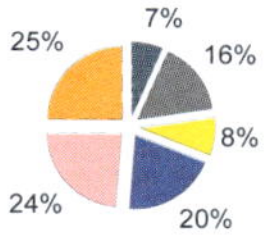

Employment in major sectors, 1997

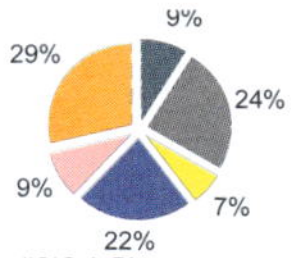

- Agriculture, hunting & forestry; fishing (ISIC A-B)
- Industry, including energy (ISIC C-E)
- Construction (ISIC F)
- Wholesale & retail trade, repairs; hotels & restaurants; transport & communications (ISIC G-I)
- Financial intermediation; real estate, renting & business activities (ISIC J-K)
- Other service activities (ISIC L-P)

Major import partners from UNECE, 2005

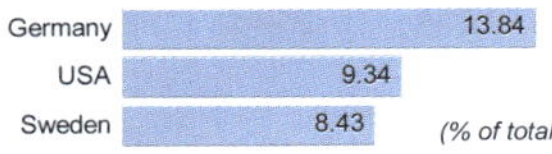

(% of total imports)

Major export partners in UNECE, 2005

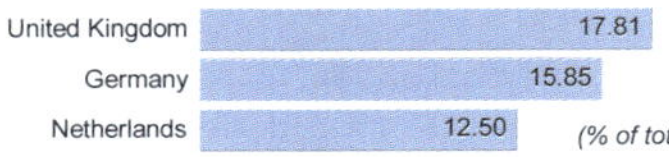

(% of total exports)

IRELAND

Capital:	Dublin (495 781)
Two largest cities:	Cork (123 062)
	Galway (65 832)
Area (km²):	70 273
Total population:	4 159 096
Population density (per km²):	59
Official languages:	Gaelic, English
Date joined UN:	14 December 1955
National currency:	Euro (EUR)
National statistical office:	Central Statistics Office Ireland http://www.cso.ie

Time: UTC

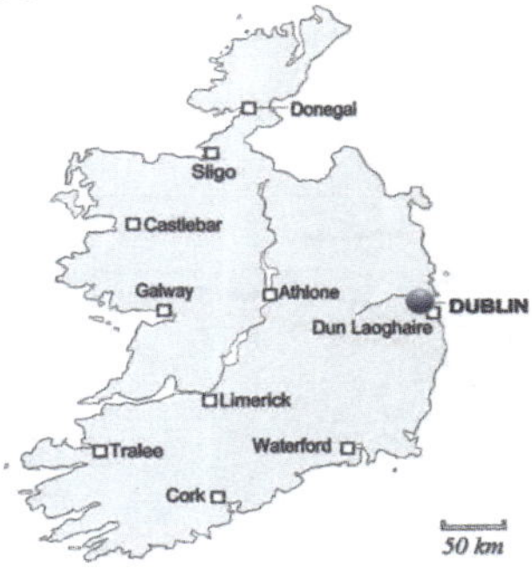

Population by age, 2005

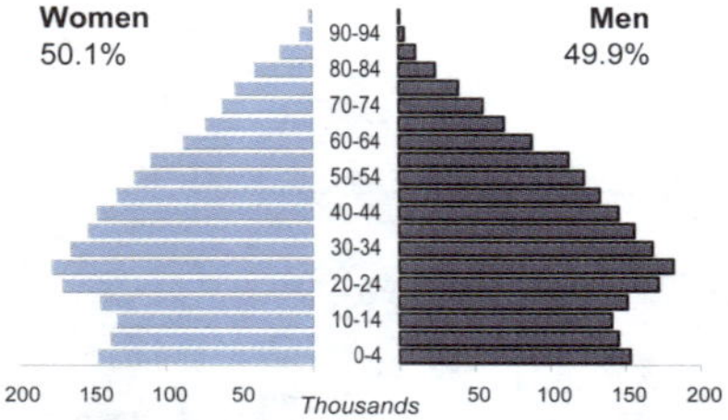

Legal marital status, population aged 18+, 2002

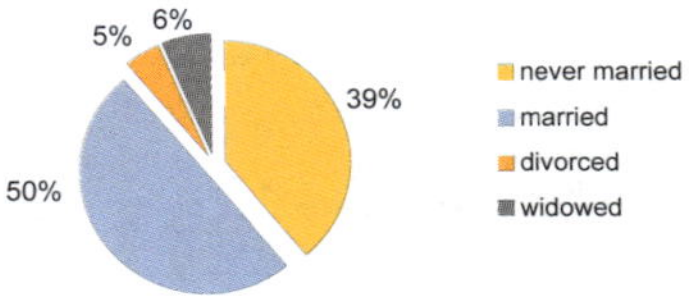

Life expectancy (in years), 2005:	at birth	at 65
Women:	82	20
Men:	77	17

Median age (in years), 2005:	
Women:	34
Men:	33

	percentage of total population
Foreign born:	..
Foreigners in population, 2005:	6.2%

Women in the labour force, 2005:	42.3%
Gender pay gap, 2005:	9%
Female government ministers, 2003: percentage of total for both sexes	20%
Female central bank board members, 2005: percentage of total for both sexes	8.3%
Female tertiary students, 2003-2004: percentage of total for both sexes	55.2%

Total fertility rate

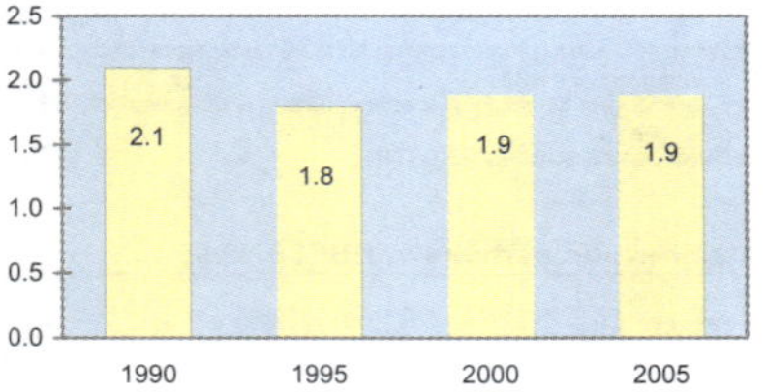

Parliament seats held by women (% of total)

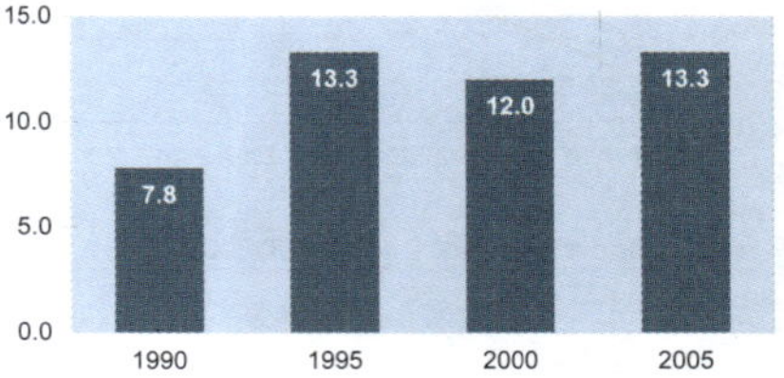

IRELAND

	1999	2000	2001	2002	2003	2004	2005
Employment (% change over previous year)	6.3	4.6	3.0	1.8	2.0	3.1	3.8
Unemployment rate (%)	5.7	4.3	4.0	4.5	4.7	4.5	4.3
Youth unemployment rate (%)	..	6.9	7.2	8.5	9.1	8.9	8.7

Economic activity rate, 2004

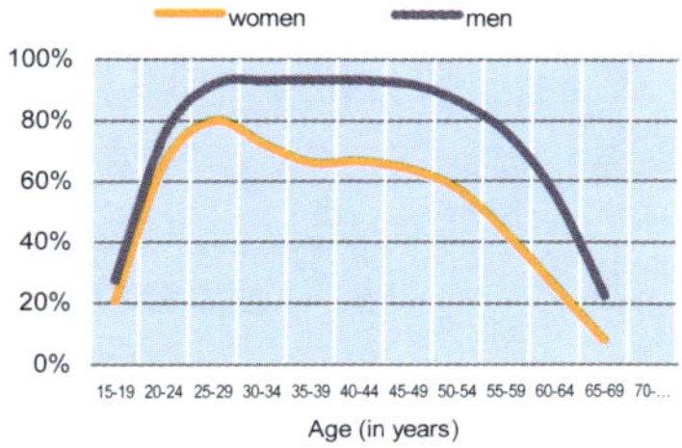

GDP at current prices	
in millions of US Dollars, PPP, 2005:	157 858
in millions of EUR, 2005:	161 163
GDP at constant 2000 prices, per capita	
US Dollars, PPP, 2005:	34 062
EUR, 2005:	32 491
Final consumption expenditure at 2000 prices, per capita, US Dollars, PPP, 2005:	20 234
Purchasing Power Parity (PPP)	
EUR per USD, 2005, US=1:	1.021
Gross external debt:	
in millions of US Dollars, 2005:	1 147 609
Exchange rate	
Annual average, EUR per USD, 2005:	0.804

Real GDP growth rate

% change over previous year

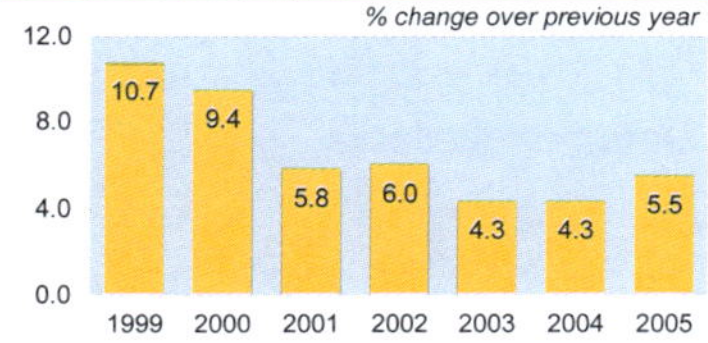

Consumer price index (annual average)

% change over previous year

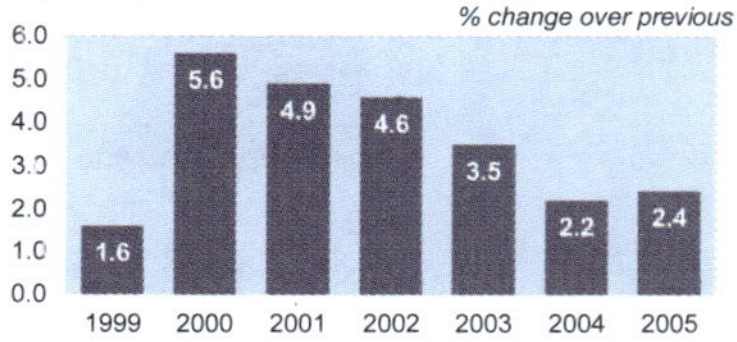

	% of GDP
Exports of goods and services, 2005:	81.3
Imports of goods and services, 2005:	68.6
External trade balance, 2005:	12.7

GDP in agriculture, industry, and services (2000=100)

Annual indices

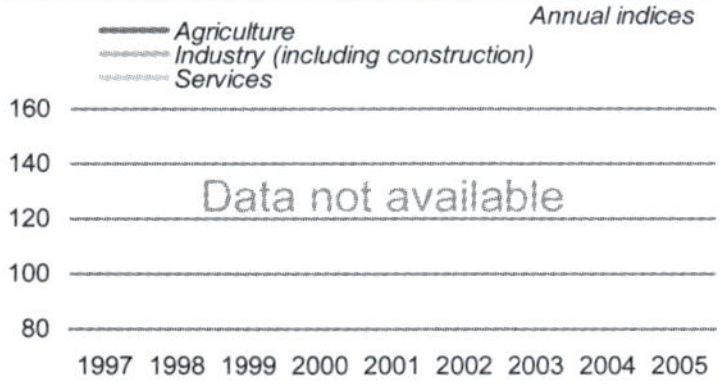

GDP by major sectors

Employment in major sectors, 2004

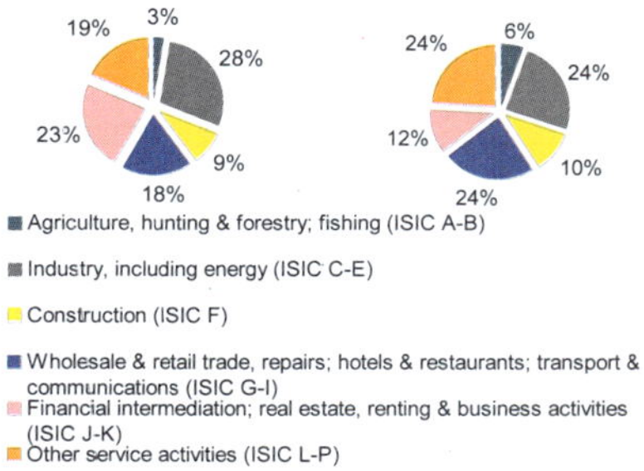

Major import partners from UNECE, 2005

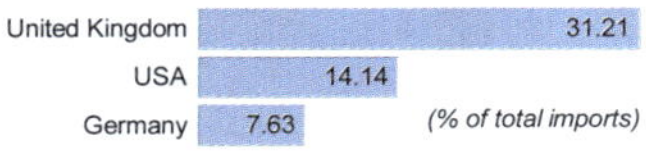

Major export partners in UNECE, 2005

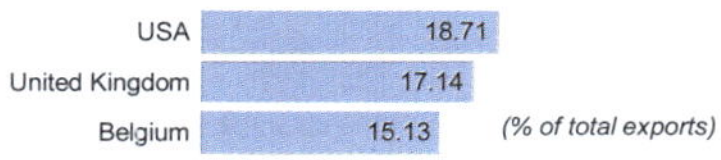

ISRAEL

Capital:	*
Two largest cities:	Tel Aviv (371 000)
	Haifa (269 300)
Area (km²):	22 145
Total population:	6 809 000
Population density (per km²):	307
Official languages:	Hebrew and Arabic
Date joined UN:	11 May 1949
National currency:	Israeli new shekel (ILS)
National statistical office:	Central Bureau of Statistics Israel http://www.cbs.gov.il

Population by age, 2004

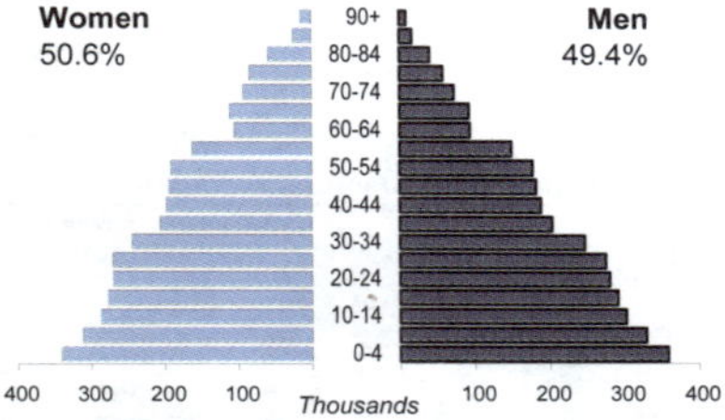

Life expectancy (in years), 2003:	at birth	at 65
Women:	82	20
Men:	78	17

Median age (in years), 2004:	
Women:	29
Men:	27

	percentage of total population
Foreign born:	..
Foreigners in population:	..

Total fertility rate

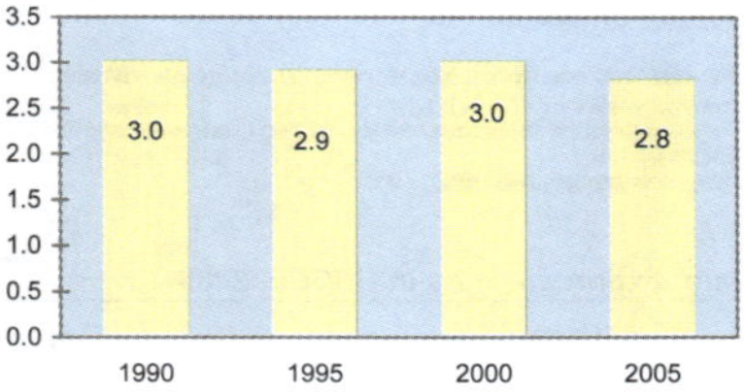

* See the country specific notes on page viii.

Time: UTC +2h

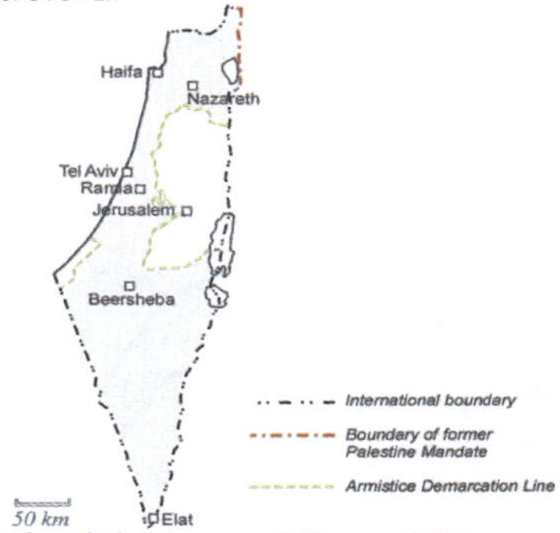

Legal marital status, population aged 18+

never married
married
divorced
widowed

Data not available

Women in the labour force, 2005:	46.5%
Gender pay gap, 2004:	36.7%
Female government ministers: percentage of total for both sexes	..
Female central bank board members: percentage of total for both sexes	..
Female tertiary students, 2000-2001: percentage of total for both sexes	54%

Parliament seats held by women (% of total)

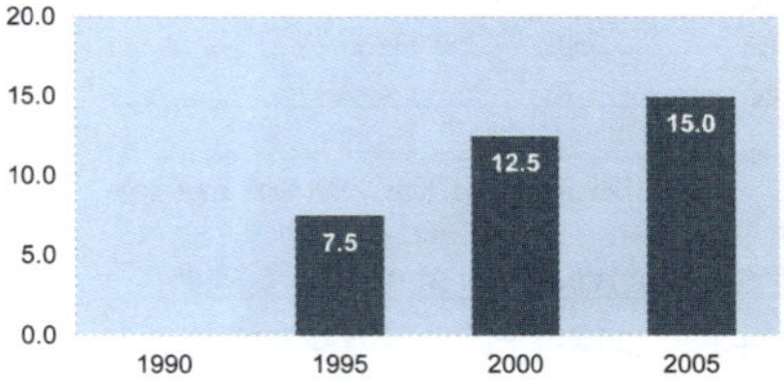

ISRAEL

	1999	2000	2001	2002	2003	2004	2005
Employment (% change over previous year)	3.1	4.0	2.0	0.9	2.0	3.0	3.9
Unemployment rate (%)	8.9	8.8	9.4	10.3	10.7	10.4	9.0
Youth unemployment rate (%)	..	17.0	..	..	..	..	..

Economic activity rate, 2004

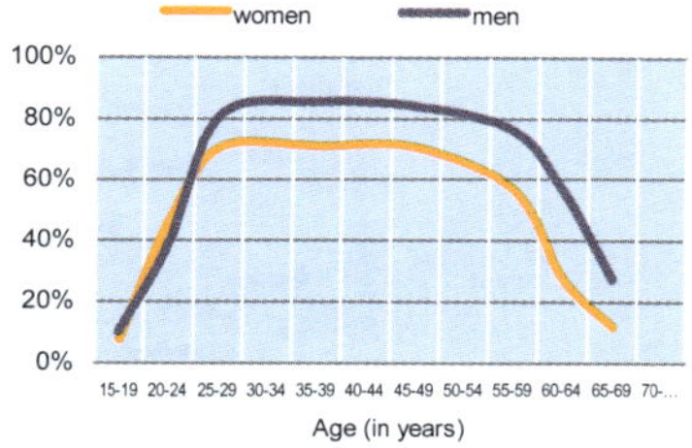

GDP at current prices	
in millions of US Dollars, PPP, 2003:	144 198
in millions of ILS, 2005:	582 291
GDP at constant 2000 prices, per capita	
US Dollars, PPP, 2005:	23 055
ILS, 2005:	83 114
Final consumption expenditure at 2000 prices, per capita, US Dollars, PPP, 2005:	18 737
Purchasing Power Parity (PPP)	
ILS per USD, 2003, US=1:	3.635
Gross external debt:	
in millions of US Dollars, 2005:	76 443
Exchange rate	
Annual average, ILS per USD, 2005:	4.488

Real GDP growth rate

% change over previous year

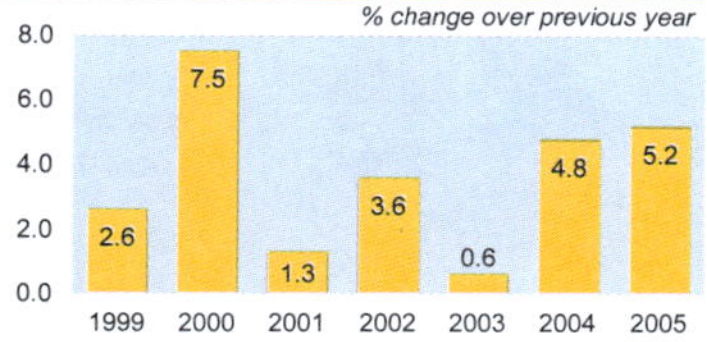

Consumer price index (annual average)

% change over previous year

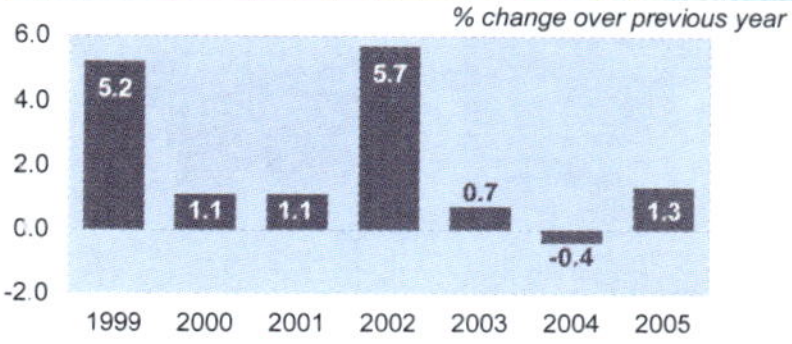

	% of GDP
Exports of goods and services, 2005:	44.6
Imports of goods and services, 2005:	44.3
External trade balance, 2005:	0.3

GDP in agriculture, industry, and services (2000=100)

Annual indices

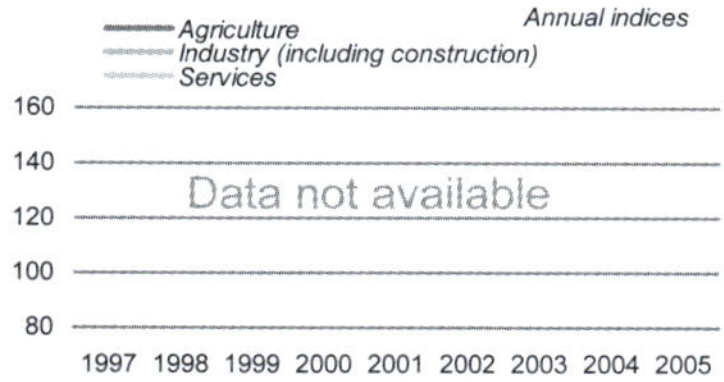

GDP by major sectors

Employment in major sectors, 2005

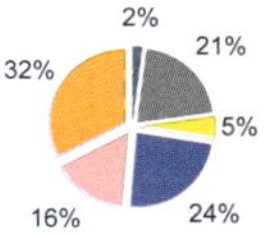

- Agriculture, hunting & forestry; fishing (ISIC A-B)
- Industry, including energy (ISIC C-E)
- Construction (ISIC F)
- Wholesale & retail trade, repairs; hotels & restaurants; transport & communications (ISIC G-I)
- Financial intermediation; real estate, renting & business activities (ISIC J-K)
- Other service activities (ISIC L-P)

Major import partners from UNECE, 2005

Major export partners in UNECE, 2005

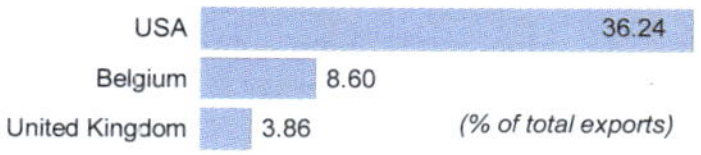

ITALY

Capital:	Rome (2 542 003)
Two largest cities:	Milano (1 271 898)
	Napoli (1 000 449)
Area (km^2):	301 337
Total population:	58 175 310
Population density (per km^2):	193
Official languages:	Italian
Date joined UN:	14 December 1955
National currency:	Euro (EUR)
National statistical office:	National Institute of Statistics Italy http://www.istat.it

Time: UTC +1h

Population by age, 2004

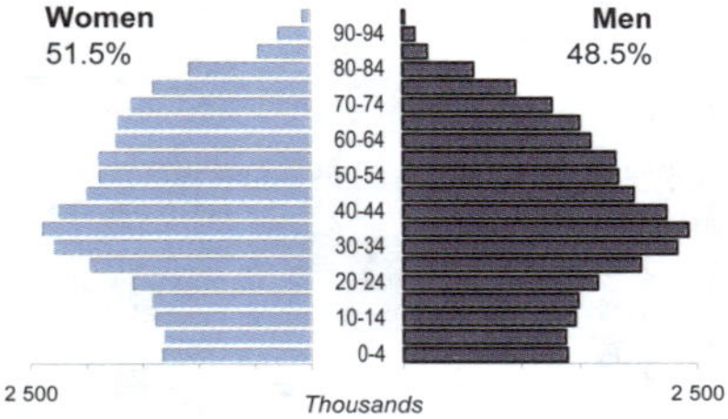

Life expectancy (in years), 2005:	at birth	at 65
Women:	83	21
Men:	78	17

Median age (in years), 2004:	
Women:	43
Men:	40

	percentage of total population
Foreign born:	..
Foreigners in population, 2005:	4.1%

Legal marital status, population aged 18+, 2003

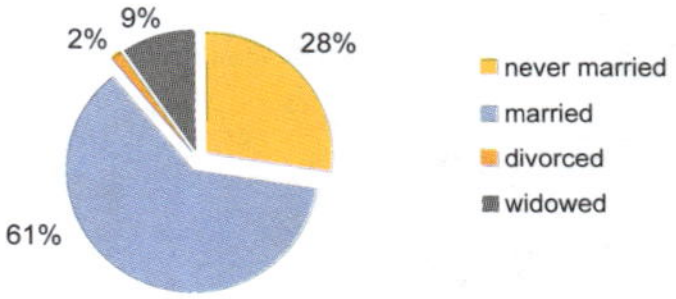

Women in the labour force, 2005:	40.1%
Gender pay gap, 2005:	9%
Female government ministers, 2006: percentage of total for both sexes	10.6%
Female central bank board members: percentage of total for both sexes	..
Female tertiary students, 2003-2004: percentage of total for both sexes	56.2%

Total fertility rate

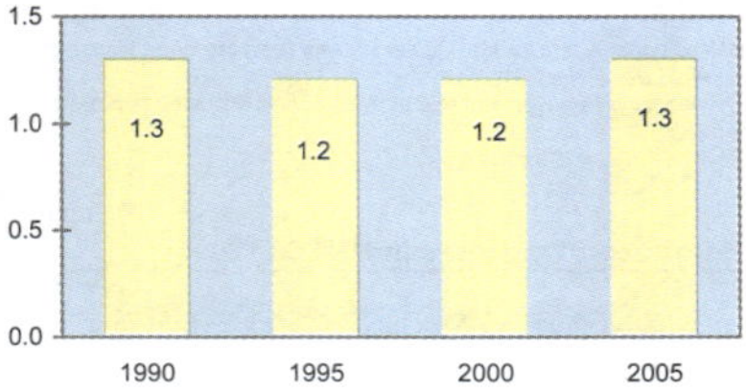

Parliament seats held by women (% of total)

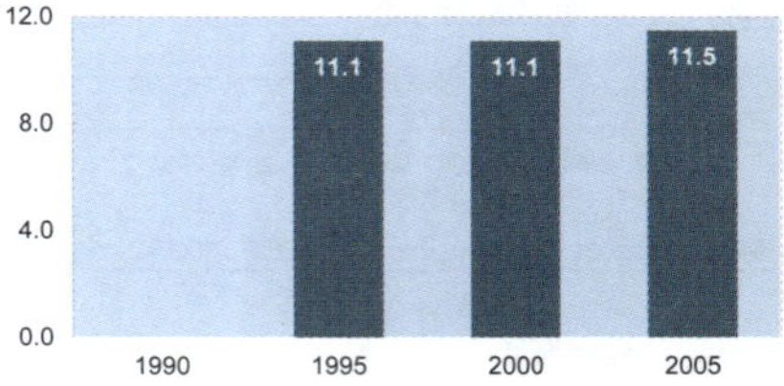

ITALY

	1999	2000	2001	2002	2003	2004	2005
Employment (% change over previous year)	1.1	1.9	2.0	1.7	1.5	0.3	0.2
Unemployment rate (%)	10.9	10.1	9.1	8.6	8.4	8.0	7.7
Youth unemployment rate (%)	..	27.0	24.1	23.1	23.7	23.5	24.0

Economic activity rate, 2004

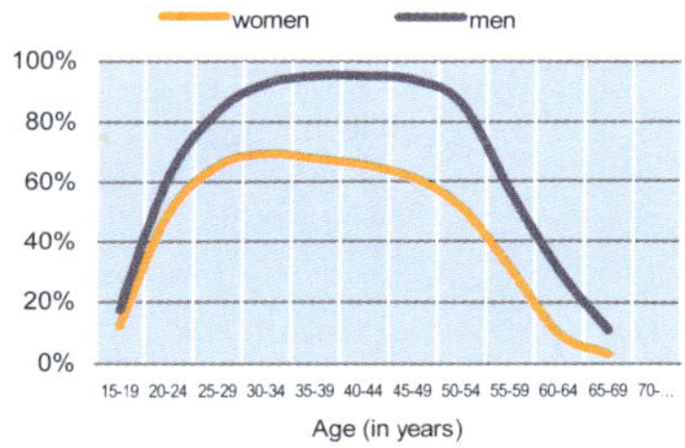

GDP at current prices	
in millions of US Dollars, PPP, 2005:	1 661 998
in millions of EUR, 2005:	1 417 241
GDP at constant 2000 prices, per capita	
US Dollars, PPP, 2005:	25 992
EUR, 2005:	21 007
Final consumption expenditure at 2000 prices, per capita, US Dollars, PPP, 2005:	20 576
Purchasing Power Parity (PPP)	
EUR per USD, 2005, US=1:	0.853
Gross external debt:	
in millions of US Dollars, 2005:	1 684 291
Exchange rate	
Annual average, EUR per USD, 2005:	0.804

Real GDP growth rate

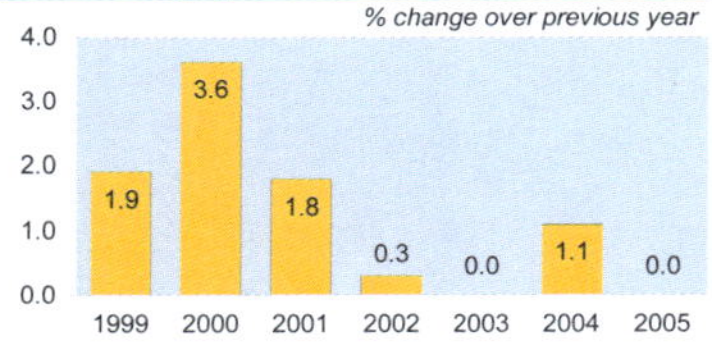

Consumer price index (annual average)

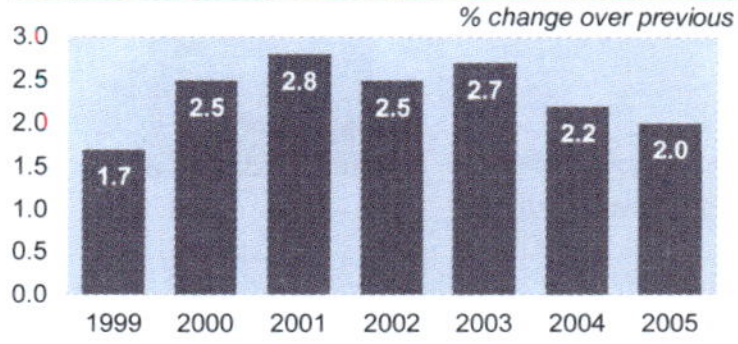

	% of GDP
Exports of goods and services, 2005:	26.3
Imports of goods and services, 2005:	26.4
External trade balance, 2005:	0.0

GDP by major sectors, 2005

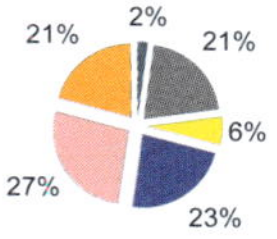

Employment in major sectors, 2005

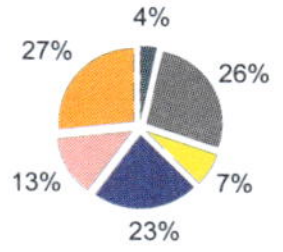

- Agriculture, hunting & forestry; fishing (ISIC A-B)
- Industry, including energy (ISIC C-E)
- Construction (ISIC F)
- Wholesale & retail trade, repairs; hotels & restaurants; transport & communications (ISIC G-I)
- Financial intermediation; real estate, renting & business activities (ISIC J-K)
- Other service activities (ISIC L-P)

GDP in agriculture, industry, and services (2000=100)

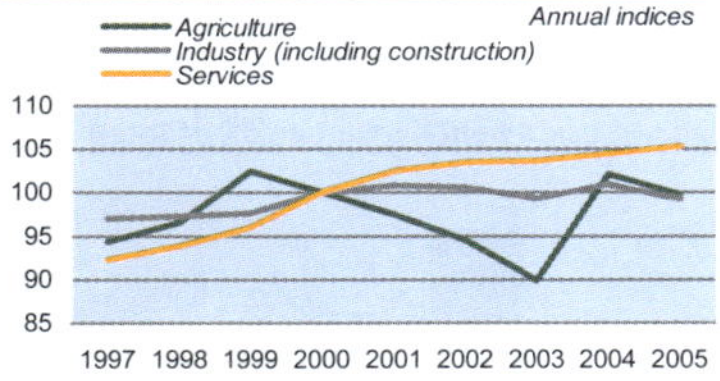

Major import partners from UNECE, 2005

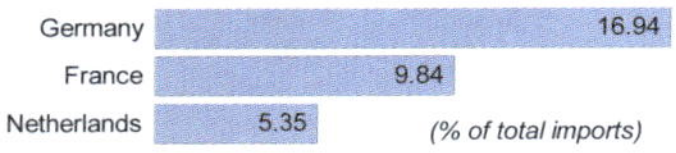

Major export partners in UNECE, 2005

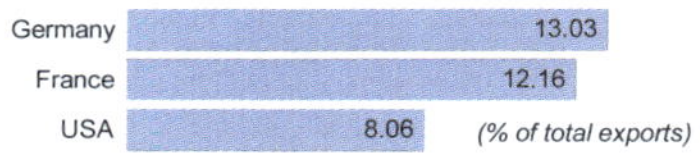

KAZAKHSTAN

Capital:	Astana (1 129 356)
Two largest cities:	Qaraghandy (436 864)
	Shymkent (360 078)
Area (km^2):	2 724 900
Total population:	15 012 985
Population density (per km^2):	6
Official languages:	Kazak
Date joined UN:	2 March 1992
National currency:	Kazakh tenge (KZT)
National statistical office:	

Agency of Statistics of the Republic of Kazakhstan
http://www.stat.kz

Time: UTC +5h

Population by age, 2004

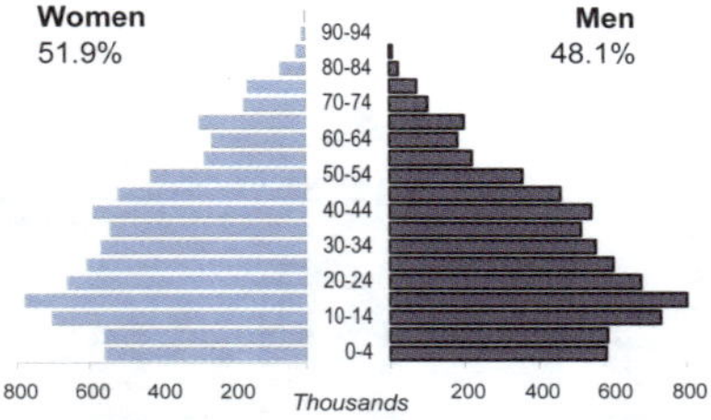

Life expectancy (in years), 2005:	at birth	at 65
Women:	72	15
Men:	60	11

Median age (in years), 2004:	
Women:	30
Men:	27

	percentage of total population
Foreign born:	..
Foreigners in population:	..

Legal marital status, population aged 18+

Data not available

never married
married
divorced
widowed

Women in the labour force, 2004:	49%
Gender pay gap, 2004:	38.1%
Female government ministers: percentage of total for both sexes	..
Female central bank board members, 2005: percentage of total for both sexes	28.6%
Female tertiary students: percentage of total for both sexes	..

Total fertility rate

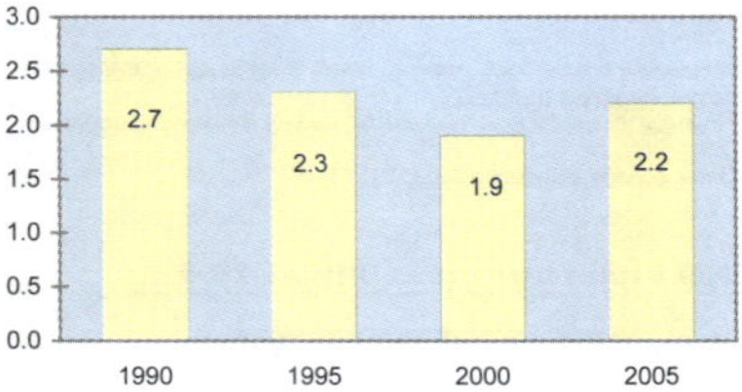

Parliament seats held by women (% of total)

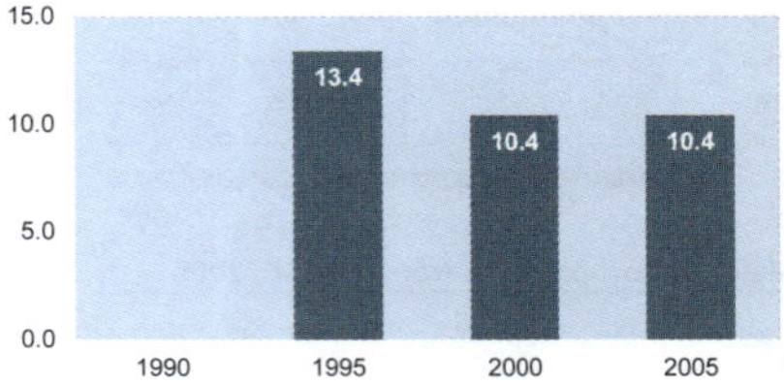

KAZAKHSTAN

	1999	2000	2001	2002	2003	2004	2005
Employment (% change over previous year)	..	..	8.0	0.2	4.1	2.8	1.1
Unemployment rate (%)	..	12.8	10.4	9.3	8.8	8.4	8.1
Youth unemployment rate (%)	..	..	19.1	17.3	14.5	14.3	13.4

Economic activity rate, 2002

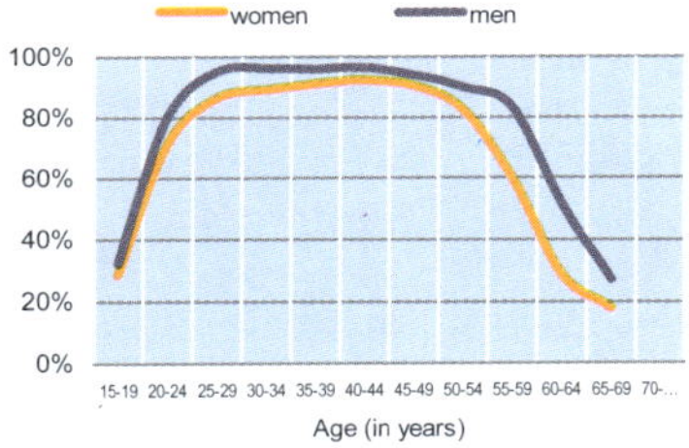

GDP at current prices	
in millions of US Dollars, PPP, 2005:	120 229
in millions of KZT, 2005:	7 590 594
GDP at constant 2000 prices, per capita	
US Dollars, PPP, 2005:	6 927
KZT, 2005:	281 129
Final consumption expenditure at 2000 prices, per capita, US Dollars, PPP, 2005:	4 936
Purchasing Power Parity (PPP)	
KZT per USD, 2005, US=1:	63.13
Gross external debt:	
in millions of US Dollars, 2005:	41 516
Exchange rate	
Annual average, KZT per USD, 2005:	132.9

Real GDP growth rate

% change over previous year

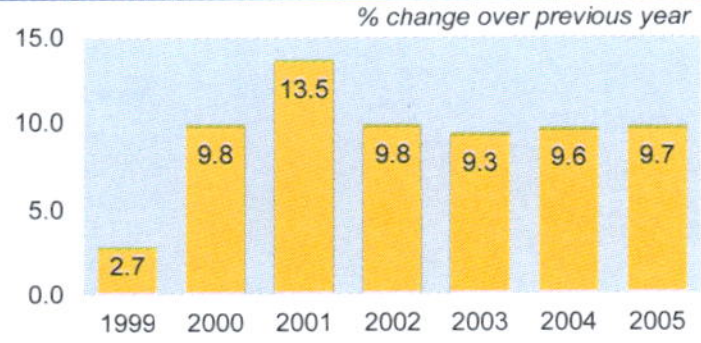

Consumer price index (annual average)

% change over previous year

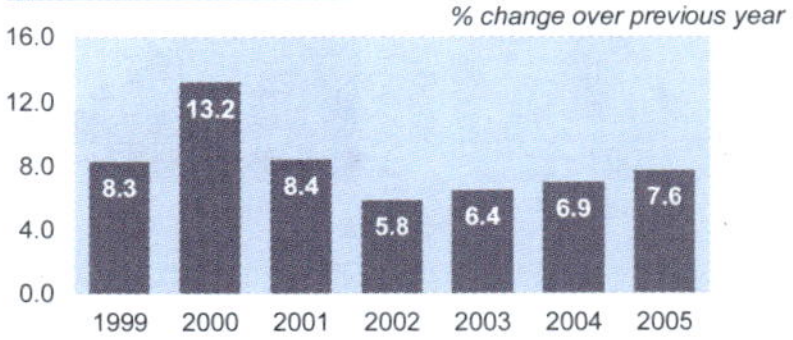

	% of GDP
Exports of goods and services, 2005:	53.5
Imports of goods and services, 2005:	44.7
External trade balance, 2005:	8.8

GDP in agriculture, industry, and services (2000=100)

Annual indices

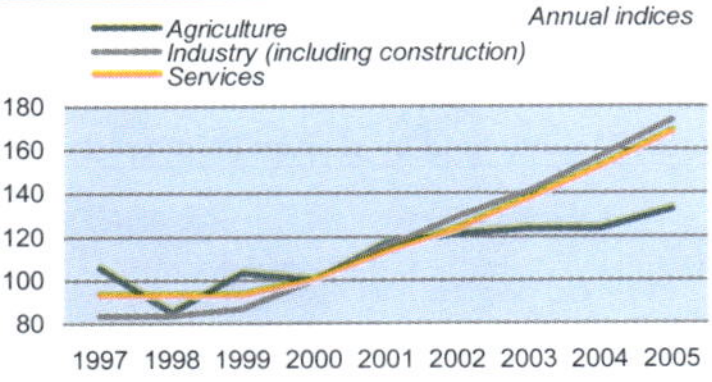

GDP by major sectors, 2005

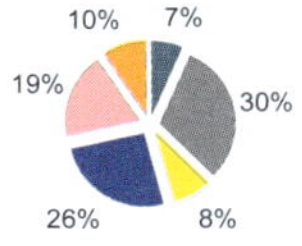

Employment in major sectors, 2005

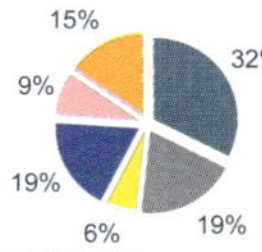

- Agriculture, hunting & forestry; fishing (ISIC A-B)
- Industry, including energy (ISIC C-E)
- Construction (ISIC F)
- Wholesale & retail trade, repairs; hotels & restaurants; transport & communications (ISIC G-I)
- Financial intermediation; real estate, renting & business activities (ISIC J-K)
- Other service activities (ISIC L-P)

Major import partners from UNECE, 2005

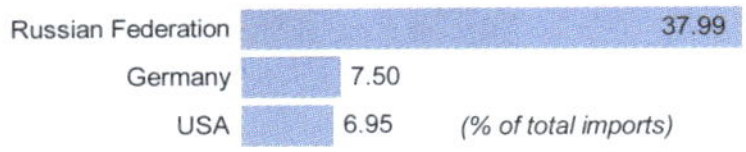

Major export partners in UNECE, 2005

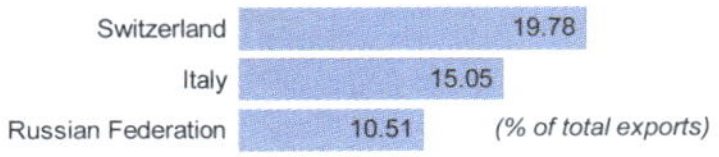

KYRGYZSTAN

Time: UTC +5h

Capital:	Bishkek (750 327)
Two largest cities:	Osh (208 520)
	Jalal-Abad (70 401)
Area (km^2):	199 900
Total population:	5 065 027
Population density (per km^2):	25
Official languages:	Kyrgyz
Date joined UN:	2 March 1992
National currency:	Kyrgyz som (KGS)
National statistical office:	National Statistical Committee Kyrgyzstan
	http://www.stat.kg

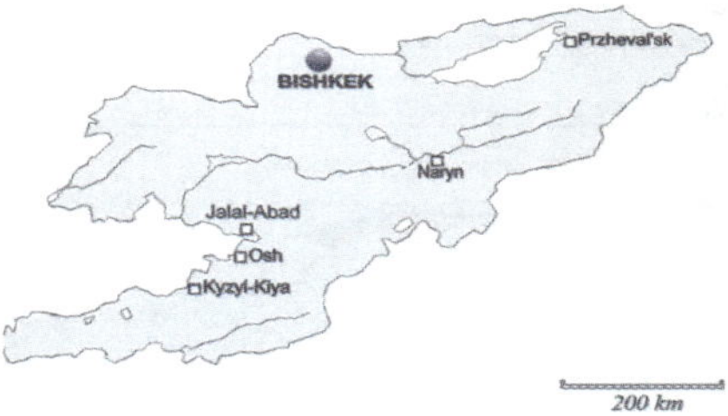

Population by age, 2004

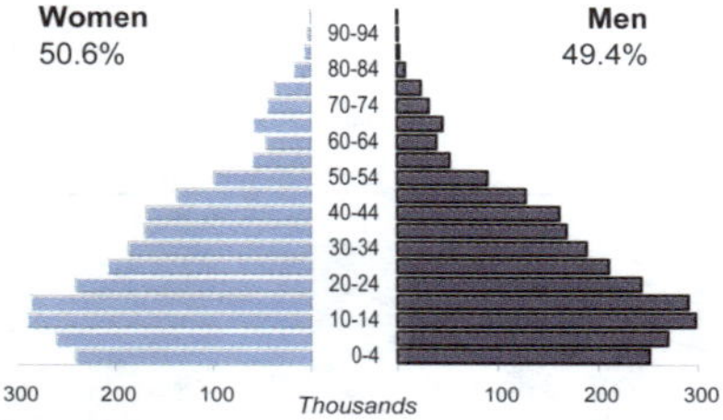

Life expectancy (in years), 2005:	at birth	at 65
Women:	72	15
Men:	64	12

Median age (in years), 2004:	
Women:	24
Men:	23

	percentage of total population
Foreign born, 2004:	0.4%
Foreigners in population, 2004:	1%

Legal marital status, population aged 18+

Data not available

never married
married
divorced
widowed

Women in the labour force, 2004:	43.1%
Gender pay gap, 2004:	33.4%
Female government ministers, 2001: percentage of total for both sexes	14.3%
Female central bank board members: percentage of total for both sexes	..
Female tertiary students: percentage of total for both sexes	..

Total fertility rate

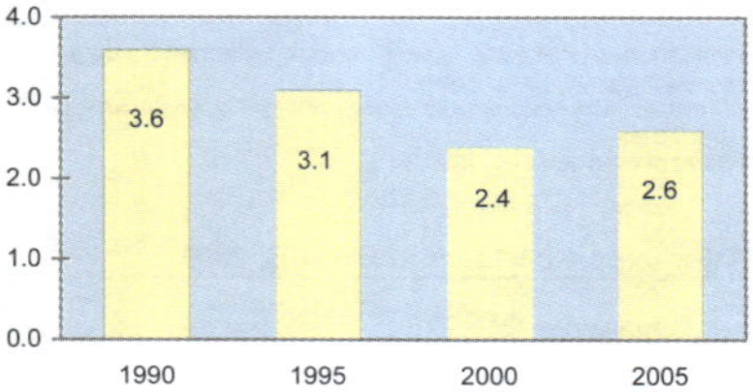

Parliament seats held by women (% of total)

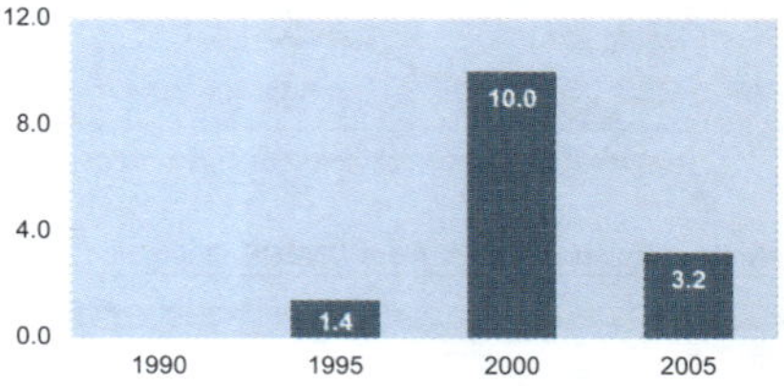

KYRGYZSTAN

	1999	2000	2001	2002	2003	2004	2005
Employment (% change over previous year)	3.5	0.2	1.1	1.1	1.7	2.3	2.8
Unemployment rate (%)	3.0	3.1	3.2	3.1	2.9	2.9	3.3
Youth unemployment rate (%)	..	..	..	20.1	15.4	15.2	14.5

Economic activity rate, 2004

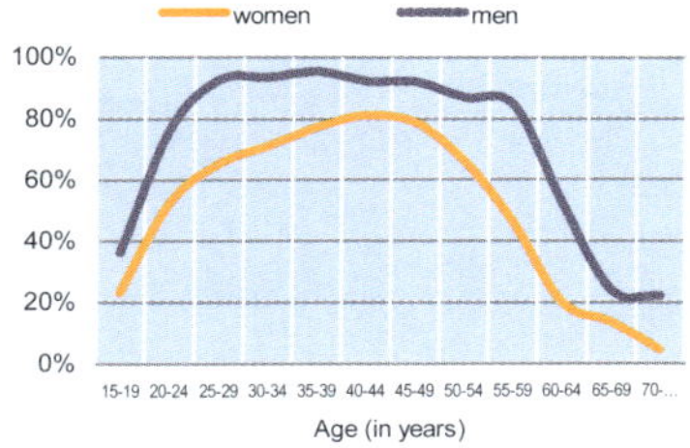

GDP at current prices	
in millions of US Dollars, PPP, 2005:	9 735
in millions of KGS, 2005:	100 116
GDP at constant 2000 prices, per capita	
US Dollars, PPP, 2005:	1 688
KGS, 2005:	15 318
Final consumption expenditure at 2000 prices, per capita, US Dollars, PPP, 2005:	1 756
Purchasing Power Parity (PPP)	
KGS per USD, 2005, US=1:	10.28
Gross external debt:	
in millions of US Dollars, 2005:	2 366
Exchange rate	
Annual average, KGS per USD, 2005:	41.01

Real GDP growth rate

% change over previous year

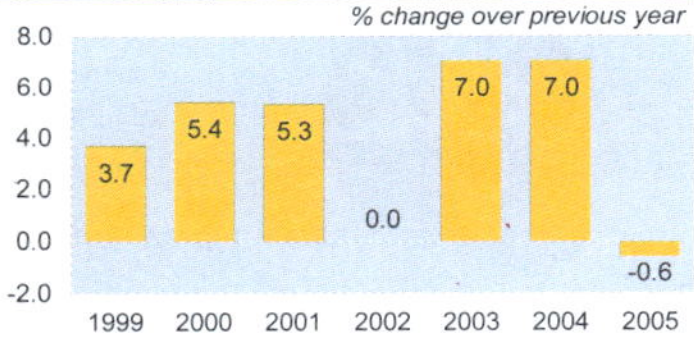

Consumer price index (annual average)

% change over previous year

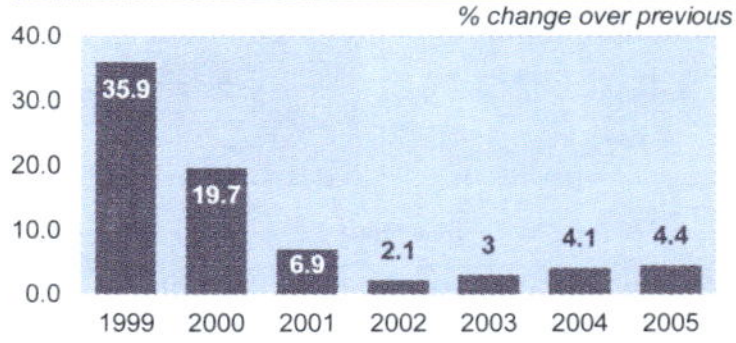

	% of GDP
Exports of goods and services, 2005:	39.0
Imports of goods and services, 2005:	58.2
External trade balance, 2005:	-19

GDP by major sectors, 2005

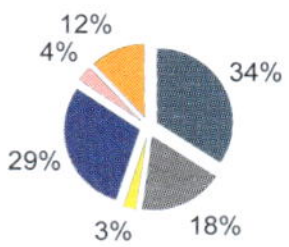

Employment in major sectors, 2003

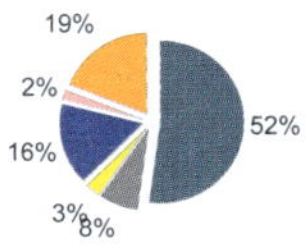

- Agriculture, hunting & forestry; fishing (ISIC A-B)
- Industry, including energy (ISIC C-E)
- Construction (ISIC F)
- Wholesale & retail trade, repairs; hotels & restaurants; transport & communications (ISIC G-I)
- Financial intermediation; real estate, renting & business activities (ISIC J-K)
- Other service activities (ISIC L-P)

GDP in agriculture, industry, and services (2000=100)

Annual indices

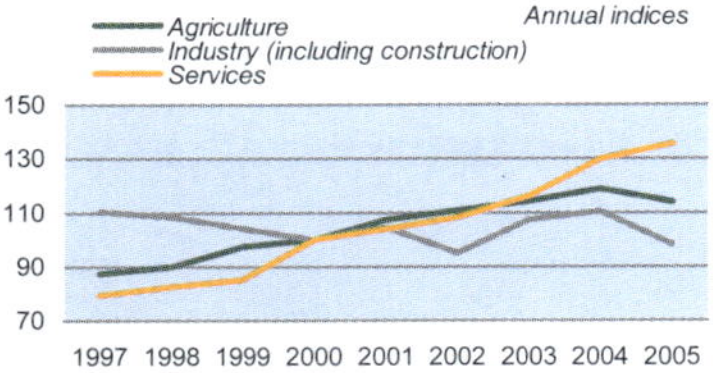

Major import partners from UNECE, 2005

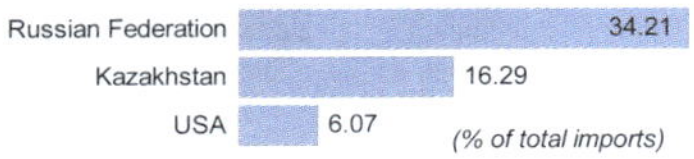

Major export partners in UNECE, 2005

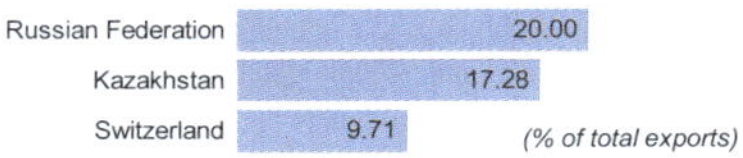

LATVIA

Capital:	Riga (727 578)
Two largest cities:	Daugavpils (109 482)
	Liepāja (85 915)
Area (km^2):	64 589
Total population:	2 300 512
Population density (per km^2):	36
Official languages:	Latvian
Date joined UN:	17 September 1991
National currency:	Latvian lats (LVL)
National statistical office:	Central Statistical Bureau of Latvia http://www.csb.lv

Time: UTC +2h

Population by age, 2005

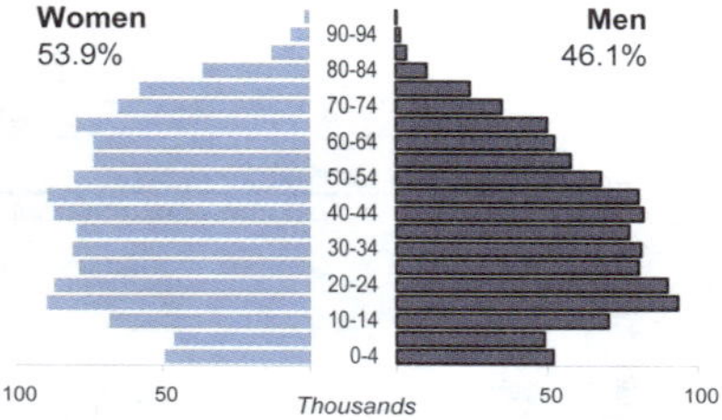

Life expectancy (in years), 2005:	at birth	at 65
Women:	77	17
Men:	66	13

Median age (in years), 2005:	
Women:	42
Men:	36

	percentage of total population
Foreign born, 2005:	16.7%
Foreigners in population, 2005:	1.5%

Legal marital status, population aged 18+, 2004

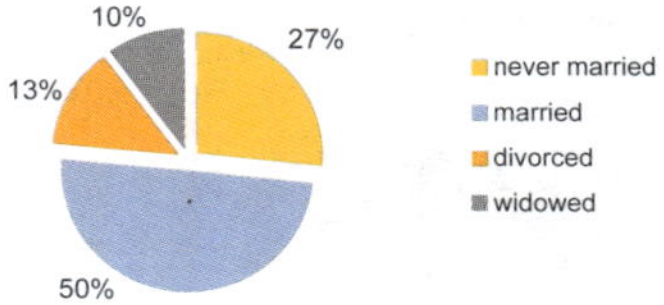

Women in the labour force, 2005:	48.3%
Gender pay gap, 2005:	17%
Female government ministers, 2005: percentage of total for both sexes	27.8%
Female central bank board members, 2005: percentage of total for both sexes	25%
Female tertiary students, 2003-2004: percentage of total for both sexes	62.3%

Total fertility rate

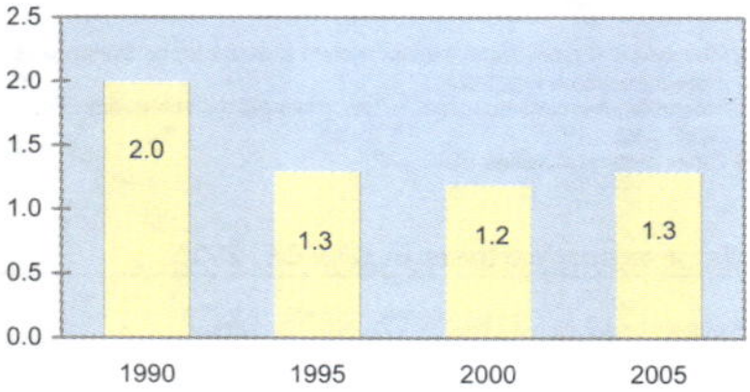

Parliament seats held by women (% of total)

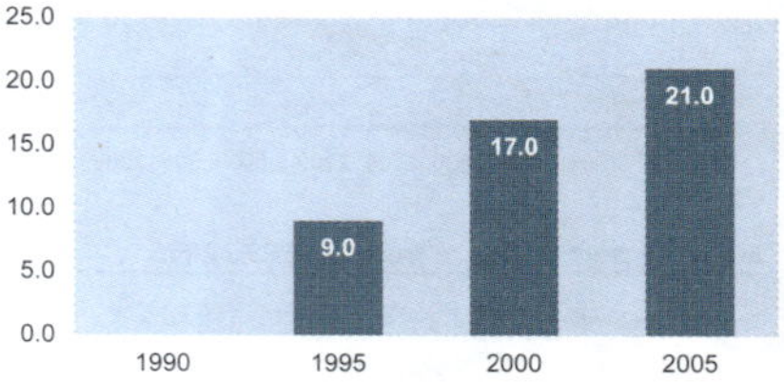

LATVIA

	1999	2000	2001	2002	2003	2004	2005
Employment (% change over previous year)	-1.8	-3.0	2.2	1.6	1.7	1.1	1.6
Unemployment rate (%)	14.0	13.7	12.9	12.2	10.5	10.4	9.0
Youth unemployment rate (%)	..	21.4	23.0	22.0	18.0	18.1	13.6

Economic activity rate, 2004

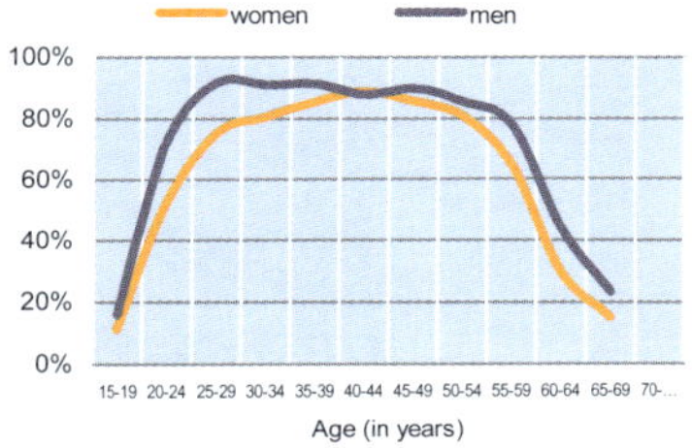

GDP at current prices	
in millions of US Dollars, PPP, 2005:	30 024
in millions of LVL, 2005:	8 937
GDP at constant 2000 prices, per capita	
US Dollars, PPP, 2005:	12 309
LVL, 2005:	3 051
Final consumption expenditure at 2000 prices, per capita, US Dollars, PPP, 2005:	9 870
Purchasing Power Parity (PPP)	
LVL per USD, 2005, US=1:	0.298
Gross external debt:	
in millions of US Dollars, 2005:	15 177
Exchange rate	
Annual average, LVL per USD, 2005:	0.565

Real GDP growth rate

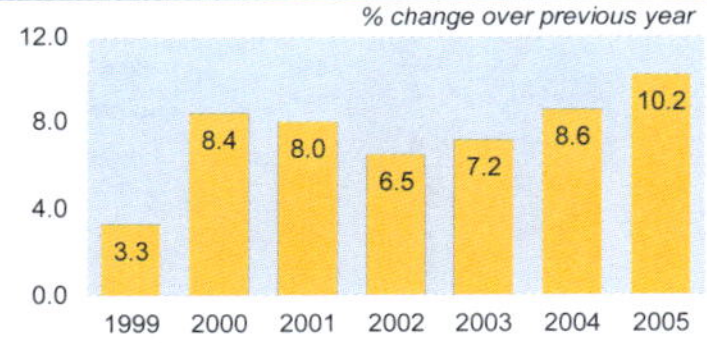

Consumer price index (annual average)

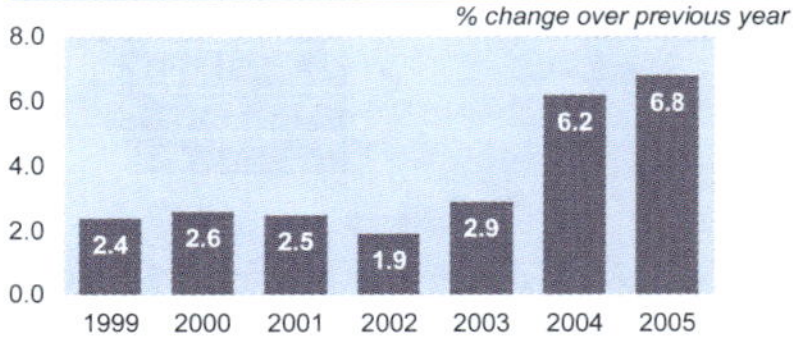

	% of GDP
Exports of goods and services, 2005:	48.1
Imports of goods and services, 2005:	62.4
External trade balance, 2005:	-14

GDP in agriculture, industry, and services (2000=100)

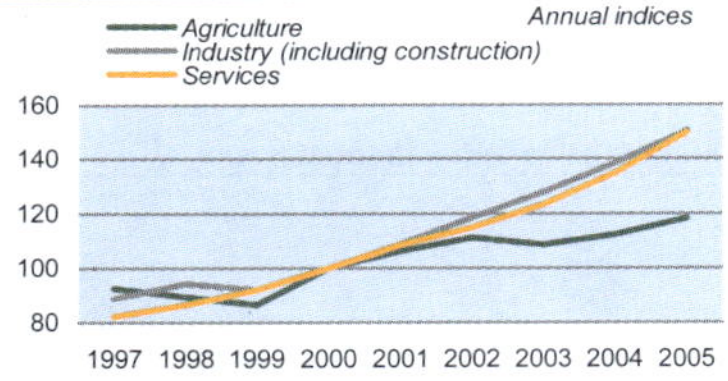

GDP by major sectors, 2005

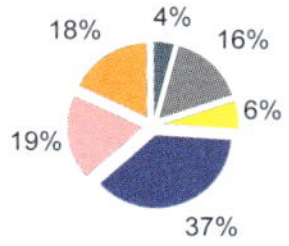

Employment in major sectors, 2005

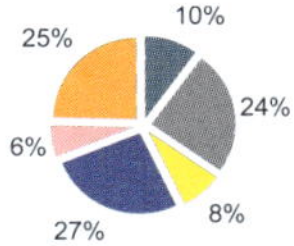

- Agriculture, hunting & forestry; fishing (ISIC A-B)
- Industry, including energy (ISIC C-E)
- Construction (ISIC F)
- Wholesale & retail trade, repairs; hotels & restaurants; transport & communications (ISIC G-I)
- Financial intermediation; real estate, renting & business activities (ISIC J-K)
- Other service activities (ISIC L-P)

Major import partners from UNECE, 2005

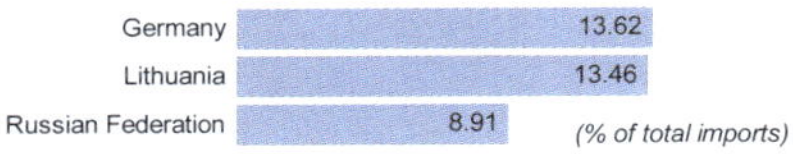

Major export partners in UNECE, 2005

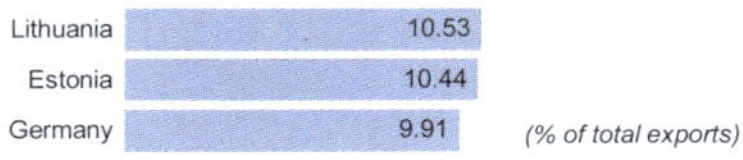

LIECHTENSTEIN

Capital:	Vaduz (5047)
Two largest cities:	Schaan (5811)
	Triesen (4643)
Area (km²):	160
Total population:	33 436
Population density (per km²):	209
Official languages:	German
Date joined UN:	18 September 1990
National currency:	Swiss franc (CHF)
National statistical office:	

Portal of the Principality of Liechtenstein

http://www.llv.li/amtsstellen/llv-avw-statistik.htm

Time: UTC +1h

Population by age, 2004

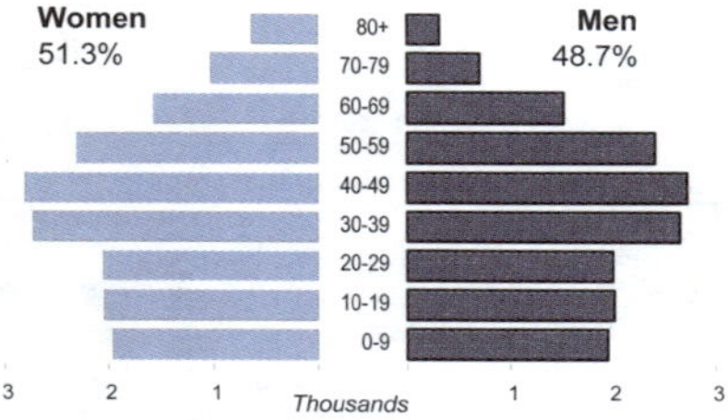

Legal marital status, population aged 18+, 2005

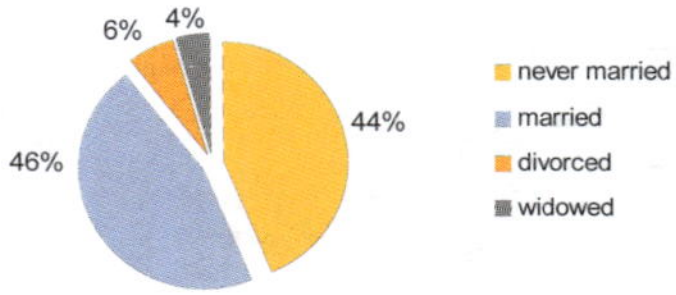

Life expectancy (in years):	at birth	at 65
Women:	..	..
Men:	..	..

Median age (in years), 2004:	
Women:	39
Men:	38

	percentage of total population
Foreign born:	..
Foreigners in population, 2004:	34%

Total fertility rate

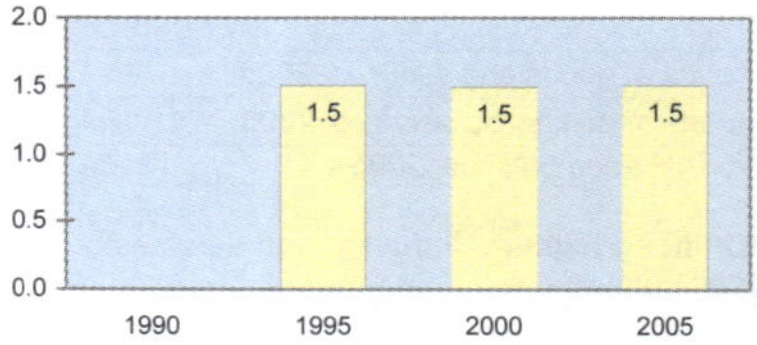

Real GDP growth rate

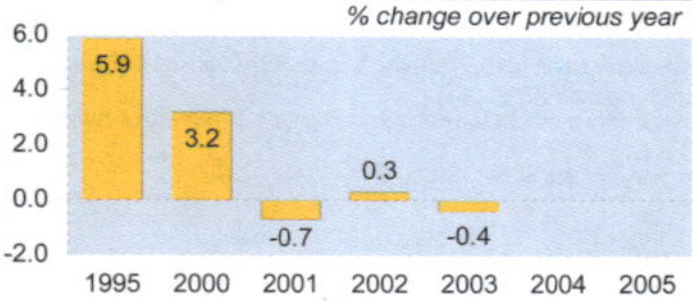

Consumer price index (annual average)

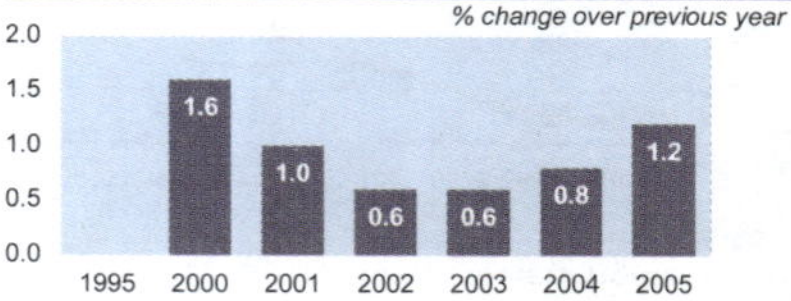

LIECHTENSTEIN

	1999	2000	2001	2002	2003	2004	2005
Employment (% change over previous year)	..	..	..	..	..	..	..
Unemployment rate (%)	1.2	1.1	1.2	1.4	2.2	2.4	2.4
Youth unemployment rate (%)	..	..	..	..	..	..	..

GDP by major sectors

Employment in major sectors, 2005

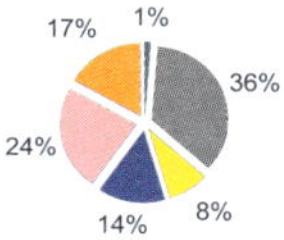

- Agriculture, hunting & forestry; fishing (ISIC A-B)
- Industry, including energy (ISIC C-E)
- Construction (ISIC F)
- Wholesale & retail trade, repairs; hotels & restaurants; transport & communications (ISIC G-I)
- Financial intermediation; real estate, renting & business activities (ISIC J-K)
- Other service activities (ISIC L-P)

GDP at current prices	
in millions of US Dollars, PPP:	..
in millions of CHF, 2002:	4 191
GDP per capita	
US Dollars, 2003:	94 532
CHF:	..
Final consumption expenditure at 2000 prices, per capita, US Dollars, PPP:	..
Purchasing Power Parity (PPP)	
CHF per USD, US=1:	..
Gross external debt:	
in millions of US Dollars:	..
Exchange rate	
Annual average, CHF per USD, 2005:	1.245

LITHUANIA

Capital:	Vilnius (541 291)
Two largest cities:	Kaunas (364 083)
	Klaipeda (188 775)
Area (km²):	65 300
Total population:	3 414 304
Population density (per km²):	52
Official languages:	Lithuanian
Date joined UN:	17 September 1991
National currency:	Lithuanian litas (LTL)
National statistical office:	Statistical Office of Lithuania http://www.std.lt

Time: UTC +2h

Population by age, 2005

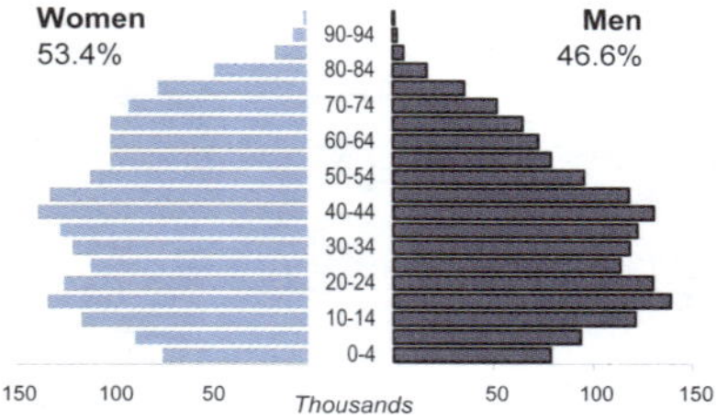

Legal marital status, population aged 18+, 2004

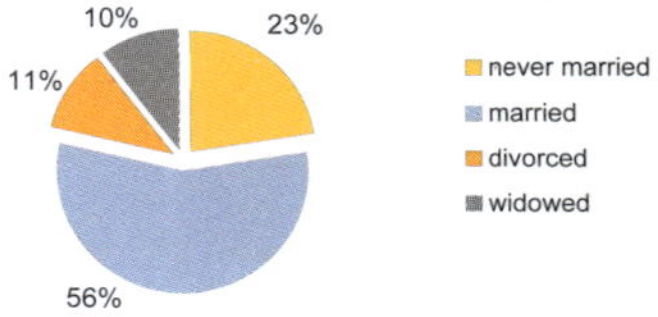

Life expectancy (in years), 2005:	at birth	at 65
Women:	77	18
Men:	65	14

Median age (in years), 2005:	
Women:	40
Men:	35

	percentage of total population
Foreign born, 2005:	6.6%
Foreigners in population, 2005:	0.9%

Women in the labour force, 2005:	49.1%
Gender pay gap, 2005:	15%
Female government ministers, 2005: percentage of total for both sexes	15.4%
Female central bank board members, 2005: percentage of total for both sexes	20%
Female tertiary students, 2003-2004: percentage of total for both sexes	60%

Total fertility rate

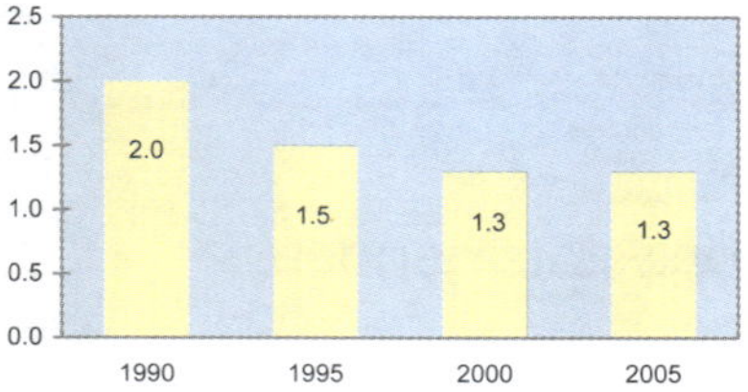

Parliament seats held by women (% of total)

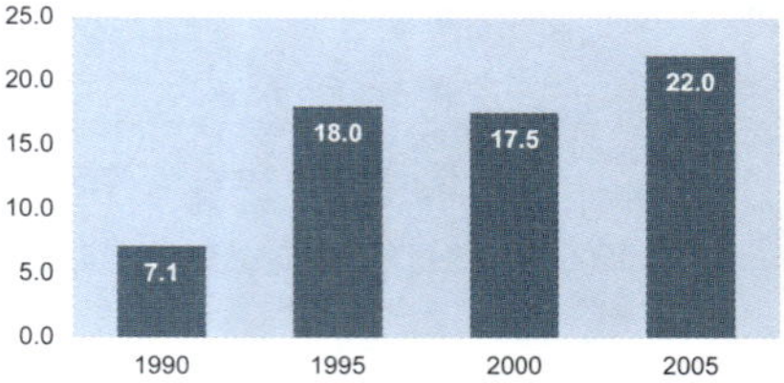

LITHUANIA

	1999	2000	2001	2002	2003	2004	2005
Employment (% change over previous year)	-2.2	-4.0	-3.3	4.0	2.3	-0.1	2.6
Unemployment rate (%)	13.7	16.4	16.5	13.5	12.4	11.4	8.3
Youth unemployment rate (%)	..	30.6	30.9	22.5	25.1	22.7	15.7

Economic activity rate, 2004

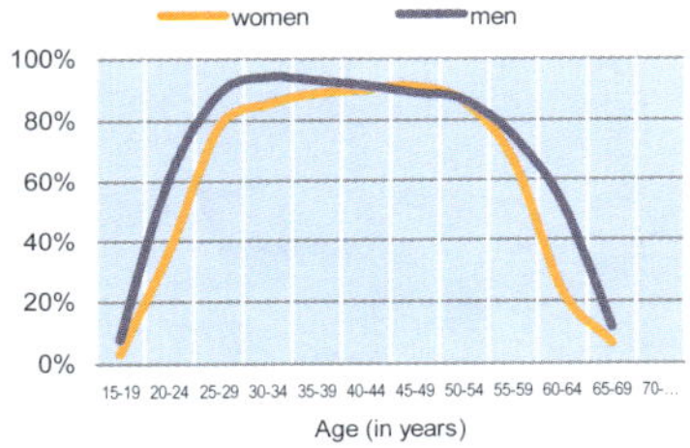

GDP at current prices	
in millions of US Dollars, PPP, 2005:	49 180
in millions of LTL, 2005:	71 200
GDP at constant 2000 prices, per capita	
US Dollars, PPP, 2005:	12 917
LTL, 2005:	19 425
Final consumption expenditure at 2000 prices, per capita, US Dollars, PPP, 2005:	10 977
Purchasing Power Parity (PPP)	
LTL per USD, 2005, US=1:	1.448
Gross external debt:	
in millions of US Dollars, 2005:	10 612
Exchange rate	
Annual average, LTL per USD, 2005:	2.774

Real GDP growth rate

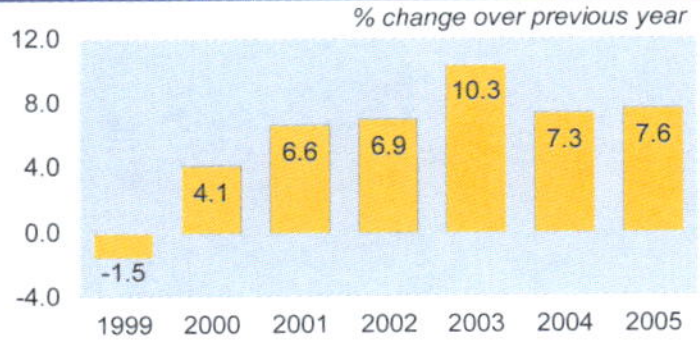

Consumer price index (annual average)

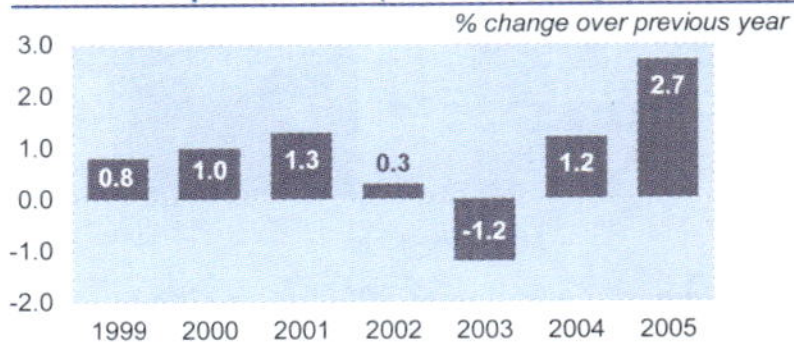

	% of GDP
Exports of goods and services, 2005:	58.3
Imports of goods and services, 2005:	65.3
External trade balance, 2005:	-7

GDP in agriculture, industry, and services (2000=100)

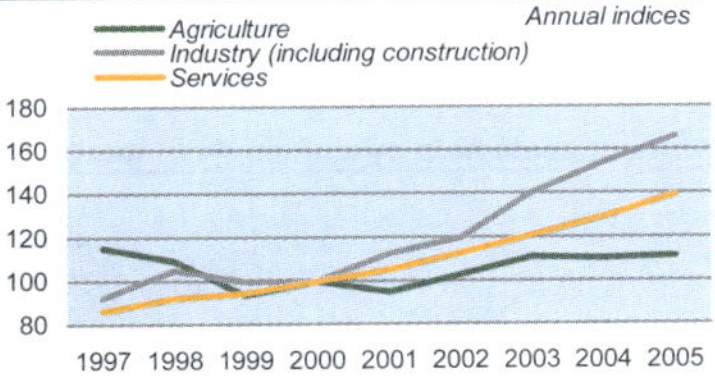

GDP by major sectors, 2005

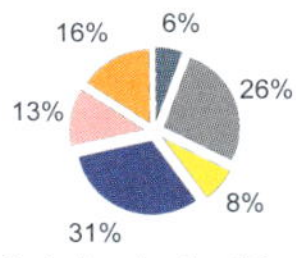

Employment in major sectors, 2005

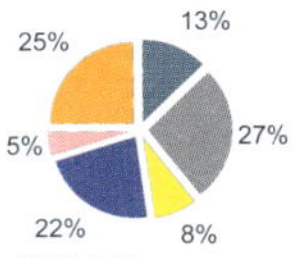

- Agriculture, hunting & forestry; fishing (ISIC A-B)
- Industry, including energy (ISIC C-E)
- Construction (ISIC F)
- Wholesale & retail trade, repairs; hotels & restaurants; transport & communications (ISIC G-I)
- Financial intermediation; real estate, renting & business activities (ISIC J-K)
- Other service activities (ISIC L-P)

Major import partners from UNECE, 2005

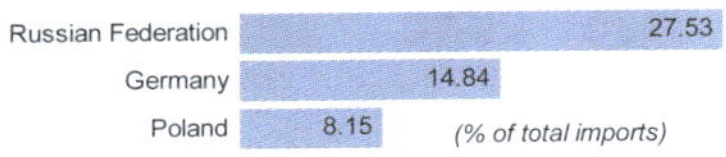

Major export partners in UNECE, 2005

LUXEMBOURG

Capital:	Luxembourg (77 325)
Two largest cities:	Esch-sur-Alzette (27 891)
	Differdange (18 891)
Area (km²):	2 586
Total population:	457 250
Population density (per km²):	177
Official languages:	French, German and Luxembourgish
Date joined UN:	24 October 1945
National currency:	Euro (EUR)
National statistical office:	

Central Service for Statistics and Economic Studies
http://www.statec.public.lu

Time: UTC +1h

Population by age, 2005

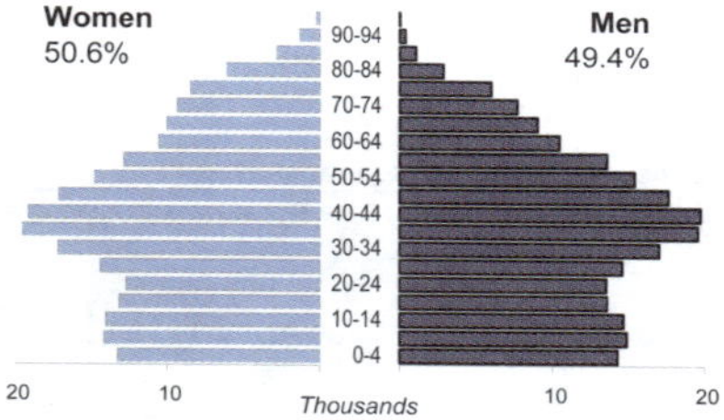

Life expectancy (in years), 2005:	at birth	at 65
Women:	82	20
Men:	76	17

Median age (in years), 2005:	
Women:	39
Men:	38

	percentage of total population
Foreign born:	..
Foreigners in population, 2005:	39%

Legal marital status, population aged 18+

Data not available

never married
married
divorced
widowed

Women in the labour force, 2005:	42.4%
Gender pay gap, 2005:	14%
Female government ministers, 2006: percentage of total for both sexes	21.3%
Female central bank board members, 2005: percentage of total for both sexes	11.1%
Female tertiary students: percentage of total for both sexes	..

Total fertility rate

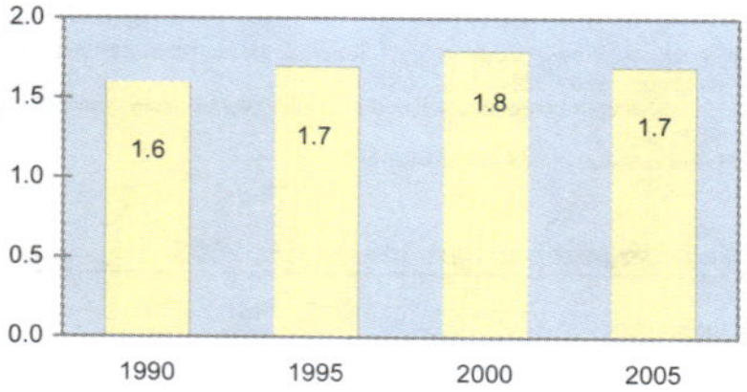

Parliament seats held by women (% of total)

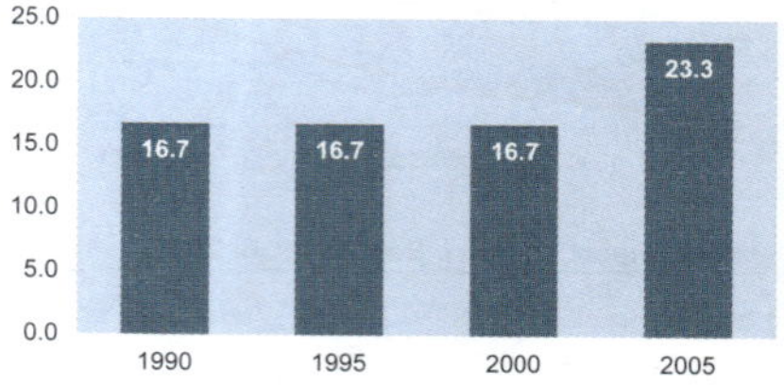

LUXEMBOURG

	1999	2000	2001	2002	2003	2004	2005
Employment (% change over previous year)	5.0	5.6	5.3	3.2	1.7	2.1	3.0
Unemployment rate (%)	2.4	2.3	2.1	2.8	3.7	5.1	4.5
Youth unemployment rate (%)	..	7.1	7.1	7.7	11.0	16.8	13.7

Economic activity rate, 2003

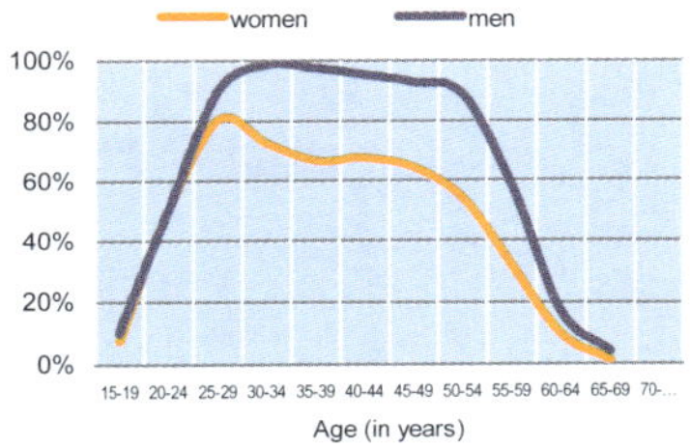

GDP at current prices	
in millions of US Dollars, PPP, 2005:	31 319
in millions of EUR, 2005:	29 396
GDP at constant 2000 prices, per capita	
US Dollars, PPP, 2005:	56 768
EUR, 2005:	56 083
Final consumption expenditure at 2000 prices, per capita, US Dollars, PPP, 2005:	32 933
Purchasing Power Parity (PPP)	
EUR per USD, 2005, US=1:	0.939
Gross external debt:	
in millions of US Dollars:	..
Exchange rate	
Annual average, EUR per USD, 2005:	0.804

Real GDP growth rate

% change over previous year

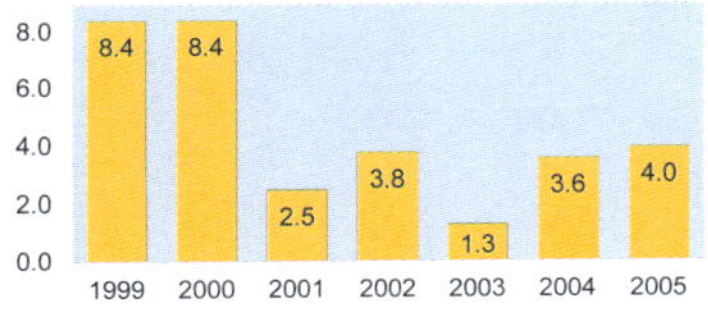

Consumer price index (annual average)

% change over previous year

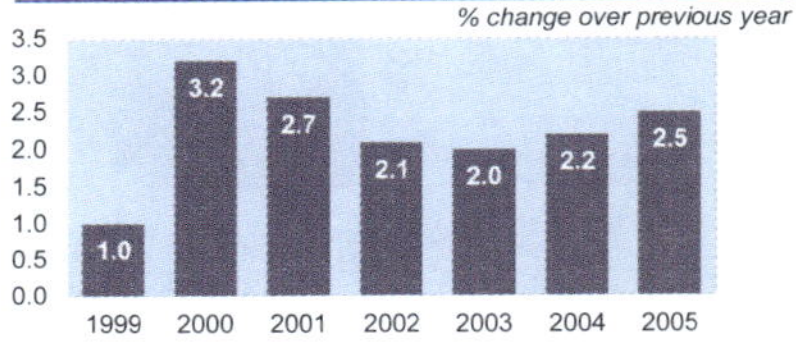

	% of GDP
Exports of goods and services, 2005:	159.3
Imports of goods and services, 2005:	138.0
External trade balance, 2005:	21.3

GDP by major sectors, 2005

Employment in major sectors, 2005

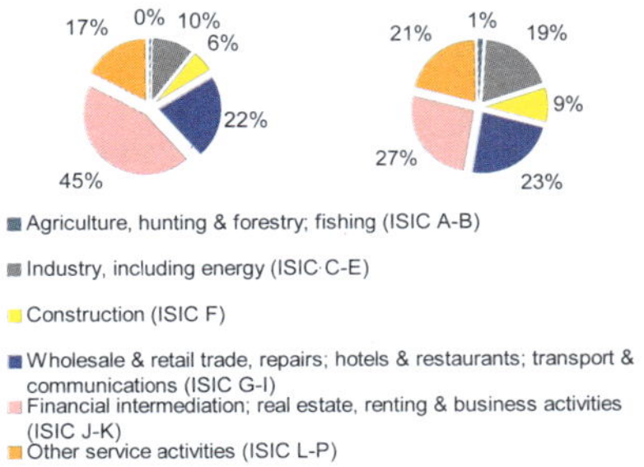

GDP in agriculture, industry, and services (2000=100)

Annual indices

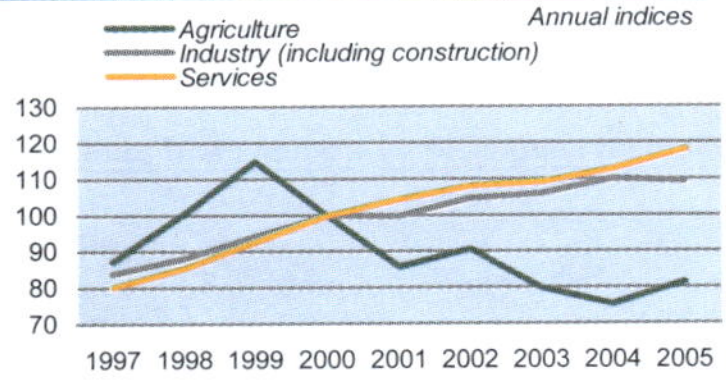

Major import partners from UNECE, 2005

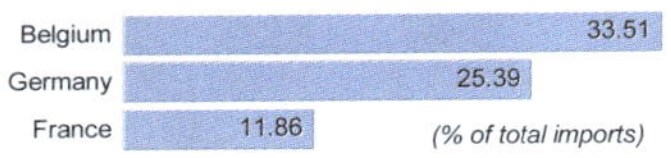

Major export partners in UNECE, 2005

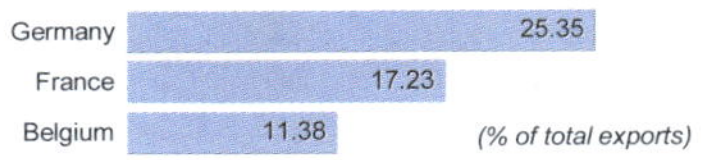

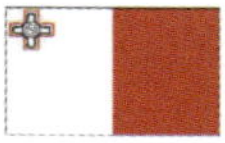

MALTA

Capital:	Valletta (6 315)
Two largest cities:	Birkirkara (21 775)
	Mosta (18 676)
Area (km^2):	316
Total population:	403 507
Population density (per km^2):	1277
Official languages:	Maltese and English
Date joined UN:	1 December 1964
National currency:	Maltese lira (MTL)
National statistical office:	National Statistics Office Malta http://www.nso.gov.mt/

Time: UTC +1h

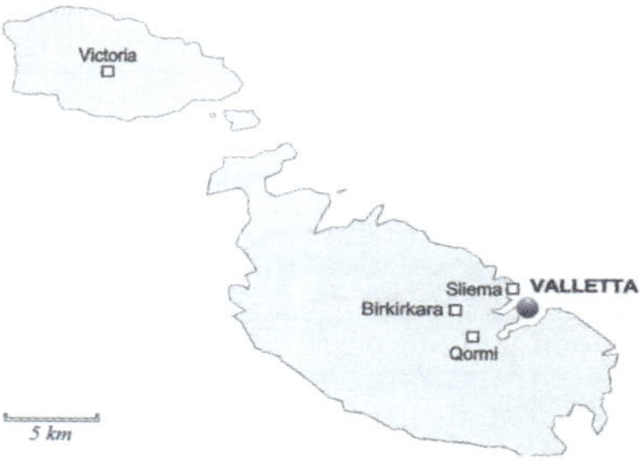

Population by age, 2005

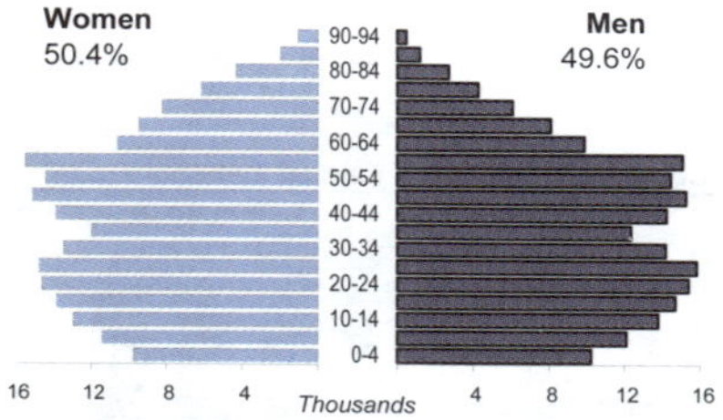

Life expectancy (in years), 2005:	at birth	at 65
Women:	81	19
Men:	78	16

Median age (in years), 2005:	
Women:	40
Men:	37

	percentage of total population
Foreign born:	..
Foreigners in population:	..

Total fertility rate

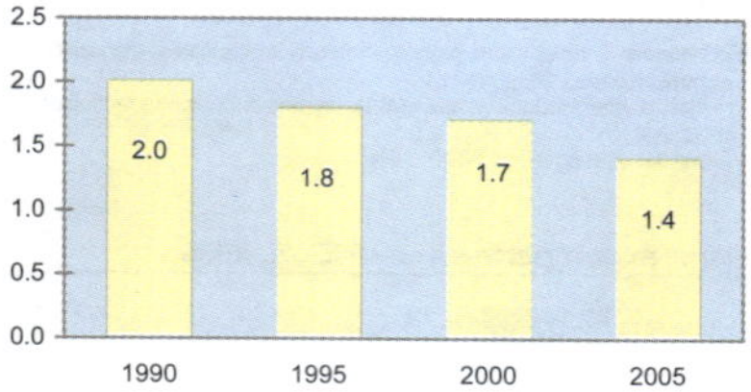

Legal marital status, population aged 18+

Data not available

never married
married
divorced
widowed

Women in the labour force, 2004:	30.8%
Gender pay gap, 2005:	4%
Female government ministers, 2006: percentage of total for both sexes	14.4%
Female central bank board members, 2005: percentage of total for both sexes	20%
Female tertiary students, 2003-2004: percentage of total for both sexes	55.9%

Parliament seats held by women (% of total)

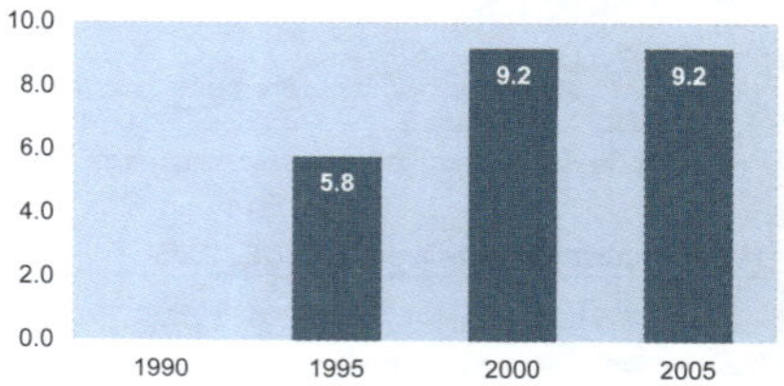

MALTA

	1999	2000	2001	2002	2003	2004	2005
Employment (% change over previous year)	0.8	1.9	2.1	-0.7	-0.7	1.4	0.7
Unemployment rate (%)	7.8	6.7	7.6	7.5	7.6	7.3	7.3
Youth unemployment rate (%)	..	13.7	18.8	17.1	17.2	16.8	16.4

Economic activity rate, 2004

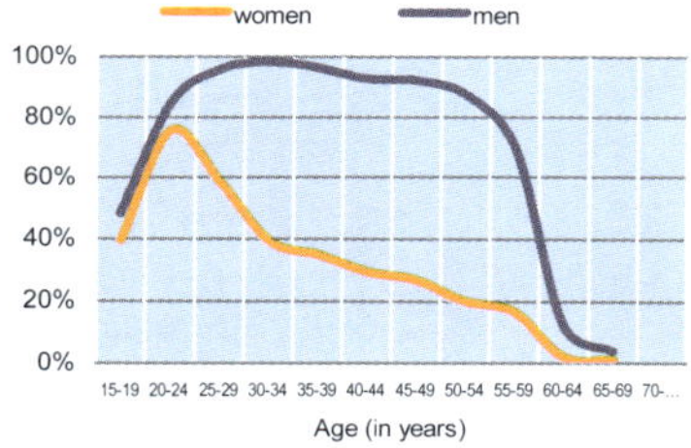

GDP at current prices	
in millions of US Dollars, PPP, 2005:	7 768
in millions of MTL, 2005:	1 941
GDP at constant 2000 prices, per capita	
US Dollars, PPP, 2005:	17 602
MTL, 2005:	4 309
Final consumption expenditure at 2000 prices, per capita, US Dollars, PPP, 2005:	15 534
Purchasing Power Parity (PPP)	
MTL per USD, 2005, US=1:	0.25
Gross external debt:	
in millions of US Dollars:	..
Exchange rate	
Annual average, MTL per USD, 2005:	0.346

Real GDP growth rate

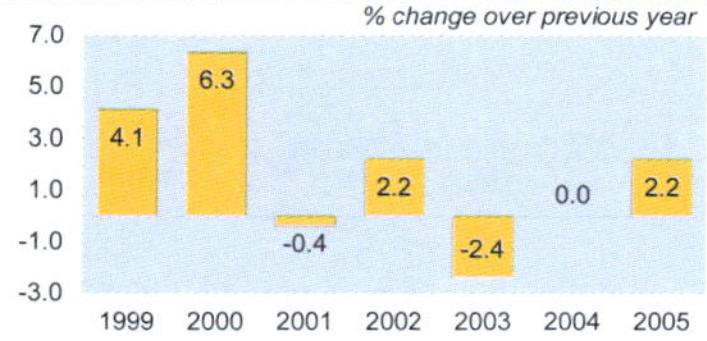

Consumer price index (annual average)

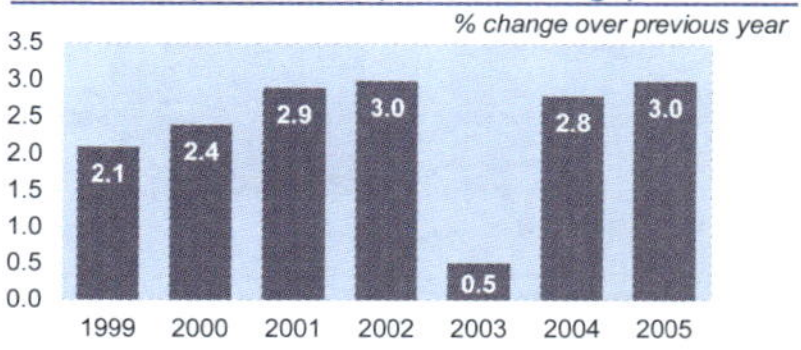

	% of GDP
Exports of goods and services, 2005:	72.5
Imports of goods and services, 2005:	82.6
External trade balance, 2005:	-10

GDP in agriculture, industry, and services (2000=100)

GDP by major sectors, 2005

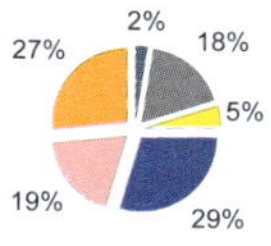

Employment in major sectors, 2000

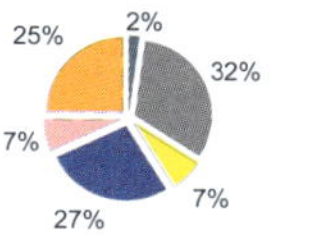

- Agriculture, hunting & forestry; fishing (ISIC A-B)
- Industry, including energy (ISIC C-E)
- Construction (ISIC F)
- Wholesale & retail trade, repairs; hotels & restaurants; transport & communications (ISIC G-I)
- Financial intermediation; real estate, renting & business activities (ISIC J-K)
- Other service activities (ISIC L-P)

Major import partners from UNECE, 2005

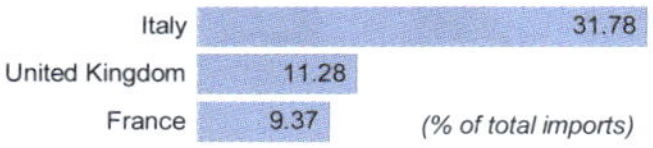

Major export partners in UNECE, 2005

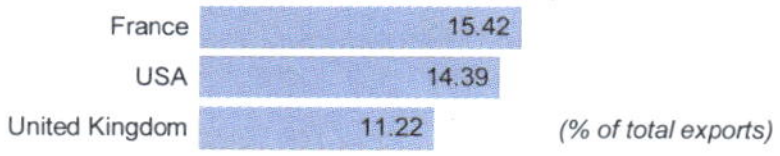

MOLDOVA

Time: UTC +2h

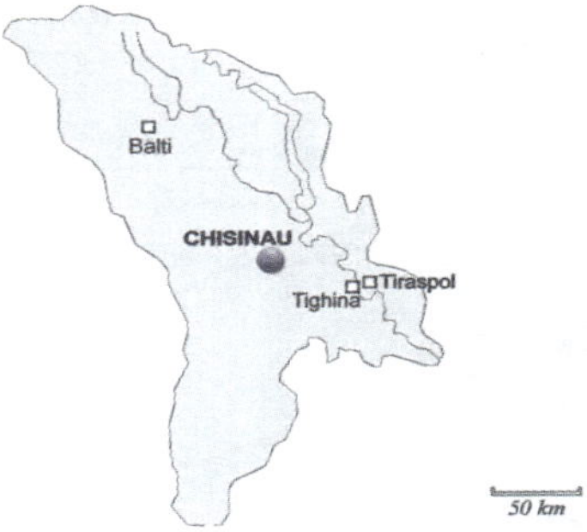

Capital:	Chisinau (601 000)
Two largest cities:	Tiraspol (185 000)
	Tighina (125 000)
Area (km^2):	33 845
Total population:	3 603 936
Population density (per km^2):	106
Official languages:	Moldavian
Date joined UN:	2 March 1992
National currency:	Moldovan leu (MDL)
National statistical office:	

National Bureau of Statistics of the Republic of Moldova
http://www.statistica.md

Population by age, 2004

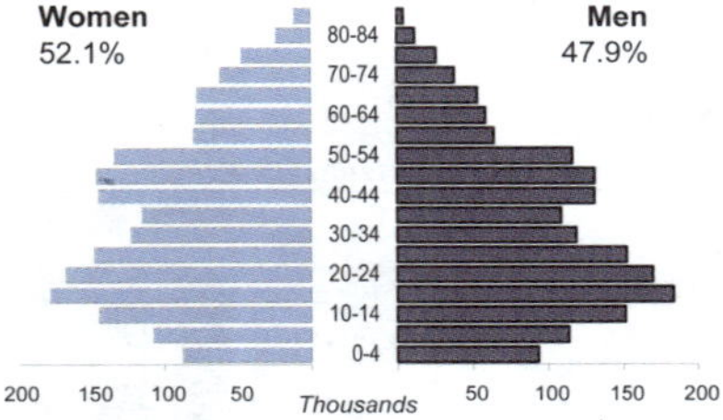

Life expectancy (in years), 2005:	at birth	at 65
Women:	72	14
Men:	64	11

Median age (in years), 2004:	
Women:	34
Men:	30

	percentage of total population
Foreign born:	..
Foreigners in population:	..

Total fertility rate

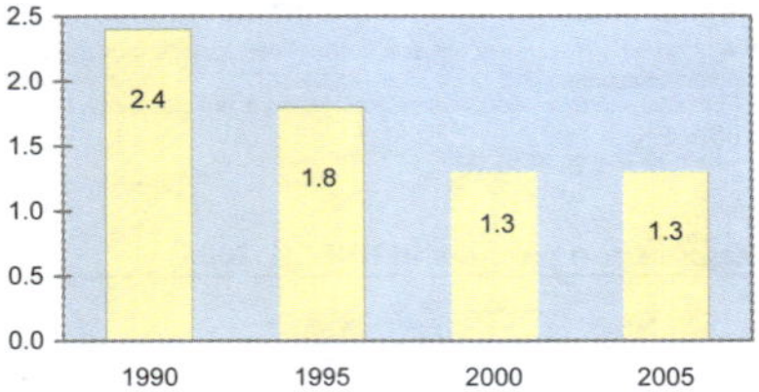

Legal marital status, population aged 18+

never married
married
divorced
widowed

Data not available

Women in the labour force, 2005:	51.5%
Gender pay gap, 2004:	28.7%
Female government ministers, 2006: percentage of total for both sexes	29.4%
Female central bank board members: percentage of total for both sexes	..
Female tertiary students, 2002-2003: percentage of total for both sexes	56.8%

Parliament seats held by women (% of total)

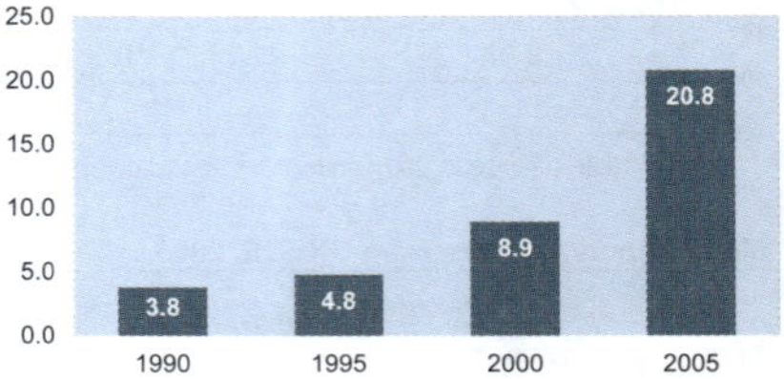

MOLDOVA

	1999	2000	2001	2002	2003	2004	2005
Employment (% change over previous year)	..	..	-1.0	0.4	-9.9	-3.0	0.2
Unemployment rate (%)	..	8.5	7.3	6.8	7.9	8.1	7.3
Youth unemployment rate (%)	..	15.8	16.3	15.2	18.1	19.7	18.7

Economic activity rate, 2004

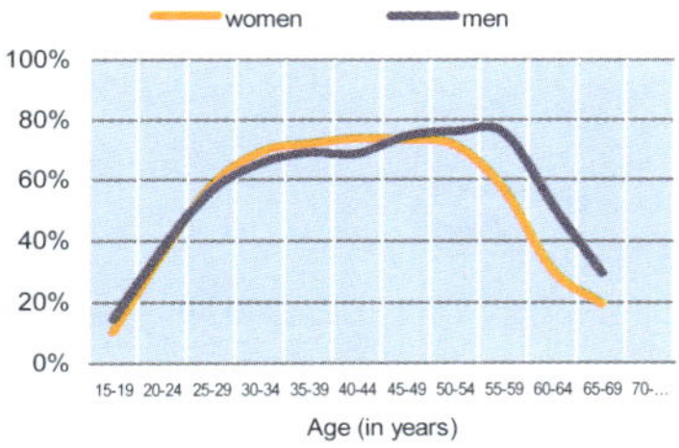

GDP at current prices	
in millions of US Dollars, PPP, 2005:	8 689
in millions of MDL, 2005:	36 755
GDP at constant 2000 prices, per capita	
US Dollars, PPP, 2005:	2 143
MDL, 2005:	6 246
Final consumption expenditure at 2000 prices, per capita, US Dollars, PPP, 2005:	2 320
Purchasing Power Parity (PPP)	
MDL per USD, 2005, US=1:	4.23
Gross external debt:	
in millions of US Dollars, 2005:	1 990
Exchange rate	
Annual average, MDL per USD, 2005:	12.6

Real GDP growth rate

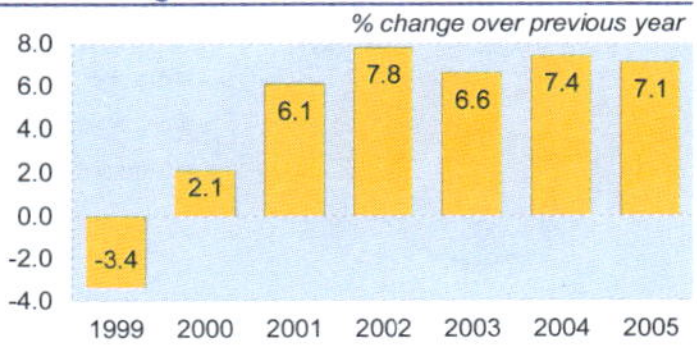

Consumer price index (annual average)

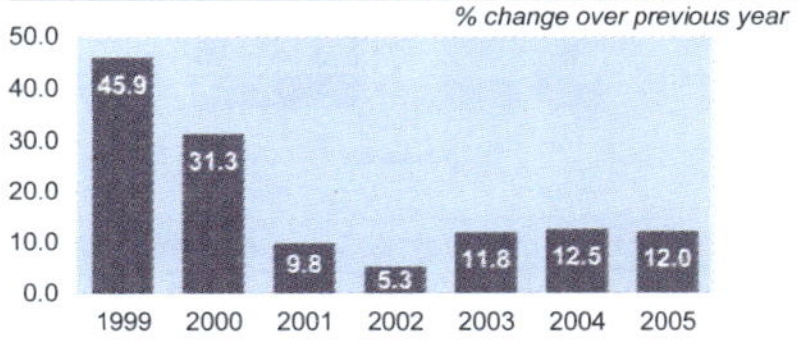

	% of GDP
Exports of goods and services, 2005:	53.1
Imports of goods and services, 2005:	91.3
External trade balance, 2005:	-38

GDP in agriculture, industry, and services (2000=100)

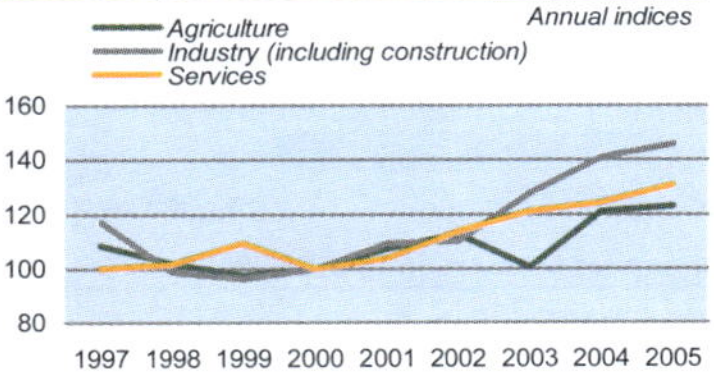

GDP by major sectors, 2005

Employment in major sectors, 2005

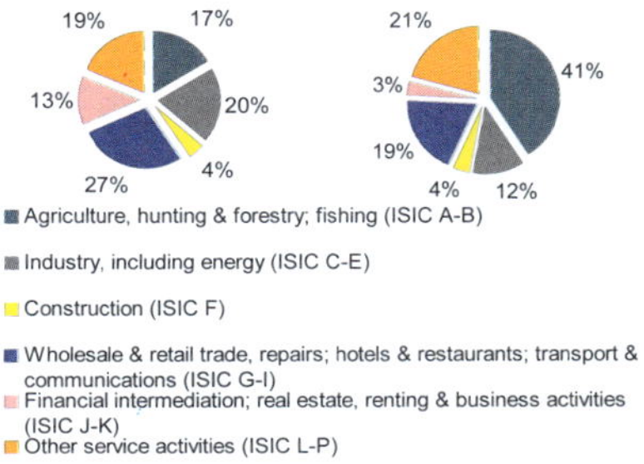

Major import partners from UNECE, 2005

Major export partners in UNECE, 2005

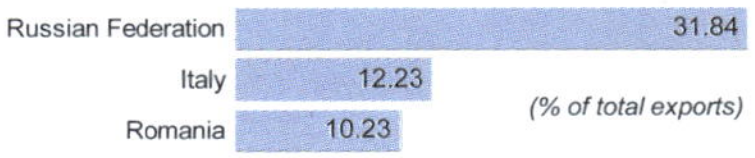

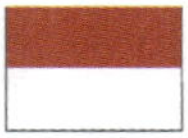

MONACO

Capital:	Monaco City (35 026)
Area (km²):	2
Total population:	31 521
Population density (per km²):	16165
Official languages:	French
Date joined UN:	28 May 1993
National currency:	Euro (EUR)
National statistical office:	State Information Service http://www.monaco.gouv.mc/

Time: UTC +1h

Population by age, 2004

Women 51.1% | **Men** 48.9%

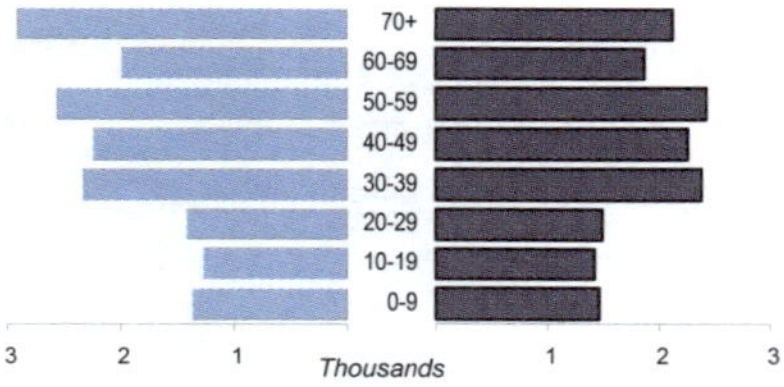

Life expectancy (in years), 2004:	at birth	at 65
Women:	85	..
Men:	78	..

Median age (in years), 2004:	
Women:	43
Men:	40

	percentage of total population
Foreign born:	..
Foreigners in population, 2000:	80.98%

Real GDP growth rate

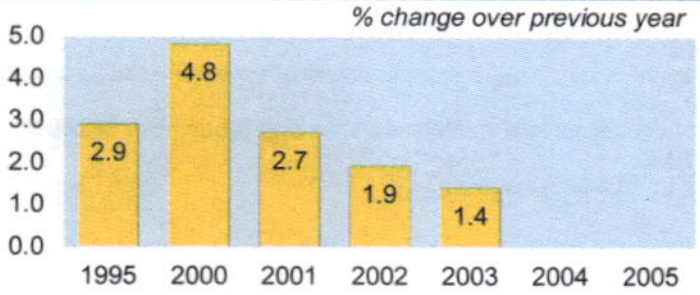

Legal marital status, population aged 18+, 2000

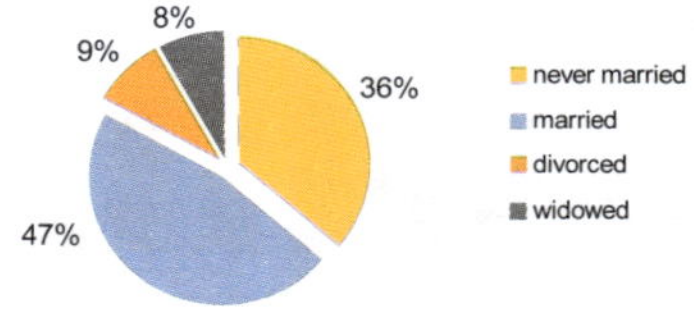

GDP per capita, current prices	
US Dollars, 2003 (UN Estimates):	28 958
EUR:	..
Purchasing Power Parity (PPP)	
EUR per USD, 2000, US=1:	0.906
Exchange rate	
Annual average, EUR per USD, 2005:	0.804

Major import partners from UNECE, 2006

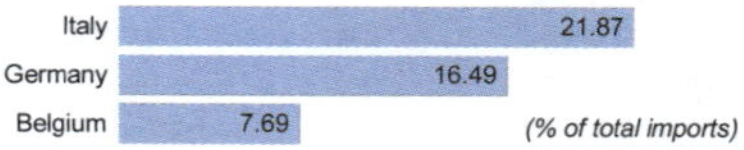

Major export partners in UNECE, 2006

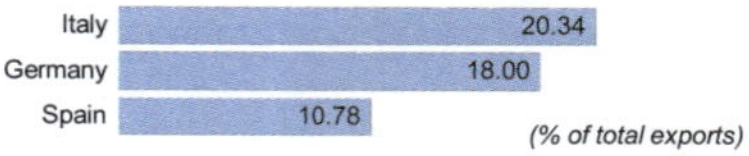

MONTENEGRO

Capital:	Podgorica (136 473)
Two largest cities:	Nikšić (58 212)
	Pljevlja (21 377)
Area (km²):	13 812
Total population:	622 118
Population density (per km²):	45
Official languages:	Serbian
Date joined UN:	28 June 2006
National currency:	Euro (EUR)
National statistical office:	
	Statistical Office of Montenegro
	www.monstat.cg.yu

Time: UTC +1h

Population by age, 2004

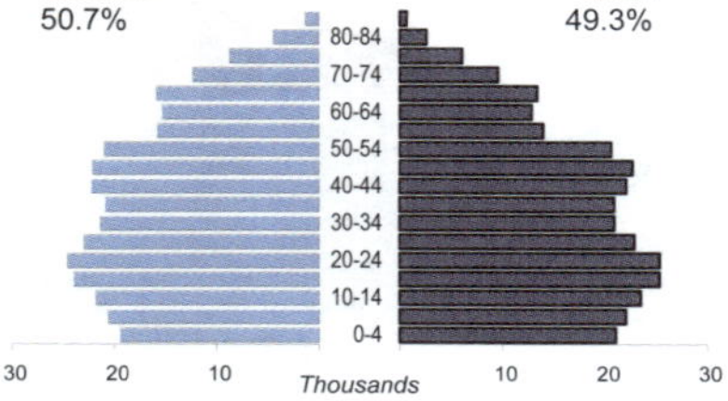

Total fertility rate

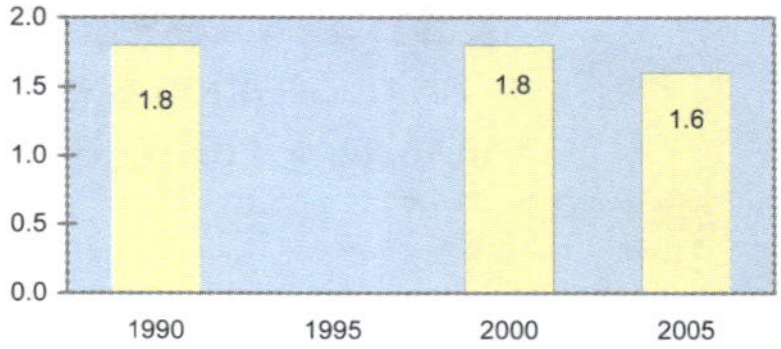

Life expectancy (in years), 2005:	at birth	at 65
Women:	75	16
Men:	70	14

Median age (in years), 2004:	
Women:	36
Men:	33

GDP at current prices	
in millions of US Dollars, PPP:	..
in millions of EUR, 2004:	1 565
Final consumption expenditure at 2000 prices, per capita, US Dollars, PPP:	..
Exchange rate Annual average, EUR per USD, 2005:	0.804

Real GDP growth rate

% change over previous year

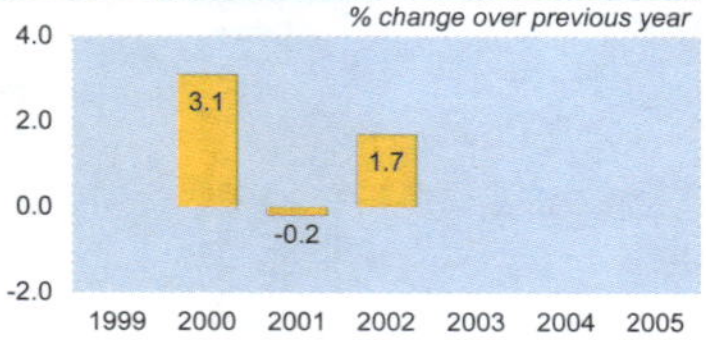

Consumer price index (annual average)

% change over previous year

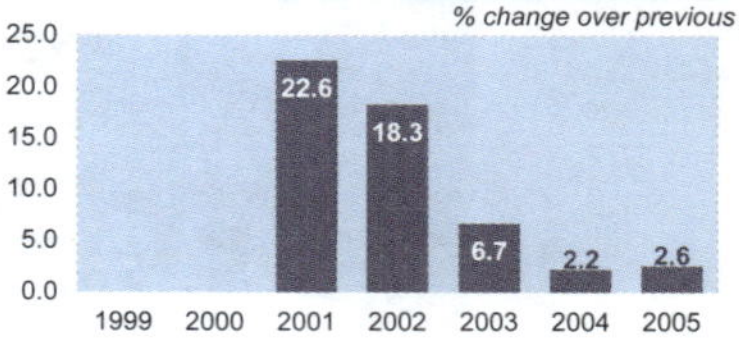

MONTENEGRO

	% of GDP
Exports of goods and services, 2004:	44.8
Imports of goods and services, 2004:	62.0
External trade balance, 2004:	-17

GDP in agriculture, industry, and services (2000=100)

GDP by major sectors

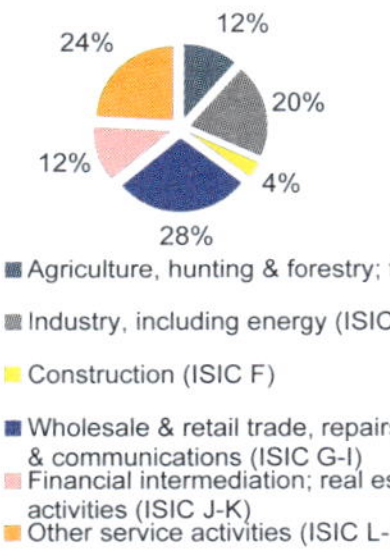

Employment in major sectors

Major import partners from UNECE, 2005

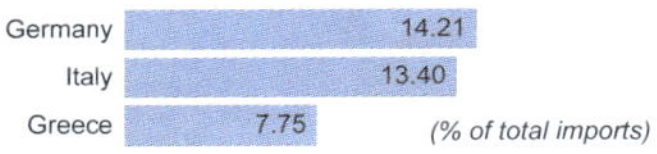

Major export partners in UNECE, 2005

NETHERLANDS

Capital:	Amsterdam (739 295)
Two largest cities:	Rotterdam (596 068)
	The Hague (468 421)
Area (km²):	41 526
Total population:	16 319 868
Population density (per km²):	393
Official languages:	Dutch
Date joined UN:	10 December 1945
National currency:	Euro (EUR)
National statistical office:	Statistics Netherlands http://www.cbs.nl

Time: UTC +1h

Population by age, 2005

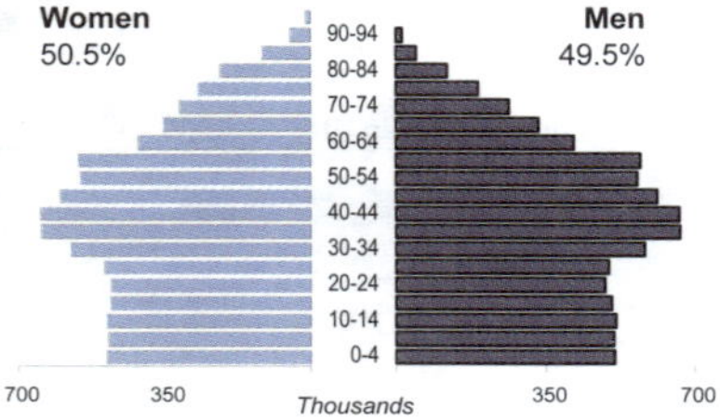

Life expectancy (in years), 2005:	at birth	at 65
Women:	82	20
Men:	77	16

Median age (in years), 2005:	
Women:	40
Men:	38

	percentage of total population
Foreign born, 2005:	10.6%
Foreigners in population, 2005:	4.3%

Legal marital status, population aged 18+, 2004

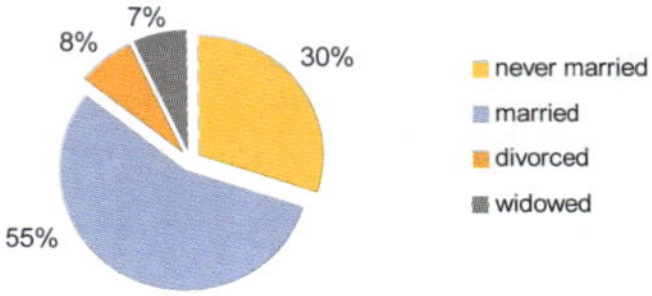

Women in the labour force, 2005:	44.9%
Gender pay gap, 2005:	18%
Female government ministers, 2003: percentage of total for both sexes	33.3%
Female central bank board members: percentage of total for both sexes	..
Female tertiary students, 2003-2004: percentage of total for both sexes	50.9%

Total fertility rate

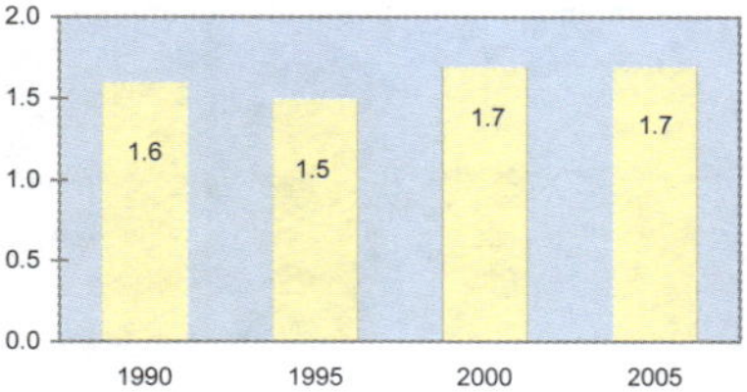

Parliament seats held by women (% of total)

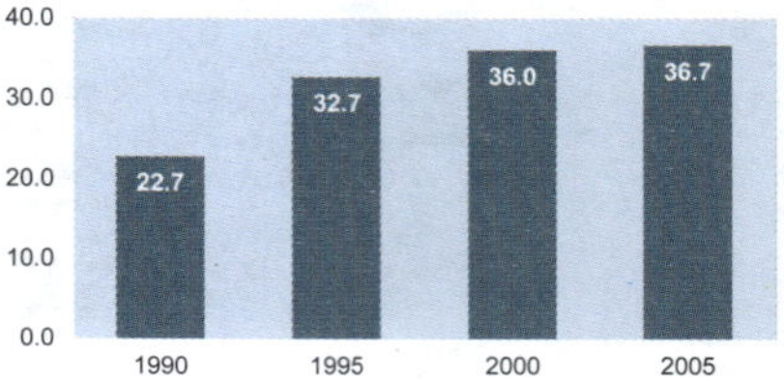

NETHERLANDS

	1999	2000	2001	2002	2003	2004	2005
Employment (% change over previous year)	2.6	2.2	1.9	0.5	-0.6	-1.4	-0.3
Unemployment rate (%)	3.2	2.8	2.2	2.8	3.7	4.6	4.8
Youth unemployment rate (%)	..	5.7	4.5	5.0	6.3	8.0	8.2

Economic activity rate, 2004

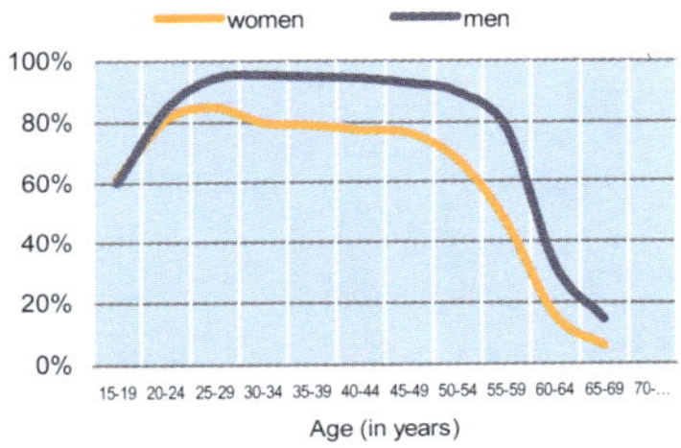

GDP at current prices	
in millions of US Dollars, PPP, 2005:	560 600
in millions of EUR, 2005:	505 646
GDP at constant 2000 prices, per capita	
US Dollars, PPP, 2005:	29 336
EUR, 2005:	27 138
Final consumption expenditure at 2000 prices, per capita, US Dollars, PPP, 2005:	21 313
Purchasing Power Parity (PPP)	
EUR per USD, 2005, US=1:	0.902
Gross external debt:	
in millions of US Dollars, 2005:	1 671 498
Exchange rate	
Annual average, EUR per USD, 2005:	0.804

Real GDP growth rate

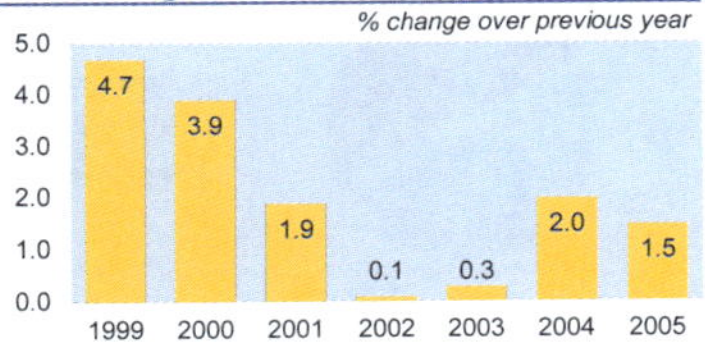

Consumer price index (annual average)

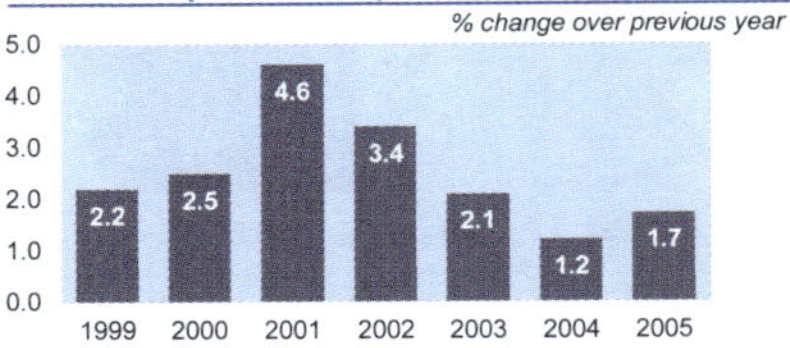

	% of GDP
Exports of goods and services, 2005:	69.9
Imports of goods and services, 2005:	62.2
External trade balance, 2005:	7.7

GDP in agriculture, industry, and services (2000=100)

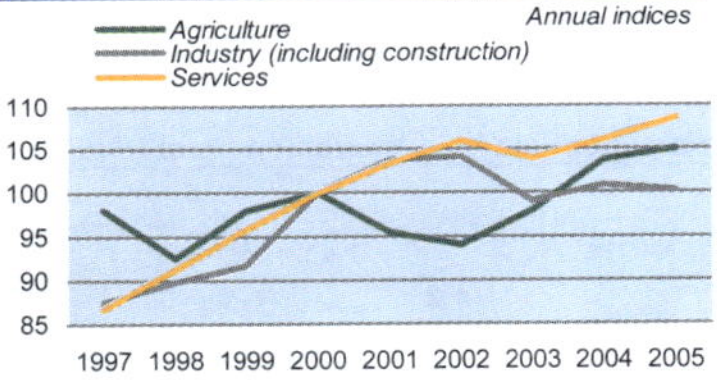

GDP by major sectors, 2005

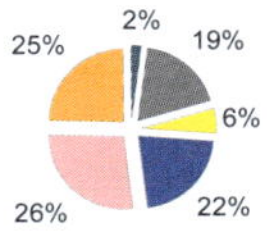

Employment in major sectors, 2005

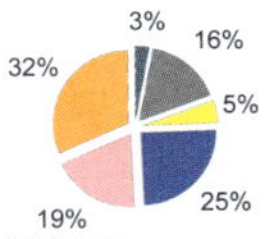

- Agriculture, hunting & forestry; fishing (ISIC A-B)
- Industry, including energy (ISIC C-E)
- Construction (ISIC F)
- Wholesale & retail trade, repairs; hotels & restaurants; transport & communications (ISIC G-I)
- Financial intermediation; real estate, renting & business activities (ISIC J-K)
- Other service activities (ISIC L-P)

Major import partners from UNECE, 2005

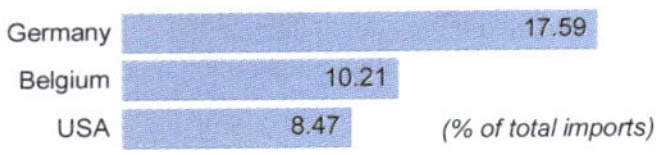

Major export partners in UNECE, 2005

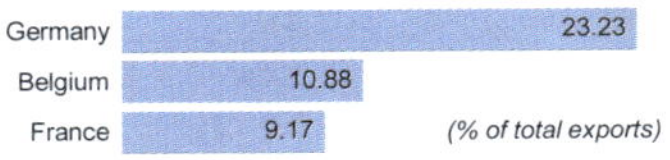

NORWAY

Capital:	Oslo (521 886)
Two largest cities:	Bergen (237 430)
	Trondheim (154 351)
Area (km²):	323 759
Total population:	4 623 291
Population density (per km²):	14
Official languages:	Norwegian
Date joined UN:	27 November 1945
National currency:	Norwegian krone (NOK)
National statistical office:	Statistics Norway http://www.ssb.no

Time: UTC +1h

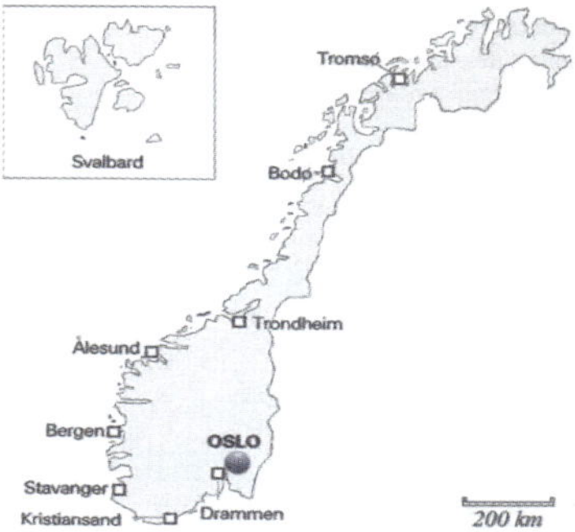

Population by age, 2005

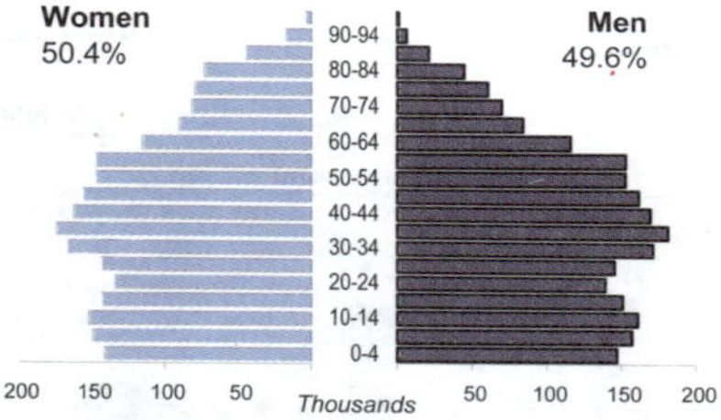

Legal marital status, population aged 18+, 2002

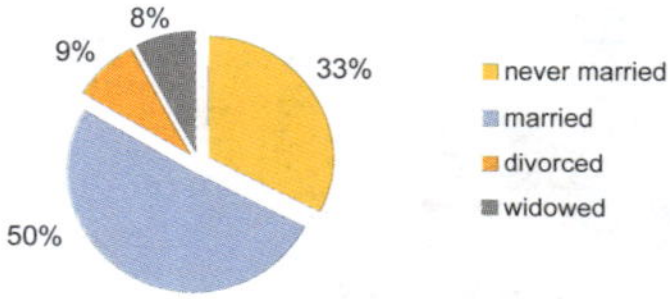

Life expectancy (in years), 2005:	at birth	at 65
Women:	83	21
Men:	78	17

Median age (in years), 2005:	
Women:	39
Men:	37

	percentage of total population
Foreign born, 2005:	7.8%
Foreigners in population, 2005:	4.6%

Women in the labour force, 2005:	47.1%
Gender pay gap, 2005:	13.3%
Female government ministers, 2006: percentage of total for both sexes	47.3%
Female central bank board members, 2005: percentage of total for both sexes	42.9%
Female tertiary students, 2003-2004: percentage of total for both sexes	59.6%

Total fertility rate

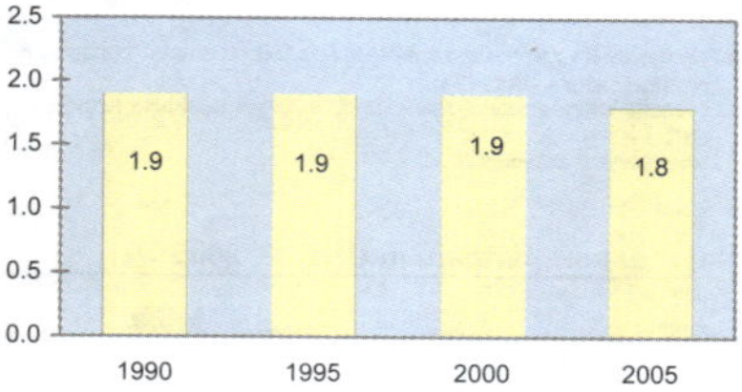

Parliament seats held by women (% of total)

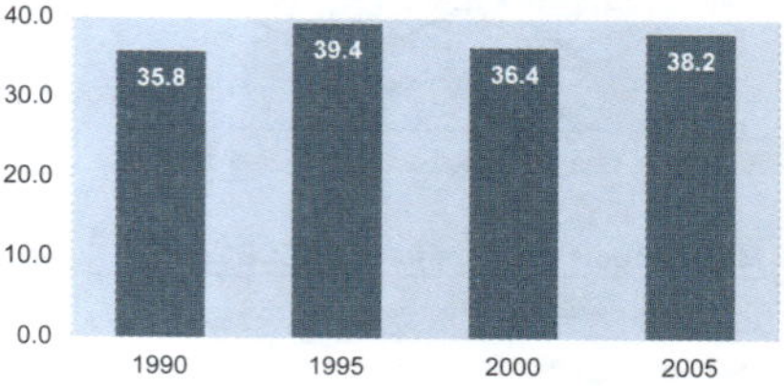

NORWAY

	1999	2000	2001	2002	2003	2004	2005
Employment (% change over previous year)	0.8	0.4	0.3	0.1	-1.0	0.3	0.7
Unemployment rate (%)	3.2	3.4	3.6	3.9	4.5	4.4	4.6
Youth unemployment rate (%)	..	9.9	10.3	11.1	11.6	11.4	11.6

Economic activity rate, 2004

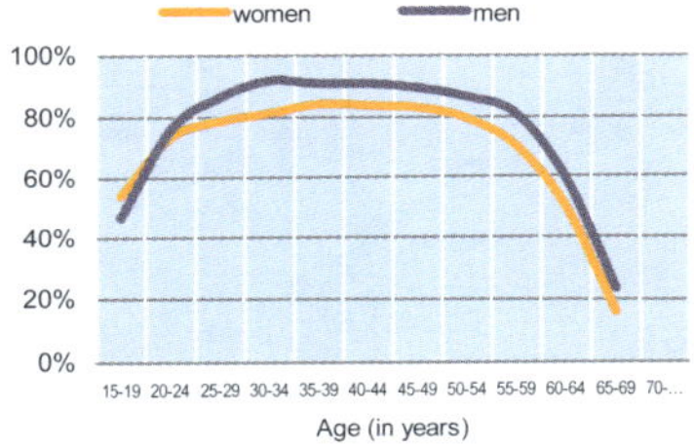

GDP at current prices	
in millions of US Dollars, PPP, 2005:	210 357
in millions of NOK, 2005:	1 903 841
GDP at constant 2000 prices, per capita	
US Dollars, PPP, 2005:	39 020
NOK, 2005:	351 895
Final consumption expenditure at 2000 prices, per capita, US Dollars, PPP, 2005:	25 292
Purchasing Power Parity (PPP)	
NOK per USD, 2005, US=1:	9.051
Gross external debt:	
in millions of US Dollars, 2005:	279 095
Exchange rate	
Annual average, NOK per USD, 2005:	6.443

Real GDP growth rate

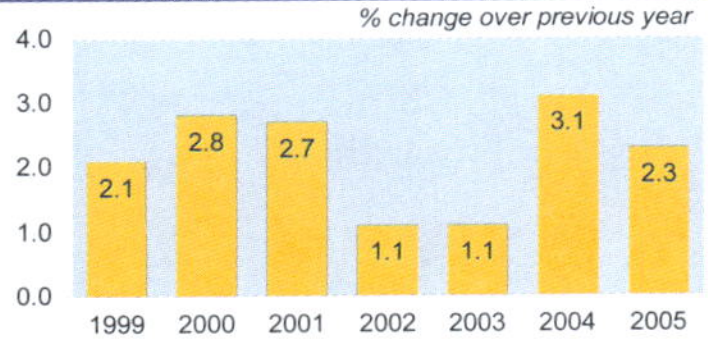

Consumer price index (annual average)

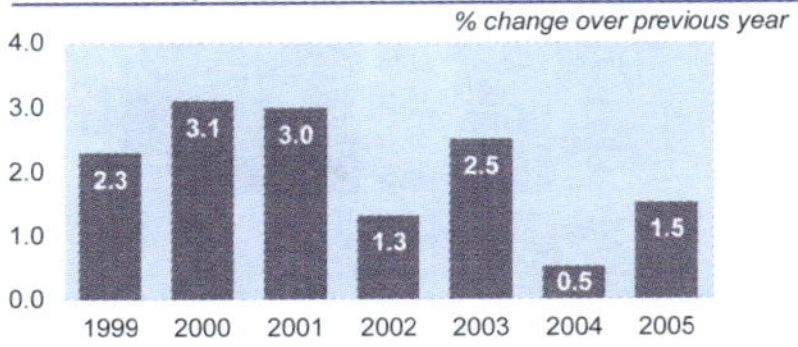

	% of GDP
Exports of goods and services, 2005:	45.3
Imports of goods and services, 2005:	28.1
External trade balance, 2005:	17.2

GDP by major sectors, 2005

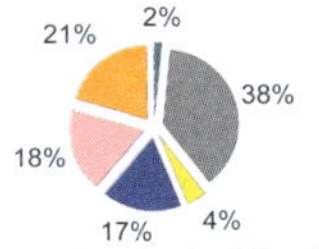

Employment in major sectors, 2005

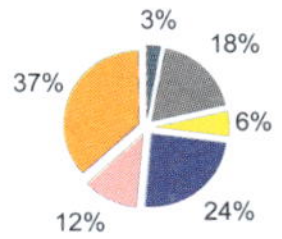

- Agriculture, hunting & forestry; fishing (ISIC A-B)
- Industry, including energy (ISIC C-E)
- Construction (ISIC F)
- Wholesale & retail trade, repairs; hotels & restaurants; transport & communications (ISIC G-I)
- Financial intermediation; real estate, renting & business activities (ISIC J-K)
- Other service activities (ISIC L-P)

GDP in agriculture, industry, and services (2000=100)

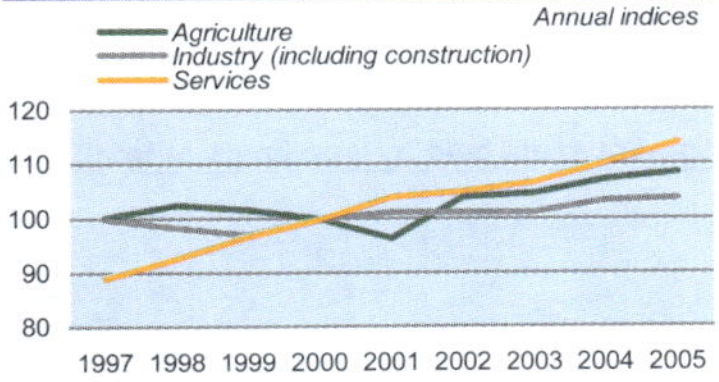

Major import partners from UNECE, 2005

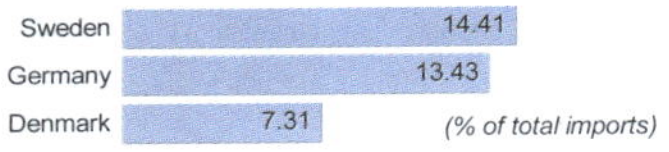

Major export partners in UNECE, 2005

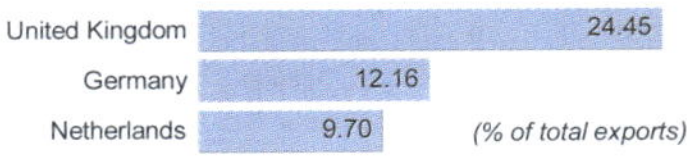

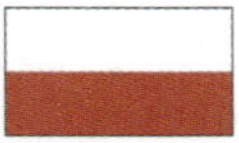

POLAND

Capital:	Warsaw (1 692 854)
Two largest cities:	Lodz (774 004)
	Krakow (757 430)
Area (km²):	312 685
Total population:	38 182 222
Population density (per km²):	122
Official languages:	Polish
Date joined UN:	24 October 1945
National currency:	Polish zloty (PLN)
National statistical office:	Central Statistical Office of Poland
	http://www.stat.gov.pl

Time: UTC +1h

Population by age, 2004

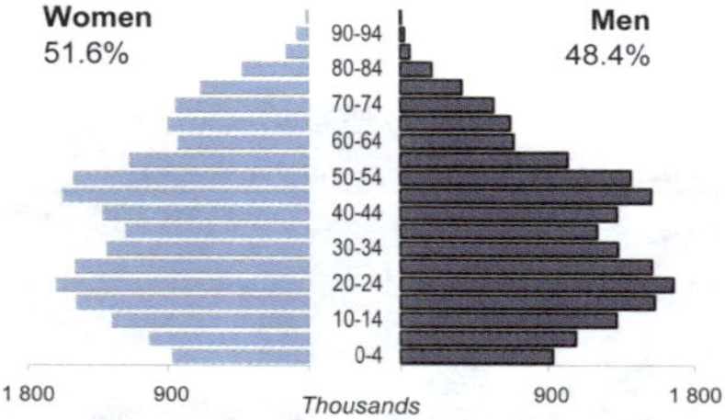

Life expectancy (in years), 2005:	at birth	at 65
Women:	79	18
Men:	71	14

Median age (in years), 2004:	
Women:	38
Men:	34

	percentage of total population
Foreign born:	..
Foreigners in population, 2002:	1.8%

Legal marital status, population aged 18+

Data not available

never married
married
divorced
widowed

Women in the labour force, 2005:	45.4%
Gender pay gap, 2005:	10%
Female government ministers, 2006: percentage of total for both sexes	18.2%
Female central bank board members, 2005: percentage of total for both sexes	11.1%
Female tertiary students, 2004-2005: percentage of total for both sexes	57.5%

Total fertility rate

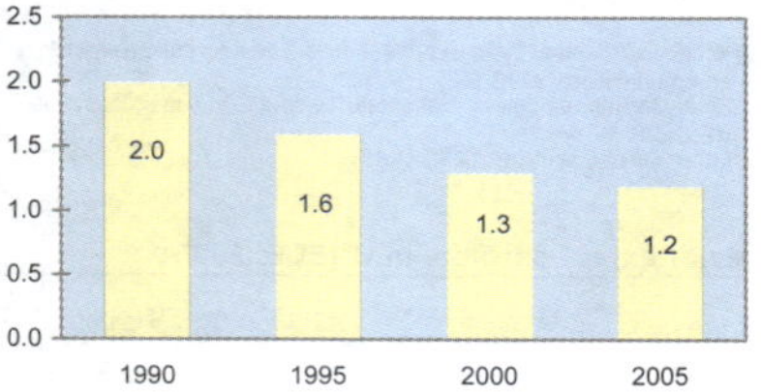

Parliament seats held by women (% of total)

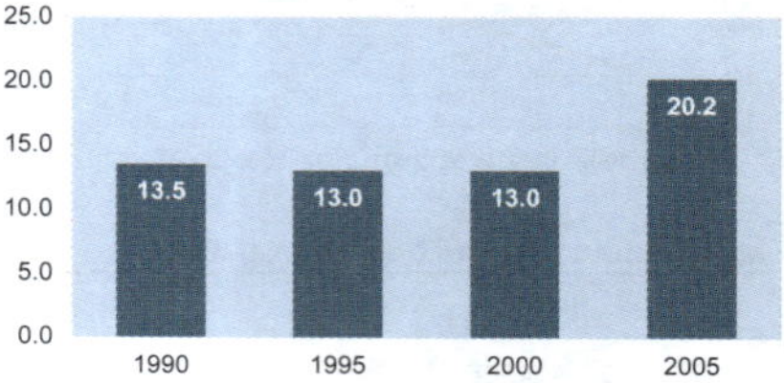

POLAND

	1999	2000	2001	2002	2003	2004	2005
Employment (% change over previous year)	-3.9	-1.6	-2.2	-3.0	-1.2	1.3	1.1
Unemployment rate (%)	13.4	16.1	18.2	19.9	19.6	19.0	17.7
Youth unemployment rate (%)	..	35.1	39.5	42.5	41.9	39.6	36.9

Economic activity rate, 2004

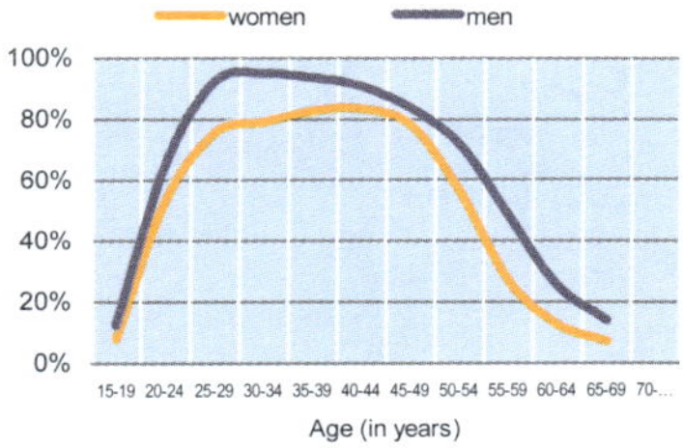

GDP at current prices	
in millions of US Dollars, PPP, 2005:	526 277
in millions of PLN, 2005:	980 666
GDP at constant 2000 prices, per capita	
US Dollars, PPP, 2005:	12 432
PLN, 2005:	22 659
Final consumption expenditure at 2000 prices, per capita, US Dollars, PPP, 2005:	10 066
Purchasing Power Parity (PPP)	
PLN per USD, 2005, US=1:	1.863
Gross external debt:	
in millions of US Dollars, 2005:	131 102
Exchange rate	
Annual average, PLN per USD, 2005:	3.236

Real GDP growth rate

% change over previous year

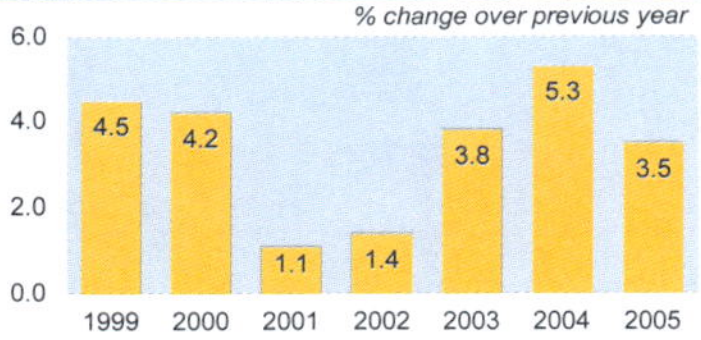

Consumer price index (annual average)

% change over previous year

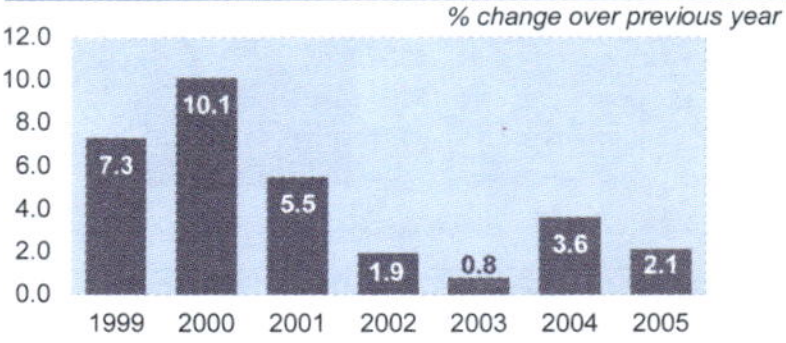

	% of GDP
Exports of goods and services, 2005:	37.2
Imports of goods and services, 2005:	37.5
External trade balance, 2005:	-0.3

GDP by major sectors, 2005 / Employment in major sectors, 2005

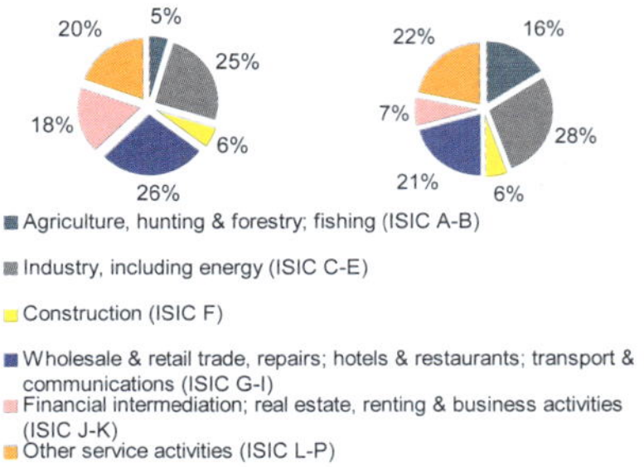

GDP in agriculture, industry, and services (2000=100)

Annual indices

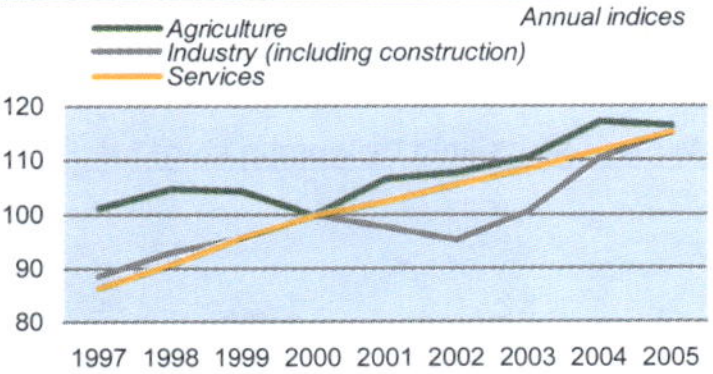

Major import partners from UNECE, 2005

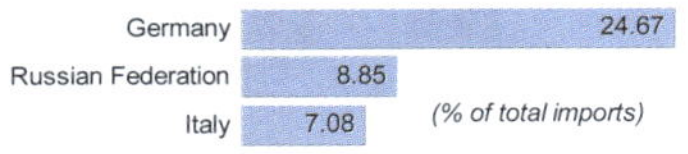

Major export partners in UNECE, 2005

PORTUGAL

Capital:	Lisbon (556 797)
Two largest cities:	Vila Nova de Gaia (287 597)
	Porto (262 928)
Area (km²):	91 982
Total population:	10 549 424
Population density (per km²):	115
Official languages:	Portuguese
Date joined UN:	14 December 1955
National currency:	Euro (EUR)
National statistical office:	National Institute of Statistics
	http://www.ine.pt

Time: UTC +1h

Population by age, 2005

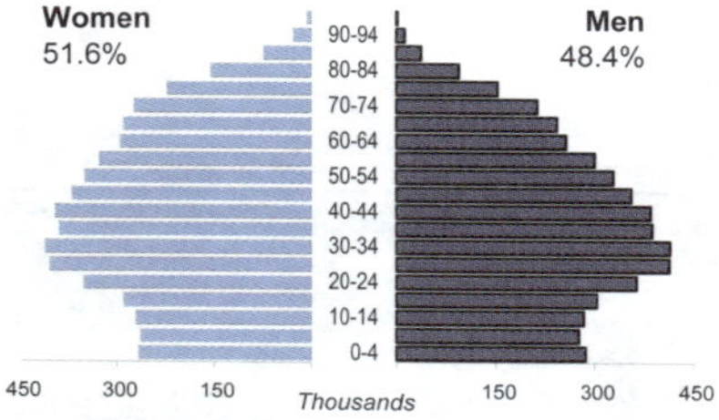

Life expectancy (in years), 2005:	at birth	at 65
Women:	81	19
Men:	75	16

Median age (in years), 2005:	
Women:	41
Men:	38

	percentage of total population
Foreign born, 2001:	5.4%
Foreigners in population, 2001:	2.2%

Total fertility rate

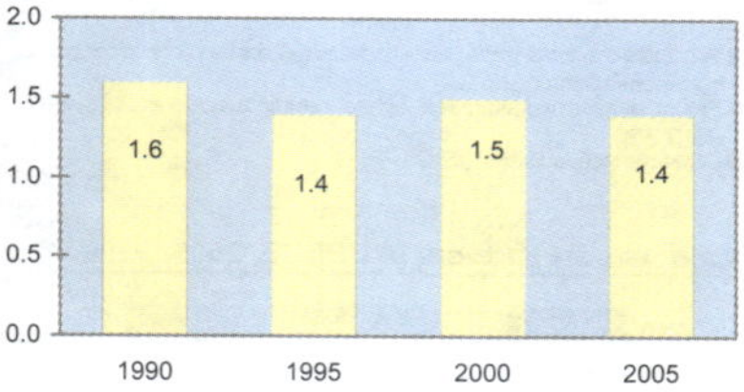

Legal marital status, population aged 18+

Data not available

never married
married
divorced
widowed

Women in the labour force, 2005:	46.6%
Gender pay gap, 2005:	9%
Female government ministers, 2006: percentage of total for both sexes	11.8%
Female central bank board members: percentage of total for both sexes	..
Female tertiary students, 2003-2004: percentage of total for both sexes	56.1%

Parliament seats held by women (% of total)

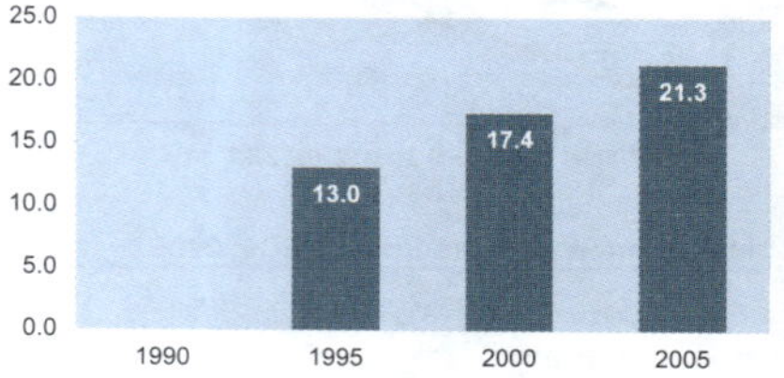

PORTUGAL

	1999	2000	2001	2002	2003	2004	2005
Employment (% change over previous year)	1.9	1.8	1.6	0.5	-0.4	0.1	0.1
Unemployment rate (%)	4.5	4.0	4.0	5.0	6.3	6.7	7.6
Youth unemployment rate (%)	..	8.8	9.4	11.6	14.5	15.3	16.1

Economic activity rate, 2004

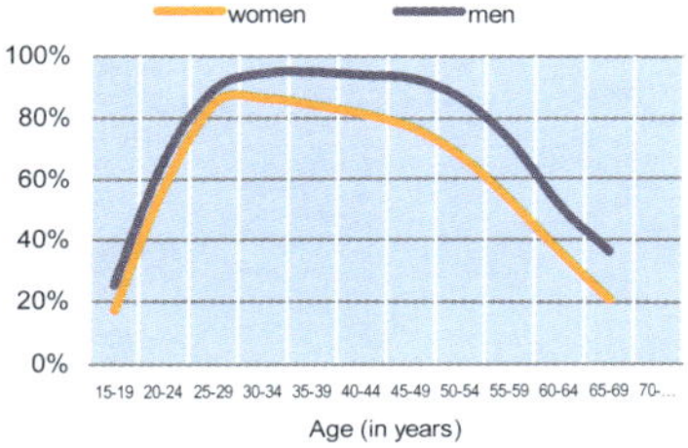

GDP at current prices	
in millions of US Dollars, PPP, 2005:	208 207
in millions of EUR, 2005:	147 378
GDP at constant 2000 prices, per capita	
US Dollars, PPP, 2005:	18 357
EUR, 2005:	11 947
Final consumption expenditure at 2000 prices, per capita, US Dollars, PPP, 2005:	16 013
Purchasing Power Parity (PPP)	
EUR per USD, 2005, US=1:	0.708
Gross external debt:	
in millions of US Dollars, 2005:	302 220
Exchange rate	
Annual average, EUR per USD, 2005:	0.804

Real GDP growth rate

% change over previous year

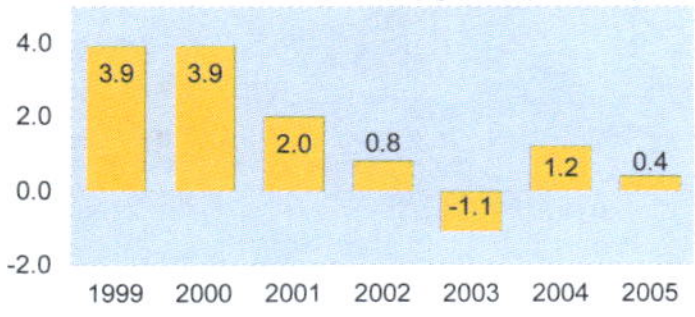

Consumer price index (annual average)

% change over previous year

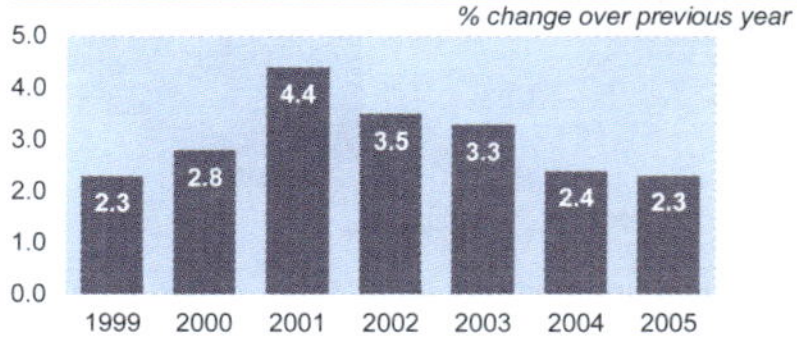

	% of GDP
Exports of goods and services, 2005:	28.6
Imports of goods and services, 2005:	37.4
External trade balance, 2005:	-8.9

GDP by major sectors, 2005

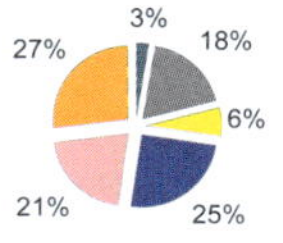

Employment in major sectors

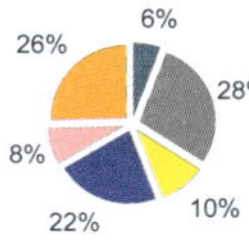

- Agriculture, hunting & forestry; fishing (ISIC A-B)
- Industry, including energy (ISIC C-E)
- Construction (ISIC F)
- Wholesale & retail trade, repairs; hotels & restaurants; transport & communications (ISIC G-I)
- Financial intermediation; real estate, renting & business activities (ISIC J-K)
- Other service activities (ISIC L-P)

GDP in agriculture, industry, and services (2000=100)

Annual indices

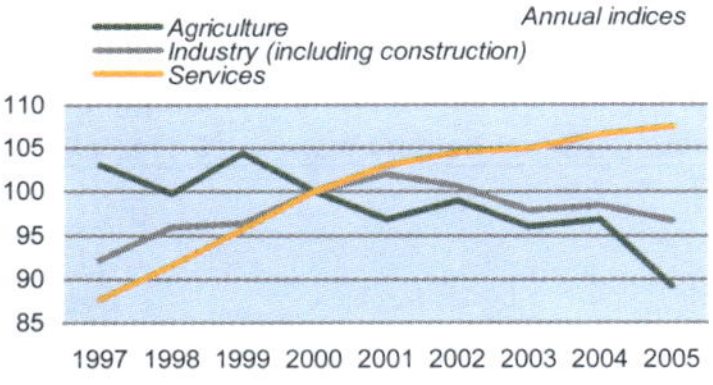

Major import partners from UNECE, 2005

Major export partners in UNECE, 2005

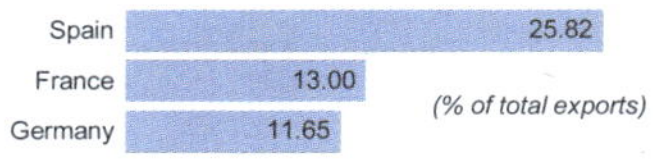

ROMANIA

Time: UTC +2h

Capital:	Bucharest (1 921 751)
Two largest cities:	Iaşi (321 580)
	Cluj-Napoca (318 027)
Area (km²):	238 391
Total population:	21 684 890
Population density (per km²):	91
Official languages:	Romanian
Date joined UN:	14 December 1955
National currency:	Romanian new leu (RON)
National statistical office:	National Institute of Statistics http://www.insse.ro

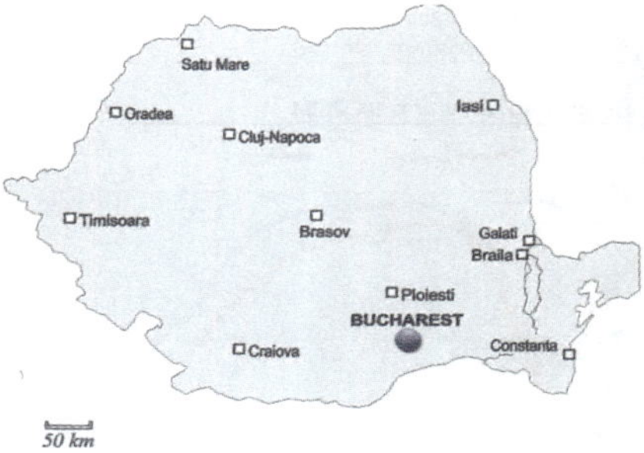

Population by age, 2004

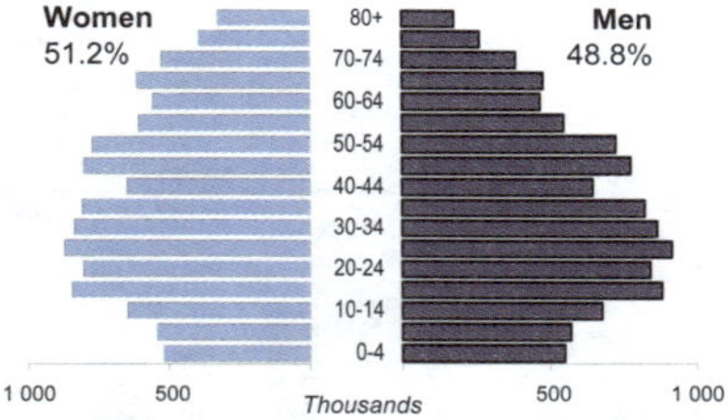

Life expectancy (in years), 2005:	at birth	at 65
Women:	75	16
Men:	68	13

Median age (in years), 2004:	
Women:	38
Men:	35

	percentage of total population
Foreign born:	..
Foreigners in population, 2005:	0.1%

Legal marital status, population aged 18+, 2004

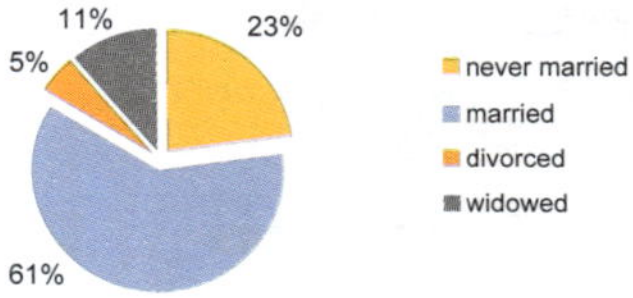

Women in the labour force, 2005:	45%
Gender pay gap, 2005:	13%
Female government ministers, 2006: percentage of total for both sexes	13.6%
Female central bank board members, 2005: percentage of total for both sexes	22.2%
Female tertiary students, 2003-2004: percentage of total for both sexes	54.8%

Total fertility rate

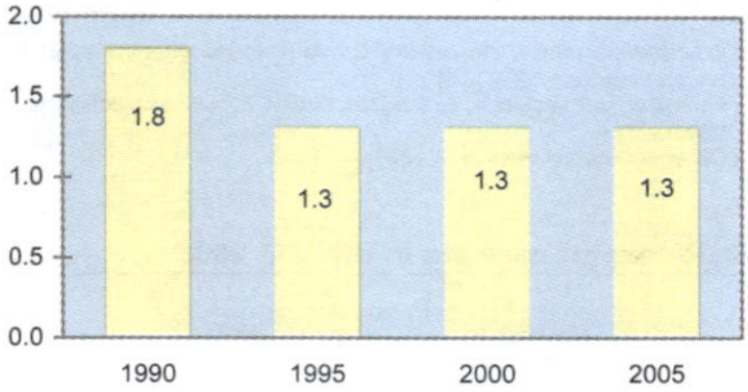

Parliament seats held by women (% of total)

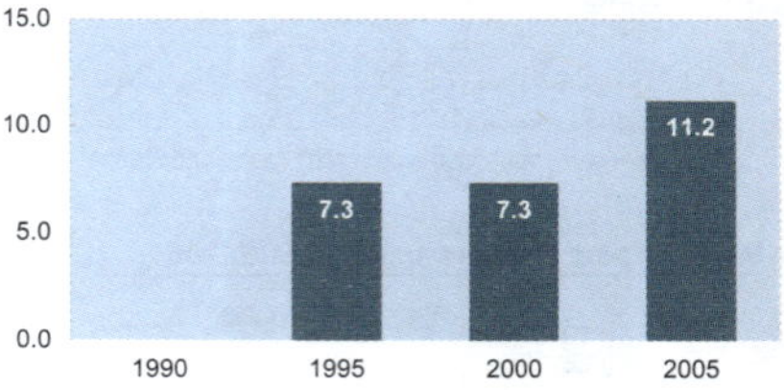

ROMANIA

	1999	2000	2001	2002	2003	2004	2005
Employment (% change over previous year)	-1.8	-1.3	-1.9	-4.2	-0.1	-0.7	-0.1
Unemployment rate (%)	6.2	6.8	6.6	7.5	6.8	7.6	7.7
Youth unemployment rate (%)	..	20.0	18.6	23.2	19.6	21.9	20.2

Economic activity rate, 2004

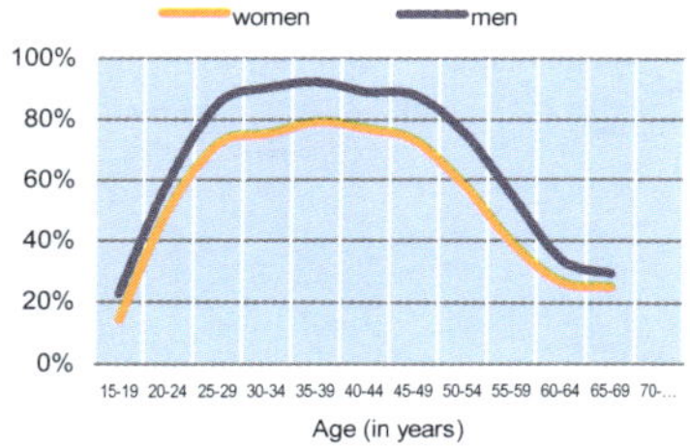

GDP at current prices	
in millions of US Dollars, PPP, 2005:	207 687
in millions of RON, 2005:	287 186
GDP at constant 2000 prices, per capita	
US Dollars, PPP, 2005:	7 765
RON, 2005:	4 887
Final consumption expenditure at 2000 prices, per capita, US Dollars, PPP, 2005:	7 510
Purchasing Power Parity (PPP)	
RON per USD, 2005, US=1:	1.383
Gross external debt:	
in millions of US Dollars, 2005:	29 126
Exchange rate	
Annual average, RON per USD, 2005:	2.914

Real GDP growth rate

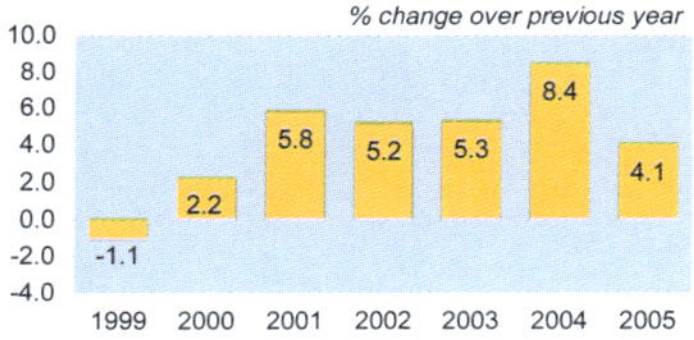

Consumer price index (annual average)

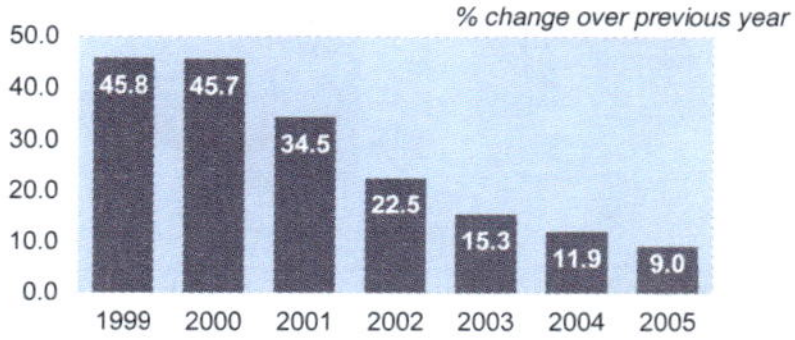

	% of GDP
Exports of goods and services, 2005:	33.0
Imports of goods and services, 2005:	43.4
External trade balance, 2005:	-10

GDP by major sectors

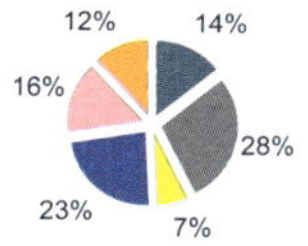

Employment in major sectors, 2005

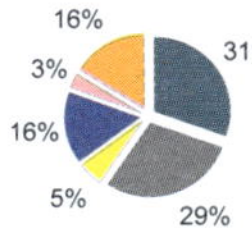

■ Agriculture, hunting & forestry; fishing (ISIC A-B)

■ Industry, including energy (ISIC C-E)

■ Construction (ISIC F)

■ Wholesale & retail trade, repairs; hotels & restaurants; transport & communications (ISIC G-I)

■ Financial intermediation; real estate, renting & business activities (ISIC J-K)

■ Other service activities (ISIC L-P)

GDP in agriculture, industry, and services (2000=100)

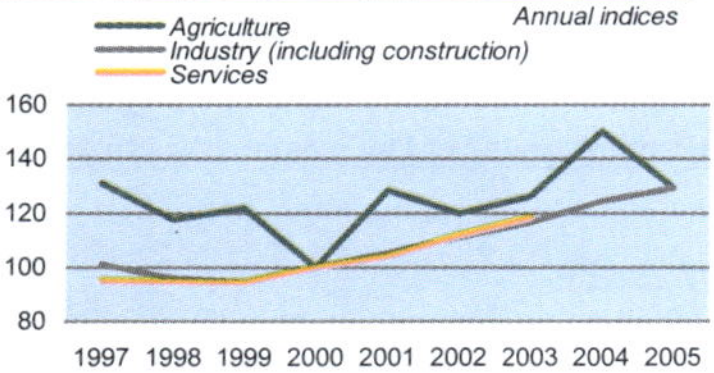

Major import partners from UNECE, 2005

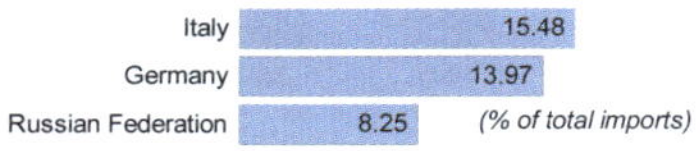

Major export partners in UNECE, 2005

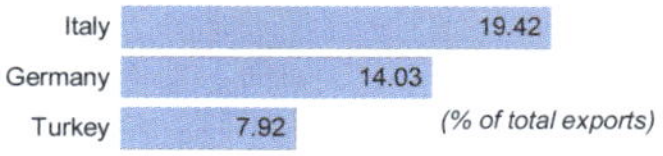

RUSSIAN FEDERATION

Capital:	Moscow (10 406 578)
Two largest cities:	St Petersburg (4 601 000)
	Novosibirsk (1 405 569)
Area (km^2):	17 075 400
Total population:	143 821 213
Population density (per km^2):	8
Official languages:	Russian
Date joined UN:	24 October 1945
National currency:	Russian ruble (RUB)
National statistical office:	Federal State Statistics Service (ROSSTAT)
	http://www.gks.ru

Time: UTC +3h

Population by age, 2004

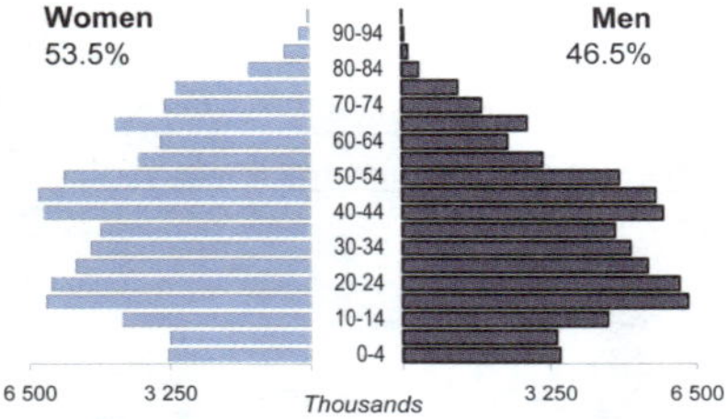

Legal marital status, population aged 18+

never married
married
divorced
widowed

Data not available

Life expectancy (in years), 2005:	at birth	at 65
Women:	72	15
Men:	59	11

Median age (in years), 2004:	
Women:	40
Men:	34

	percentage of total population
Foreign born, 2002:	9.3%
Foreigners in population, 2002:	0.7%

Women in the labour force, 2005:	49.2%
Gender pay gap, 2003:	35.5%
Female government ministers, 2006: percentage of total for both sexes	..
Female central bank board members: percentage of total for both sexes	..
Female tertiary students, 2002-2003: percentage of total for both sexes	55.8%

Total fertility rate

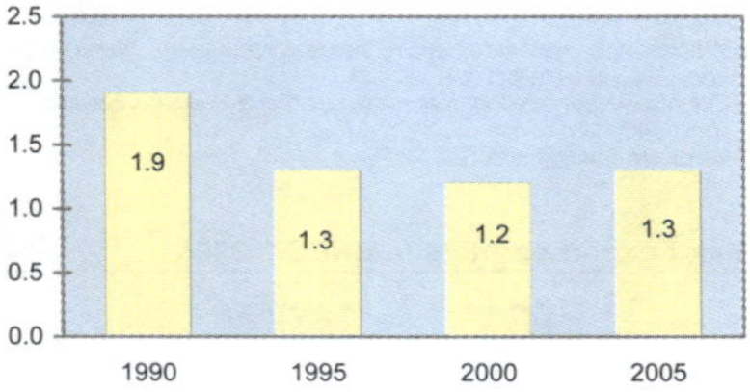

Parliament seats held by women (% of total)

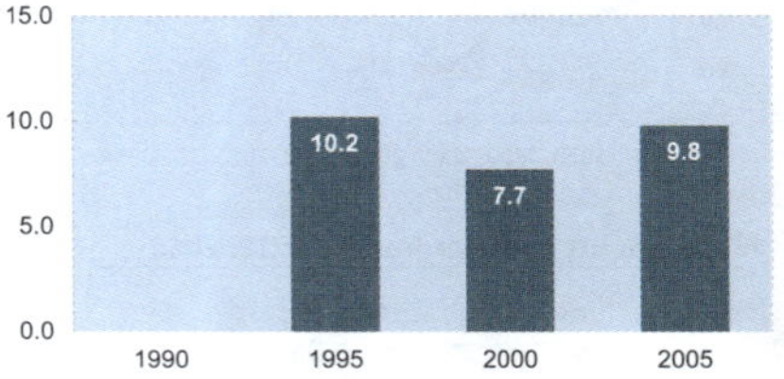

RUSSIAN FEDERATION

	1999	2000	2001	2002	2003	2004	2005
Employment (% change over previous year)	6.9	4.2	0.1	2.4	-0.3	1.3	1.3
Unemployment rate (%)	12.6	10.6	9.0	7.9	8.2	7.9	7.2
Youth unemployment rate (%)	..	20.7	18.0	15.6	17.5	17.2	15.7

Economic activity rate, 2001

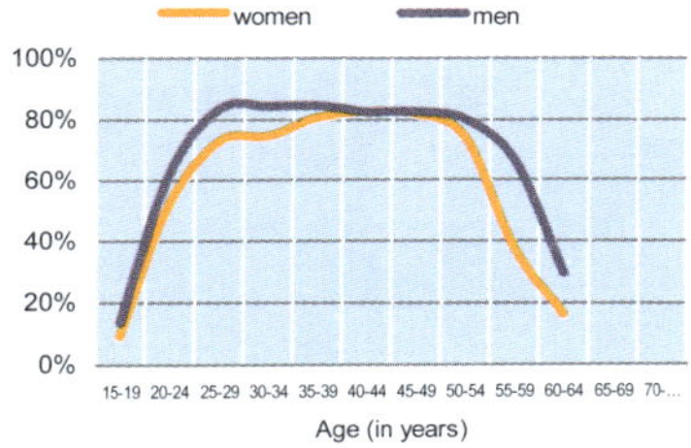

GDP at current prices	
in millions of US Dollars, PPP, 2005:	1 541 285
in millions of RUB, 2005:	21 597 968
GDP at constant 2000 prices, per capita	
US Dollars, PPP, 2005:	9 596
RUB, 2005:	68 737
Final consumption expenditure at 2000 prices, per capita, US Dollars, PPP, 2005:	6 258
Purchasing Power Parity (PPP)	
RUB per USD, 2005, US=1:	14.01
Gross external debt:	
in millions of US Dollars, 2005:	258 440
Exchange rate	
Annual average, RUB per USD, 2005:	28.28

Real GDP growth rate

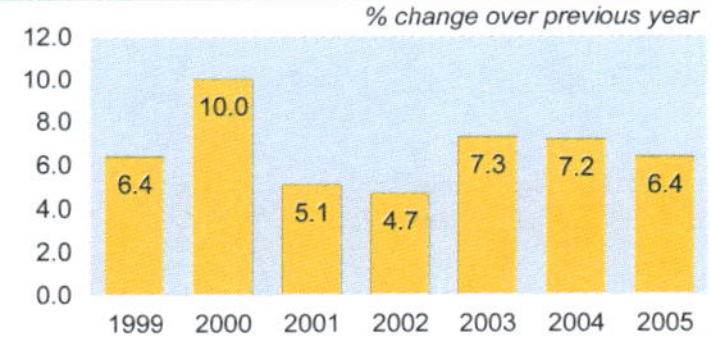

Consumer price index (annual average)

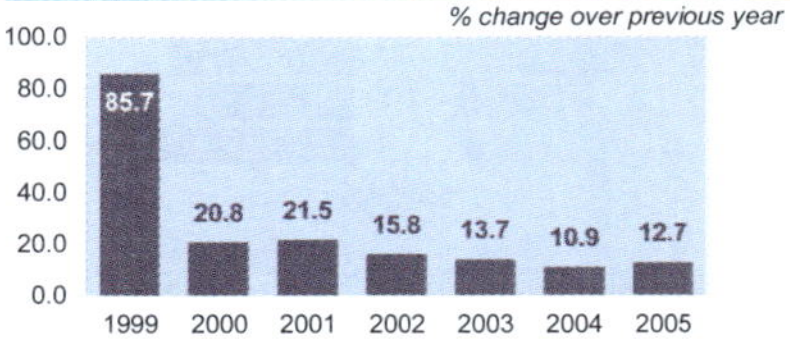

	% of GDP
Exports of goods and services, 2005:	35.1
Imports of goods and services, 2005:	21.6
External trade balance, 2005:	13.6

GDP in agriculture, industry, and services (2000=100)

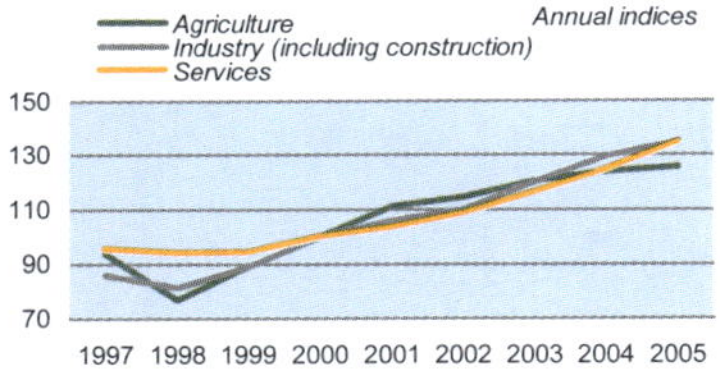

GDP by major sectors, 2005

Employment in major sectors, 2005

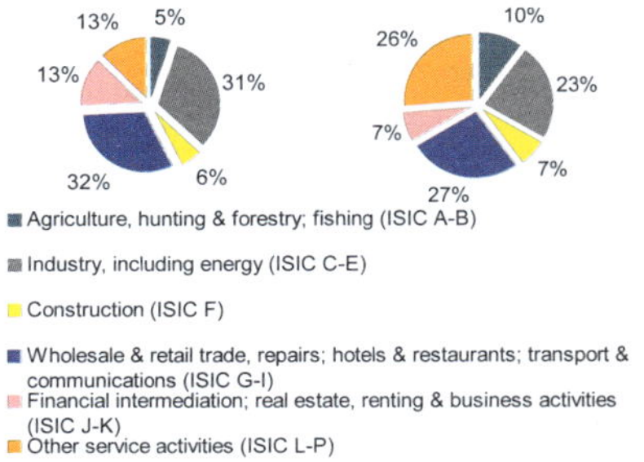

Major import partners from UNECE, 2005

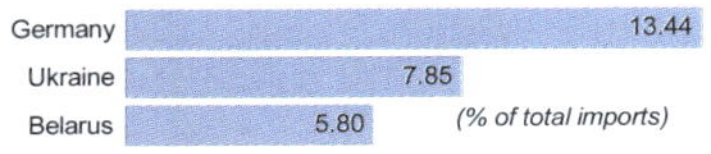

Major export partners in UNECE, 2005

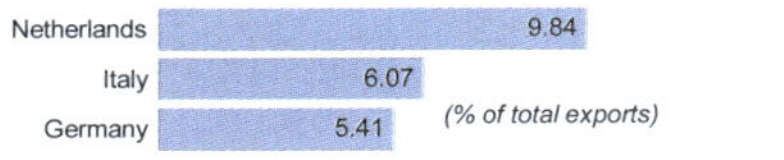

SAN MARINO

Capital:	San Marino (2 294)
Two largest cities:	Serravalle/Dogano (4 802)
	Borgo Maggiore (2 394)
Area (km^2):	61
Total population:	28 503
Population density (per km^2):	467
Official languages:	Italian
Date joined UN:	2 March 1992
National currency:	Euro (EUR)
National Statistical Office:	-

Time: UTC +1h

Population by age, 2004

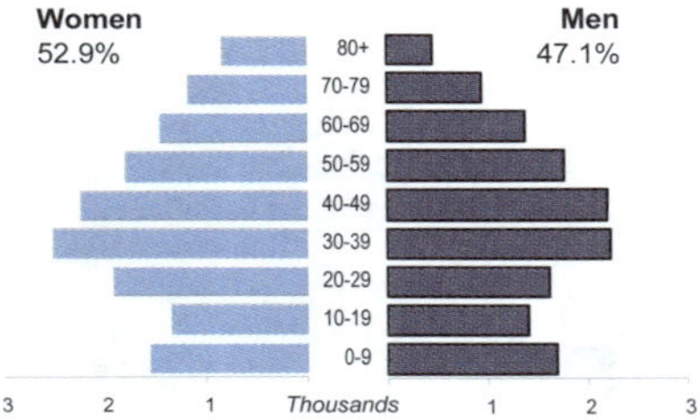

Life expectancy (in years), 2004:	at birth	at 65
Women:	84	..
Men:	79	..

Median age (in years), 2004:	
Women:	39
Men:	37

	percentage of total population
Foreign born:	..
Foreigners in population:	..

Economic activity rate

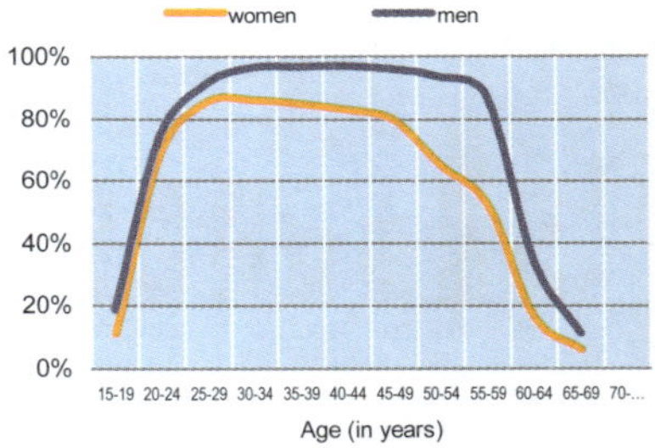

GDP at constant 2000 prices, per capita	
US Dollars, PPP, 2004:	40 552
Purchasing Power Parities (PPP)	
EUR per USD, 2000, US=1:	0.853
Exchange rate	
Annual average, EUR per USD, 2005:	0.804

SAN MARINO

Total fertility rate

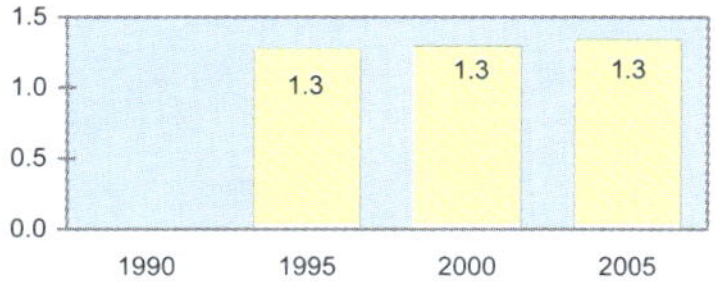

Real GDP growth rate

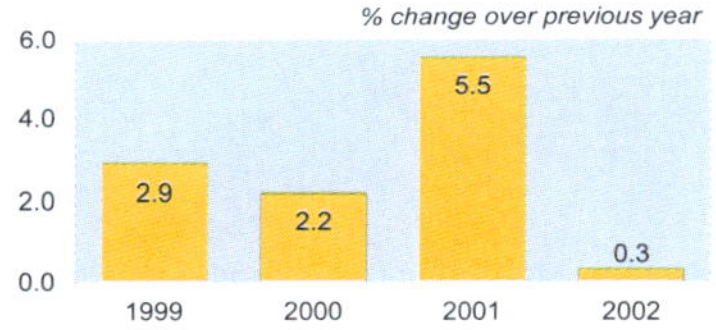

GDP by major sectors

Employment in major sectors, 2004

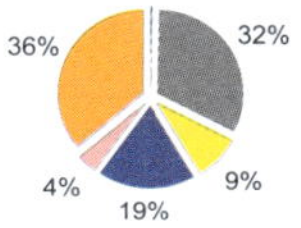

- Agriculture, hunting & forestry; fishing (ISIC A-B)
- Industry, including energy (ISIC C-E)
- Construction (ISIC F)
- Wholesale & retail trade, repairs; hotels & restaurants; transport & communications (ISIC G-I)
- Financial, real estate, renting & business activities (ISIC J-K)
- Other service activities (ISIC L-P)

SERBIA

Capital:	Belgrade (1 120 092)
Two largest cities:	Novi Sad (191 405)
	Niš (173 724)
Area (km²):	88 361
Total population:	7 463 157
Population density (per km²):	84
Official languages:	Serbian
Date joined UN:	1 November 2000*
National currency:	Serbian dinar (RSD)
National statistical office:	Statistical Office of the Republic of Serbia http://www.statserb.sr.gov.yu

Time: UTC +1h

Population by age, 2004

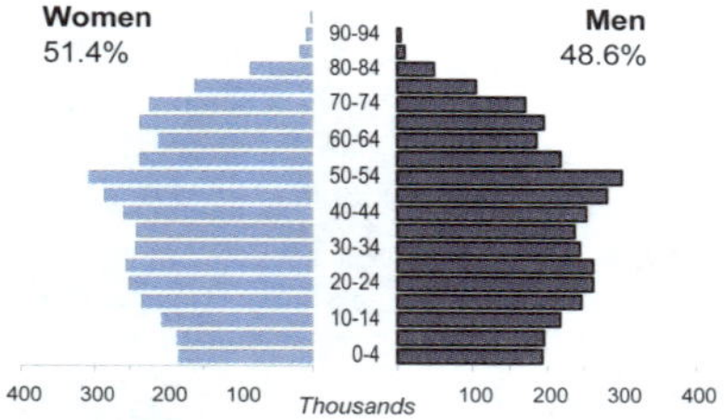

Life expectancy (in years):	at birth	at 65
Women:	75	..
Men:	70	..

Median age (in years), 2004:	
Women:	42
Men:	39

	percentage of total population
Foreign born:	..
Foreigners in population:	..

Legal marital status, population aged 15+, 2002

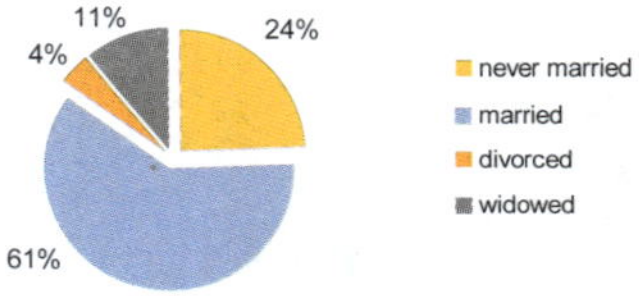

Women in the labour force:	..
Gender pay gap:	..
Female government ministers, 2004: percentage of total for both sexes	11.8%
Female central bank board members: percentage of total for both sexes	..
Female tertiary students, 2002: percentage of total for both sexes	52.9%

Total fertility rate

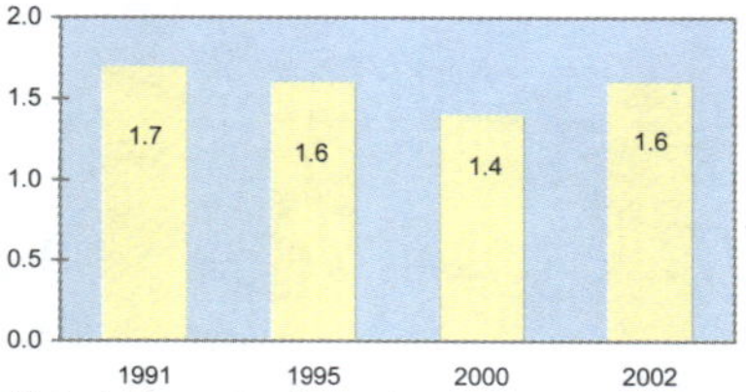

* Refer to the explanatory notes.

Parliament seats held by women (% of total)

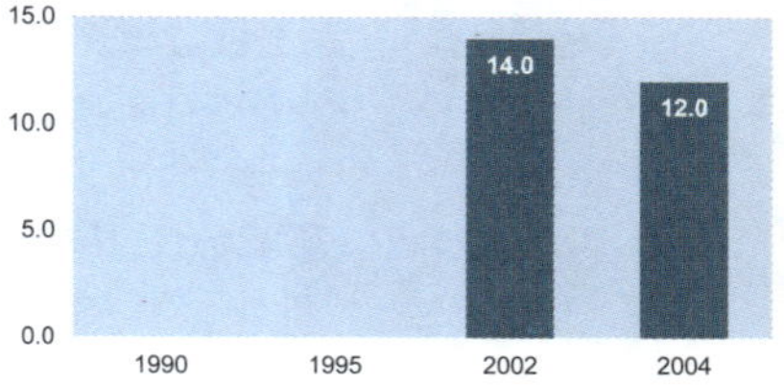

SERBIA

	1999	2000	2001	2002	2003	2004	2005
Employment (% change over previous year)	..	..	..	..	..	..	..
Unemployment rate (%)	..	..	..	..	..	..	..
Youth unemployment rate (%)	..	..	..	..	..	..	..

Economic activity rate

GDP at current prices	
in millions of US Dollars, PPP:	..
in millions of RSD, 2005:	1 750 000
GDP at constant 2000 prices, per capita	
US Dollars, PPP:	..
RSD, 2005:	68 938
Final consumption expenditure at 2000 prices, per capita, US Dollars, PPP:	..
Purchasing Power Parity (PPP)	
RSD per USD, US=1:	..
Gross external debt:	
in millions of US Dollars:	..
Exchange rate	
Annual average, RSD per USD, 2005:	66.71

Real GDP growth rate

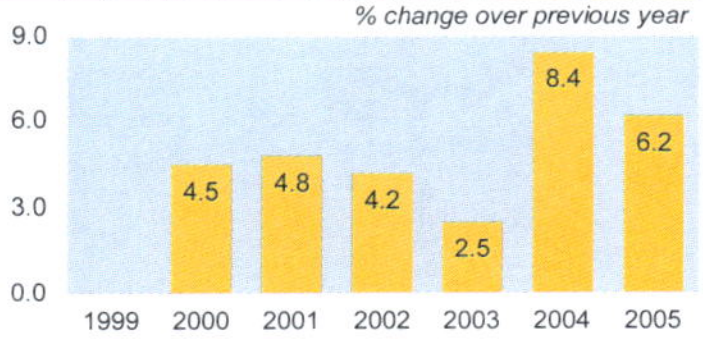

Consumer price index (annual average)

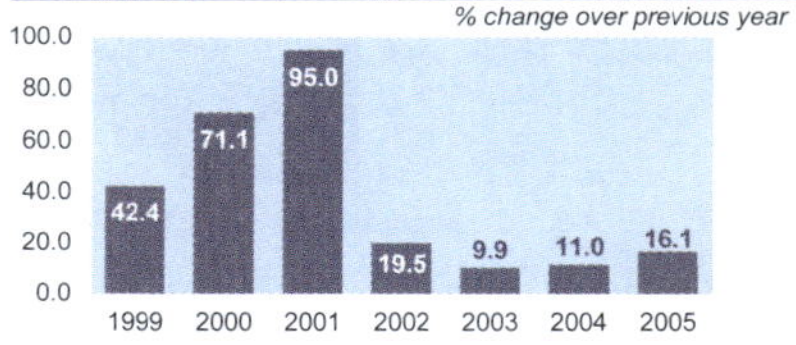

	% of GDP
Exports of goods and services, 2004:	22.2
Imports of goods and services, 2004:	50.6
External trade balance, 2004:	-28

GDP by major sectors

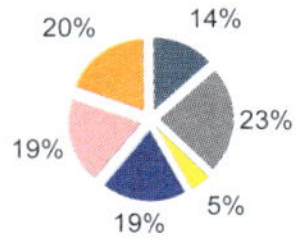

Employment in major sectors

- Agriculture, hunting & forestry; fishing (ISIC A-B)
- Industry, including energy (ISIC C-E)
- Construction (ISIC F)
- Wholesale & retail trade, repairs; hotels & restaurants; transport & communications (ISIC G-I)
- Financial intermediation; real estate, renting & business activities (ISIC J-K)
- Other service activities (ISIC L-P)

GDP in agriculture, industry, and services (2000=100)

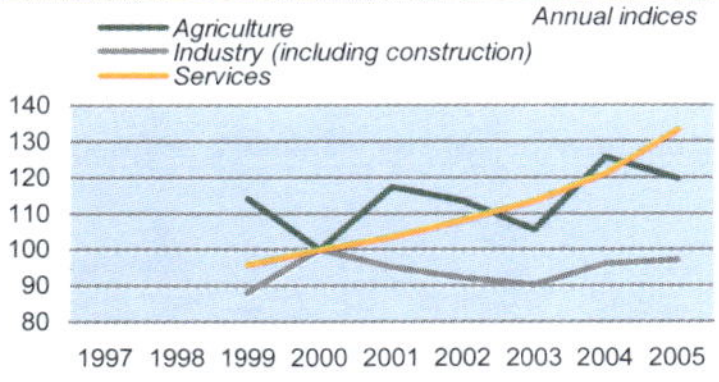

Major import partners from UNECE, 2006

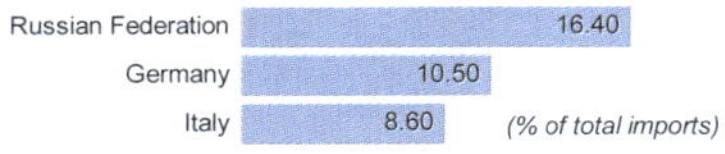

Major export partners in UNECE, 2006

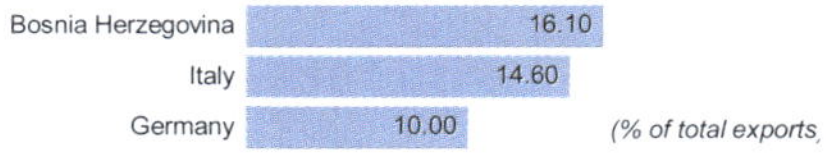

SLOVAKIA

Capital:	Bratislava (425 533)
Two largest cities:	Košice (235 281)
	Prešov (92 147)
Area (km^2):	49 012
Total population:	5 387 285
Population density (per km^2):	110
Official languages:	Slovak
Date joined UN:	19 January 1993
National currency:	Slovak koruna (SKK)
National statistical office:	Statistical Office of the Slovak Republic http://www.statistics.sk

Time: UTC +1h

Population by age, 2005

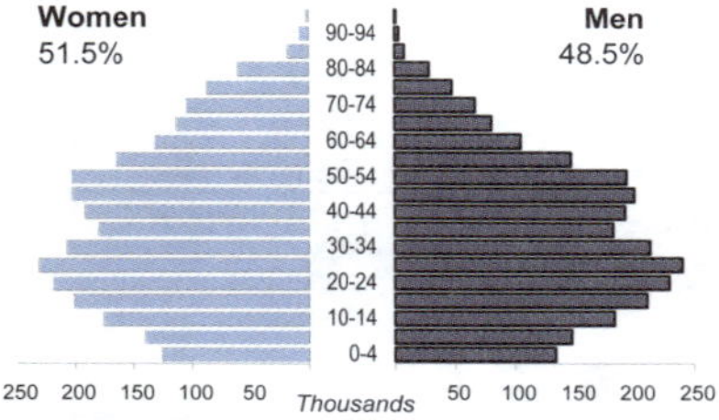

Life expectancy (in years), 2005:	at birth	at 65
Women:	78	17
Men:	70	13

Median age (in years), 2005:	
Women:	37
Men:	34

	percentage of total population
Foreign born, 2005:	9%
Foreigners in population, 2005:	0.4%

Legal marital status, population aged 18+, 2004

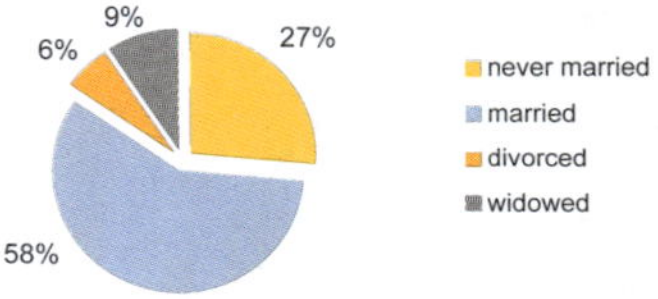

Women in the labour force, 2005:	44.9%
Gender pay gap, 2005:	24%
Female government ministers, 2006: percentage of total for both sexes	12.5%
Female central bank board members: percentage of total for both sexes	..
Female tertiary students, 2003-2004: percentage of total for both sexes	54.1%

Total fertility rate

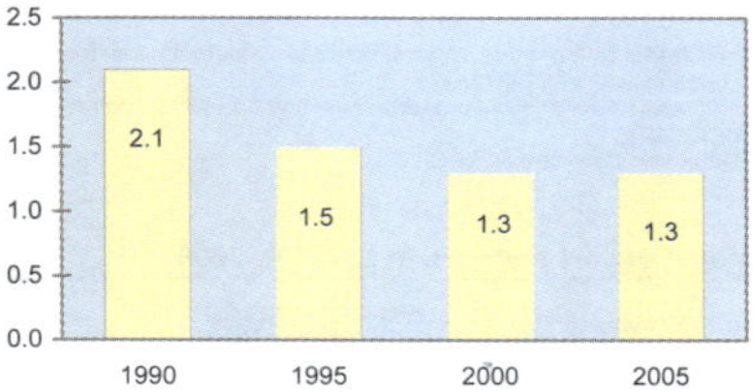

Parliament seats held by women (% of total)

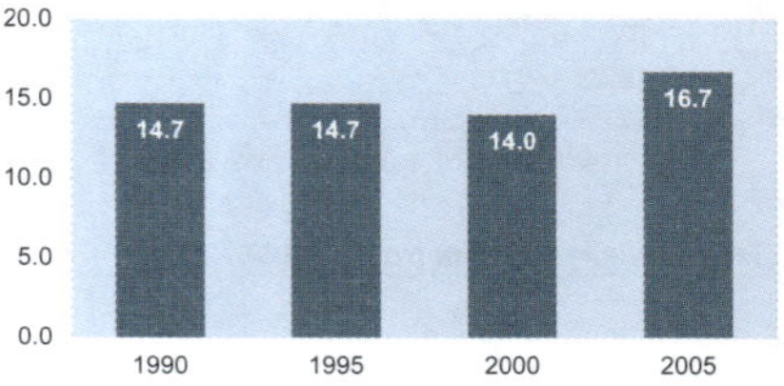

SLOVAKIA

	1999	2000	2001	2002	2003	2004	2005
Employment (% change over previous year)	-2.7	-1.8	0.6	-0.5	1.8	-0.3	1.8
Unemployment rate (%)	16.4	18.8	19.3	18.7	17.6	18.2	16.4
Youth unemployment rate (%)	..	36.9	39.2	37.7	33.4	33.1	30.1

Economic activity rate, 2004

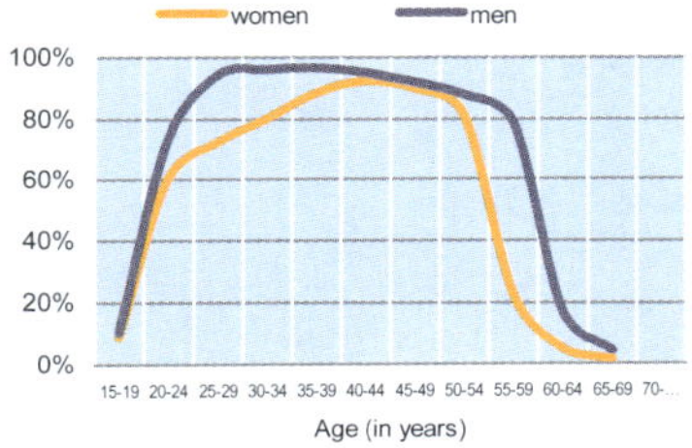

GDP at current prices	
in millions of US Dollars, PPP, 2005:	81 956
in millions of SKK, 2005:	1 471 131
GDP at constant 2000 prices, per capita	
US Dollars, PPP, 2005:	13 595
SKK, 2005:	218 655
Final consumption expenditure at 2000 prices, per capita, US Dollars, PPP, 2005:	10 127
Purchasing Power Parity (PPP)	
SKK per USD, 2005, US=1:	17.95
Gross external debt:	
in millions of US Dollars, 2005:	27 053
Exchange rate	
Annual average, SKK per USD, 2005:	31.02

Real GDP growth rate

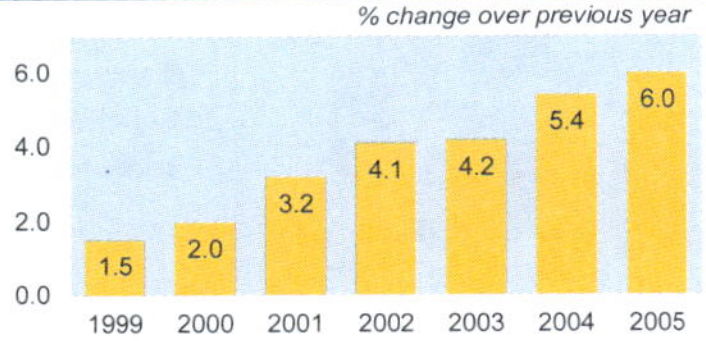

Consumer price index (annual average)

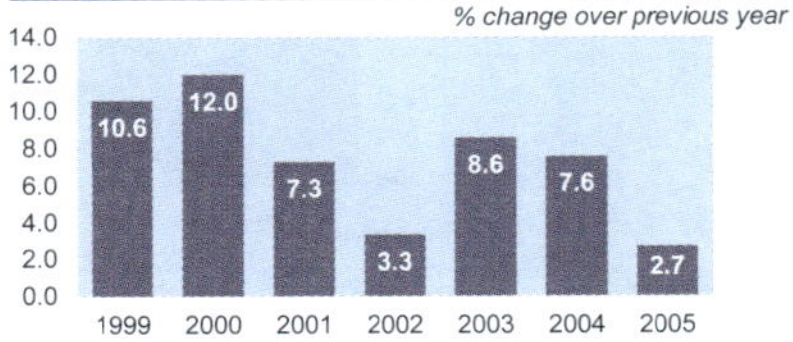

	% of GDP
Exports of goods and services, 2005:	77.3
Imports of goods and services, 2005:	82.4
External trade balance, 2005:	-5.1

GDP in agriculture, industry, and services (2000=100)

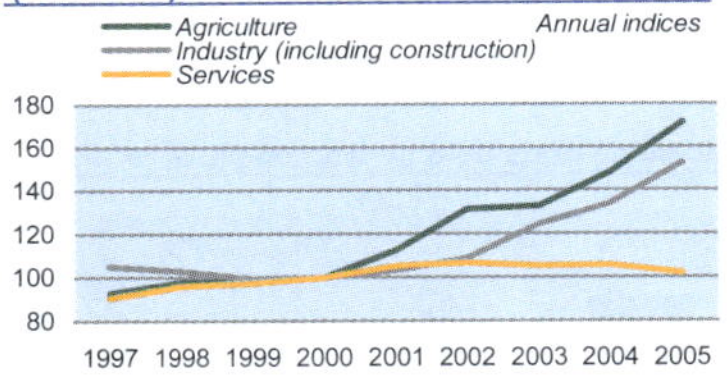

GDP by major sectors, 2005

Employment in major sectors, 2005

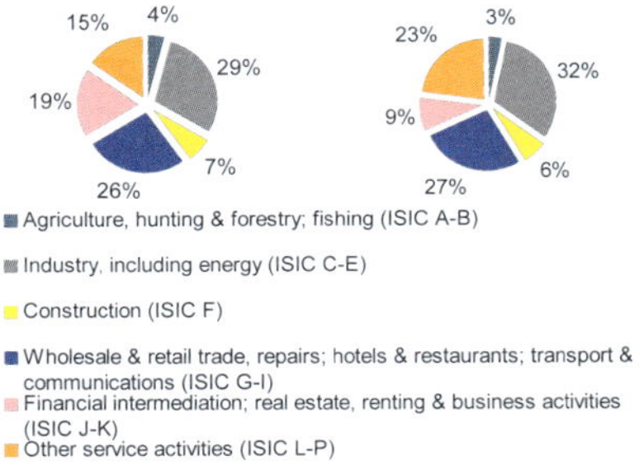

Major import partners from UNECE, 2005

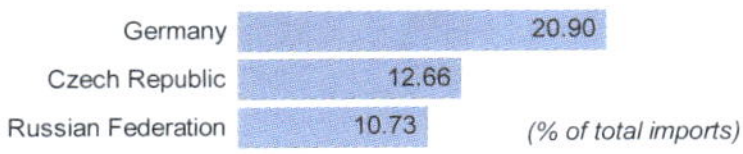

Major export partners in UNECE, 2005

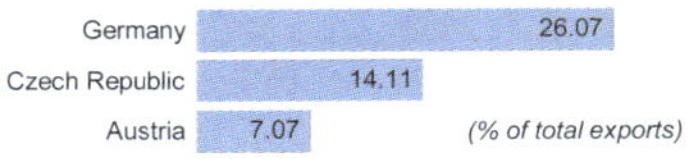

SLOVENIA

Capital:	Ljubljana (258 873)
Two largest cities:	Maribor (93 847)
	Celje (37 834)
Area (km²):	20 253
Total population:	2 000 474
Population density (per km²):	99
Official languages:	Slovenian
Date joined UN:	22 May 1992
National currency:	Euro (EUR)
National statistical office:	Statistical Office of the Republic of Slovenia http://www.stat.si

Time: UTC +1h

Population by age, 2005

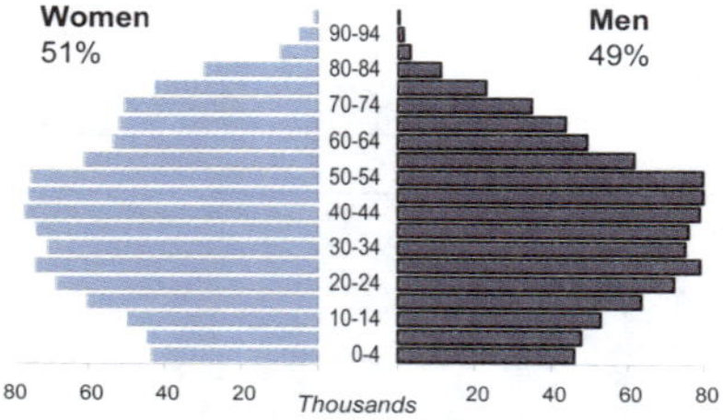

Life expectancy (in years), 2005:	at birth	at 65
Women:	81	19
Men:	74	14

Median age (in years), 2005:	
Women:	42
Men:	39

	percentage of total population
Foreign born, 2005:	10.9%
Foreigners in population, 2005:	2.2%

Legal marital status, population aged 18+, 2004

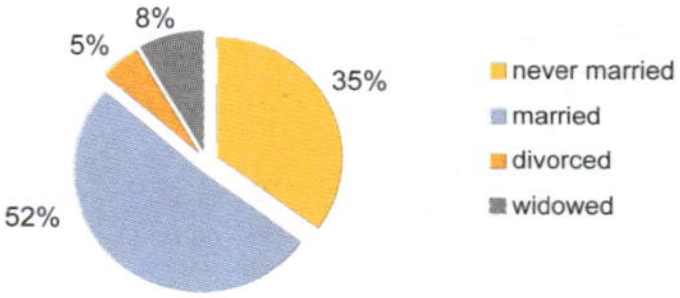

Women in the labour force, 2005:	45.9%
Gender pay gap, 2005:	8%
Female government ministers, 2006: percentage of total for both sexes	6.2%
Female central bank board members: percentage of total for both sexes	..
Female tertiary students, 2003-2004: percentage of total for both sexes	56.9%

Total fertility rate

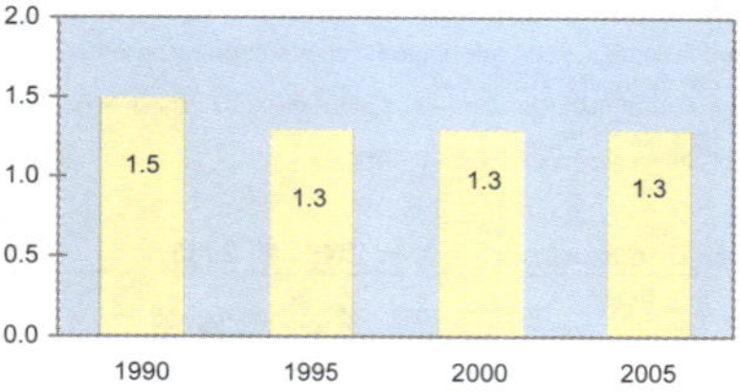

Parliament seats held by women (% of total)

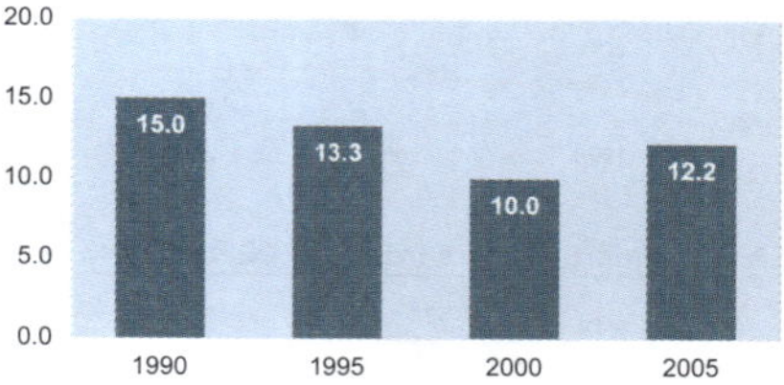

* The currency of Slovenia changed to euro (EUR) from 1 January 2007. Figures relating to national currency may be expressed in Slovenian tolar (SIT).

SLOVENIA

	1999	2000	2001	2002	2003	2004	2005
Employment (% change over previous year)	1.5	0.8	0.4	1.4	-0.2	0.4	0.8
Unemployment rate (%)	7.3	6.7	6.2	6.3	6.7	6.3	6.3
Youth unemployment rate (%)	..	16.3	17.8	16.5	17.3	16.1	15.9

Economic activity rate, 2004

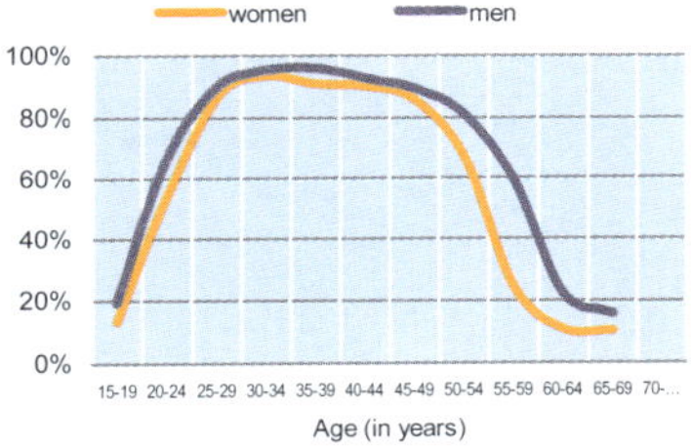

GDP at current prices	
in millions of US Dollars, PPP, 2005:	44 608
in millions of SIT*, 2005:	6 620 145
GDP at constant 2000 prices, per capita	
US Dollars, PPP, 2005:	19 587
SIT*, 2005:	2 545 123
Final consumption expenditure at 2000 prices, per capita, US Dollars, PPP, 2005:	14 484
Purchasing Power Parity (PPP)	
SIT* per USD, 2005, US=1:	148.4
Gross external debt:	
in millions of US Dollars, 2005:	23 081
Exchange rate	
Annual average, EUR per USD, 2005:	0.804

Real GDP growth rate

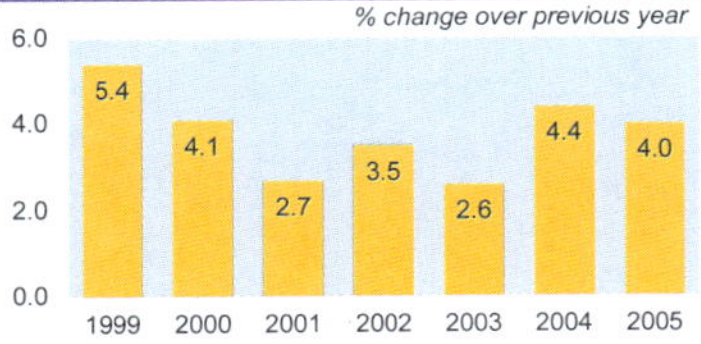

Consumer price index (annual average)

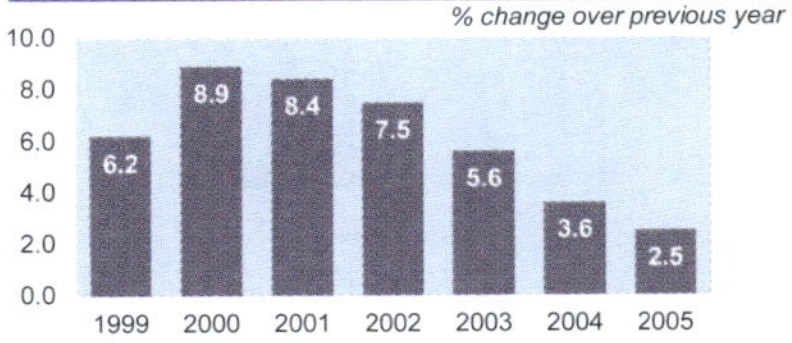

	% of GDP
Exports of goods and services, 2005:	64.6
Imports of goods and services, 2005:	65.1
External trade balance, 2005:	-0.5

GDP by major sectors, 2005

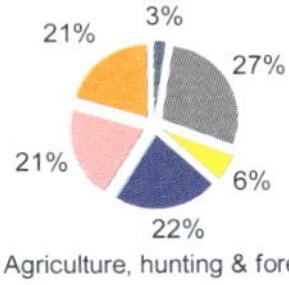

Employment in major sectors, 2005

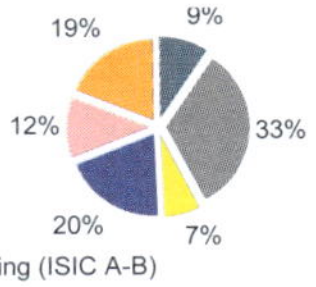

- Agriculture, hunting & forestry; fishing (ISIC A-B)
- Industry, including energy (ISIC C-E)
- Construction (ISIC F)
- Wholesale & retail trade, repairs; hotels & restaurants; transport & communications (ISIC G-I)
- Financial intermediation; real estate, renting & business activities (ISIC J-K)
- Other service activities (ISIC L-P)

GDP in agriculture, industry, and services (2000=100)

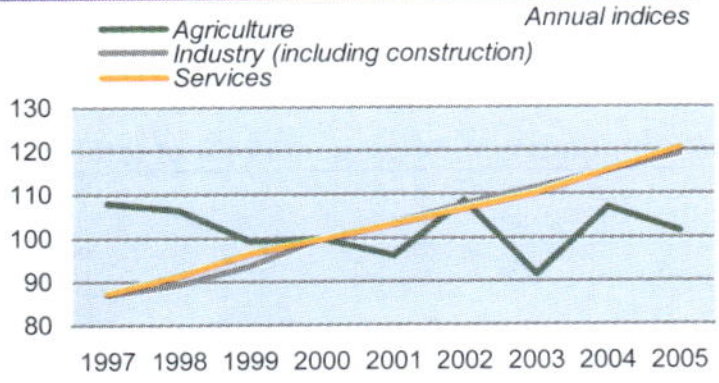

Major import partners from UNECE, 2005

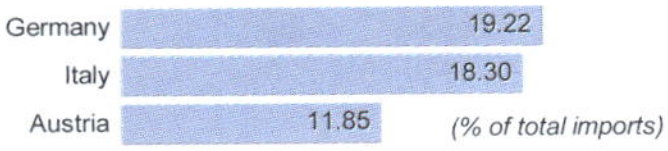

Major export partners in UNECE, 2005

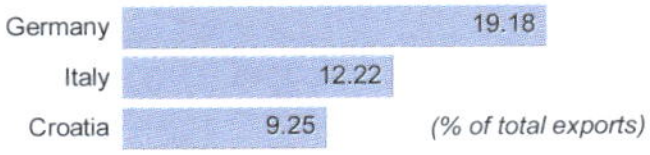

SPAIN

Time: UTC +1h

Capital:	Madrid (3 155 359)
Two largest cities:	Barcelona (1 593 075)
	Valencia (796 549)
Area (km²):	505 992
Total population:	43 398 143
Population density (per km²):	86
Official languages:	Spanish
Date joined UN:	14 December 1955
National currency:	Euro (EUR)
National statistical office:	National Institute of Statistics http://www.ine.es

Population by age, 2005

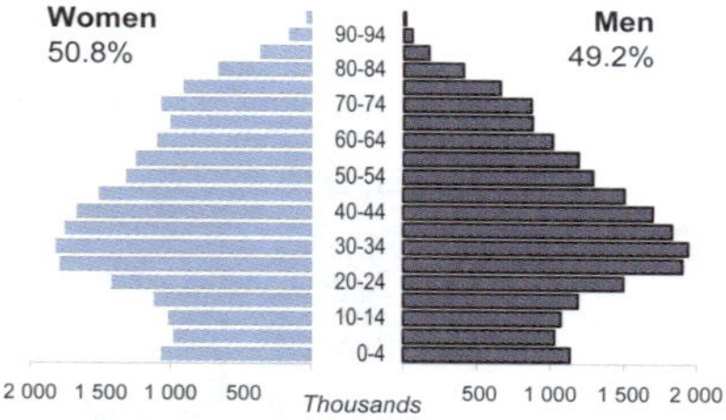

Legal marital status, population aged 18+

never married
married
divorced
widowed

Data not available

Life expectancy (in years), 2005:	at birth	at 65
Women:	84	22
Men:	77	17

Median age (in years), 2005:	
Women:	40
Men:	38

	percentage of total population
Foreign born, 2005:	9.9%
Foreigners in population, 2005:	7.8%

Women in the labour force, 2005:	41.3%
Gender pay gap, 2005:	13%
Female government ministers, 2006: percentage of total for both sexes	38.1%
Female central bank board members, 2005: percentage of total for both sexes	10%
Female tertiary students, 2003-2004: percentage of total for both sexes	53.8%

Total fertility rate

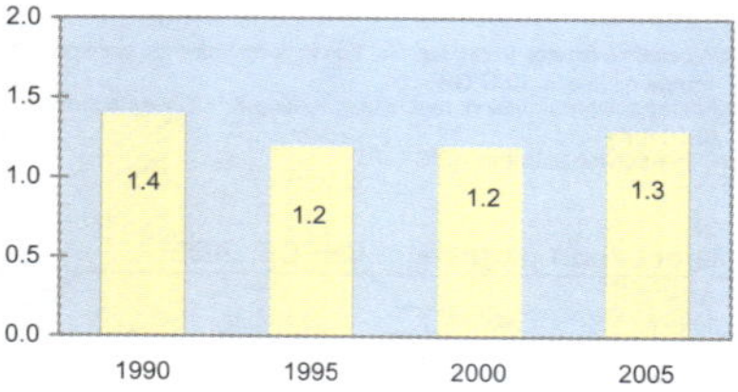

Parliament seats held by women (% of total)

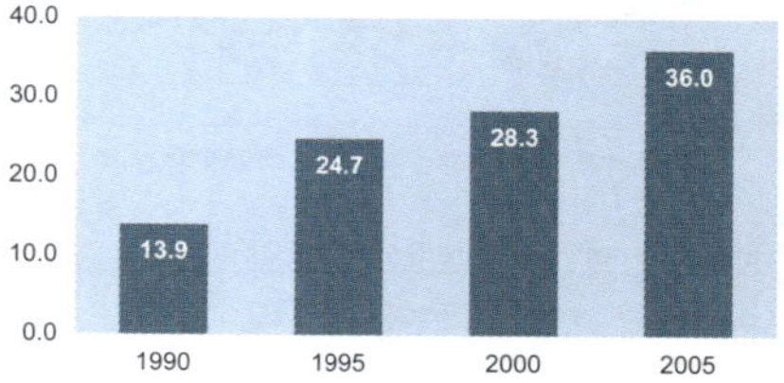

SPAIN

	1999	2000	2001	2002	2003	2004	2005
Employment (% change over previous year)	3.5	3.5	3.2	2.4	2.6	2.6	3.6
Unemployment rate (%)	12.5	11.1	10.3	11.1	11.1	10.6	9.2
Youth unemployment rate (%)	..	24.3	23.2	24.2	24.6	23.9	19.7

Economic activity rate, 2004

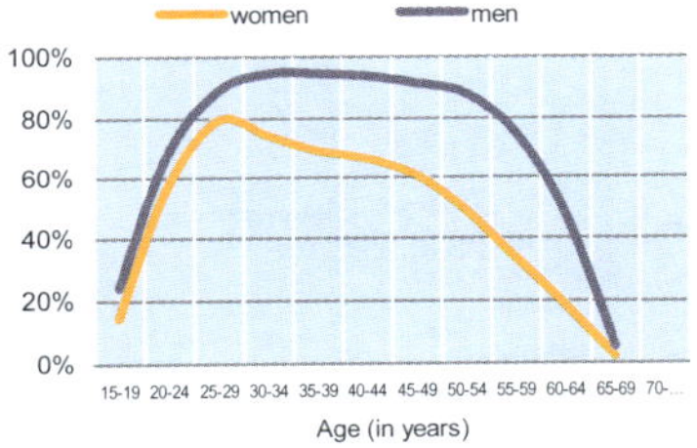

GDP at current prices	
in millions of US Dollars, PPP, 2005:	1 184 085
in millions of EUR, 2005:	905 455
GDP at constant 2000 prices, per capita	
US Dollars, PPP, 2005:	22 931
EUR, 2005:	17 028
Final consumption expenditure at 2000 prices, per capita, US Dollars, PPP, 2005:	18 112
Purchasing Power Parity (PPP)	
EUR per USD, 2005, US=1:	0.765
Gross external debt:	
in millions of US Dollars, 2005:	1 369 564
Exchange rate	
Annual average, EUR per USD, 2005:	0.804

Real GDP growth rate

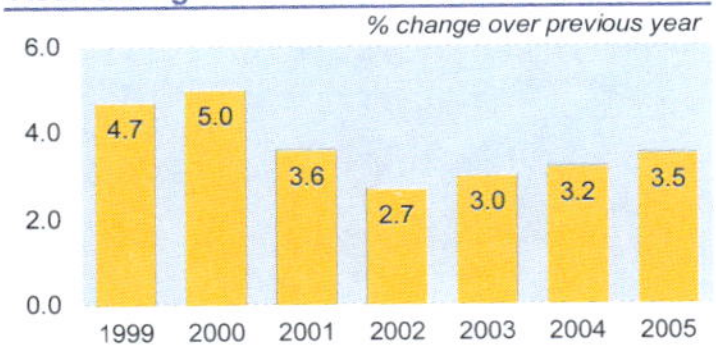

Consumer price index (annual average)

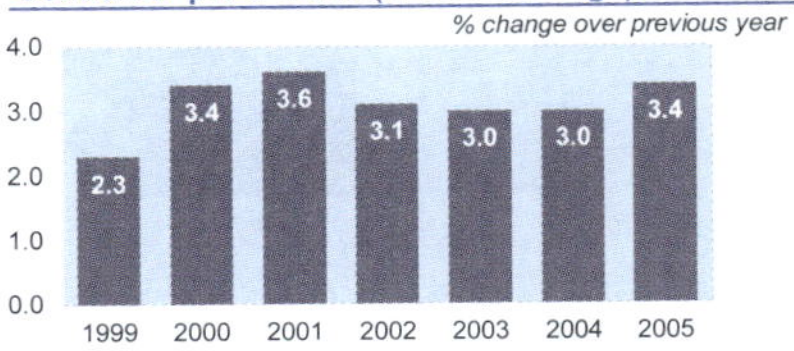

	% of GDP
Exports of goods and services, 2005:	25.5
Imports of goods and services, 2005:	30.9
External trade balance, 2005:	-5.4

GDP by major sectors

Employment in major sectors, 2005

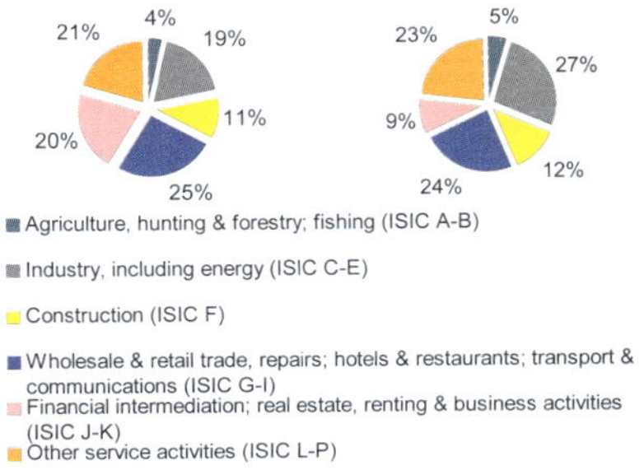

GDP in agriculture, industry, and services (2000=100)

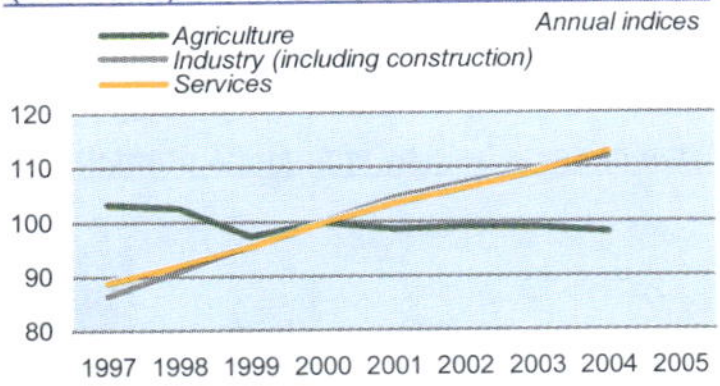

Major import partners from UNECE, 2005

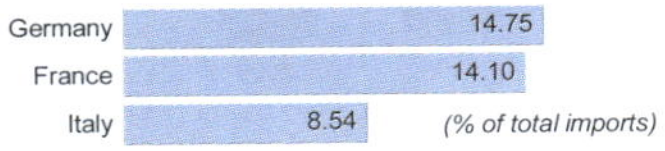

Major export partners in UNECE, 2005

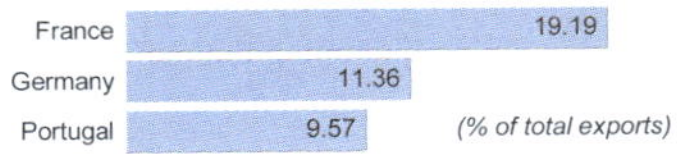

SWEDEN

Capital:	Stockholm (765 044)
Two largest cities:	Göteborg (481 410)
	Malmö (269 142)
Area (km^2):	449 964
Total population:	9 029 572
Population density (per km^2):	20
Official languages:	Swedish
Date joined UN:	19 November 1946
National currency:	Swedish krona (SEK)
National statistical office:	Statistics Sweden http://www.scb.se

Time: UTC +1h

Population by age, 2005

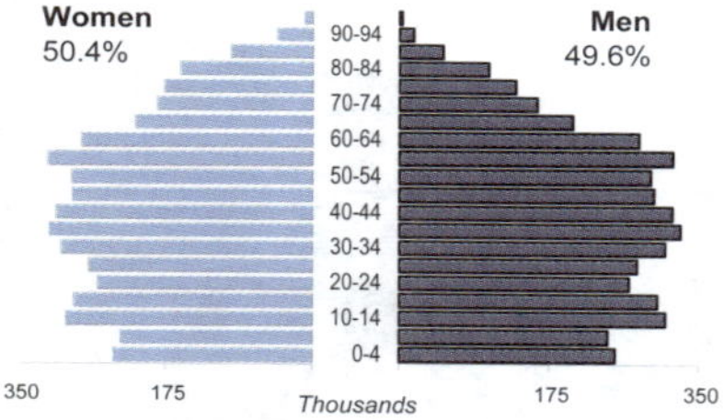

Legal marital status, population aged 18+, 2004

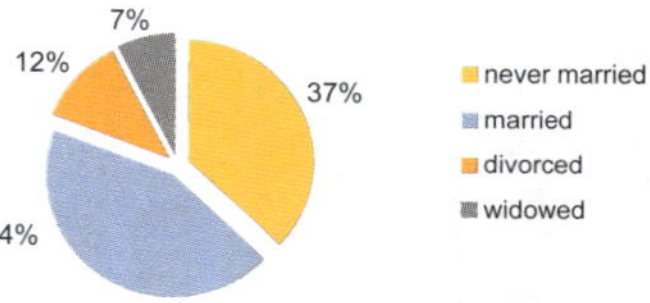

Life expectancy (in years), 2005:	at birth	at 65
Women:	83	20
Men:	78	17

Median age (in years), 2005:	
Women:	41
Men:	39

	percentage of total population
Foreign born, 2005:	12.2%
Foreigners in population, 2005:	5.3%

Women in the labour force, 2005:	47.5%
Gender pay gap, 2005:	16%
Female government ministers, 2006: percentage of total for both sexes	40.9%
Female central bank board members, 2005: percentage of total for both sexes	50%
Female tertiary students, 2003-2004: percentage of total for both sexes	59.5%

Total fertility rate

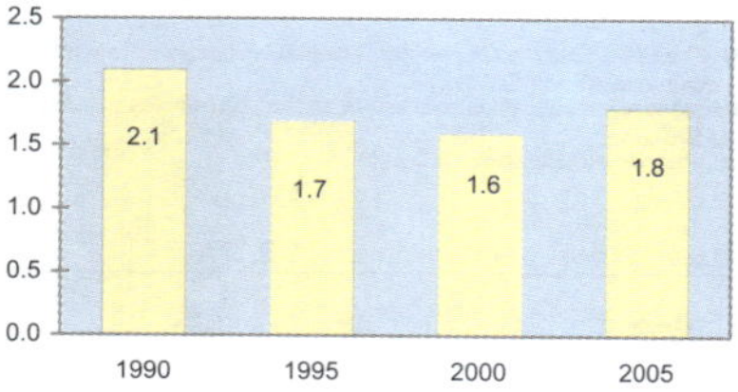

Parliament seats held by women (% of total)

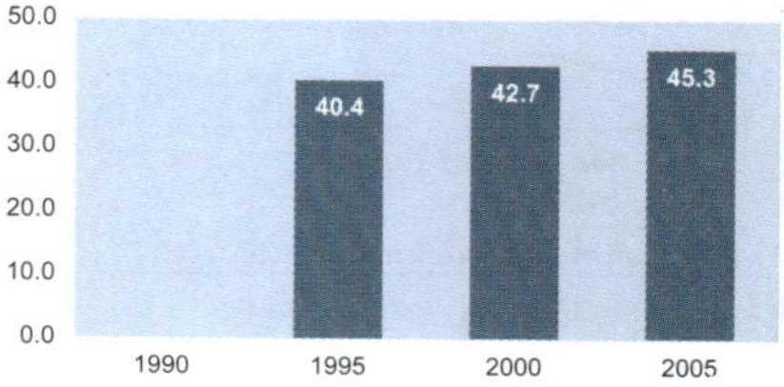

SWEDEN

	1999	2000	2001	2002	2003	2004	2005
Employment (% change over previous year)	2.1	2.4	1.9	0.2	-0.3	-0.5	0.5
Unemployment rate (%)	6.7	5.6	4.9	4.9	5.6	6.3	7.8
Youth unemployment rate (%)	..	10.5	10.9	11.9	13.4	16.3	21.8

Economic activity rate, 2004

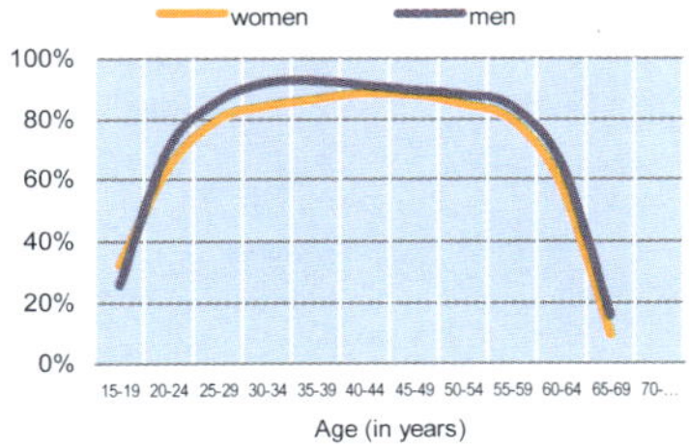

GDP at current prices	
in millions of US Dollars, PPP, 2005:	286 167
in millions of SEK, 2005:	2 672 998
GDP at constant 2000 prices, per capita	
US Dollars, PPP, 2005:	29 991
SEK, 2005:	275 816
Final consumption expenditure at 2000 prices, per capita, US Dollars, PPP, 2005:	21 680
Purchasing Power Parity (PPP)	
SEK per USD, 2005, US=1:	9.341
Gross external debt:	
in millions of US Dollars, 2005:	522 172
Exchange rate	
Annual average, SEK per USD, 2005:	7.473

Real GDP growth rate

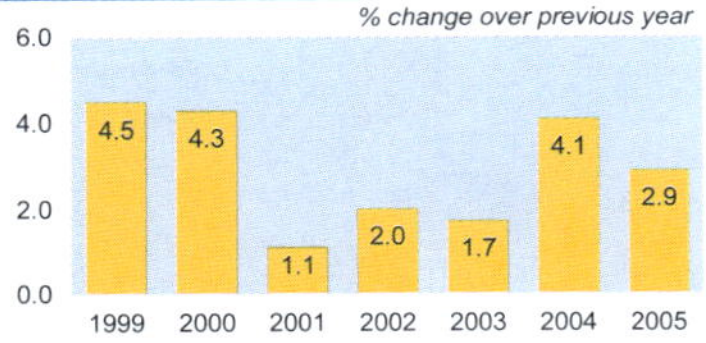

Consumer price index (annual average)

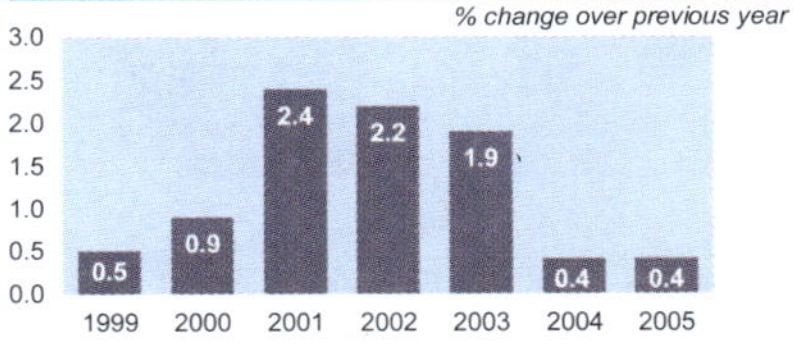

	% of GDP
Exports of goods and services, 2005:	48.6
Imports of goods and services, 2005:	40.9
External trade balance, 2005:	7.7

GDP in agriculture, industry, and services (2000=100)

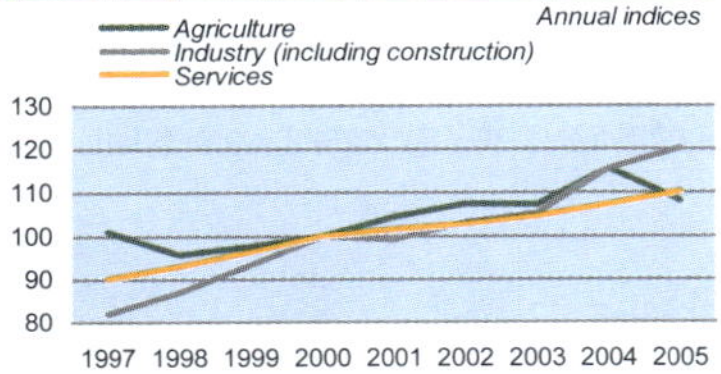

GDP by major sectors, 2005

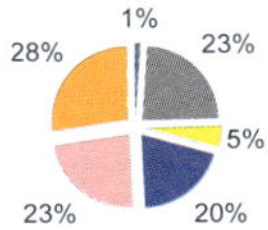

Employment in major sectors, 2005

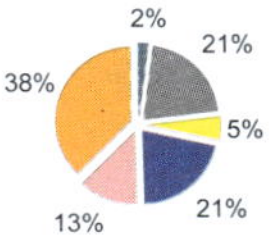

- Agriculture, hunting & forestry; fishing (ISIC A-B)
- Industry, including energy (ISIC C-E)
- Construction (ISIC F)
- Wholesale & retail trade, repairs; hotels & restaurants; transport & communications (ISIC G-I)
- Financial intermediation; real estate, renting & business activities (ISIC J-K)
- Other service activities (ISIC L-P)

Major import partners from UNECE, 2005

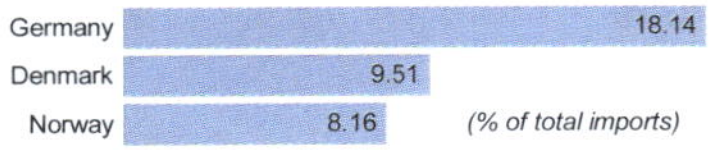

Major export partners in UNECE, 2005

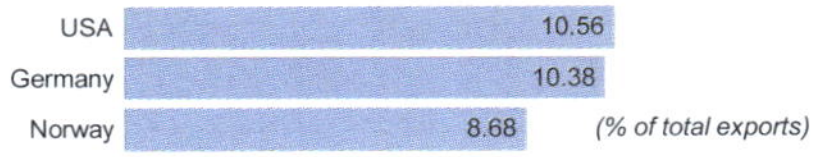

SWITZERLAND

Capital:	Bern (122 707)
Two largest cities:	Zurich (342 518)
	Geneva (177 535)
Area (km²):	41 285
Total population:	7 437 115
Population density (per km²):	180
Official languages:	German, French, Italian, Romansh
Date joined UN:	10 September 2002
National currency:	Swiss franc (CHF)
National statistical office:	Swiss Federal Statistical Office http://www.bfs.admin.ch

Time: UTC +1h

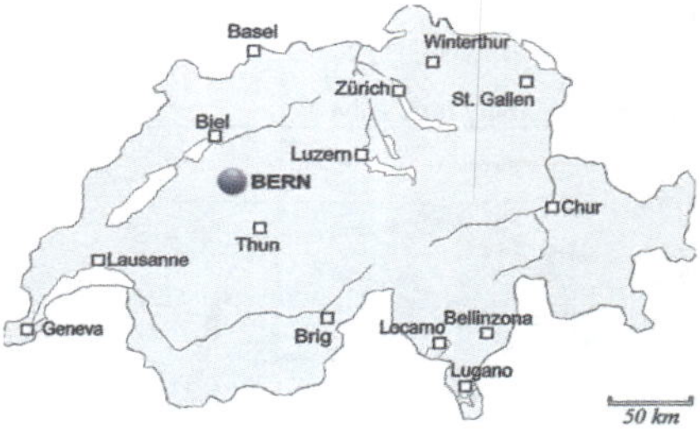

Population by age, 2005

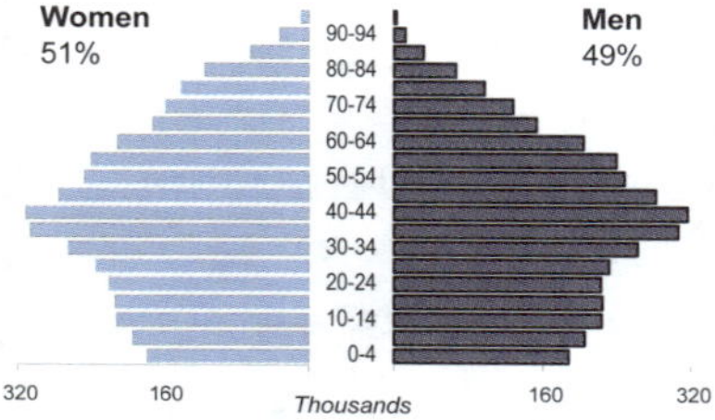

Legal marital status, population aged 18+, 2004

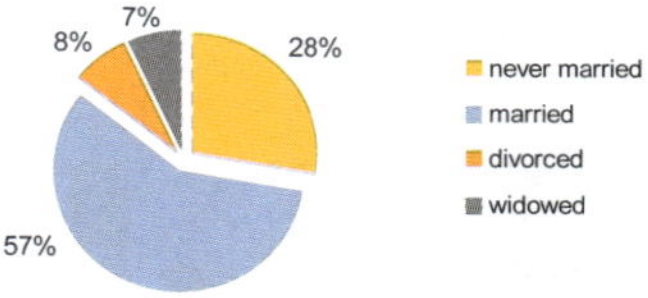

Life expectancy (in years), 2005:	at birth	at 65
Women:	84	21
Men:	79	18

Median age (in years), 2005:	
Women:	41
Men:	39

	percentage of total population
Foreign born:	..
Foreigners in population, 2005:	20.6%

Women in the labour force, 2005:	45.7%
Gender pay gap, 2002:	20.7%
Female government ministers, 2006: percentage of total for both sexes	42.8%
Female central bank board members: percentage of total for both sexes	..
Female tertiary students, 2003-2004: percentage of total for both sexes	44.9%

Total fertility rate

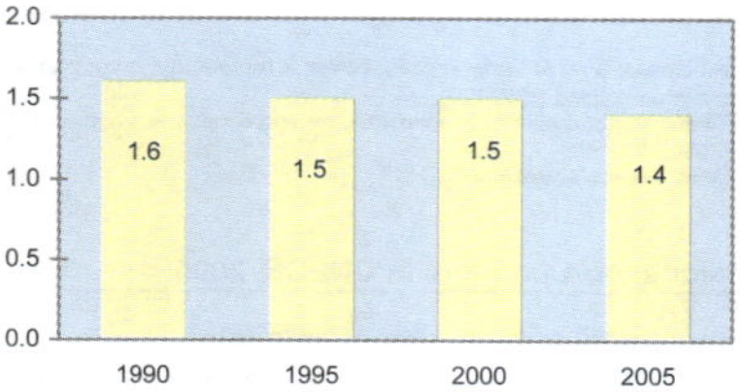

Parliament seats held by women (% of total)

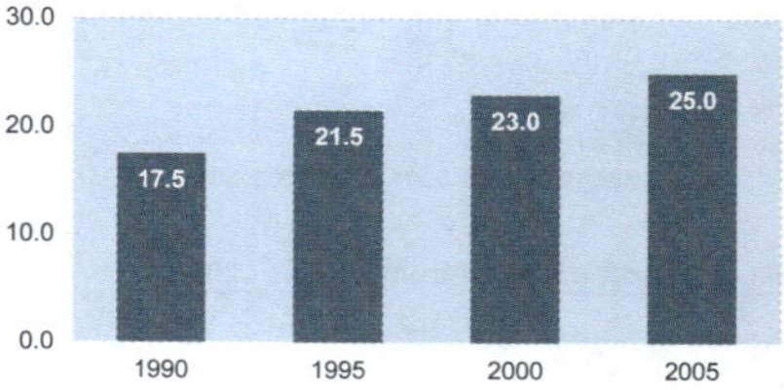

SWITZERLAND

	1999	2000	2001	2002	2003	2004	2005
Employment (% change over previous year)	0.8	1.0	1.6	0.6	-0.1	0.2	1.1
Unemployment rate (%)	3.0	2.7	2.6	3.2	4.2	4.4	4.5
Youth unemployment rate (%)	..	5.0	5.7	5.6	8.6	..	..

Economic activity rate, 2004

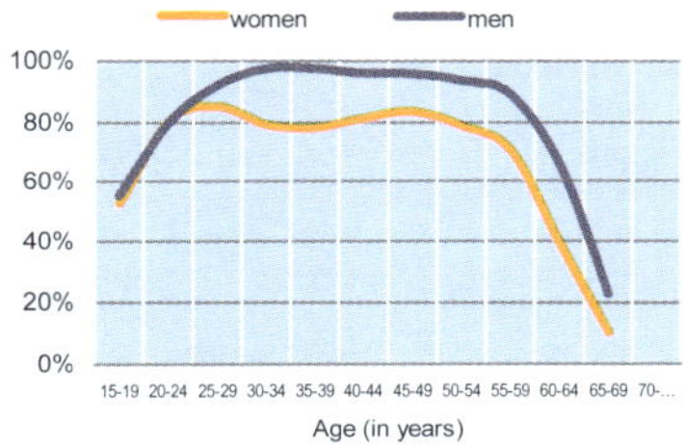

GDP at current prices	
in millions of US Dollars, PPP, 2005:	262 723
in millions of CHF, 2005:	455 594
GDP at constant 2000 prices, per capita	
US Dollars, PPP, 2005:	30 935
CHF, 2005:	58 731
Final consumption expenditure at 2000 prices, per capita, US Dollars, PPP, 2005:	22 049
Purchasing Power Parity (PPP)	
CHF per USD, 2005, US=1:	1.734
Gross external debt:	
in millions of US Dollars, 2005:	925 305
Exchange rate	
Annual average, CHF per USD, 2005:	1.245

Real GDP growth rate

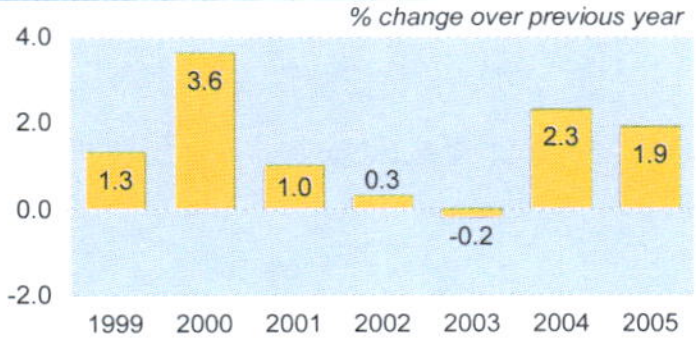

Consumer price index (annual average)

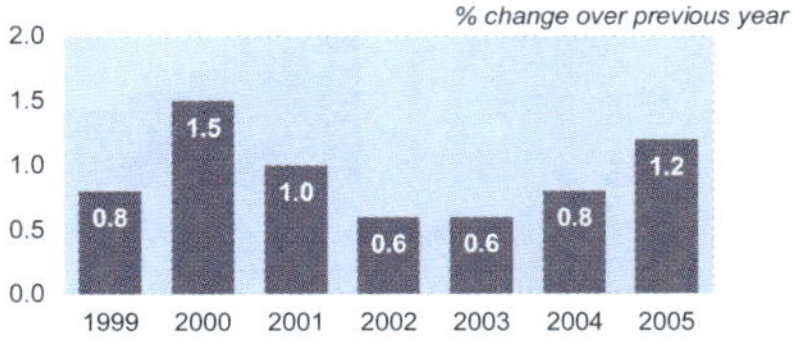

	% of GDP
Exports of goods and services, 2005:	47.9
Imports of goods and services, 2005:	41.1
External trade balance, 2005:	6.8

GDP in agriculture, industry, and services (2000=100)

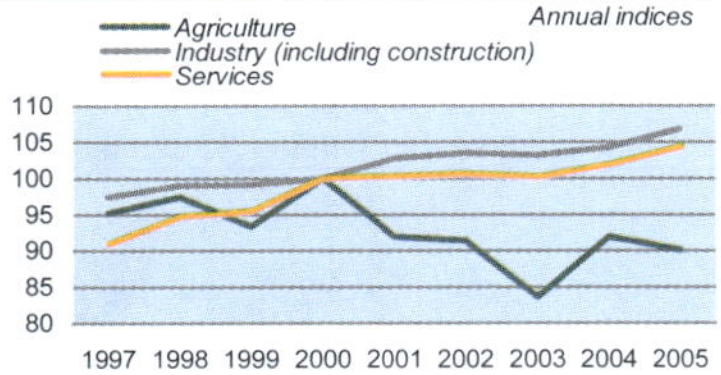

GDP by major sectors, 2005

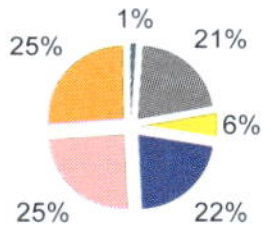

Employment in major sectors, 2003

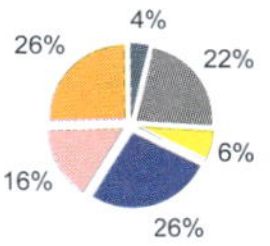

- Agriculture, hunting & forestry; fishing (ISIC A-B)
- Industry, including energy (ISIC C-E)
- Construction (ISIC F)
- Wholesale & retail trade, repairs; hotels & restaurants; transport & communications (ISIC G-I)
- Financial intermediation; real estate, renting & business activities (ISIC J-K)
- Other service activities (ISIC L-P)

Major import partners from UNECE, 2005

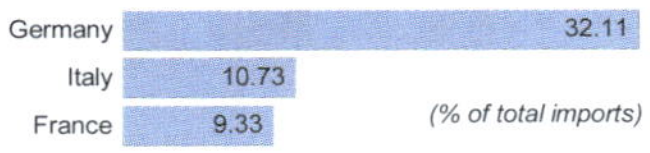

Major export partners in UNECE, 2005

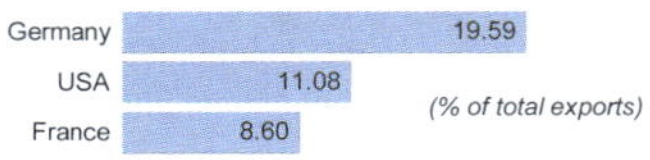

TAJIKISTAN

Capital:	Dushanbe (575 900)
Two largest cities:	Khujand (147 400)
	Kulob (79 500)
Area (km^2):	143 100
Total population:	6 503 000
Population density (per km^2):	45
Official languages:	Tajik
Date joined UN:	2 March 1992
National currency:	Tajik somoni (TJS)
National statistical office:	State Statistical Committee of Tajikistan http://www.stat.tj/

Time: UTC +5h

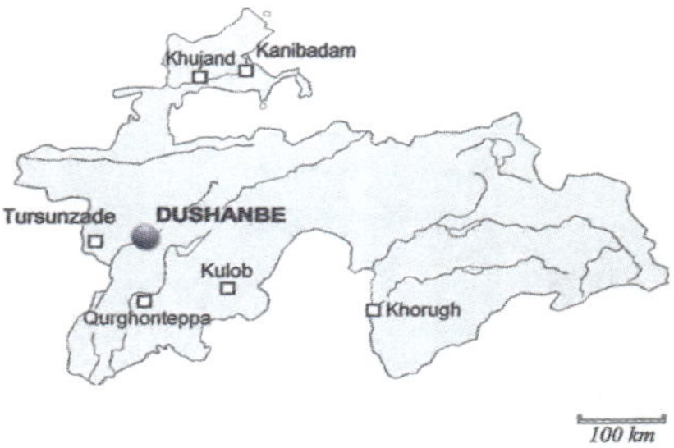

Population by age, 2005

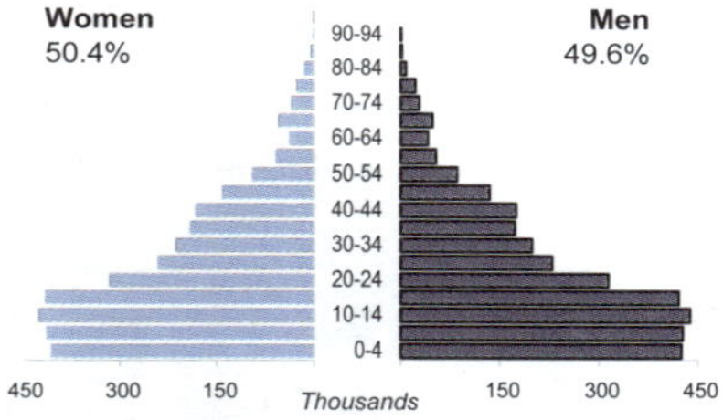

Life expectancy (in years), 2001:	at birth	at 65
Women:	74	16
Men:	70	14

Median age (in years), 2005:	
Women:	20
Men:	19

	percentage of total population
Foreign born:	..
Foreigners in population:	..

Legal marital status, population aged 18+

Data not available

never married
married
divorced
widowed

Women in the labour force:	..
Gender pay gap, 2000:	56.8%
Female government ministers: percentage of total for both sexes	..
Female central bank board members: percentage of total for both sexes	..
Female tertiary students: percentage of total for both sexes	..

Total fertility rate

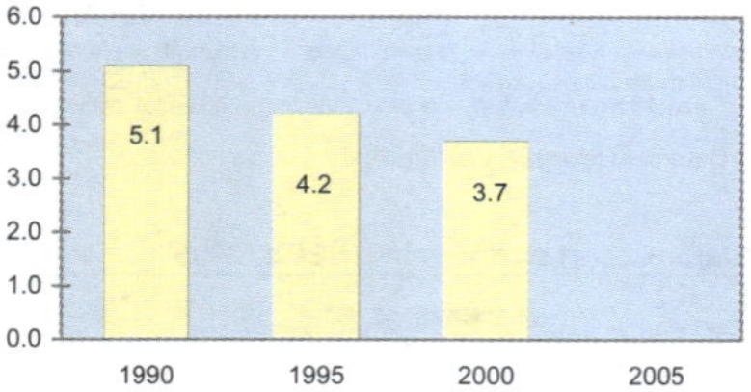

Parliament seats held by women (% of total)

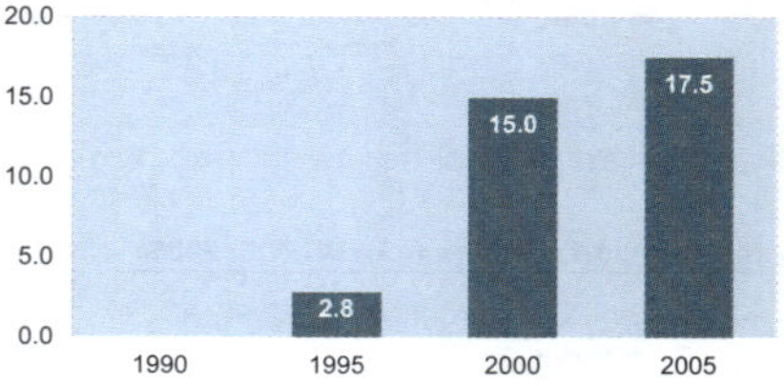

TAJIKISTAN

	1999	2000	2001	2002	2003	2004	2005
Employment (% change over previous year)	-3.3	0.5	4.8	1.5	1.5	10.8	1.1
Unemployment rate (%)	3.0	2.7	2.3	2.6	2.3	2.0	2.1
Youth unemployment rate (%)	..	12.8	..	..	..	10.0	..

Economic activity rate

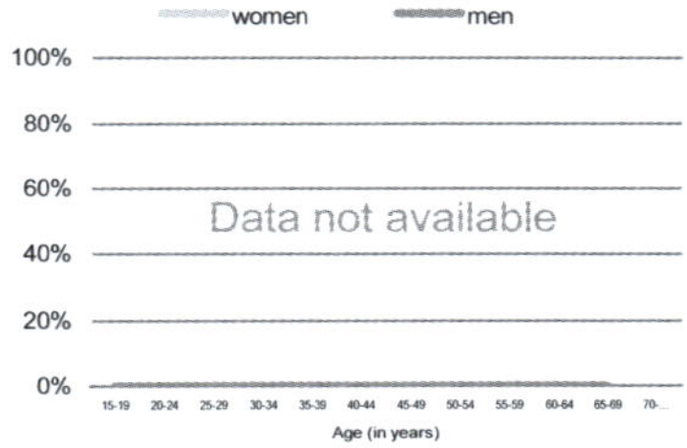

GDP at current prices	
in millions of US Dollars, PPP, 2005:	8 751
in millions of TJS, 2005:	7 207
GDP at constant 2000 prices, per capita	
US Dollars, PPP, 2005:	1 134
TJS, 2005:	414
Final consumption expenditure at 2000 prices, per capita, US Dollars, PPP, 2005:	1 287
Purchasing Power Parity (PPP)	
TJS per USD, 2005, US=1:	0.824
Gross external debt:	
in millions of US Dollars, 2004:	871
Exchange rate	
Annual average, TJS per USD, 2005:	3.115

Real GDP growth rate

% change over previous year

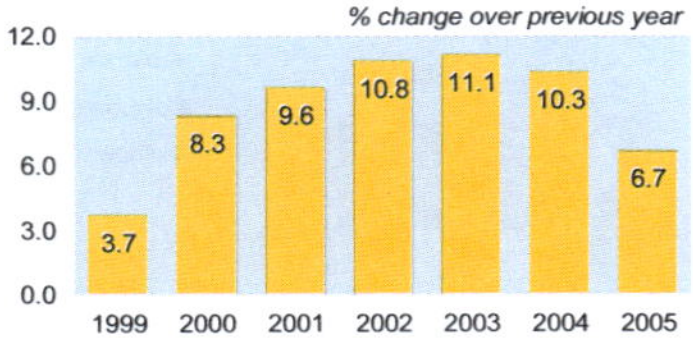

Consumer price index (annual average)

% change over previous year

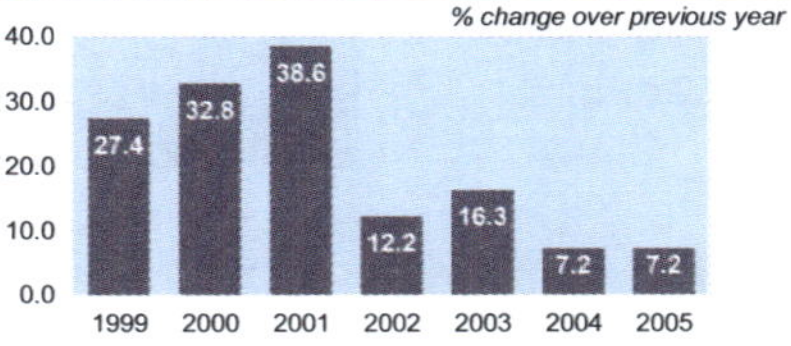

	% of GDP
Exports of goods and services, 2005:	54.3
Imports of goods and services, 2005:	72.8
External trade balance, 2005:	-19

GDP in agriculture, industry, and services (2000=100)

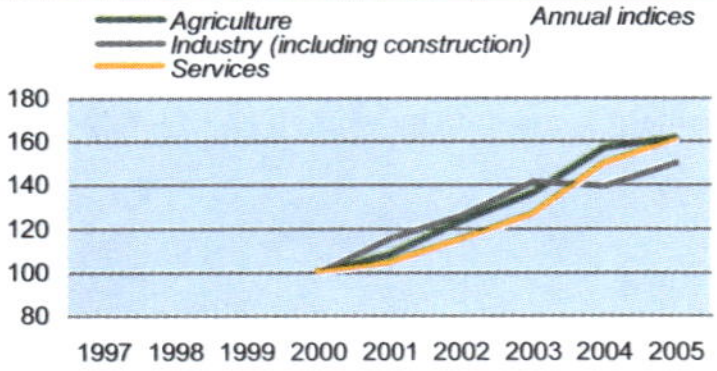

GDP by major sectors, 2005

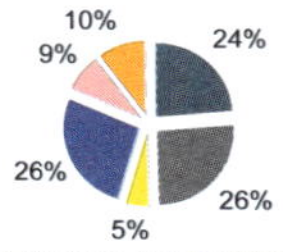

Employment in major sectors

- Agriculture, hunting & forestry; fishing (ISIC A-B)
- Industry, including energy (ISIC C-E)
- Construction (ISIC F)
- Wholesale & retail trade, repairs; hotels & restaurants; transport & communications (ISIC G-I)
- Financial intermediation; real estate, renting & business activities (ISIC J-K)
- Other service activities (ISIC L-P)

Major import partners from UNECE, 2005

(% of total imports)

Major export partners in UNECE, 2005

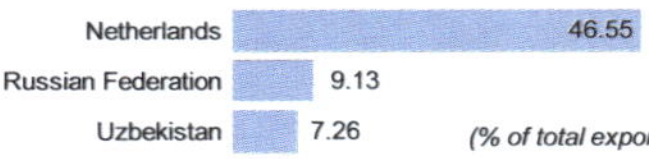

(% of total exports)

THE FORMER YUGOSLAV REPUBLIC OF MACEDONIA

Capital:	Skopje (467 257)
Two largest cities:	Kumanovo (103 205)
	Bitola (86 408)
Area (km²):	25 713
Total population:	2 036 855
Population density (per km²):	79
Official languages:	Macedonian
Date joined UN:	8 April 1993
National currency:	Macedonian denar (MKD)
National statistical office:	State Statistical Office http://www.stat.gov.mk/

Time: UTC +1h

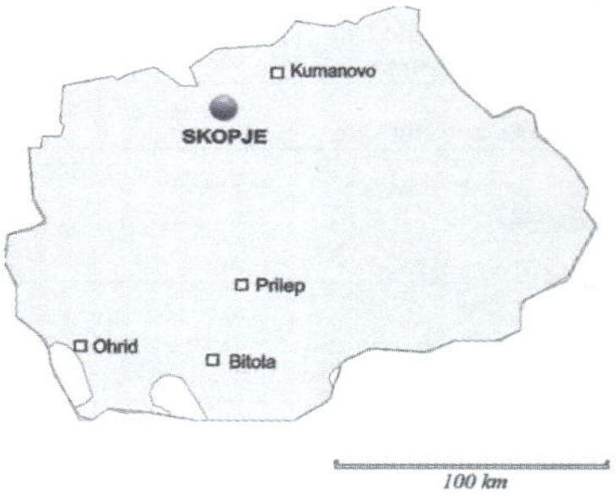

Population by age, 2005

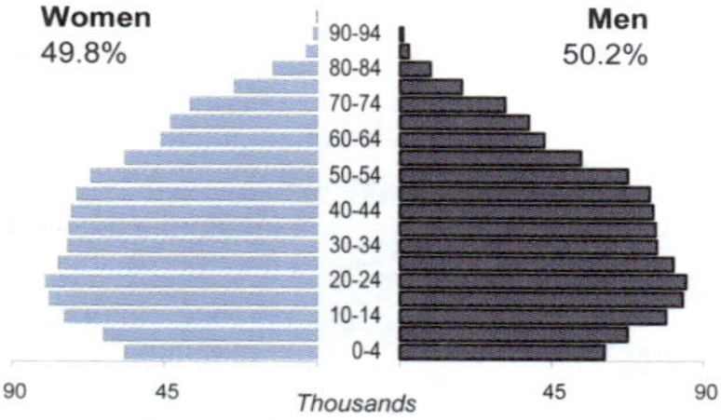

Legal marital status, population aged 18+, 2002

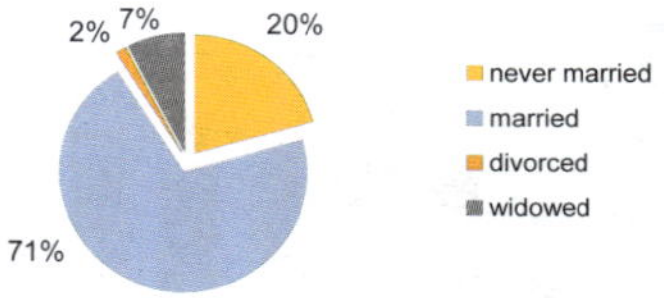

Life expectancy (in years), 2003:	at birth	at 65
Women:	76	15
Men:	71	13

Median age (in years), 2005:	
Women:	35
Men:	34

	percentage of total population
Foreign born:	..
Foreigners in population:	..

Women in the labour force, 2004:	39.1%
Gender pay gap, 2002:	17.5%
Female government ministers: percentage of total for both sexes	..
Female central bank board members: percentage of total for both sexes	..
Female tertiary students, 2003-2004: percentage of total for both sexes	57%

Total fertility rate

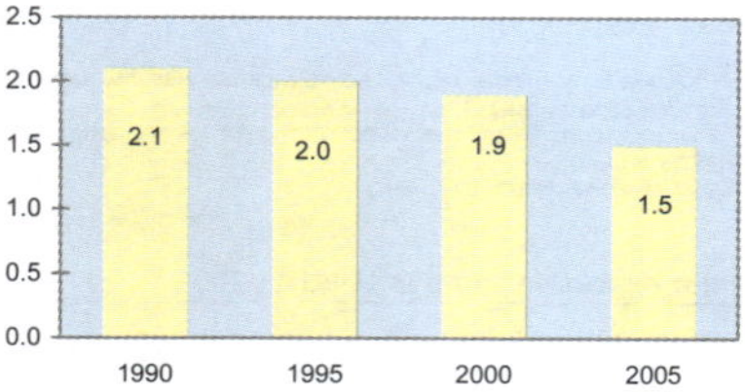

Parliament seats held by women (% of total)

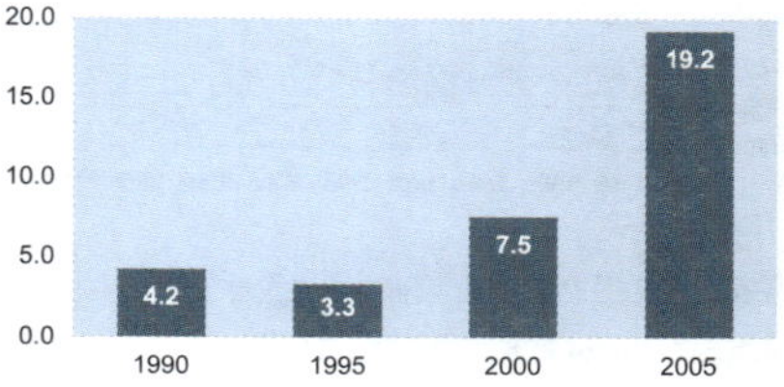

THE FORMER YUGOSLAV REPUBLIC OF MACEDONIA

	1999	2000	2001	2002	2003	2004	2005
Employment (% change over previous year)	..	0.8	9.0	-6.3	-2.9	-4.1	4.3
Unemployment rate (%)	32.4	32.2	30.5	31.9	36.7	37.2	37.3
Youth unemployment rate (%)	..	59.9	56.1	..	..	64.8	62.6

Economic activity rate, 2000

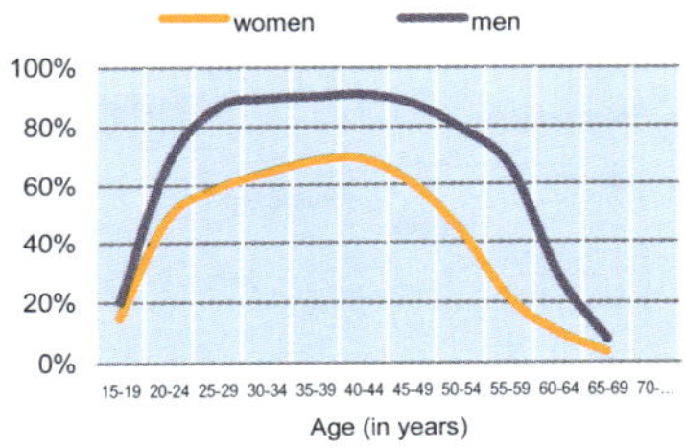

GDP at current prices	
in millions of US Dollars, PPP, 2005:	14 644
in millions of MKD, 2005:	284 226
GDP at constant 2000 prices, per capita	
US Dollars, PPP, 2005:	6 487
MKD, 2005:	128 191
Final consumption expenditure at 2000 prices, per capita, US Dollars, PPP, 2004:	5 750
Purchasing Power Parity (PPP)	
MKD per USD, 2005, US=1:	19.41
Gross external debt:	
in millions of US Dollars, 2005:	2 181
Exchange rate	
Annual average, MKD per USD, 2005:	49.28

Real GDP growth rate

% change over previous year

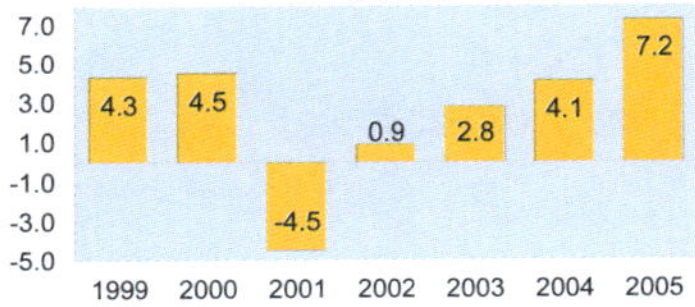

Consumer price index (annual average)

% change over previous year

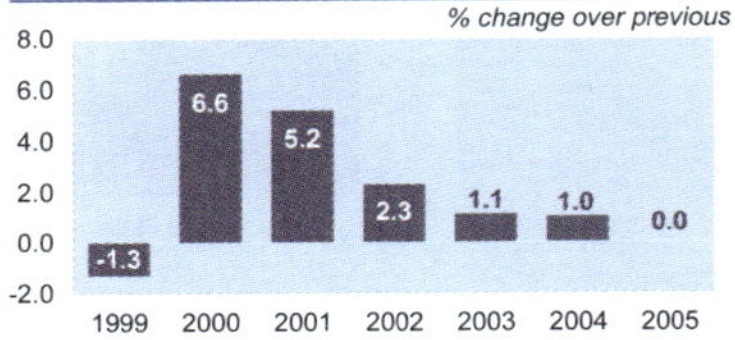

	% of GDP
Exports of goods and services, 2004:	40.2
Imports of goods and services, 2004:	60.5
External trade balance, 2004:	-20

GDP by major sectors, 2005

Employment in major sectors, 2005

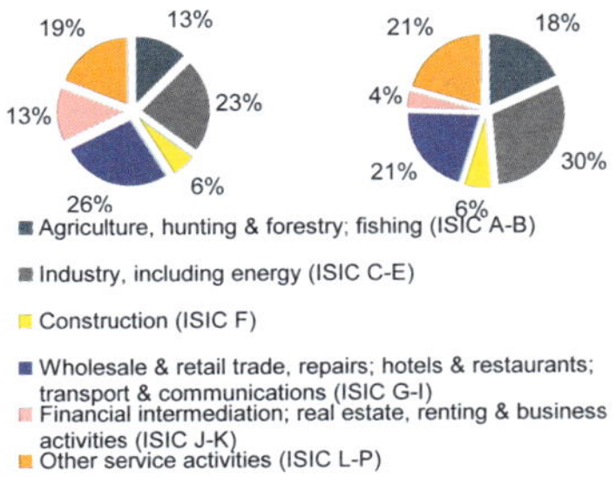

GDP in agriculture, industry, and services (2000=100)

Annual indices

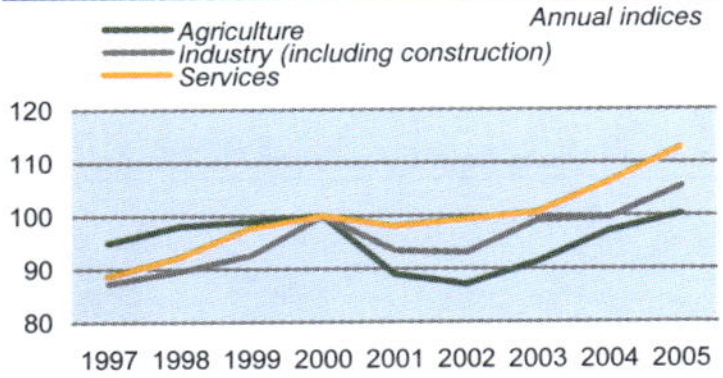

Major import partners from UNECE, 2005

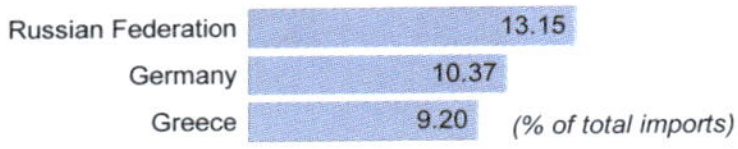

Major export partners in UNECE, 2005

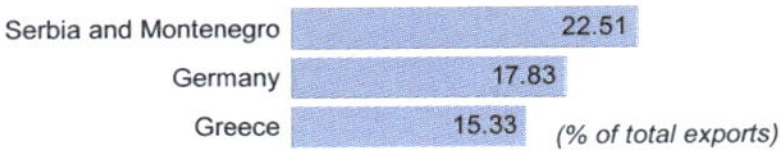

TURKEY

Capital:	Ankara (3 203 362)
Two largest cities:	Istanbul (8 803 468)
	Izmir (2 232 265)
Area (km²):	774 815
Total population:	73 195 000
Population density (per km²):	94
Official languages:	Turkish
Date joined UN:	24 October 1945
National currency:	New Turkish lira (TRY)
National statistical office:	Turkish Statistical Institute (TURKSTAT)
	http://www.die.gov.tr

Time: UTC +2h

Population by age, 2005

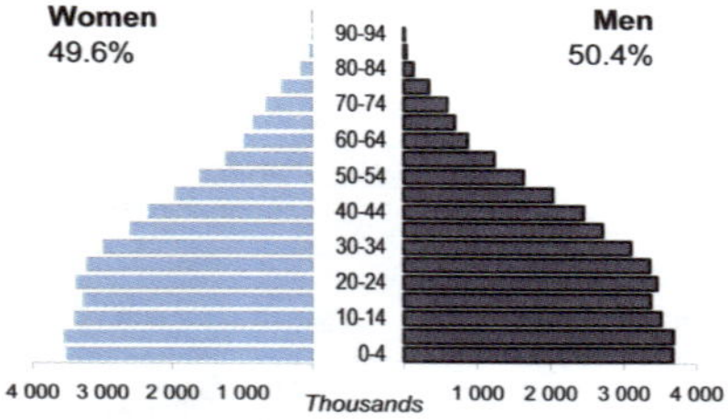

Legal marital status, population aged 18+

never married
married
divorced
widowed

Data not available

Life expectancy (in years), 2004:	at birth	at 65
Women:	74	n/a
Men:	69	n/a

Median age (in years), 2005:	
Women:	27
Men:	26

	percentage of total population
Foreign born, 2004:	0.15%
Foreigners in population, 2004:	0.4%

Women in the labour force, 2005:	25.9%
Gender pay gap:	..
Female government ministers, 2001: percentage of total for both sexes	0%
Female central bank board members, 2005: percentage of total for both sexes	20%
Female tertiary students, 2003-2004: percentage of total for both sexes	41.4%

Total fertility rate

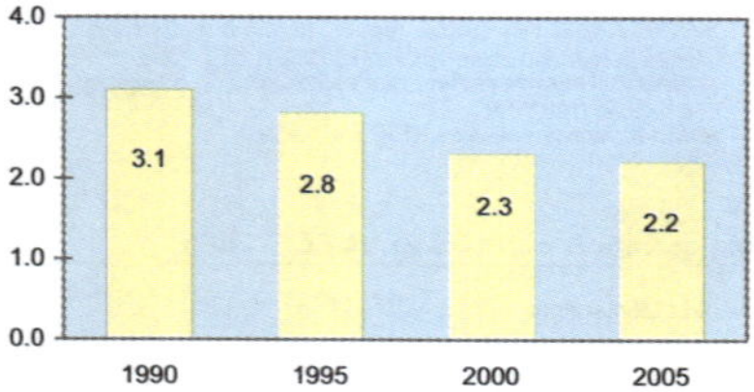

Parliament seats held by women (% of total)

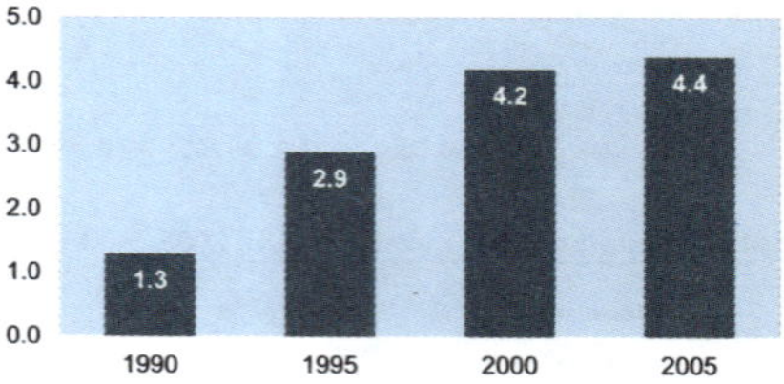

TURKEY

	1999	2000	2001	2002	2003	2004	2005
Employment (% change over previous year)	2.1	-0.4	-1.0	-1.8	-1.0	2.6	2.0
Unemployment rate (%)	7.6	6.5	8.3	10.3	10.5	10.3	10.3
Youth unemployment rate (%)	..	13.1	16.2	19.2	20.5	19.7	19.3

Economic activity rate, 2004

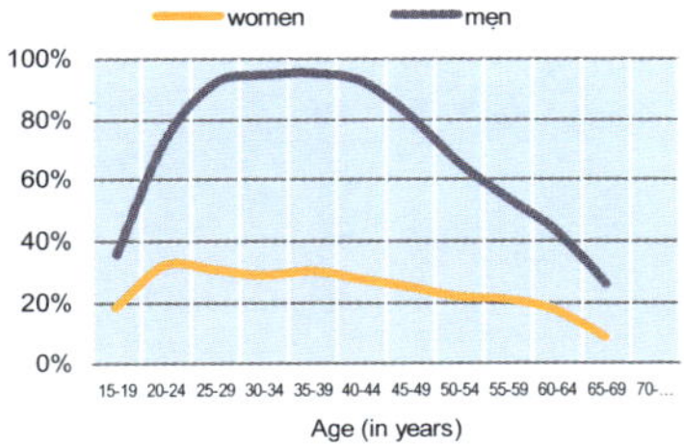

GDP at current prices	
in millions of US Dollars, PPP, 2005:	612 713
in millions of TRY, 2005:	487 202
GDP at constant 2000 prices, per capita	
US Dollars, PPP, 2005:	7 760
TRY, 2005:	2 104
Final consumption expenditure at 2000 prices, per capita, US Dollars, PPP, 2004:	5 839
Purchasing Power Parity (PPP)	
TRY per USD, 2005, US=1:	0.795
Gross external debt:	
in millions of US Dollars, 2005:	170 594
Exchange rate	
Annual average, TRY per USD, 2005:	1.344

Real GDP growth rate

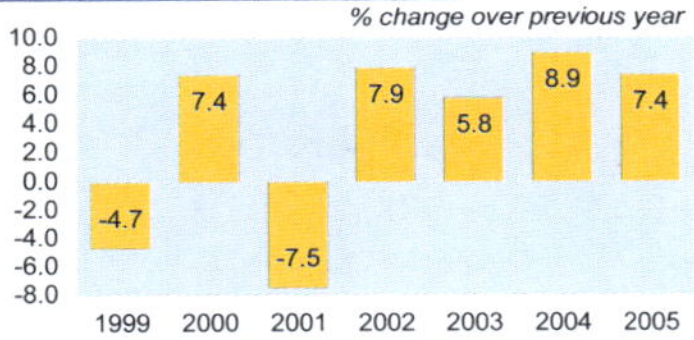

Consumer price index (annual average)

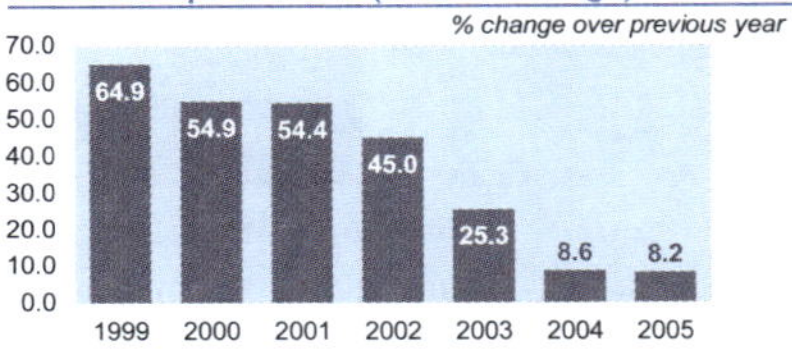

	% of GDP
Exports of goods and services, 2004:	28.9
Imports of goods and services, 2004:	34.7
External trade balance, 2004:	-5.8

GDP by major sectors, 2005

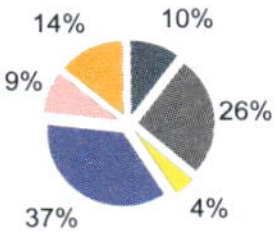

Employment in major sectors, 2005

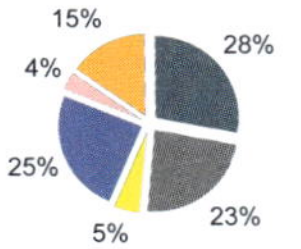

- Agriculture, hunting & forestry; fishing (ISIC A-B)
- Industry, including energy (ISIC C-E)
- Construction (ISIC F)
- Wholesale & retail trade, repairs; hotels & restaurants; transport & communications (ISIC G-I)
- Financial intermediation; real estate, renting & business activities (ISIC J-K)
- Other service activities (ISIC L-P)

GDP in agriculture, industry, and services (2000=100)

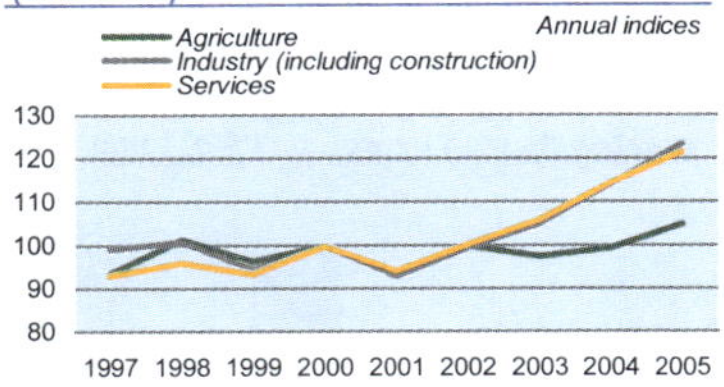

Major import partners from UNECE, 2005

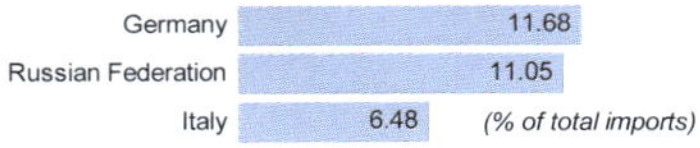

Major export partners in UNECE, 2005

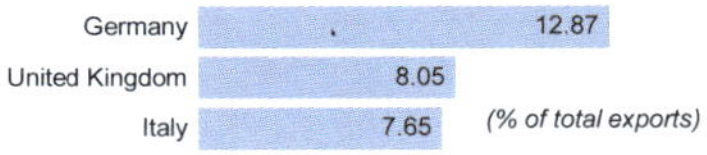

TURKMENISTAN

Capital:	Ashgabat (604 700)
Two largest cities:	Turkmenbashi (203 000)
	Dashhowuz (165 400)
Area (km²):	488 100
Total population:	4 834 000
Population density (per km²):	10
Official languages:	Turkmen
Date joined UN:	2 March 1992
National currency:	Turkmen manat (TMM)
National statistical office:	State Committee of Turkmenistan on Statistics
	http://www.turkmenistan.gov.tm

Time: UTC +5h

Population by age, 2005

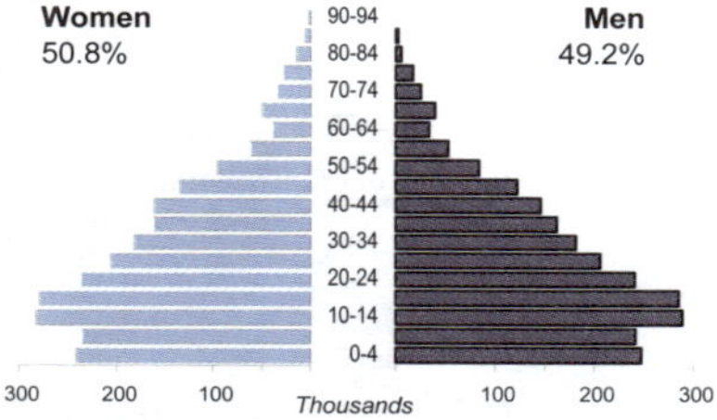

Life expectancy (in years), 2003:	at birth	at 65
Women:	72	15
Men:	66	12

Median age (in years), 2005:	
Women:	24
Men:	23

	percentage of total population
Foreign born:	..
Foreigners in population:	..

Total fertility rate

Legal marital status, population aged 18+

Data not available

never married
married
divorced
widowed

Women in the labour force:	..
Gender pay gap:	..
Female government ministers: percentage of total for both sexes	..
Female central bank board members: percentage of total for both sexes	..
Female tertiary students: percentage of total for both sexes	..

Parliament seats held by women (% of total)

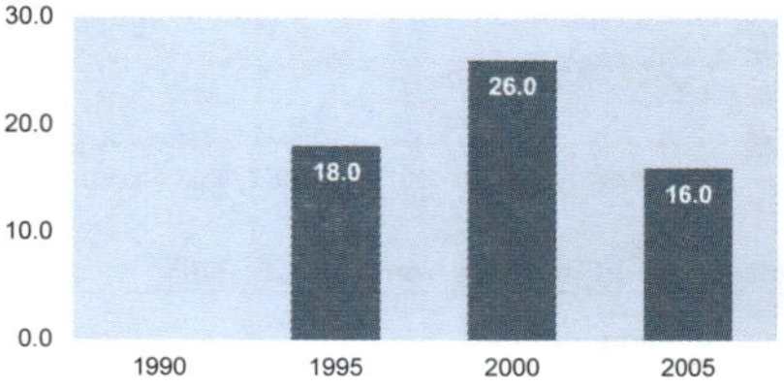

TURKMENISTAN

	1999	2000	2001	2002	2003	2004	2005
Employment (% change over previous year)	0.7	3.0	2.0	2.5	2.2	..	..
Unemployment rate (%)	..	..	..	..	..	..	..
Youth unemployment rate (%)	..	..	..	..	..	..	..

Economic activity rate

Real GDP growth rate

% change over previous year

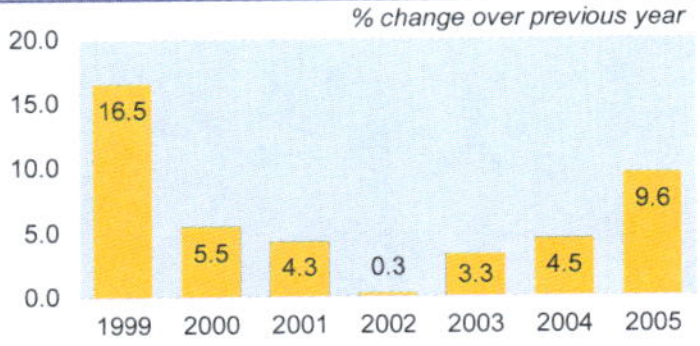

% of GDP

Exports of goods and services:	..
Imports of goods and services:	..
External trade balance:	..

GDP in agriculture, industry, and services (2000=100)

Annual indices

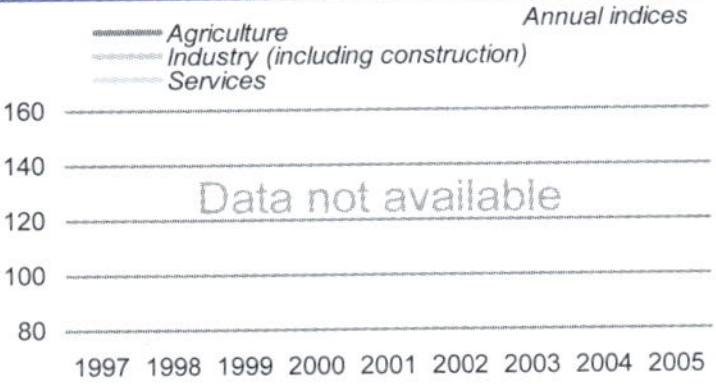

Major import partners from UNECE, 2000

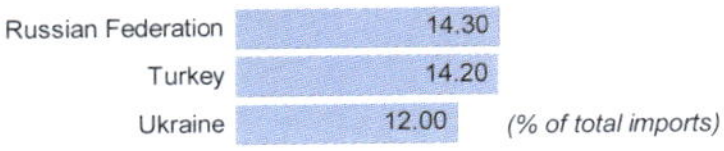

(% of total imports)

GDP at current prices	
in millions of US Dollars, PPP, 2004:	24 453
in millions of TMM, 2004:	64 032 495
GDP at constant 2000 prices, per capita	
US Dollars, PPP, 2005:	5 067
TMM, 2005:	6 565 645
Final consumption expenditure at 2000 prices, per capita, US Dollars, PPP:	..
Purchasing Power Parity (PPP)	
TMM per USD, 2004, US=1:	2 619
Gross external debt:	
in millions of US Dollars, 2004:	2 500
Exchange rate	
Annual average, TMM per USD, 2005:	5 200

Consumer price index (annual average)

% change over previous year

GDP by major sectors

Employment in major sectors

- Agriculture, hunting & forestry; fishing (ISIC A-B)
- Industry, including energy (ISIC C-E)
- Construction (ISIC F)
- Wholesale & retail trade, repairs; hotels & restaurants; transport & communications (ISIC G-I)
- Financial intermediation; real estate, renting & business activities (ISIC J-K)
- Other service activities (ISIC L-P)

Major export partners in UNECE, 2000

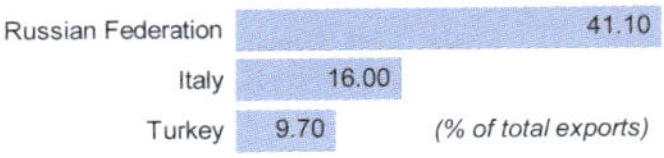

(% of total exports)

UKRAINE

Capital:	Kiev (2 660 401)
Two largest cities:	Kharkiv (1 464 740)
	Dnipropétrovsk (1 056 497)
Area (km²):	603 700
Total population:	47 271 271
Population density (per km²):	78
Official languages:	Ukrainian
Date joined UN:	24 October 1945
National currency:	Ukrainian hryvnia (UAH)
National statistical office:	The State Committee of Statistics
	http://www.ukrstat.gov.ua/

Time: UTC +2h

Population by age, 2004

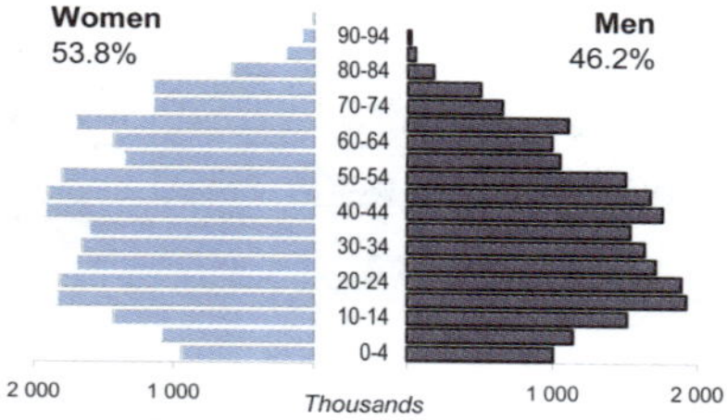

Life expectancy (in years), 2005:	at birth	at 65
Women:	73	15
Men:	62	12

Median age (in years), 2004:	
Women:	42
Men:	35

	percentage of total population
Foreign born:	..
Foreigners in population, 2004:	0.6%

Total fertility rate

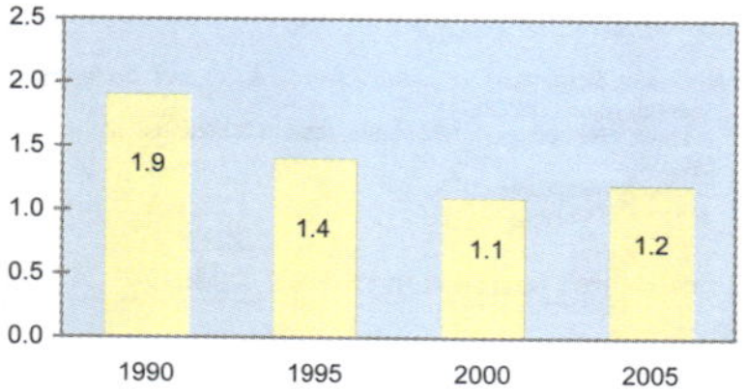

Legal marital status, population aged 18+

never married
married
divorced
widowed

Data not available

Women in the labour force, 2005:	48.5%
Gender pay gap, 2005:	29.1%
Female government ministers, 2006: percentage of total for both sexes	0%
Female central bank board members, 2005: percentage of total for both sexes	7.1%
Female tertiary students: percentage of total for both sexes	..

Parliament seats held by women (% of total)

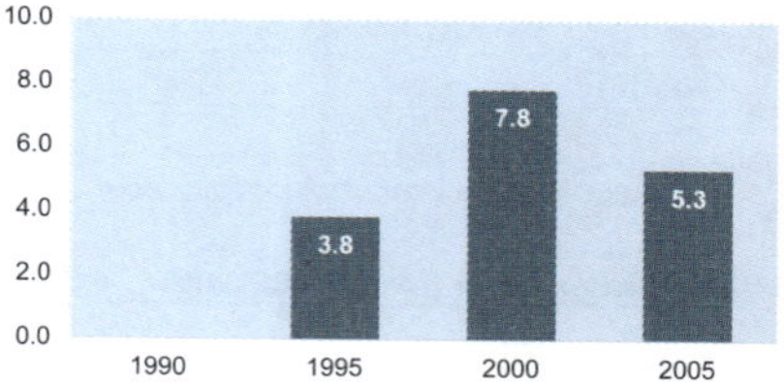

UKRAINE

	1999	2000	2001	2002	2003	2004	2005
Employment (% change over previous year)	..	1.1	-1.0	0.6	0.4	0.7	1.9
Unemployment rate (%)	11.6	11.6	10.9	9.6	9.1	8.6	7.2
Youth unemployment rate (%)	..	24.2	22.3	19.1	16.7	15.7	14.9

Economic activity rate, 2002

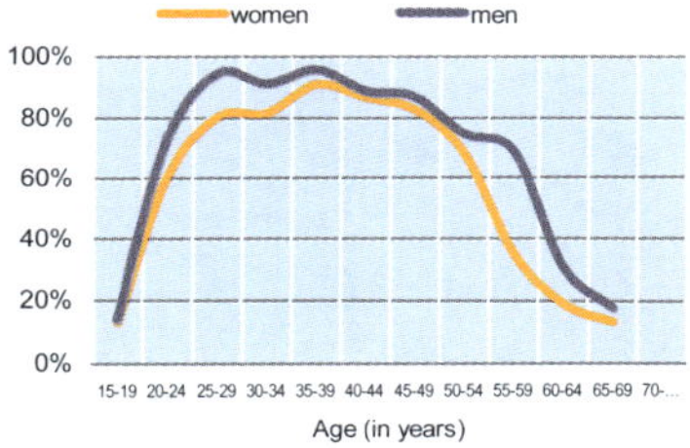

GDP at current prices	
in millions of US Dollars, PPP, 2005:	332 181
in millions of UAH, 2005:	424 741
GDP at constant 2000 prices, per capita	
US Dollars, PPP, 2005:	6 188
UAH, 2005:	5 257
Final consumption expenditure at 2000 prices, per capita, US Dollars, PPP, 2005:	5 018
Purchasing Power Parity (PPP)	
UAH per USD, 2005, US=1:	1.279
Gross external debt:	
in millions of US Dollars, 2005:	38 818
Exchange rate	
Annual average, UAH per USD, 2005:	5.125

Real GDP growth rate

% change over previous year

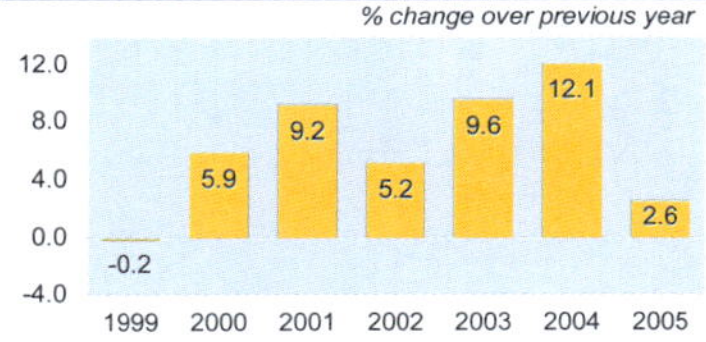

Consumer price index (annual average)

% change over previous year

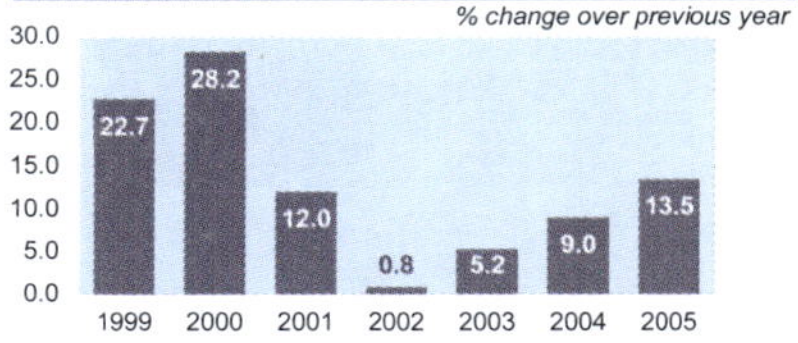

	% of GDP
Exports of goods and services, 2005:	53.5
Imports of goods and services, 2005:	52.6
External trade balance, 2005:	0.9

GDP in agriculture, industry, and services (2000=100)

Annual indices

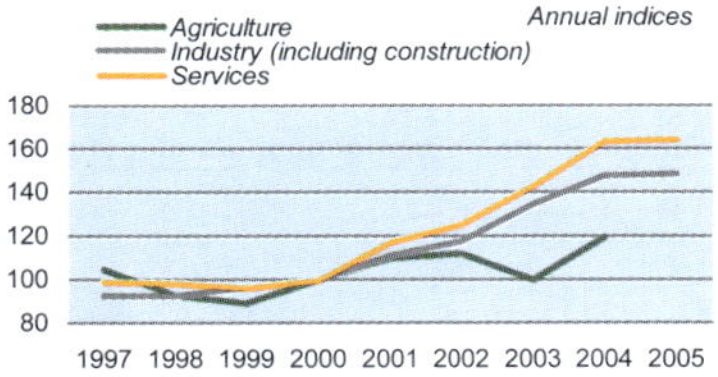

GDP by major sectors

Employment in major sectors, 2005

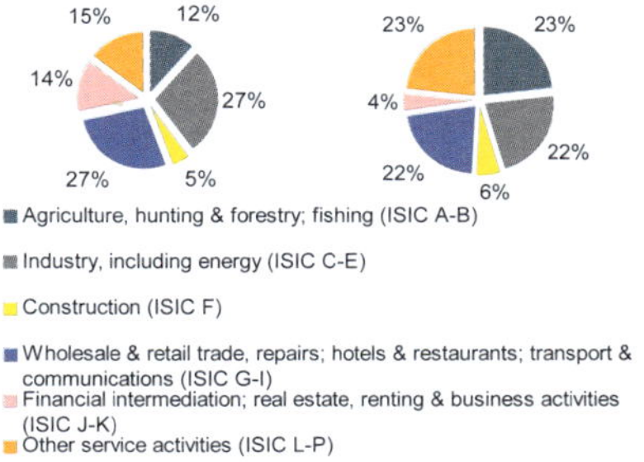

Major import partners from UNECE, 2005

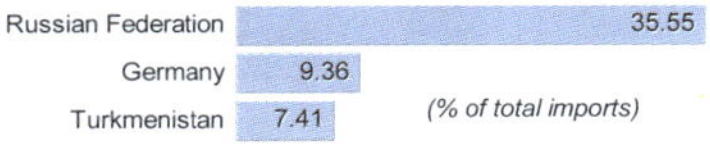

Major export partners in UNECE, 2005

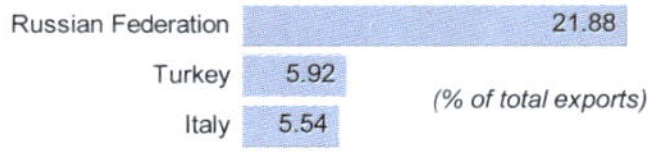

UNITED KINGDOM

Capital:	London (7 172 091)
Two largest cities:	Birmingham (970 892)
	Glasgow (629 501)
Area (km²):	242 910
Total population:	60 226 500
Population density (per km²):	248
Official languages:	English
Date joined UN:	24 October 1945
National currency:	Pound sterling (GBP)
National statistical office:	Office for National Statistics http://www.statistics.gov.uk/

Time: UTC

Population by age, 2005

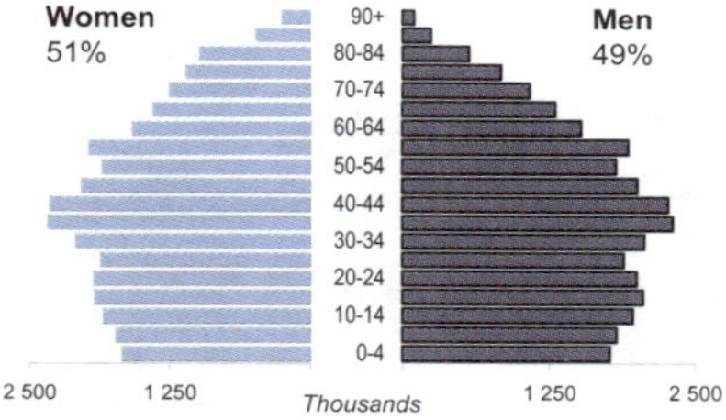

Life expectancy (in years), 2005:	at birth	at 65
Women:	81	20
Men:	77	17

Median age (in years), 2005:	
Women:	40
Men:	38

	percentage of total population
Foreign born, 2004:	8.8%
Foreigners in population, 2004:	5%

Legal marital status, population aged 18+

never married
married
divorced
widowed

Data not available

Women in the labour force, 2005:	46.2%
Gender pay gap, 2005:	20%
Female government ministers: percentage of total for both sexes	..
Female central bank board members, 2005: percentage of total for both sexes	36.8%
Female tertiary students, 2004-2005: percentage of total for both sexes	57.2%

Total fertility rate

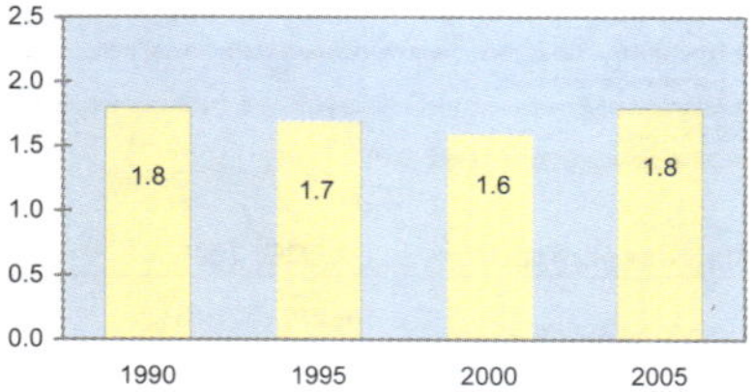

Parliament seats held by women (% of total)

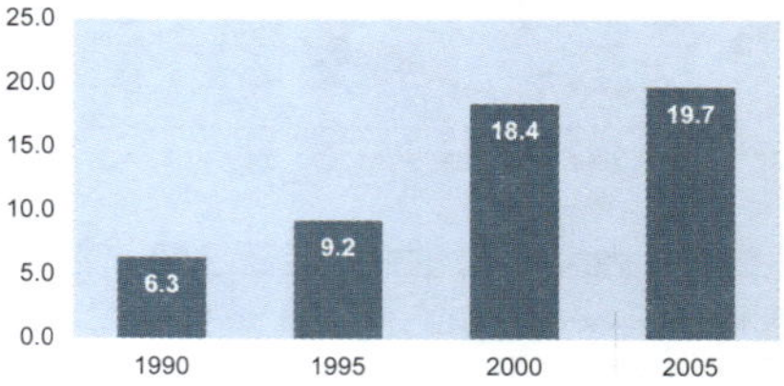

UNITED KINGDOM

	1999	2000	2001	2002	2003	2004	2005
Employment (% change over previous year)	1.4	1.2	0.8	0.8	1.0	1.0	0.6
Unemployment rate (%)	5.9	5.4	5.0	5.1	4.9	4.7	4.7
Youth unemployment rate (%)	..	12.1	11.7	12.0	12.2	12.1	12.9

Economic activity rate, 2004

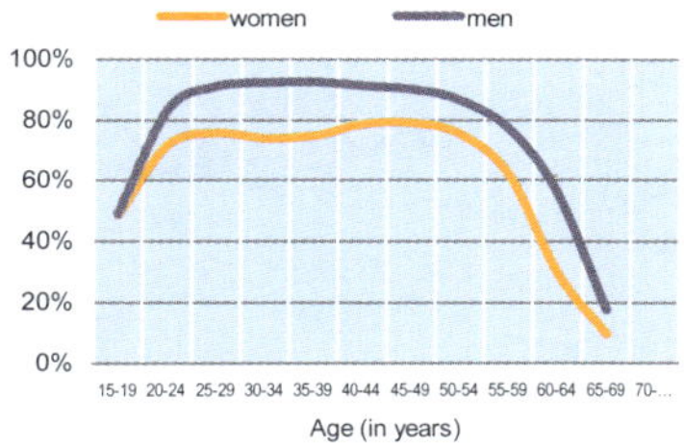

GDP at current prices	
in millions of US Dollars, PPP, 2005:	1 941 954
in millions of GBP, 2005:	1 225 339
GDP at constant 2000 prices, per capita	
US Dollars, PPP, 2005:	28 247
GBP, 2005:	17 878
Final consumption expenditure at 2000 prices, per capita, US Dollars, PPP, 2005:	24 394
Purchasing Power Parity (PPP)	
GBP per USD, 2005, US=1:	0.631
Gross external debt:	
in millions of US Dollars, 2005:	7 313 767
Exchange rate	
Annual average, GBP per USD, 2005:	0.55

Real GDP growth rate

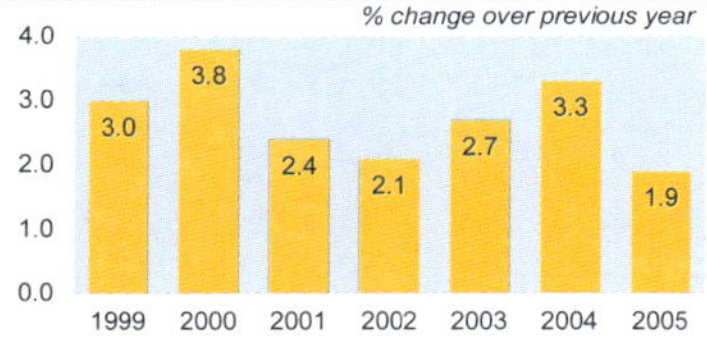

Consumer price index (annual average)

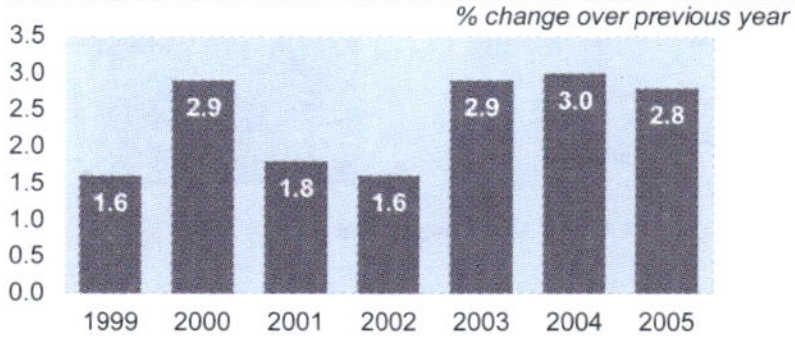

	% of GDP
Exports of goods and services, 2005:	26.6
Imports of goods and services, 2005:	30.2
External trade balance, 2005:	-3.7

GDP by major sectors

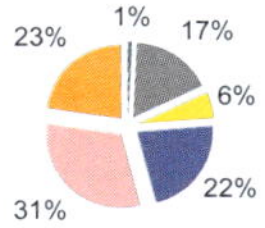

Employment in major sectors, 2004

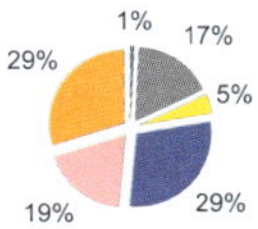

- Agriculture, hunting & forestry; fishing (ISIC A-B)
- Industry, including energy (ISIC C-E)
- Construction (ISIC F)
- Wholesale & retail trade, repairs; hotels & restaurants; transport & communications (ISIC G-I)
- Financial intermediation; real estate, renting & business activities (ISIC J-K)
- Other service activities (ISIC L-P)

GDP in agriculture, industry, and services (2000=100)

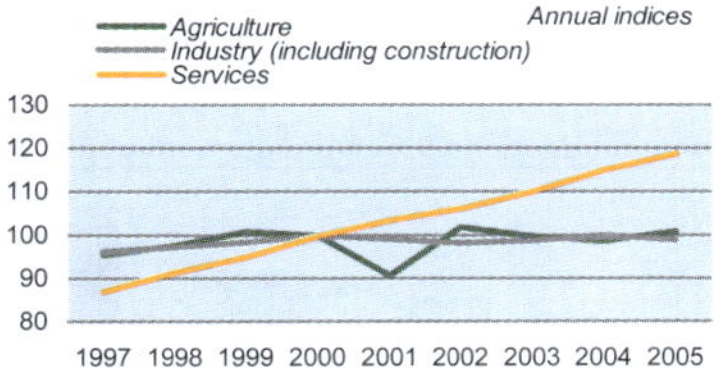

Major import partners from UNECE, 2005

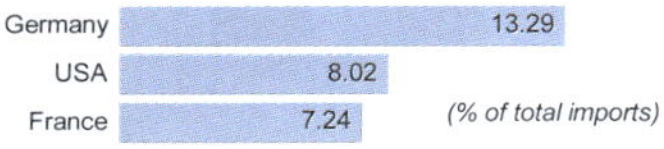

Major export partners in UNECE, 2005

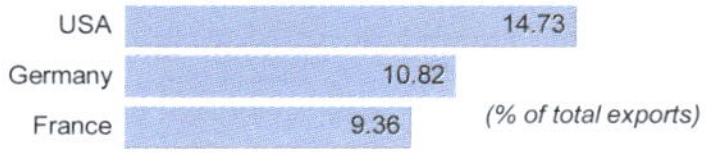

UNITED STATES

Capital:	Washington, D.C. (563 364)
Two largest cities:	New York (8 085 742)
	Los Angeles (3 819 951)
Area (km²):	9 629 090
Total population:	296 410 404
Population density (per km²):	31
Official languages:	English
Date joined UN:	24 October 1945
National currency:	US dollar (USD)
National statistical office:	
	Federal Statistical Office of the United States of America
	http://www.fedstats.gov/

Time: UTC -10h to -5h

Population by age, 2005

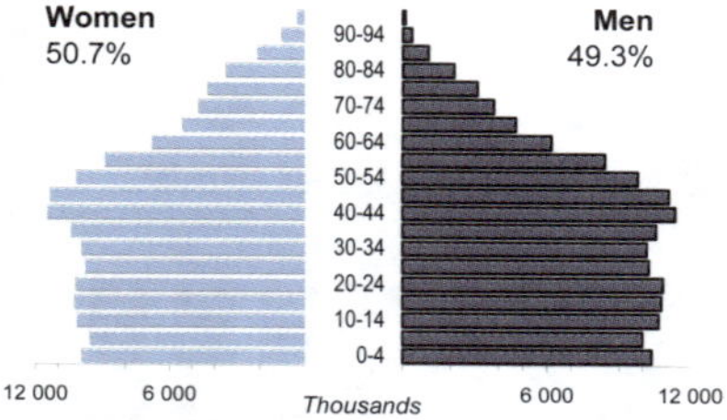

Life expectancy (in years), 2004:	at birth	at 65
Women:	80	20
Men:	75	17

Median age (in years), 2005:	
Women:	38
Men:	35

	percentage of total population
Foreign born, 2005:	12.4%
Foreigners in population, 2005:	7.2%

Legal marital status, population aged 18+

Data not available

never married
married
divorced
widowed

Women in the labour force, 2005:	46.4%
Gender pay gap, 2004:	21.4%
Female government ministers: percentage of total for both sexes	..
Female central bank board members, 2005: percentage of total for both sexes	20%
Female tertiary students, 2003-2004: percentage of total for both sexes	57.1%

Total fertility rate

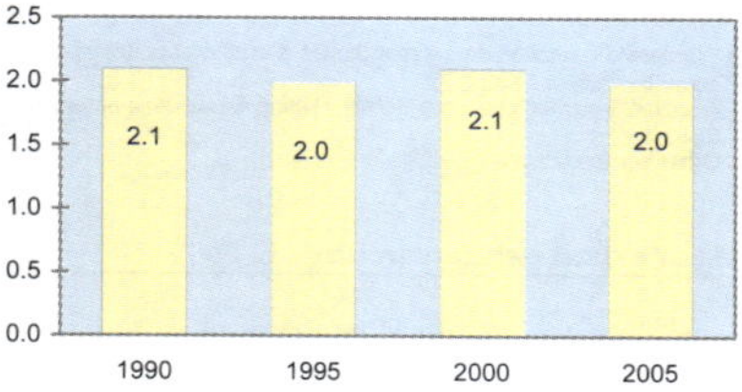

Parliament seats held by women (% of total)

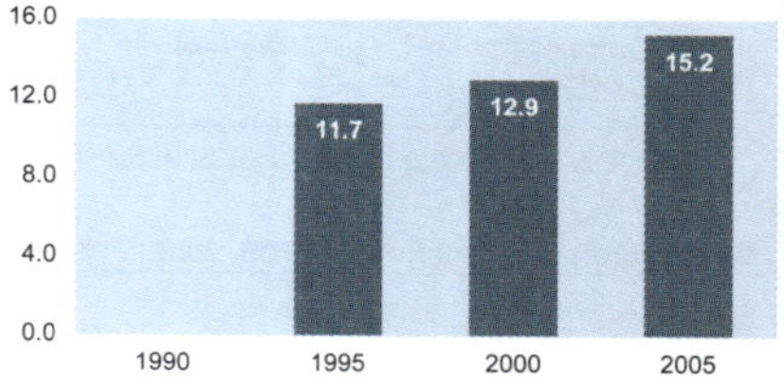

UNITED STATES

	1999	2000	2001	2002	2003	2004	2005
Employment (% change over previous year)	1.5	2.5	0.0	-0.3	0.9	1.1	..
Unemployment rate (%)	4.2	4.0	4.8	5.8	6.0	5.5	5.1
Youth unemployment rate (%)	..	9.3	10.6	12.0	12.4	11.8	11.3

Economic activity rate, 2001

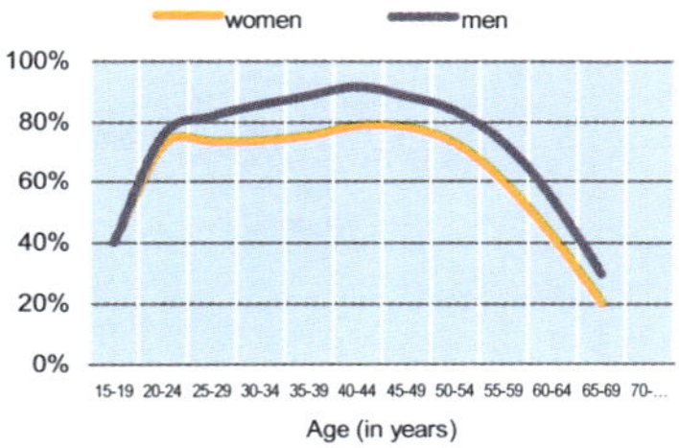

GDP at current prices	
in millions of US Dollars, PPP, 2005:	12 455 800
in millions of USD, 2005:	12 455 800
GDP at constant 2000 prices, per capita	
US Dollars, PPP, 2005:	37 241
USD, 2005:	37 241
Final consumption expenditure at 2000 prices, per capita, US Dollars, PPP, 2005:	31 855
Purchasing Power Parity (PPP)	
USD per USD, 2005, US=1:	1
Gross external debt:	
in millions of US Dollars, 2005:	9 476 403
Exchange rate	
Annual average, USD per USD, 2005:	1

Real GDP growth rate

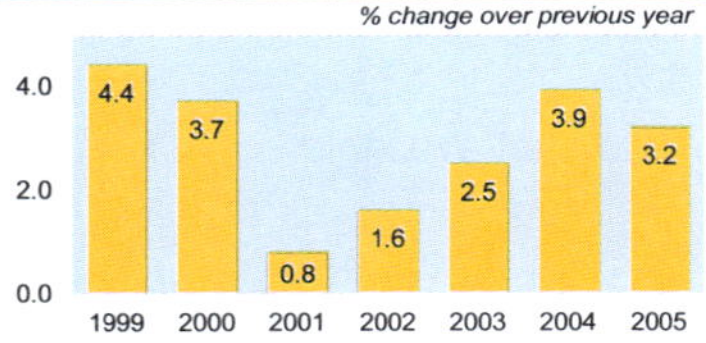

Consumer price index (annual average)

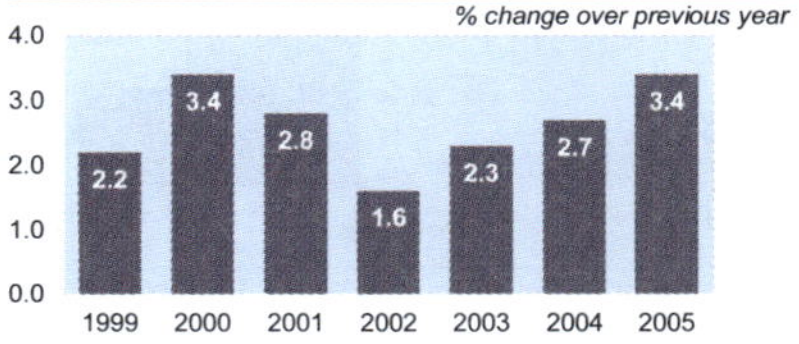

	% of GDP
Exports of goods and services, 2005:	10.5
Imports of goods and services, 2005:	16.2
External trade balance, 2005:	-5.8

GDP in agriculture, industry, and services (2000=100)

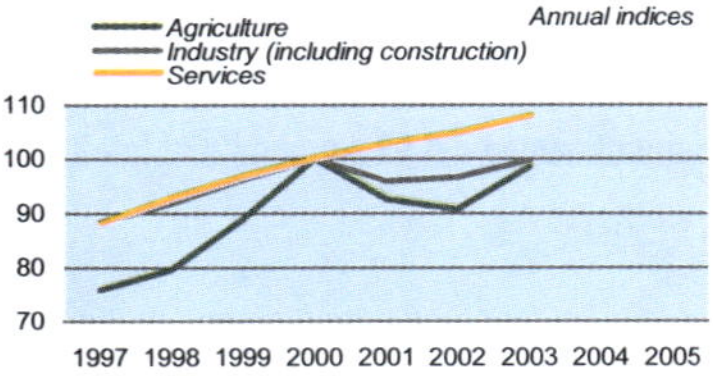

GDP by major sectors, 2003

Employment in major sectors, 2004

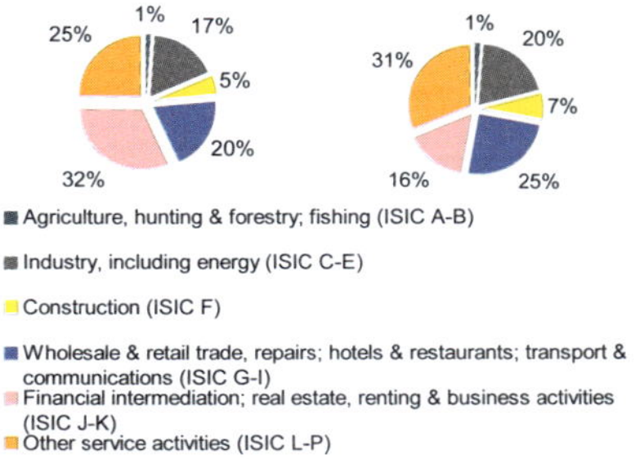

Major import partners from UNECE, 2005

Major export partners in UNECE, 2005

UZBEKISTAN

Capital:	Tashkent (2 147 700)
Two largest cities:	Namangan (376 600)
	Samarqand (362 200)
Area (km²):	447 400
Total population:	26 590 000
Population density (per km²):	59
Official languages:	Uzbek
Date joined UN:	2 March 1992
National currency:	Uzbekistani sum (UZS)
National statistical office:	

State Committee on Statistics of the Republic of Uzbekistan

http://www.stat.uz/

Time: UTC +5h

Population by age, 2005

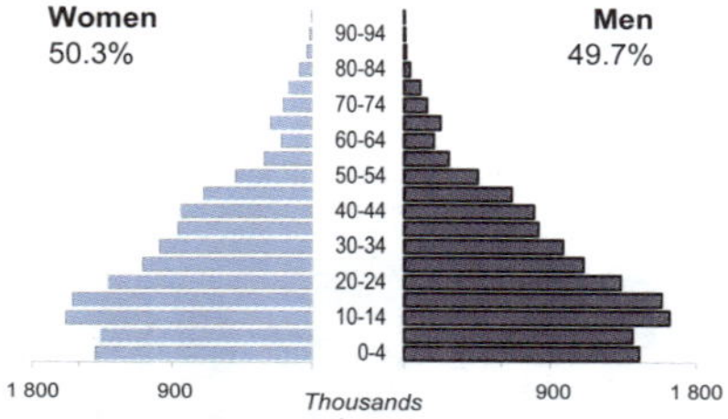

Life expectancy (in years), 2005:	at birth	at 65
Women:	73	15
Men:	68	13

Median age (in years), 2005:	
Women:	23
Men:	22

	percentage of total population
Foreign born:	..
Foreigners in population:	..

Total fertility rate

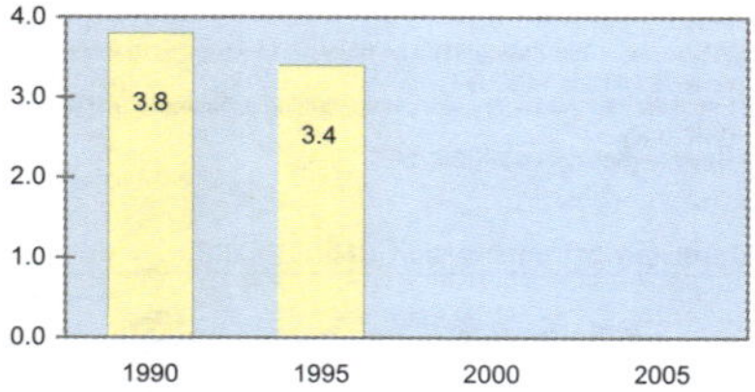

Legal marital status, population aged 18+

Data not available

never married
married
divorced
widowed

Women in the labour force:	..
Gender pay gap:	..
Female government ministers: percentage of total for both sexes	..
Female central bank board members: percentage of total for both sexes	..
Female tertiary students: percentage of total for both sexes	..

Parliament seats held by women (% of total)

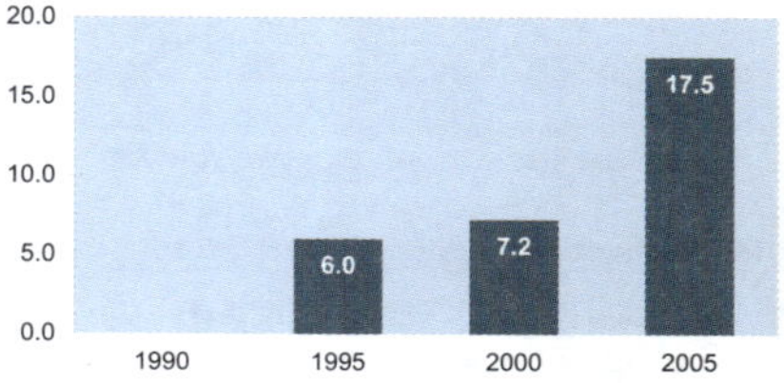

UZBEKISTAN

	1999	2000	2001	2002	2003	2004	2005
Employment (% change over previous year)	1.0	1.1	1.7	2.2	2.7	3.4	..
Unemployment rate (%)	0.4	0.4	0.4	0.4	0.3	..	..
Youth unemployment rate (%)	..	..	..	..	..	..	..

Economic activity rate

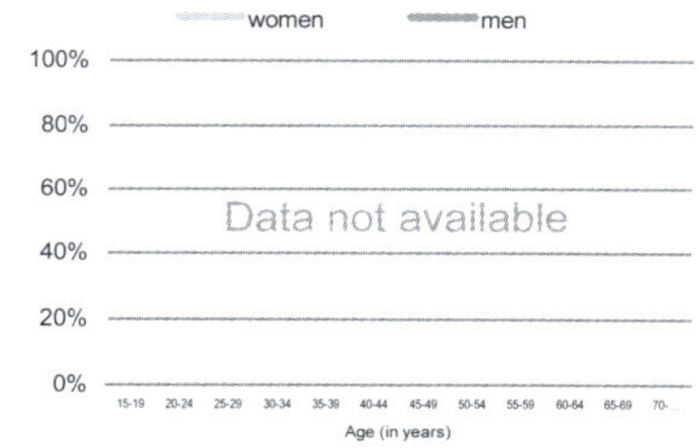

GDP at current prices	
in millions of US Dollars, PPP:	..
in millions of UZS, 2005:	15 210 000
GDP at constant 2000 prices, per capita	
US Dollars, PPP:	..
UZS, 2005:	160 378
Final consumption expenditure at 2000 prices, per capita, US Dollars, PPP:	..
Purchasing Power Parity (PPP)	
UZS per USD, US=1:	..
Gross external debt:	
in millions of US Dollars, 2004:	4 800
Exchange rate	
Annual average, UZS per USD, 2005:	1 114

Real GDP growth rate

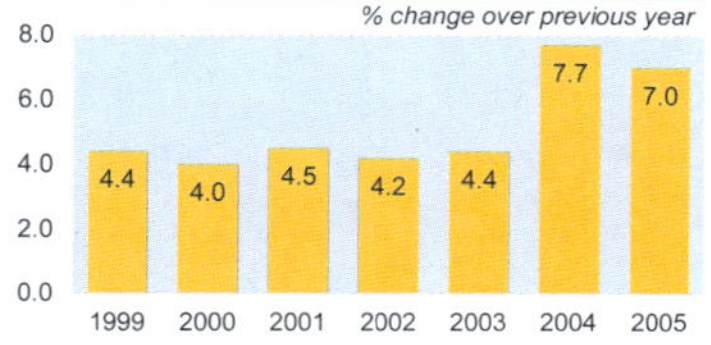

Consumer price index (annual average)

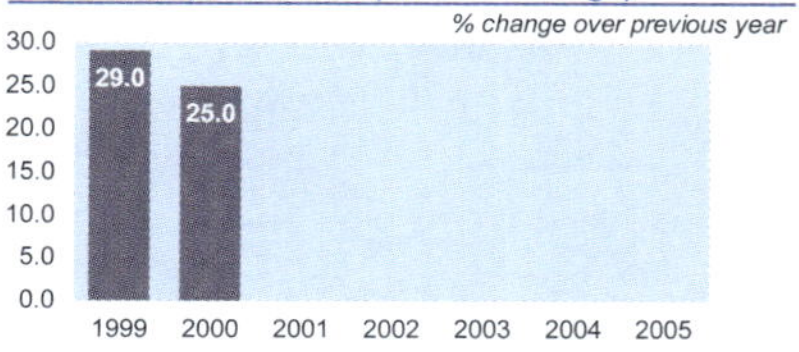

	% of GDP
Exports of goods and services:	..
Imports of goods and services:	..
External trade balance, 2001:	-0.3

GDP by major sectors

Employment in major sectors, 2004

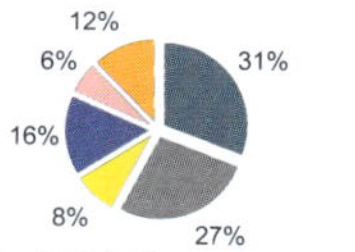

- Agriculture, hunting & forestry; fishing (ISIC A-B)
- Industry, including energy (ISIC C-E)
- Construction (ISIC F)
- Wholesale & retail trade, repairs; hotels & restaurants; transport & communications (ISIC G-I)
- Financial intermediation; real estate, renting & business activities (ISIC J-K)
- Other service activities (ISIC L-P)

GDP in agriculture, industry, and services (2000=100)

Major import partners from UNECE, 2005

Major export partners in UNECE, 2005

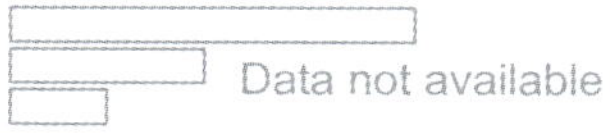

A territory is an area that is constitutionally linked to one of the UNECE member countries and does not possess full political independence. Overseas territories of UNECE member countries that meet the following criteria are included in this publication:

- the governing country is a member of the UNECE
- the territory is located within the geographical region of the UNECE
- profiles of the governing country, with the exception of the data mentioned in the explanatory notes, do not include data related to the territory
- the territory is separately reported in the United Nations Demographic Yearbook (Department of Economic and Social Affairs, 0Hhttp://unstats.un.org/unsd/demographic/products/dyb/default.htm).

TERRITORIES PROFILES

FAROE ISLANDS (DENMARK)

Time: UTC

Capital:	Torshavn (Hoyvik and Argir) (17422)
Two largest cities:	Klaksvik (4670)
	Fuglafjoerdur (1532)
Area (km²):	1 400
Total population:	48 219
Population density (per km²):	35
Official languages:	Faroese and Danish
Date joined UN:	n/a
Currency:	Danish krone (DKK)
Statistical Office:	Statistical Office of the Faroe Islands http://www.hagstova.fo

Population by age, 2004

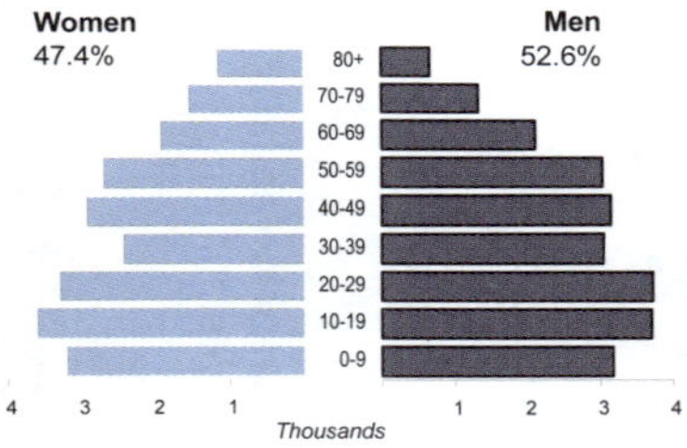

Major import partners from UNECE, 2004

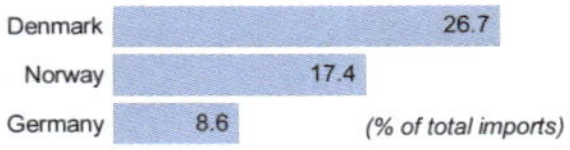

Major export partners in UNECE, 2004

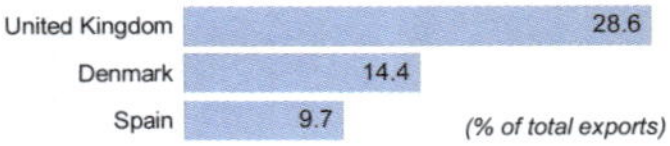

Life expectancy (in years), 2003: at birth		at 65
Women:	81	20
Men:	77	17

Median age (in years), 2004:	
Women:	36
Men:	35

GREENLAND (DENMARK)

Time: UTC

Capital:	Nuuk (14 874)
Two largest cities:	Sisimiut (6 109)
	Ilulissat (5 005)
Area (km²):	2 166 000
Total population:	56 901
Population density (per km²):	0.03
Official languages:	Greenlandic and Danish
Date joined UN:	n/a
Currency:	Danish krone (DKK)
Statistical Office:	Statistical office of Greenland http://www.statgreen.gl

Population by age, 2005

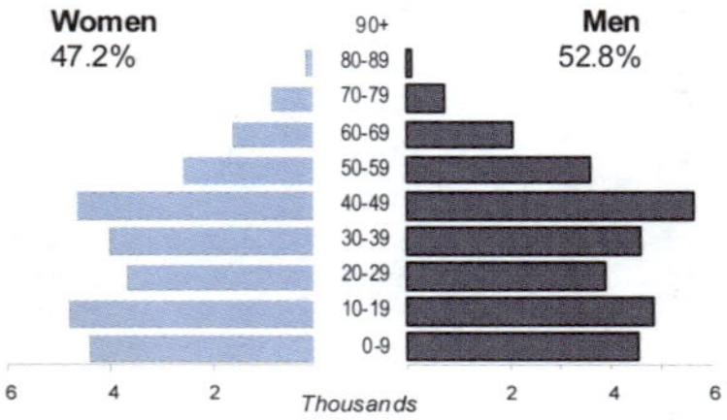

Major import partners from UNECE, 2006

Major export partners in UNECE, 2006

Life expectancy (in years), 2004: at birth		at 65
Women:	70	14
Men:	65	11

Median age (in years), 2006:	
Women:	32
Men:	33

SAINT PIERRE AND MIQUELON (FRANCE)

Time: UTC - 3h

Capital:	Saint Pierre (5618)
Second municipality:	Miquelon-Langlade (698)
Area (km²):	242
Total population:	6 316
Population density (per km²):	26
Official languages:	French
Date joined UN:	n/a
Currency:	Euro (EUR)
Statistical Office:	Prefecture de Saint-Pierre-et-Miquelon http://www.saint-pierre-et-miquelon.pref.gouv.fr/

Major import partners from UNECE, 2002

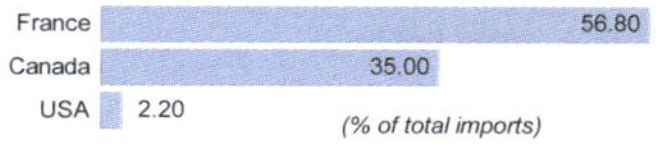

Major export partners in UNECE, 2002

Population by age, 1999:

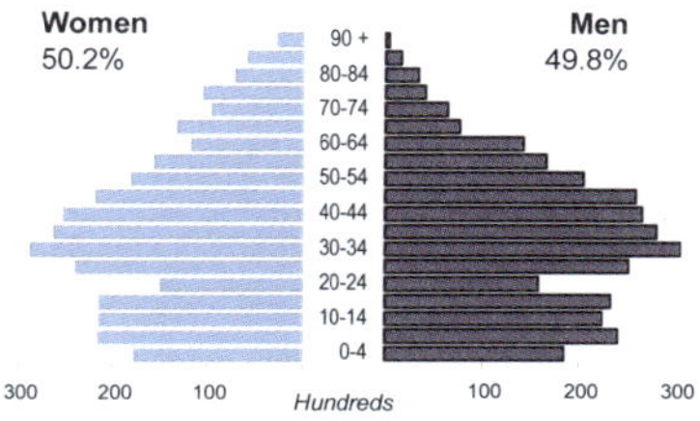

Life expectancy (in years), 2006:	at birth	at 65
Women:	81	..
Men:	76	..

Median age (in years), 1999:	
Women:	37
Men:	35

BERMUDA (UNITED KINGDOM)

Time: UTC -4

Capital:	Hamilton
Area (km²):	53
Total population:	65 365
Population density (per km²):	1 233
Official languages:	English
Date joined UN:	n/a
Currency:	Bermuda dollar (BMD)
Statistical office:	Department of Statistics http://www.statistics.gov.bm/

Major import partners from UNECE, 2005

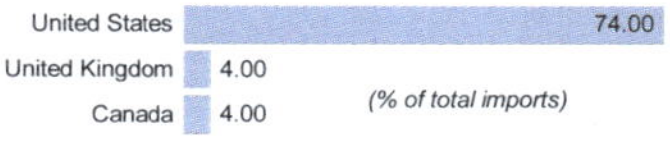

Population by age, 2005

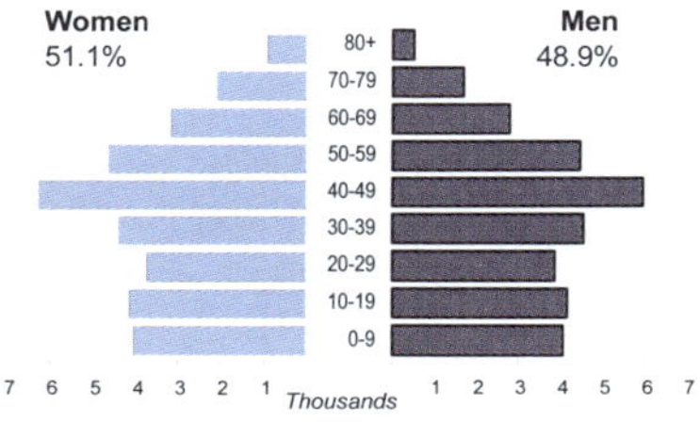

Life expectancy (in years), 2000: at birth		at 65
Women:	80	..
Men:	75	..

Median age (in years), 2005:	
Women:	41
Men:	39

GIBRALTAR (UNITED KINGDOM)

Time: UTC +1h

Capital:	Gibraltar
Area (km^2):	6
Total population:	27 447
Population density (per km^2):	4732
Official languages:	English
Date joined UN:	n/a
Currency:	Pound sterling (GBP)
Statistical Office:	Government of Gibraltar Statistics Office http://www.gibraltar.gov.gi/

Major import partners from UNECE, 2005

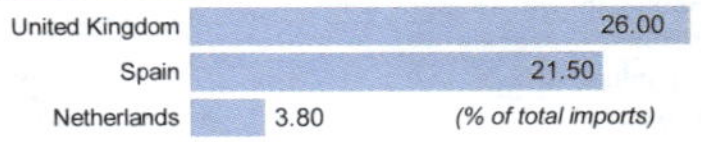

Population by age, 2001

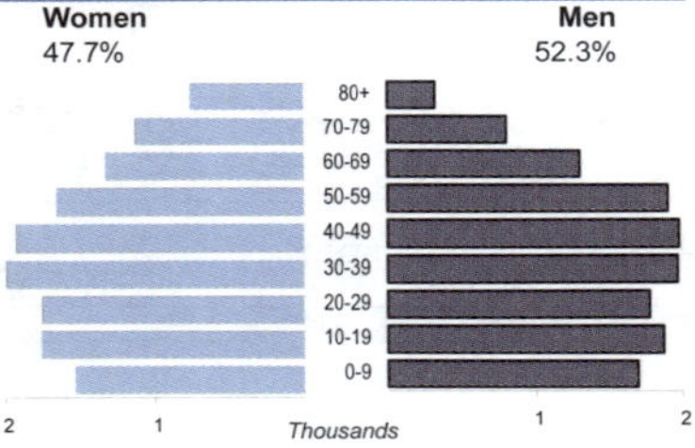

Life expectancy (in years), 2001:	at birth	at 65
Women:	83	21
Men:	79	18

Median age (in years), 2001:	
Women:	38
Men:	35

GUERNSEY (UNITED KINGDOM)

Time: UTC

Capital:	St. Peter Port (16 488)
Two largest cities:	Vale (9 573)
	Castel (8 975)
Area (km^2):	63
Total population:	60 382
Population density (per km^2):	958
Official languages:	English
Date joined UN:	n/a
Currency:	Pound sterling (GBP)
Statistical Office:	States of Guernsey Policy and Research Unit http://www.gov.gg/ccm/navigation/government/facts---figures/

Life expectancy (in years):	at birth	at 65
Women:	82	..
Men:	78	..

Median age (in years):	
Women:	38
Men:	36

Population by age, 2004

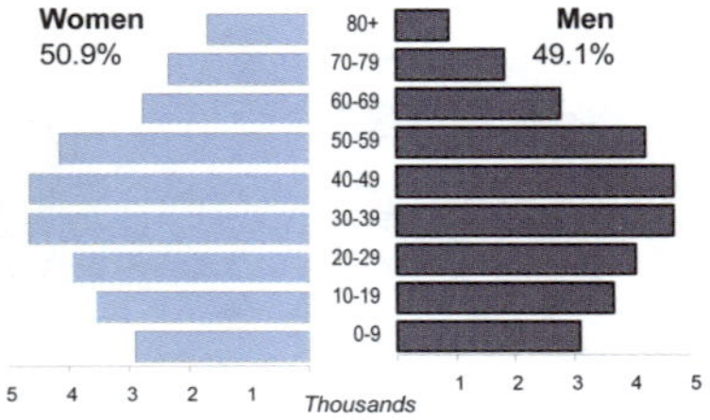

ISLE OF MAN (UNITED KINGDOM)

Capital:	Douglas (25308)
Two largest cities:	Onchan (8706)
	Ramsey (7626)
Area (km²):	572
Total population:	76 315
Population density (per km²):	133
Official languages:	English, Manx
Date joined UN:	n/a
Currency:	Pound sterling (GBP)
Statistical Office:	
	Isle of Man Treasury Department, Economic Affairs Division
	http://www.gov.im/treasury/economic/

Time: UTC

Median age (in years), 2001:	
Women:	39
Men:	36

Population by age, 2001

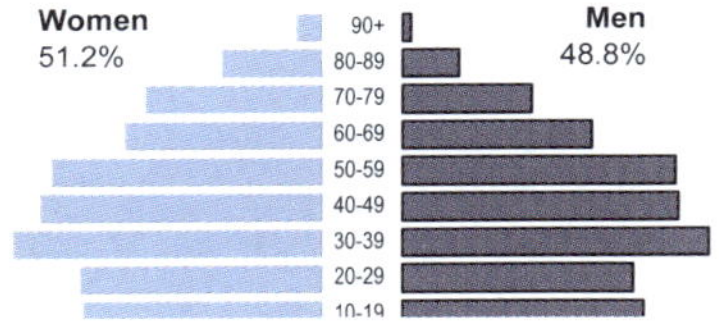

JERSEY (UNITED KINGDOM)

Capital:	St Helier (28 310)
Two largest cities:	St Saviour (12 491)
	St Brelade (10 134)
Area (km²):	118
Total population:	87 186
Population density (per km²):	739
Official languages:	English
Date joined UN:	n/a
Currency:	Pound sterling (GBP)
Statistical office:	
	States of Jersey Statistics Unit
	http://www.gov.je/statistics/

Time: UTC

Life expectancy (in years), 2004:	at birth	at 65
Women:	79	..
Men:	72	..

Median age (in years), 2005:	
Women:	42
Men:	40

Population by age, 2005

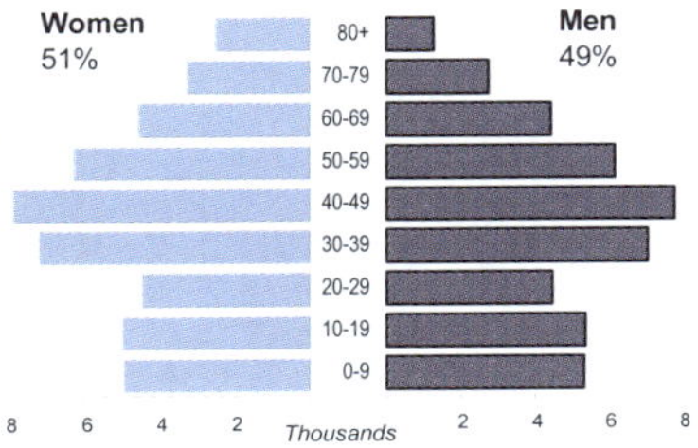

The United Nations Security Council Resolution 1266 (1999) authorized the Secretary-General, with the assistance of relevant international organizations, to establish an international civil presence in Kosovo in order to provide an interim administration for Kosovo under which the people of Kosovo can enjoy substantial autonomy within the Federal Republic of Yugoslavia (from 2003 to 2006: State Union Serbia and Montenegro; since 3 June 2006: Republic of Serbia)

KOSOVO

Capital:	Pristina
Area (km²):	10 908
Total population[1]:	2 100 000
Population density (per km²):	193
Official languages:	Albanian, Serbian, English
Date joined UN:	n/a
Currency:	Euro (EUR)
Statistical office:	Statistical Office of Kosovo http://www.ks-gov.net/esk

Life expectancy (in years), 2003:	at birth	at 65
Women:	71	..
Men:	67	..

Time: UTC +1

Major import partners from UNECE, 2004

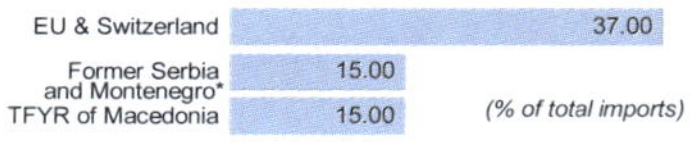

Major export partners in UNECE, 2004

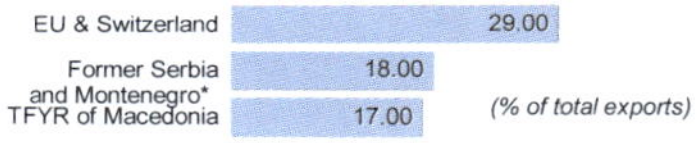

* Refers to trade with the former State Union Serbia and Montenegro (excluding Kosovo).
1. Estimation published by the Statistical Office of Kosovo, 2007 (http://www.ks-gov.net/esk/).

Glossary

Area: Area comprising land area and inland water.

Capital: This entry gives the location of the capital city, usually the seat of government.

Central Bank: The Central Bank is the institution that is charged with regulating the size of the money supply in a nation, the availability and cost of credit, and the foreign exchange value of its currency. The boards of Central Banks are the decision making bodies.

Consumer price index: The Consumer Price Index (CPI) aims to measure the average changes over time in the general level of prices of goods and services purchased by the households for their own final consumption. The prices of a representative sample of goods and services are collected in monthly surveys and the CPI is compiled and published monthly. It is usually not revised or seasonally adjusted. To some extent, differences in compilation methods and in the coverage (of goods and services, geographical area and population groups) may influence the international comparability of the data.

Date joined UN: The date on which a particular country joined the United Nations.

Divorce: A final legal dissolution of a marriage, that is, the separation of married persons which confers on the parties the right to remarriage under civil, religious and/or other provisions, according to the laws of each country.

Economic activity rate: Percentage of the population aged 15 years or more which supplies, or are available to supply, labour for the production of goods and services.

Employment: The employed comprise all persons above a specified age who, during a specified brief period, either one week or one day, were in the following categories:

a) paid employment:
   (a.1) at work: persons who during the reference period performed some work for wage or salary, in cash or in kind;
   (a.2) with a job but not at work: persons who, having already worked in their present job, were temporarily

not at work during the reference period and had a formal attachment to their job.

b) self-employment:

(b.1) at work: persons who during the reference period performed some work for profit or family gain, in cash or in kind;

(b.2) with an enterprise but not at work: persons with an enterprise, which may be a business enterprise, a farm or a service undertaking, who were temporarily not at work during the reference period for any specific reason.

Exchange rate: Annual average exchange rate expressed in national currency units per US dollar. Depending on the country, the exchange rates are market rates, that is, largely determined by market forces, or official rates, that is, determined by authorities.

Exports of goods and services: Exports of goods and services consist of sales, barter, gifts or grants, of goods and services from residents to non-residents.

External debt: Gross external debt, at any given time, is the outstanding amount of those actual current, and not contingent, liabilities that require payment(s) of principal and/or interest by the debtor at some point(s) in the future and that are owed to non-residents by residents of an economy.

External trade balance, or net trade: The value of exports of goods and services less imports of goods and services.

Final consumption expenditure: The final consumption expenditure consists of the expenditure, including imputed expenditure, incurred by resident households and non-profit institutions servicing households (NPISHs) on individual consumption goods and services and incurred by general government on both individual consumption goods and services and collective consumption services.

Foreign born: The foreign-born population of a country includes all persons who have that country as country of usual residence and whose place of birth is located in another country.

Foreigners in population: The foreign population of a country includes all persons who have that country as country of usual residence and who are the citizens of another country.

Gender pay gap: Gender pay gap is the difference between average monthly earnings of male employees and of female employees as a percentage of average monthly earnings of male employees.

Government ministers: Ministers are high-level officers of the State entrusted with the management of a division of governmental activities.

Gross Domestic Product (GDP): Gross domestic product is an aggregate measure of production equal to the sum of the gross value added of all resident institutional units engaged in production (plus any taxes, and minus any subsidies, on products not included in the value of their outputs). It can also be defined as the sum of the final uses of goods and services (all uses except intermediate consumption) measured in purchasers' prices, less the value of imports of goods and services, or the sum of primary incomes distributed by resident producer units. GDP at market prices as measured by production, expenditure and income has to be identical.

GDP at current prices, in millions of US Dollars, PPP: The current price GDP of a country converted into US dollars on the basis of the purchasing power parity (PPP) of the country's currency. PPP is a method to eliminate price level differences in currency conversion of GDP. See glossary term *Purchasing power parity*.

GDP in agriculture, industry and services: Measures the produced value added in respective economic sectors. Agriculture covers agriculture, hunting, forestry and fishing; Industry comprises the production industries (including electricity, gas, and water supply), mining and quarrying and construction; Services comprise market services and non-market services.

GDP per capita: This entry shows GDP divided by annual average population.

Imports of goods and services: Import of goods and services consist of purchases, barter, or receipts of gifts or grants, of goods and services by residents from non-residents.

Labour Force: The labour force/economically active population comprises all persons above 15 years of age who supply, or are available to supply, labour for the production of goods and services.

Legal marital status of total population aged 18+: Refers to marital status, defined as the legal conjugal status of each individual aged 18 years or more in relation to the marriage laws (or customs) in the country. The following categories of marital status are used: Never married; Married; Widowed and not remarried; Divorced and not remarried. In some countries the legal status of separated also exists and in this publication, persons of this group are included in the group of married. Data refer to 1 January of the indicated year.

Life Expectancy: Life expectancy is the average number of years of life remaining to be lived by a female or male at a specific age (at birth or at 65 years), based on current age-specific mortality rates.

Major export partners in UNECE: The three UNECE member countries in receipt of majority of exports from the particular country. Shares are presented in percentage of total export to all worldwide trading partners. Data are sourced from the United Nations Comtrade Database (comtrade.un.org/).

Major import partners from UNECE: The three UNECE member countries where most imports to the particular country come from. Shares are presented in percentage of total imports from all worldwide trading partners. Data are sourced from the United Nations Comtrade Database (comtrade.un.org/).

Major sectors: Groupings used to measure GDP and Employment in major sectors according to the International Standard Industrial Classification of all Economic Activities (ISIC), version 3.1.

ISIC A-B:	Agriculture, hunting & forestry; fishing
ISIC C-E:	Industry, including energy
ISIC F:	Construction
ISIC G-I:	Wholesale & retail trade, repairs; hotels & restaurants; transport & communications
ISIC J-K:	Financial intermediation; real estate, renting & business activities
ISIC L-P:	Other service activities

Marriage: The act, ceremony or process by which the legal conjugal relationship between two persons is constituted according to the marriage laws in the country.

Median age: The median divides the age distribution of the population into two equal parts: one-half of the cases falling below the median age and one-half above the median.

National currency: This entry identifies the national medium of exchange and its basic subunit.

Official languages: This entry provides the official languages of the country or territory.

Parliament: Legislative or deliberative assembly. One or more chambers or assemblies that form (or form part of) the legislature of a country. The term may also be applied to multinational legislative bodies.

Population by age: This graph provides the distribution of the population according to 5-year age groups and gender.

Population density: Average number of residents within a unit of area.

Purchasing power parity (PPP): In broad terms, PPP is the relative cost of the same representative basket of goods when valued at the domestic prices of two different countries. In other words, PPPs are the rates of currency conversion that equalize the purchasing power of different currencies. PPPs, and not exchange rates, should be used in international comparisons of GDP and its components.

Real GDP growth rate: Real GDP refers to GDP at constant prices. Constant prices estimates are obtained by expressing GDP value in the prices of a base period. They are used to show the growth (percentage change over previous year) in a country's economy.

Territory: A territory that is constitutionally linked to one of the UNECE member countries and does not possess full political independence.

Tertiary student: Tertiary students are those enrolled in university level courses.

Total fertility rate: The average number of children that would be born alive to a woman during her lifetime if she were to pass through her childbearing years conforming to the age-specific fertility rates of a given year.

Total population: Total mid-year or annual average population.

Unemployment: The unemployed comprise all persons of working age who during the reference period were:

a) without work – that is, were not in paid employment or self-employment; and
b) currently available for work – that is, were available for paid employment or self-employment during the reference period; and
c) seeking work – that is, had taken specific steps in a specified reference period to seek paid employment or self-employment.

Unless otherwise stated, all data on unemployment are from Labour Force Surveys. Registered unemployment comprises unemployed population registered at Employment or Labour Offices. This administrative approach to unemployment reflects national rules and conditions and usually yields different results from those of surveys using the ILO concept of unemployment, which includes persons often not covered in registered unemployment statistics, such as persons seeking work for the first time.

Unemployment rate: Percentage share of unemployed persons in the active population.

UTC: Co-ordinated Universal Time (UTC), maintained by the Bureau International des Poids et Mesures (BIPM), is the time scale that forms the basis for the co-ordinated dissemination of standard frequencies and time signals.

Widowed: A type of marital status indicating the person is single due to the death of a spouse.

Youth unemployment: Unemployment amongst persons aged 15-24 years.

References and Data Sources

The majority of statistical data in these profiles were extracted from the UNECE Statistical Database (www.unece.org/stats/data.htm): an online collection of official statistics from national and international sources. Additional sources for this publication are listed below.

General data

Coordinated Universal Time	www.bipm.org/en/scientific/tai/time_server.html
United Nations	www.un.org/Overview/unmember.html

Population

World Health Organization (WHO)	Core Health Indicators www3.who.int/whosis/core/
United Nations Economic Commission for Europe, Statistical Division	Joint UNSD-Eurostat-UNECE-Council of Europe-ILO questionnaire on international migration statistics for 2004
United States Census Bureau	International Data Base (IDB) www.census.gov/ipc/www/idbnew.html
United Nations Statistics Division	Demographic Yearbook unstats.un.org/unsd/demographic/

Economy

United Nations Statistics Division	United Nations Common Database (UNCDB) unstats.un.org/unsd/cdb/
World Health Organization (WHO)	Core Health Indicators www3.who.int/whosis/core/

Trade

United Nations Statistics Division Comtrade Database	unstats.un.org/unsd/comtrade/

Internet addresses of National Statistical Offices

Albania	www.instat.gov.al/
Andorra	www.estadistica.ad
Armenia	www.armstat.am/
Austria	www.statistik.at
Azerbaijan	www.azstat.org
Belarus	www.belstat.gov.by
Belgium	www.statbel.fgov.be
Bosnia and Herzegovina	www.fzs.ba/
Bulgaria	www.nsi.bg/
Canada	www.statcan.ca
Croatia	www.dzs.hr
Cyprus	www.mof.gov.cy
Czech Republic	www.czso.cz
Denmark	www.dst.dk
Estonia	www.stat.ee
Finland	www.stat.fi
France	www.insee.fr
Georgia	www.statistics.ge
Germany	www.destatis.de
Greece	www.statistics.gr
Hungary	www.ksh.hu
Iceland	www.statice.is
Ireland	www.cso.ie
Israel	www.cbs.gov.il
Italy	www.istat.it
Kazakhstan	www.stat.kz
Kyrgyzstan	www.stat.kg
Latvia	www.csb.lv
Liechtenstein	www.llv.li/amtsstellen/llv-avw-statistik.htm
Lithuania	www.std.lt
Luxembourg	www.statec.public.lu
Malta	www.nso.gov.mt/
Moldova	www.statistica.md
Monaco	www.monaco.gouv.mc
Montenegro	www.monstat.cg.yu

Netherlands	www.cbs.nl
Norway	www.ssb.no
Poland	www.stat.gov.pl
Portugal	www.ine.pt
Romania	www.insse.ro
Russian Federation	www.gks.ru
San Marino	-
Serbia	www.statserb.sr.gov.yu
Slovakia	www.statistics.sk
Slovenia	www.stat.si
Spain	www.ine.es
Sweden	www.scb.se
Switzerland	www.bfs.admin.ch
Tajikistan	www.stat.tj/
The former Yugoslav Republic of Macedonia	www.stat.gov.mk/
Turkey	www.die.gov.tr
Turkmenistan	www.turkmenistan.gov.tm
Ukraine	www.ukrstat.gov.ua/
United Kingdom	www.statistics.gov.uk/
United States	www.fedstats.gov/
Uzbekistan	www.stat.uz/

Statistical Offices of Territories

Faroe Islands	www.hagstova.fo
Greenland	www.statgreen.gl
St Pierre and Miquelon	www.saint-pierre-et-miquelon.pref.gouv.fr
Bermuda	www.statistics.gov.bm
Gibraltar	www.gibraltar.gov.gi/
Guernsey	www.gov.gg
Isle of Man	www.gov.im/treasury/economic/
Jersey	www.gov.je/statistics/
Kosovo	www.ks-gov.net/esk

Indicators

English	French	Russian
Capital	Capitale	Столица
Two largest cities	Les deux plus grandes villes	Два наиболее крупно заселенных города
Area (km^2)	Superficie (km^2)	Площадь ($км^2$)
Total population	Population totale	Общая численность населения
Population density (per km^2)	Densité de population (Hab/km^2)	Плотность населения (на $км^2$)
Official languages	Langues officielles	Официальный язык
Date joined UN	Date d'adhésion à l'ONU	Дата вхождения в ООН
National currency	Unité monétaire	Национальная валюта
National Statistical Office	Office National de Statistique	Национальный статистический комитет
Population by age	Population par groupe d'âge	Возрастная структура населения
Women	Femmes	Женщины
Men	Hommes	Мужчины
Thousands	En milliers	В тысячах
Life expectancy (in years) at birth, at 65	Espérance de vie (en années) à la naissance, à 65 ans	Ожидаемая продолжительность жизни (кол-во. лет) на момент рождения, в возрасте 65 лет
Median age (in years):	Âge médian (en années)	Средний возраст
Foreign born	Résidents nés à l'étranger	Родившиеся в другой стране
Foreigners in population	Population étrangère	Количество иностранцев, проживающих в стране
Total fertility rate	Taux de fécondité.	Общий коэффициент рождаемости
Legal marital status of total population aged 18+	Situation matrimoniale légale (18 ans et plus)	Семейное положение населения в возрасте более 18 лет
Never married	Célibataires	Не состоящие в браке
Married	Mariées/Mariés	Состоящие в браке
Divorced	Divorcées/Divorcés	Разведенные
Widowed	Veuves/Veufs	Овдовевшие

Women in the labour force	Proportion de femmes dans la population active	Процентное соотношение женщин к рабочей силе
Gender pay gap	Ecart salarial hommes/femmes	Разница в оплате труда между полами
Female government ministers	Nombre de femmes ministres	Количество женщин на посту министра
Percentage of total	Part dans le total	Процентное отношение к общему количеству
Female central bank board members	Nombre de femmes dans le conseil d'administration de la banque centrale	Количество женщин в совете директоров центрального банка
Female tertiary students	Femmes étudiantes dans l'enseignement supérieur	количество женщин, обучающихся в высших учебных заведениях
Parliament seats held by women (% of total)	Proportion de femmes députées (%)	Количество женщин членов парламента
Employment (% change over previous year)	Emploi (variation annuelle en %)	Занятость населения (процентное изменение по отношению к прошлому году)
Unemployment rate (%)	Taux de chômage (%)	Уровень безработицы
Youth unemployment rate (%)	Taux de chômage des jeunes (%)	Уровень безработицы молодежи
Economic activity rate	Taux d'activité économique	Коэффициент экономической активности
Real GDP growth rate	Taux de croissance du PIB réel	Изменение реального ВВП
Exports of goods and services	Exportations de biens et services	Экспорт товаров и услуг
Imports of goods and services	Importations de biens et services	Импорт товаров и услуг
External trade balance	Solde des échanges extérieurs	Внешний баланс товаров и услуг
% of GDP	% du PIB	% ВВП
GDP in agriculture, industry, and services (2000=100)	PIB dans l'Agriculture, l'industrie et les services (2000=100)	ВВП, произведенный в сельском хозяйстве, промышленности и сфере услуг
Annual indices	Indices annuels	Годовые индексы
Agriculture	Agriculture	Сельское хозяйство
Industry (including construction)	Industrie (y compris la construction)	Промышленность, включая строительство
Service	Services	Услуги
Major import partners from UNECE	Principaux partenaires à l'importation (%)	Основные партнеры по импорту (%)

GDP at current prices	PIB à prix courants	ВВП в текущих ценах
In millions of US-Dollars, PPP:	en millions de Dollars des Etats Unis d'Amérique aux prix, PPA	В миллионах долларов США, ППС
GDP at constant 2000 prices, per capita	PIB par habitant aux prix constants de 2000	ВВП в сопоставимых ценах 2000 года на душу населения
Final consumption expenditure at 2000 prices, per capita, US-Dollars, PPP	Dépense de consommation finale par tête aux prix de 2000, en Dollars des Etats Unis d'Amérique, PPA	Расходы на конечное потребление в сопоставимых ценах 2000, года на душу населения, US$, ППС
Purchasing Power Parity (PPP)	Parité de pouvoir d'achat (PPA)	Паритет покупательной способности
Gross external debt	Dette extérieure	Внешний долг
Exchange rate	Taux de change	Валютный курс
Consumer price index (annual average)	Indice des prix à la consommation (moyenne annuelle)	Индекс потребительских цен (среднегодовой)
% change over previous year	Taux de croissance annuel (%)	Процентное изменение по отношению к прошлому году
GDP by major sectors	PIB par secteurs	Доля основных секторов экономики от ВВП
Employment in major sectors	Emploi par secteurs	Занятость населения в основных секторах экономики
Agriculture, Hunting & forestry, fishing	Agriculture, chasse, sylviculture et pêche	Сельское хозяйство, охота и лесоводство, рыболовство
Industry, including energy	Industrie, électricité et eau	Промышленность, включая энергетику
Construction	Construction	Строительство
Wholesale & retail trade, repairs; hotels & restaurants; transport & communications	Commerce, réparations automobile et d'articles domestiques; hôtels et restaurants; transports et communications	Оптовая и в розничная торговля, ремонт гостиницы и рестораны, транспорт и связь
Financial, real estate, renting & business activities	Activités financières, Immobilier, locations et activités de services aux entreprises	Финансовое посредничество в операциях с недвижимостью, аренда и услуги предприятиям
Other service activities	Autres services	Иная деятельность в сфере услуг
Major export partners in UNECE	Principaux partenaires à l'exportation appartenant à UNECE	Основные партнеры по экспорту (%)
% of total imports / exports	% du l'importation / l'exportation total	% всех импортов / экспортов

NOTES

NOTES

NOTES

NOTES

NOTES

NOTES

NOTES